# THE RESISTANCE

# THE RESISTANCE

## TEN YEARS OF POP CULTURE THAT SHOOK THE WORLD

### ARMOND WHITE

THE OVERLOOK PRESS
WOODSTOCK • NEW YORK

First published in 1995 by
The Overlook Press
Lewis Hollow Road
Woodstock, New York 12498

Library of Congress Cataloging-in-Publication Data

White, Armond
The resistance : ten years of pop culture that shook the world / Armond White.
p. cm.
Includes index.
1. Popular culture–United States.  2. Arts, Modern–20th century–United
States.  3. Arts, American.  I. Title.
E169.04.W488   1995
306.4'7--dc20
94-46280              CIP
ISBN: 0-87951-586-4

Book design by Bernard Schleifer
Typeset by AeroType, Inc.

First Edition
10 9 8 7 6 5 4 3 2 1

## Author's Note

The author wishes the thank the following publications where many of the articles in this book first appeared: *The City Sun, Film Comment, L.A. Weekly, The Village Voice* and *Emerge Magazine*.

## Dedication

To
Sandra Short
Shirley Allen
Jannett Gaines

# CONTENTS

Contents                                    □  xi

# INTRODUCTION

D ETERMINED TO OPPOSE the standard of journalism by which writers unwittingly support the system of privilege and oppression that hires them and constructs middle-class public opinion, I approached *Film Comment* editor Harlan Jacobson with the idea to permanently change my byline to "The Resistance." I thought readers should always be confronted with the possibility of dissent. Jacobson responded that if I felt moved to this position, it was worth serious consideration. Still cautious about such a radical tactic, I next asked Keith Gardner, who advised, "It doesn't matter what you call yourself; it's what you say that matters." Rather than refuse my name, I resolved to pursue a difficult path as a culture writer. Thus, "The Resistance" took the form of my approach to the arts, to journalism, and eventually to this book.

In 1984 Jesse Jackson ran for president of the United States, and I began writing for *The City Sun*. Both auspicious beginnings, they announced the most significant change in popular culture in three decades—specifically, a new moment when Black Americans asserted their ideas in the public arena. What a remarkable, coincidental interstice of politics and culture! A preacher became a politician, and a critic wrote on politics—each endeavoring to prove, against the odds, that Americans were ready for their contribution. The only way to make sense of the eighties' inescapable cultural and political turmoil was to jump into it. My method was to defend and agitate—to address the public without a plebiscite but with a personal conviction that all the established voices of cultural commentary were missing the point. I didn't want to add to the pop discourse; like an uncompromised politician, I wanted to change the terms of the discussion. My motives, then and now, reflect the civil rights era and seventies protest ethic; these formed my responses to culture as much as home, school, or church. Not so much inspired by Jackson's national bid, I identified with the opportunity—the necessity—to make private thought into public expression. This political action regarding culture was often, I can't deny, resistance.

Resistance meant defying the standard "objective" approach to art as innocuous entertainment. Resistance was also evident in artists who changed the norm of popular entertainment by making it reflect the country's variety rather than some conformist fantasy. The distinctions were primarily ethnic, but in this period female artists asserted themselves significantly, so did gay artists—the race and sex issues being paramount to the political sensitivities in all areas of American living.

Startled by the commanding tones of Public Enemy, pulled into Morrissey's subtly shaded expressions, roused by Marcus Nispel's and Steven Spielberg's vivid imagery, one feels the shackles of hegemony fall away. There is frisson, there is joy, there is freedom in the art. And beauty in a new, different approach to the world. Not one of these artists is a simple hero; rather, each represents the complex changes in the temper of this era's pop culture. *The Resistance* chronicles cultural changes since 1984, the year Hollywood—the institution representing America's consciousness—woke up to the reality of nonmainstream expression. Nineteen eighty-four had its cultural revanchism—the right's unfortunate appropriation of Bruce Springsteen's too ambivalent *Born in the U.S.A.*, Arnold Schwarzenegger's ascension in *The Terminator*—but these events were reactions, not resistance.

The 1984 Hollywood watershed consisted of Alex Cox's *Repo Man*, Prince's *Purple Rain*, Billy Woodberry–Charles Burnett's *Bless Their Little Hearts*, the Norman Jewison–Charles Fuller *A Soldier's Story*, Robert Benton's *Places in the Heart*. Each film announced a new consciousness about race, history, sexuality, and each movie connected to the way other media had, or would, express these concerns: *Repo Man* used punk anarchy to counter eighties conservatism, *Purple Rain*'s play with androgyny and misogyny made those issues central to public discussion by additionally broadcasting them through the music industry and on television via music video; *Bless Their Little Hearts* was a significant statement of America's ethnic-independent filmmakers; *A Solider's Story* reflected the "live theater's" contribution to racial and historical consciousness; and *Places in the Heart* established mainstream Hollywood awareness. These films entered the air and had their effect on public thinking and every fresh art event of the past few years—Public Enemy's *It Takes a Nation of Millions to Hold Us Back*, Spike Lee's *Do the Right Thing*, Madonna's *Like a Prayer*, Wendell B. Harris's *Chameleon Street*, Michael Jackson's *Black or White*, Willie D's *Rodney K*, Morrissey's *Your Arsenal*, RuPaul's *Back to My Roots*, among many—set a new standard for oppositional art.

Week after week I was able to follow and comment on these developments in a way only journalism made possible—frequently, immediately—catching the gist of a cultural moment by attending its weekly metamorphoses and thrill. Most pop criticism of this period belonged to the school of ecstatic culture writing from the sixties but misapplied that hard-won advocacy by emphasizing the *pleasure* of the arts. I took it for granted that people know these films, records, videos, and plays are meant to be enjoyed; what the school of ecstatic culture writing leaves out is that these works mean something and I tried—always—to search out and interpret the political secrets and emotional value of artists expressing themselves through resistance aesthetics. I identified with filmmaker Alain Cavalier's *Libera Me,* a montage of gestures in underground liberation movements from the time of the French Occupation to Somewhere Today, made spellbinding by Cavalier's rapt, devoted cataloging.

So often the changes in nonmainstream ideology go unrecorded. The truth gets lost or buried in history. For example, the significant embrace of Black independent filmmakers by Hollywood is generally marked from the feature film debut of Spike Lee's *She's Gotta Have It,* but that misrepresents the way the past decade evolved. Certainly the impetus for pluralizing Hollywood mythology started in 1984 with *Purple Rain,* but it was ratified the next year by the success of Steven Spielberg's *The Color Purple.* And Lee, like many other contemporary Black filmmakers, was inspired by the example of Charles Burnett's 1975 *Killer of Sheep.* There is an artistic continuity here, and too often the mainstream media's treatment of Black cultural developments leaves out the connections. Counterculture icon Bob Dylan acerbically referred to the modern pop era as a period when "the insane world of entertainment exploded." But the boom also blew together Dylan and many unlikely peers, rivals, and antagonists; the fallout being an ideological free-for-all. Through the rise of rap, music video, and the greater visibility of artists of color, white creators such as Dylan no longer held the center of pop culture. It was a marketplace where third-world filmmakers competed with Hollywood,

Morrissey shared the political distress of Public Enemy. The failed—or collapsed—moral leadership in government only replicated the marketplace reality of *caveat emptor,* leaving each record purchaser, moviegoer, TV watcher—like each voter—on his or her own.

As the past decade progressed, hiphop, the primary creative force in pop, was appropriated for various kinds of commercial advancement without conscientious acknowledgment of hiphop's significance as a means of political and historical expression. *The Resistance* concentrates on hiphop culture because it is so important to understanding late-twentieth-century modernity.

Hiphop artists exemplify the paradox of a society's marginal citizens staking out the entire country's—and the world's—imagination. A groundswell of the dispossessed and the pissed-off found voices and images to express their condition. Pop-art legitimacy not only furthered their discontent but confirmed its reality in a society where "racism" and "homophobia" are disruptive words. I use them without shame to provoke a political discussion that is usually discouraged around the arts. A lot of fear (and thus movements toward censorship) came in reaction to this era's pop, but a greater result was that people were forced to recognize how art became politics unapologetically, breathtakingly. No longer the obsession of fringe-group radicals, politics is an everyday fact of cultural life.

There is still a lot to be understood about the nature, obligation, and pleasure of pop culture in a multicultural, multipolitical, *volatile* society. I have tried to make sense of things and to pin down the elusive victories and assaults, the fleeting clarity and flaring passions, to report/review the details of art experience. This includes the problem of Black solidarity (the *Coming to America* contretemps, in which Eddie Murphy responded to my review in a three-page *City Sun* advertisement); the developing potential for artists crossing over their own ethnic boundaries (Spielberg's controversial *The Color Purple*); and the awful rut of class ruining pop discourse (as when hiphop critics contribute to the form's debasing).

Writing through this chaos was a challenge to everything I thought I knew about art, politics, and people. The effort to understand what was going on is what kept me going, because Public Enemy, De La Soul, Son of Bazerk, Whoopi Goldberg, Steven Spielberg, Eddie Murphy, Morrissey, Pedro Almodovar, RuPaul, Terence Davies, Ice Cube, Alex Cox, and Michael Jackson were doing things that seemed new and certainly were turning the world upside down. Most of these artists have more than their share of detractors, and the particular kind of opposition they face—a defense of traditional art and politics—only reinvigorated my position. A review became a confrontation with the culture's prevailing ideology. Simply in describing an artist's style one could not overlook a concern with nonmainstream virtues. Thus, aesthetics were freighted with the facts of sociology. This is where writing primarily for *The City Sun* made such an important difference in the development of a resistor's attitude. *The City Sun*'s motto, "Speaking Truth to Power," became a necessary dictum. The *Sun* offered me as much expressive freedom as some record managements offered some rappers. The ability to effect my own statements felt as much like the privilege of rap as a journalist's honorable mandate, so in this book I flaunt the pleasure and thank God for the privilege.

*The Resistance* reflects the influence of the good people who shared their intelligence and caring from way back. At *The City Sun,* Utrice Leid and Angela Briggins made invaluable contributions. Elsewhere, Jack Barth and Harlan Jacobson provided a boost—continued by Gavin Smith, Richard Pena, Robin Little, and especially Barbara Zitwer. There are many more I can't thank enough, among them Keith Gardner, Matthew Bernstein, Judy Gelman, Jerry Green, Bob Lazzaro, Dennis Myers, Judy Richheimer, Richard Torres. Particularly, Gregory Solman and Benj DeMott both combined support with persistent challenge. And Kevin McDonnell always knew what was needed.

# PLACES IN THE ART

*I'm working on [a film] about an American Indian. Again it's a comic story, but we'll have scenes that will be as terrible as the lot of the American Indian really is—and really was—in Custer's time. Of course, the analogy is to the American Negro, but at the moment I don't know how to do a film about the American Negro that wouldn't be a distortion or a romance, or too limited in its views. . . . I have to have perspective. I don't have a view sufficiently complete to be able to know how to make a film about the American Negro. I can tell lots of incidents that would be terrible and unpleasant and show injustice, but they wouldn't be saying anything because I don't know the end. Making a film about the Indians might help me to understand that.*

—ARTHUR PENN, 1968

A FTER SEX, race is probably the most powerful and confusing issue an American movie can deal with. Some of the best known and most representative American films combine sex and race. The two create the central friction of *The Birth of a Nation*. Race is, of course, part of *Gone With the Wind* and *The Searchers*. Between Travis Bickle's wild reveries over blondes in *Taxi Driver* are his dazed, unsettling confrontations with Blacks, the combination of sexual and racial tension precipitating his violent climax. And the unspoken racial dynamics of the *Rocky* films are their only real force and account for their popular success. But how race became the gainsaid element in contemporary American movies—the element conspicuous by its absence, and currently by its emphasis—is a story of the complacence, fear, and rigidity in the industry's practical and aesthetic conventions.

Since Penn spoke in '68, Vietnam and the women's movement have taken precedence over racial issues as social and cultural preoccupations. The trepidation Penn expressed doesn't even occur to most filmmakers today. It can't simply be that demographics put Black people in the background of most Hollywood movies; race is pushed to the background of most filmmakers' consciousness. The problem is satirized in *Fast*

*Times at Ridgemont High:* a little white kid amazed at seeing the school's Black football star in the local mall, says, incredulously, "He lives here! I thought he only flew in for games."

The life and history depicted in American movies is largely a matter of fantasy. Contemporary films are less a direct reflection of the world than a reification of current ideas and feelings. Movies reveal what the filmmakers think but might not express. From the race-shy reviews of *Taxi Driver* and *Moscow on the Hudson,* from the Punch and Judy show of harmlessly flung epithets in *48 HRS* (known as "Phony-eight Hours" in my neighborhood), to the curiously astute moment in *1941* when Dan Aykroyd gives an anti-Japanese speech on Hollywood Boulevard and director Steven Spielberg reveals an anomalous Japanese-American in the crowd, listening, it's obvious that race is strangely muted in our films and that no one is talking about it in movie culture.

Until now. The recent string of movies that stand out for the prominence of Black faces in them—*Breakin', Beat Street, Purple Rain, The Brother from Another Planet, Cotton Club, A Soldier's Story, Places in the Heart*—provides an instructive measure of the reticent acceptance of Blacks and racial themes. None is a great or daringly honest picture (this isn't the era for daring), and all are unresolved about whether Blacks should be portrayed in movies as individuals or historical symbols. At best, the films are cultural documents, empirical evidence of the society's values and tensions.

Even so meek a film as Robert Benton's *Places in the Heart* is propelled by tension. The threat of racial hostility is braided through a filigreed enactment of this country's kindliest platitudes and sentiments. Benton distills them into a tale of the Great Depression, used here as a distanced representation of authentic American struggle. *Places in the Heart* might be the grand apologia for Hollywood's large-scale disregard of racial matters in the past dozen years. Unfortunately, it's a sixties *To Kill a Mockingbird–Lilies of the Field* apology. Because Benton doesn't make the necessary, long overdue imaginative leap into Moze (Danny Glover), the Black itinerant who helps widow Edna (Sally Field) farm her cotton fields, the Black characters seem recessed, abstract figments—a human problem the white characters (and the film's author) stare at without comprehending.

In *Places'* social awareness, Benton may be paces ahead of his contemporaries: the shocking events that open the film are played in a kind of psychological dumb show using, without addressing, assumptions about the social interaction of Blacks and whites. Yet Benton's ellipsis also seems the inevitable retardation of films and filmmakers ignoring race for so long. *Places* attempts an early-movie simplicity in action and expression; that the themes of the sketchy beginning are so easily understood is frightening, proving Benton knows there's much about social-racial complexity and its typical use in popular fiction that we accept without openly acknowledging it. His sophistication is based in condescension, another facet of the low awareness and timid admittance of race in movies. Perhaps, in racial matters Hollywood hasn't moved forward since the sixties, because in essence, society hasn't either. There's hardly an American movie in the past ten years that does not evidence a certain moral lethargy in this respect: *Bad Boys* builds its racial consciousness upside-down; *Manhattan* and *Kramer vs. Kramer* describe a bizarrely homogenous society; *The Right Stuff* reviews history myopically; *Arthur* constructs an indeterminate fantasy world.

Sidney Poitier's march through fifties and sixties Hollywood left not a mammy or Uncle Tom in sight, but he didn't stamp out the problem of stereotype. Poitier only (some only!) punched a hole in the screen's superstitious segregation. His image on screen denied legitimacy to easy preconceptions about Black people and Black characters—the ones *A Soldier's Story* identifies as shiftless, lazy Negroes. But most radically, Poitier's image refused invisibility and disregard. His figure was perhaps a natural indication of the Black man's Other status in the white world, but a reminder of the Other's dignity. Poitier provided a color and temperamental contrast that suggested a Black character could never again appear on screen negligibly or without indicating the schisms and anxieties that control and structure his place in society.

Poitier's diminished profile since 1967—the year *In the Heat of the Night, Guess Who's Coming to Dinner?* and *To Sir, With Love* made him the country's top box-office attraction—can be viewed by the cynical as the inevitable suppression of the industry's racism; by the naive as just one good Black man's self-effacing decision; and by the foolish as fair exchange for his contribution as a director. Unarguably, his passing from prominence has seen his advances subsumed, normalized, and almost forgotten. The Black man in today's movies is Sidney Poitier's carelessly employed, indistinctly perceived poor relation: seated at the table, yes, but at the far end and in a short-legged chair.

These would be the tokens. Seen in government or service-industry roles but never central to the plot, Black people occupy peripheral positions on screen. In high school, just before the Blaxploitation surge of the seventies, we used to watch the screen intently for Black faces. If we saw just *one,* that somehow legitimized the film as acceptable, forward-thinking, and not indifferent or altogether disdainful of our kind. After Blaxploitation the habit of those pathetic stake-outs had become unnecessary, but today one can keep as busy at it as before and still for a reason that aches: to substantiate a deficient art form you can't seem to do without.

The rewards can be depressing. Even favorite recent films come up short: *Blow Out* had none; *Pennies from Heaven*, one; *Excalibur*, none (of course); *Reds*, none; *E.T.*, one; *Shoot the Moon*, none; *Diva*, one; *The Right Stuff*, none; *Repo Man*, two. And in such popular films as *Tootsie*, I counted two; *Terms of Endearment*, none; *Return of the Jedi*, one; *Indiana Jones and the Temple of Doom*, none; *Gremlins*, one. One plays this game and learns that the sideline position given to Blacks in film, while insufficient, is yet significant.

Our art, like our journalism, is diseased by the assumption that every legitimate, visible person is white. As movies represent a conceptualized, ordered reality, it becomes apparent that there are world concepts (belonging to those media-employed many) that do not include "minorities." The resulting films indicate a racism that can be variously traced and argued, perhaps even back to the Euro-immigrant ancestors who started this business (but who even then preferred scrubbed-up, bleached-out dream images rather than real pictures of what they themselves were).

Updating that tradition, *Places in the Heart* ends with a Griffith-like idealized tableau of an America with all wounds healed by love. The wish itself is powerfully moving, although the film doesn't earn that effect. *Places'* "honesty" (emblematized in the contrasts of Lindsay Crouse's stern eyeballing and Sally Field's generous apology when they both first speak to Moze through the screen door) admits and finds succinct visual correlatives to the problems of racial division, neglect, and obscureness. But the film also commits those errors. The irritation of providing Moze with only the tiniest interior life and history makes sense only in relation to his equals in the household: a blind veteran, two children, and a widow. The band of struggling misfits suggests liberal solicitation, figures in a bleeding-heart campaign poster. The bit of a Black man that Benton wrote and Danny Glover plays so solidly has less personality than Robert DoQui in the few scenes in *Nashville* that Robert Altman says he regretted cutting and at one time hoped to restore in a five-hour TV version.

From *The Birth of a Nation* to *Nashville* to *Places in the Heart*, the grandest, most sincere attempts to create a wide, encompassing view of American life all falter on racial matters. Yet these films openly confront facts of social division (though to different ends) that every film either attempts or else deliberately dodges. In the generalized view of American life that we see most often, and most repeatedly, social discord is discouraged and social unity is stressed—to the exclusion, if necessary, of possibly dissident factors or people. The beguiling but questionable wishfulness of *Places in the Heart* relays, of course, white middle-class charitable complaisance. Its idealism may be central to mainstream filmmaking, which always (if only by implication) conveys the socio-economic interests of the people involved. But this is not idealism or filmmaking that calls for change. Moze conveniently disappears into the night, as do the Ku Klux Klansmen who beat him and threaten his life, to be replaced on screen by lyrical sap. Those stealthy exits (with Moze, like Paul Muni in *I Am a Fugitive from a Chain Gang,* provoking the question "Where will you go, how will you live?") are easy, evasive, and ideologically contradictory.

The film's pretense of understanding its characters and milieu is undercut by the neat avoidance of character complication or further exposition of either Moze or the Texas Klansmen. Benton's effort to deal in simple portraiture and communicate on a basic level is booby-trapped by fear of the characters' complexities. Hal Ashby's comparably idyllic *Bound for Glory* featured the rigorous contrasts of characters cracking under the psychic stress of the period. The man complaining of newsreels in his head and the truculent Black hobo seemed stunned and haunted – their pain made poignant the film's nostalgic yearning. When Benton's filmmaking is not obviously sentimental, it is extremely canny, rather accurately embodying current problems and dissatisfaction regarding race relations, female assertiveness, and economic stress – without, of course, even coming close to solutions anyone might imagine.

Though *Places* is set in the past, its inconclusiveness is certainly of today; it is an acknowledgment of social frustration that achieves only a limited catharsis. *Places* proves that you can be shaken by archetypes and still long for deeper satisfaction and personal transformation. Benton does a lot but never really gets so close to his characters – the way Vittorio DeSica did in *Shoeshine,* or Luchino Visconti in *La Terra Trema,* or Satyajit Ray in *Pather Panchali* – that you sense their emotions in your own. *Places* creates a type of emotion, an idea of patriotism, that we can recognize and approve without feeling. Benton's reticence is too humble, too conciliatory either to make a real advance or to express a profound mood. When Edna bids farewell to Moze, praising his work in her cotton fields and admonishing, "Don't you forget that," the picture's maudlin obviousness does it in. How could Moze – callused, beaten, tired, and bloody – not forget? Shouldn't Edna have said "*I* won't forget" as a more generous tribute and as Benton's instruction to the audience rather than, again, condescension to Blacks (and to history)?

"My sympathies are with the dispossessed – unabashedly," Martin Ritt has said. That interest may explain the humanist shape of his work

(*Sounder, Conrack, Norma Rae, The Molly Maguires*) that has come the closest yet in American movies to DeSica's and Ray's concern for low-caste people's best qualities. Ritt's attitude of proud Jewish liberalism (as American filmmaking, it shows a rather socialist patriotism) might explain American films' success and failure in addressing so-called minorities. Only the motivation to question popular assumptions about American experience can make filmmakers characterize people of color more imaginatively—crossing the Ideal Color bar. Otherwise, movies will continue their soporific reassurance that everything is OK and Tom Cruise, Elizabeth McGovern, and Robert Redford will function cease-lessly as the representative American citizens joining the Walter Brennan, Jeanne Crain, and Fay Bainter Hall of Fame.

Filmmaking that projects lily-white ideal national images, admitting ethnicity only as a problem, is an insidious practice. Complexes of self-hate hide in the white image's self-denial and ethnic denial. When James Toback and Paul Schrader romanticize and embellish Black characters as an ultimate purgation or libidinal fulfillment, they reverse the logic in Hollywood's avoidance of racial issues: they invite chaos by a screwy affirmation of ethnicity (wholly preferable to the soda cracker optimism of, say, *The Natural*). Most filmmakers deny ethnicity to preserve a synthetic social fabric, and so deny appearance and dimension to Blacks—immediately the most visually contrasting and most militant group—as a way of maintaining their own composure and illusions.

Blacks, more than other ethnic groups, have served as an objective correlative for some Jewish filmmakers ("I thought of my own parents' immigrant experience and related that way," Ritt said of *Sounder*) and as a primary focus for their political consciousness. The scarcity of Black screen figures indicates not only the absence of true political consciousness but also the absence of curiosity and concern. A cultural form based on altruism is, of course, suspect. It is in the highest artistic interest that such insults as the 1982 *Kiss Me Goodbye* (Jeff Bridges learns a lesson in love from a tap-dancing Black janitor) and the 1983 *WarGames* (a Black air force officer conducts a weapons demonstration in arch ghettoese) don't happen again. And certainly not, as in those cases, as cute, well-intended liberal sop.

Stupid as it is for filmmakers to exclude Blacks from depictions of our society and its ideals, how much stupider it is to include Blacks suspiciously, stereotypically, or inanely. It is not just the socially conscious epics like *Places in the Heart* that need a broadened sense of national character. In the effort to give cinematic life to America, filmmakers need to become smarter about the people who live here and how society shapes their thought and behavior.

Those noble intentions imbue Paul Mazursky's *Moscow on the Hudson* with enormous goodwill, but its Family of Man brotherhood is annoyingly quaint. Mazursky confuses cuteness with depth, and (hard to believe in the year of the Simpson-Mazzoli immigration bill and the Statue of Liberty's dilapidation) he insists on the most jejune democratic platitudes about that wacky melting pot, the U.S.A. Unlike his best film, *Next Stop, Greenwich Village,* Mazursky simplifies these characters' complexes. His funny jokes and sweet anecdotes hardly admit the characters' struggles for recognition; it submerges them all in a sea of homiletic banality in which every ethnic trait is seemingly cashed in as a joke. If not for its rah-rah Americanism, *Moscow on the Hudson* would seem a gross, insensitive comedy of xenophobia; the film has the unctuousness of Don Rickles's "Just kidding, folks—we're all brothers under the skin" wrap-up. Clevant Derricks' raucous stereotype as a Bloomingdale's security guard, whose Harlem family eats Cocoa Puffs, is shockingly regressive. His Black cartoon, like the picture's gay, Italian, and Cuban cartoons, conveys an at-least-we-aren't-Communist complacency—and sets a trap.

*Moscow on the Hudson*'s strange utopia, free of ethnic antagonism and aggression (in New York City!) strikes a resoundingly false note. The picture is not so naive as it is mindless. Superficially perceived, Mazursky's ethnics (foreigners to him and us) have superficial differences, superficial essences. They're slight, and slighted. The film is, after all, about an easily assimilated type; by making Robin Williams's Russian Jew nonspecific, it supports the racist myths of easy assimilation, and promotes the tradition of white movie hero as well as the high visibility and larger dimension of only the white American. The distortion of liberal impulses that *Moscow on the Hudson* represents makes the appearance of a one-dimensional Black character more clearly offensive as the product of short, insincere thinking and a narrow world view.

Usually present onscreen only as stereotype or efficient caricature, a Black character is often hard to react to. Is the gang of punks in *Dressed to Kill* threatening—apart from being Black? Is the film's screaming cleaning lady a comical Black hysteric or just simply frightened? In *King of Comedy* is Diahann Abbott a thief because she is Black or because some other motivation was left on the cutting-room floor? Are the killings of Frank McRae in *Red Dawn* and Scatman Crothers in *The Shining* plot necessities or racist conveniences? The stunted history of Black presentation in movies confuses most interpretations when the characterizations are sketchy or incidental. The past conditions us to have prejudiced responses that disrupt a film and make suspicious some filmmaker's intentions. A character like Madge Sinclair's self-deluded schoolteacher in *Conrack* transcends liberal accounting of whether a Black characterization is positive or demeaning because there are differing aspects of the character that involve your sense of humanity. Achieving that on film takes a miracle of understanding, but that's what I thought movies were all about.

Louis Gossett Jr.'s Oscar-winning performance in *An Officer and a Gentleman* created one of the most confounding enigmas in movie history: an ethnic cipher, he had no particularity except skin color. Although we hear about Gere's "Mayo the wop" and Winger's "Paula the polack," Gossett's ethnicity is never mentioned. Yet the movie—especially the high-contrast-prone cinematographer Donald Thorin—gets lots of mileage out of Gossett's fly-in-the-buttermilk circumstance. You can practically hear Taylor Hackford, the director, revving his engine when Gere calls Gossett a "motherfucker"—a reversal of roles sick enough for a Fassbinder movie but plenty provocative and shrewdly manipulative of applause (almost a decade after *Mandingo*) or the get-whitey tactic of Gossett's kicking Gere in the groin. Gossett's performance as a pure disciplinarian seemed less an act of suppressed instincts than erasure: here was *Roots*'s Old Fiddler without roots.

Among other archaic notions, *An Officer and a Gentleman* resurrected the idea of a military with no use for racial enmity. That lie may be key to its popularity; certainly the unmistakable fact of race in Robert Altman's *Streamers* did nothing to increase its box-office life. Race may have been too prominent by being so powerfully dramatized. David Rabe's play expressed a unity of social changes—political, sexual, and racial—that haven't yet converged in our movies: sexual revolution, Vietnam, and Black concerns are kept separate (except now in the genteel *Places in the Heart*). Rabe's combustible interaction expresses a fearfulness of these changes (as does David Mamet's neglected *Edmond*). Yet *Streamers* (maybe the most powerful American play written in the seventies) really does clear the air, or else puts an unsettling charge into it. Last fall *Streamers* was almost embarrassingly gauche. Its race concern was one that was not talked about in polite society anymore. Altman's daring in bringing this play to the screen went unnoticed, even as the play's exacerbation brought the artistic pretenses of the New York Film Festival up short: two months later *Streamers*' demystification of the military was proved anachronistic by the surprise success of the war fantasy *Uncommon Valor.*

This year, *A Soldier's Story* combines the microcosmic theatrics of *Streamers* with *An Officer and a Gentleman*'s ethnic riddle. It's a psychological mystery investigating the 1944 murder of a Black technical sergeant at a Tynin, Louisiana, army base. This minority interest seems so much more possible (or at least frequent) in theater; it sticks out at the movies. Charles Fuller, adapting his own Pulitzer Prize–winning play, and director Norman Jewison take a distressingly conventional approach. Howard E. Rollins Jr. is Captain Davenport, a Black officer from Washington, D.C., assigned to investigate the controversial case and quell potential friction between the Black platoon and area whites. Davenport's investigation reveals that the dead sergeant, Vernon Waters (Adolph Caesar), was a harsh martinet held in place by white officers. He is widely disliked by his Black platoon, which he scolds and ridicules for lack of pride and ambition and slackness in the struggle for Black manhood and dignity.

The play is a consideration of behavioral modes and philosophies, including Waters's Spartan segregationism, the soldiers laissez-faire-to-militant reactionism, and Davenport's self-conscious integrationism. In 1984, these don't count as major revelations. The destruction that their conflict engenders isn't apparent in the film's tame revelations. The parts of himself that Davenport recognizes in either Waters or the soldiers don't collide; he doesn't suffer the disintegration of his race (the torment of a Black man restricted in his social role) that he witnesses. Davenport is supposed to represent the new breed of recently evolved middle-class Black man brought back in touch with the persistent struggle for respect by other Black men, and reminded that the struggle has not finished for himself either. ("Any man uncertain about where he belongs got to be in a whole lot of pain.")

More parochial in its concern than any other major film about Blacks, *A Soldier's Story* expresses the state of awareness current in contemporary Black theater. *A Soldier's Play* speaks one kind of rhetoric, a colloquy on social values and Black American ethics. But now it speaks another: since the dearth of significant Black cultural figures in the past decade, the play takes on meaning as a contest of role models — with Davenport at the pivot. In essence, this movie reacts to the figure of Sidney Poitier, the last major Black cultural figure that communicated to the world with the minority's general approval and assent. The *Shaft* and *Superfly* heroes were bogus folk-art heroes without an authentic political, or useful, social profile. Self-centered opportunists, Shaft and Superfly had no revolutionary principles. (The distinction might be best understood as similar to that between the figures of Joe and Humphrey Bogart.) Movie culture, and the nation, has yet to get over the phenomenon of Sidney Poitier, because nothing since has equaled his achievement, his ambassadorship.

Norman Jewison parallels *A Soldier's Story* to his 1967 *In the Heat of the Night* (the opening-up scenes touring the surrounding parish, the tense-yet-tangential foot chases), understanding very well the chronological distance between the films and the racial gap that has not been closed.

Despite Jewison's efforts, *Story* can't ameliorate Fuller's script. The World War II setting restricts the picture's impact, encasing the film and its characters in amber (the Vietnam-era setting of *Streamers* had an opposite, intensifying effect). Fuller fails to use the past to spring thoughts about any of the characters' future. The movie seems set in the past because, as with *Places in the Heart,* we can't or won't understand or think about the issues dealt with in contemporary terms, and *A Soldier's Story*'s issues are inescapably contemporary—one can think nostalgically about anything *except* identity and suffering. Unless the purpose is to uncover schizophrenia, the conflicts Davenport experiences (understanding Waters's harshness, sympathizing with the soldiers' resentment) are both too neatly drawn and unclear. Fuller is stymied by the situation he means to define: the self-consciousness, the rectitude, the heroic cunning of a modern Black man's survival in white-dominated circumstances—the situation Sidney Poitier brought to light at the peak of his career both onscreen and existentially. ("I represent millions of people," Poitier once said. "I'll never do anything to embarrass any of them.")

To have brought off this coup Jewison needed to see the parallel to *In the Heat of the Night* all the way through and beg Sidney Poitier to take the role of Davenport, even with age. Movie history cries out for Poitier's return to acting in a role that would clarify and explore his Supernegro image and expose the prudence Fuller conceives but that none of Poitier's previous screenwriters could imagine or dare.

The personality conflicts Fuller dramatizes reflect Poitier's own debate in fashioning Black characters for mainstream audiences written by white screenwriters in a scarcely established tradition of noncomic, Black screen portraiture. Poitier must have known Davenport's mental vacillation. The great good fortune of Poitier's talent is that he smoothly expressed the tensions of his roles and his career in *A Raisin in the Sun* and *In the Heat of the Night*—his hand gestures and body stance possess extraordinary grace and nuanced psychology. Hopped-up or fluid, Poitier moved with his emotions, cadencing them (as Bette Davis did) and becoming, along with Paul Newman, one of the two best American film actors of the sixties. The Davenport of Howard E. Rollins Jr.—a good actor but not a commanding screen presence—isn't variegated enough. Poitier's was a well-developed, resilient acting style to which all other Black screen performers draw inevitable comparison. In *A Soldier's Story,* Denzel Washington, Art Evans, and Larry Riley have a believable naturalism. Adolph Caesar, as Waters, is disastrously stagebound through a snarling, roaring caricature that denies the humanity of the tortured sergeant. Caesar's too-rhetorical style (favored by writers of the contemporary Black theater and better suited for comedy) negates what he says onscreen. Unfortunately, he speaks Fuller's most pointed lines. He's what Louis Gossett Jr. might have been with real dialogue in *An Officer and a Gentleman:* a Black cartoon.

The real shock of *Purple Rain* is not Prince's ejaculating guitar, but that the trashy atmosphere, crude dialogue, and tawdry plot are exciting, enjoyable, and not a racial affront. Race is the novelty that makes *Purple Rain* special. This is the most financially successful movie without a white principal player ever and an achievement that can't be ignored. It knocks silly the belief that Black pictures don't cross over to white audiences and therefore have a predictable performance ceiling. That *Purple Rain* is more a musical event than a movie becomes less significant in the face of the film's box-office success ($62 million grossed by its third month) and the pleasure it affords. The movie succeeds, unlike such popular record setters as *Guess Who's Coming to Dinner?* and *To Sir, With Love,* without benefit of racial exploitation. This exception should influence industry thinking regarding the marketability of Black protagonists and, more important, the racial mixture of the films we see from now on.

*Purple Rain* inspires the question whether American movies can continue interestingly without a Black contribution. What filmmaker can pretend to American authenticity without using figures as native and as entertaining as Prince, Morris Day, and Jerome Benton? Sex is palpably at issue in *Purple Rain,* but race is not; it is accepted as natural. The characters are observed at the personality level—not profoundly, but arrestingly—with the way these people talk and interact as just another aspect of American society to be regarded and understood. They are not drawn in depth but embody history and cultural associations that have particular fascination and seem a slap to the staidness and homogeneity of recent films.

Strutting across a spectrum of feminine coquettishness and masculine dynamism, Prince is as incendiary an icon as ever existed on film. He has Dietrich's campy glamour and self-allure, genuine musicianship, and a singing and performance style to match all the musical legends. Morris Day and Jerome Benton resurrect and refine an ethnic performing style (a Cab Calloway–Lester Young hipsterism) that signifies social change as much as it amuses. In their way, these men and the German-Hispanic Apollonia Kotero, as the sought-after woman, bring to the screen the gaudiest, most provocative sexual melodrama in memory. The brazen salaciousness of Prince's music pushes movie candidness forward.

As The Kid, Prince enacts a showbiz-bio that takes generously from the stockpile of backstage clichés but transforms it with his music and renews it with his infusion of spirit and ethnic inflection and signification.

The macho chauvinist tradition of rock is also a part of Prince's blend of funk, rock, gospel, and soul music. While rock seems perfect for film, few pictures use it well; *Purple Rain* percolates with the music's intensity and thrill, using that as its subject. There is a new perspective on sex and on music. (Diana Ross and *Lady Sings the Blues* missed it by a mile; with the routine use of generic and musical commonplaces, no faith was put in the essence of that music.) Prince has brought rock and soul to the center of movies when, after Elvis Presley, *Sgt. Pepper's Lonely Hearts Club Band, Grease, Xanadu, The Blues Brothers, Hard to Hold* and *One Trick Pony*, it looked like it would never happen.

Once again music, before movies, has proved the breakthrough medium for minority artists, with everybody benefiting; *Purple Rain* is the first convincing movie about the lifestyle rock culture has afforded young people. Its rise-to-stardom storyline focuses on how The Kid, now able to make his wildest sexual, financial, and musical dreams possible, has to struggle to make them—and himself—bearable. The script (by director-editor Albert Magnoli and William Blinn) sketches this, and the music amplifies the idea and gives it feeling. Those who can appreciate the meaning of Barbra Streisand's torch song at the end of *Funny Girl* but not Prince's tough-airy, ecstatic guitar solo during this film's title number may not understand the significance of *Purple Rain* working on its own terms, but that is the picture's greatest value.

Produced for $7 million, *Purple Rain* is an object lesson for the method needed to achieve Black expression and visibility in American movies. Financed outside the industry, concerned with its own sphere of activity (quick: name another film set in Minneapolis), it proceeds without ever qualifying or excusing its characters or story first. The film is also rather electrically mounted, disproving the technical wretchedness that seemed part and parcel of the Blaxploitation films and even John Sayles's well-meant but muffled and murkily lit *The Brother From Another Planet*.

*Purple Rain* doesn't avoid the white world; it is included without self-impeding awareness and recalls Lorraine Hansberry's "I don't go around thinking about being Black 24 hours a day" as much as it fulfills Prince's utopian manifesto. The Black characters here are liberated from the hegemony of white movie creativity responsible for the depiction of Black characters as strange and different—not because of their social oppression, but out of the Invisible Man conventions in which Blacks don't really belong in the picture, so if they appear at all it is with diminished character and for unstated purposes. After *Purple Rain,* one can imagine movies where race adds to characterization rather than defines it.

Isolated yet ambitious, Prince has vaulted over the morass in which Black people interested in their movie image usually flounder, stuck in limbo between character and stereotype. Despite their exclusive studio contracts, Richard Pryor (in *The Toy* and *Superman III*) and Eddie Murphy (in anything to date) seem unable to simply appear in movies without first paying for it with a joke. Stan Lathan, the director of *Beat Street,* says, "It's been easy . . . for movies about Blacks to be entertainment films because that is their first area of acceptance and success." What Pryor and Murphy have yet to achieve is a film performance that makes good on the privilege they already have—to oppose or outwit the system of production that means to control or contain them. The horror of watching Pryor in *Superman III* and Murphy in *Best Defense* is not the unfunny lines and ridiculous stunts but the apparent ease with which they submit to their exploitation, cooperating with the Hollywood processes that make every Black a specialty act, a monkey on a string.

The problem is not Pryor's or Murphy's failure to become role models (in America, every millionaire is a role model) but the loss of dignity that results when they traduce the social history we intuit looking at them. Their funny, funny travesties are all we ever get. As entertainers they must know about systematic exploitation and the psychology behind using your talent as a means to success; it is the market value of racial exploitation. They shouldn't deny it, because their audience knows it. The facts of exploitation are an authentic American experience and the kind of story people cherish. Richard Pryor has not had a fiction film to match the appeal of his concert movies (*Live in Concert* shows him at the peak of his art and audience contact), in which the drama of exploitation is out front.

Beyond doubt, the most significantly communicative Black film in recent years, *Sparkle,* dramatizes the dialectics of exploitation and ambition. Directed by Sam O'Steen and written by Joel Schumacher, with music by Curtis Mayfield, *Sparkle* featured Irene Cara and Lonette McKee as sisters in a late-fifties pop singing group. It has a historical significance that even the films of Oscar Micheaux cannot claim: It is the first Black cult movie. In the eight years since its release the film has played with unusual frequency in neighborhood playhouses and inner-city theaters across the country. Only this year, after the success of the similarly themed Broadway show *Dreamgirls* (Mike Nichols congratulated Schumacher on the similarities taken), has *Sparkle* seen repertory bookings in New York City. But among Black moviegoers it's a well-known, well-liked picture. I programmed a film series at the Henry Street Settlement last summer and attendance more than tripled at the *Sparkle* showing. The crowd anticipated the dialogue and sang the lyrics as fanatically as audiences at the Regency act along with *All About Eve*.

*Sparkle*'s success having taken root and *Purple Rain*'s more recently ablaze success ascribe a near aesthetic by which Blacks, just now, can most effectively work in film. *Purple Rain*'s success makes the crucial point that the work Blacks do in movies needn't have a superficial air of worthiness or seriousness; the disgrace of Blaxploitation was not the trash formats but the lack of authenticity and expressiveness. (The best films of that period were the fast, funny, and unpretentious *The Landlord* and *Cotton Comes to Harlem*.) The showbiz milieux of *Sparkle* and *Purple Rain* establish a forum in which Black social and spiritual aspirations receive natural expression as well as evoking a generally recognizable history. The objectification of performance in this setting seizes and vanquishes the aesthetic problem of beauty and appearance—the last frontier of movie acceptance.

*Sparkle*'s most powerful moment arrives when Lonette McKee takes the lead on "What Can I Do with This Feeling?" The stage lights warm her flesh and the camera basks in her sultry radiance. Though McKee is not dark-skinned, her apparent ethnicity mixes with her light complexion and transfixes the audience. The scene creates waves of awe not just from the force of new talent but from once-secure standards of beauty and sex melting down. First-time viewers of *Sparkle* wonder that McKee did not become a major screen presence; *Which Way Is Up* and *Cuba* were her only follow-ups until *The Cotton Club*. Apparently, filmmakers could not use a challenging, sexy, nonwhite woman as easily as young, Black male clowns.

*Sparkle* itself uses McKee and show business as metaphors for the plight of minority existence in racist institutions with very handy parallels to the movie business and to the costuming, mannerisms, and idioms Black performers adopt to both succeed and fulfill their artistic and emotional needs. Like Jean Genet's self-reflexive stage play *The Blacks* (a legendary New York production in 1961 introduced James Earl Jones, Cicely Tyson, Lou Gossett, Raymond St. Jacques, Maya Angelou, Godfrey Cambridge, Charles Gordone, and Roscoe Lee Browne), *Sparkle* and *Purple Rain* make the showbiz genre as viable as it is ironic. Browne's speech in *The Blacks* was prophetic: "They tell us we're grown-up children. In that case, what's left for us? The theater! We'll play at being reflected in it, and we'll see ourselves—big Black narcissists—slowly disappearing into its waters."

There's an undercurrent of dread in these films, unlike such faux-naif, minstrel-plantation shows as *Cabin in the Sky* and *Stormy Weather*, that allows uninhibited and very rich expression. *Purple Rain* might be the kind of movie that can only happen once in a generation. With Prince dancing upon layers of musical history and style and Albert Magnoli consciously evoking the show-within-a-show staging of *Cabaret* and the kinetics of *Mean Streets* and *Taxi Driver, Purple Rain* is like a whirling cultural vortex siphoning bits from assorted areas of pop culture. Prince's title-song performance combines the picture's filial and sexual themes, extends the musical motifs heard throughout, and sums up various plot conflicts with a coherent, expressive magnitude not seen in any movie since *Nashville*. The title number's vision of racial and sexual harmony — in which Prince captures the audience's emotions and literally sways it as one — surpasses Benton's coda in *Places in the Heart*. It shows how a performer on stage controls his projection as either character or stereotype. In this way Prince, Richard Pryor in *Live in Concert,* and the singers in *Sparkle,* more than any Blacks on film in the past decade, achieve full dimensionality.

Perhaps the only Black film artists now possible will be those willing to risk and exploit notions of performance — as Genet intuited in *The Blacks,* but perhaps also like Godard and Fassbinder, though not nearly so didactically. In the perversely homogeneous universe of American movies, Blacks appear awkwardly and apologetically, as outsiders. This enforced restriction on character (with its real-world similarity) creates an extended theater — a heightened existentialism — for Blacks to inhabit.

Only when Blacks are seen on stage can movies accommodate the irony within Black characters. The "Be Black Baby" sequence of Brian DePalma's *Hi, Mom!* satirized the complications of such role playing even, most remarkably, its patronizing acceptance by whites. *Hi, Mom!* was probably the first movie to recognize the calculation, deliberateness, and self-consciousness with which Black people move through white society, and DePalma missed none of the attendant rage. He showed how the absurdity of a social structure, in which racist behavior exists but is transformed into a polite sophisticated routine, required quickened means to expose and explain it. The actors and screenwriters found the means in *Sounder* and *The Landlord,* where the uneven parallels of Black consciousness and social roles are made clear. The showbiz institutions in *Sparkle* and *Purple Rain* make the duality especially vivid.

There are exceptions. Patti LaBelle's eagerness to perform and awesome voice are turned against her by the one-dimensional role she's given in *A Soldier's Story,* and Taylor Hackford's staging of Kid Creole and the Coconuts in *Against All Odds* wasted a great opportunity, catching none of their politics and camp irony. The summer's break-dancing movies also lacked the nerve and scandal of punkish street art. "If art is a crime may

God forgive me" appears on a wall in *Beat Street,* but the exploiters who produced the breakdance movies proved innocent of art. They came up with classic howlers (the mother in *Beat Street* tells breakers the value of school, saying, "Get something to fall back on") but not a story or character congruent with or capable of the anger and political consciousness of rap music. Movies promised rappers a chance to show the world a vision and to celebrate their art (Charlie Ahearn came closest in the basketball improvisation of *Wild Style*), but the filmmakers couldn't translate the music's point, and the didactic songs discouraged further dramatic exposition or humanizing.

The art of the performance in *Purple Rain* is in Prince: playing out the complexities of his character on stage, expressing personal thoughts without private mutterings, standing uniquely but completely human. Black performance art is uninterested in formalistic structure, and Prince expresses himself in *Purple Rain* as great blues artists did: without letting the seams or construct of his junk-movie bio show. This is not a reprise of the deceptive caricature some claim as the true militancy of Stepin Fetchit and Butterfly McQueen—working on someone else's terms, animating false conceptions. It is instead an active demonstration of where Black people stand in American movies: performing, but for their lives.

*Film Comment*
December 1984

# JOYRIDE THROUGH L.A.'S FREAKDOM

*R*EPO *MAN,* a mainstream movie with subculture consciousness, is more like the music of George Clinton, Tonio K., and Ian Dury than it is like other movies.

In fact, its "plot" is reminiscent of the way I once heard a pop-cult musician introduce a tune, saying, "This is an antiwar song that doubles as a science-fiction number about an anorexic person."

The action in *Repo Man* takes similarly lighthearted but genuinely strange twists, much the way Clinton's records make up and sustain their own logic, evincing a unique, almost private, comic vision.

The movie follows Otto (Emilio Estevez), an eighteen-year-old L.A. punk who drifts into half-responsible employment as a car repossessor. He becomes witness to the assorted underworlds of punks, mystics, cranks, and working-class blowhards.

Each of Otto's repo colleagues (particularly Harry Dean Stanton as Bud, and Tracey Walter as Miller, a Stan Laurel-ish visionary) guide him through the various L.A. subcults.

Each one's behavior is idiosyncratic to the point of surreality. When scared Otto runs from a shooting at a repo site, a partner has to talk him through finishing the job, all the while returning the gunfire.

This is the Twilight Zone, all right, where an individual neurosis hooks up with something actually in the streets, though you can never guess how. Everyone is after something, and the elusive object for the repo men turns out to be a Chevy Malibu with an atomic surprise in its trunk.

*Repo Man*'s English-born writer-director, Alex Cox, comes down hard on targets that are easily scored (such as generic food and TV evangelism). But Cox—an idiosyncratic filmmaker if ever there was one—appears sincerely fond of weirdness and its permutations, so that *Repo Man* seems less a comment on American society than an emanation from it.

He doesn't root the society's peculiar energies in full-drawn characters, yet his intelligence is such a terrific lightning rod that he intercepts all the warped, crackled energies running through our thick cultural smog.

Unlike most foreign directors who make films here, Alex Cox gets the lowdown. He makes *Repo Man* subtly, authentically potent in its off-the-wall perspective and humor.

The mix here of technological conspiracies, sex, and social paranoia is a bizarre cultural summation and very up-to-date (right down to *The Day After* special effects and the rhinestone Michael Jackson glove worn by a bureaucrat). It makes for the strangest kind of comedy—a tense one that some may find perversely overloaded and driven, like Tonio K's Sunset Strip humor or a Funkadelic record.

Like George Clinton's sci-fi funk, *Repo Man* operates within a narrow range while also being richly expressive.

Its exaggerated language, unsettled rhythms, and aggressive lunacy that finds sense in nonsense all convey a subculture's unusual vitality. The movie strains between *Taxi Driver* nihilism and *Close Encounters* hope, making both extremes seem authentic and funny, dirty yet bright, like Ian Dury's best songs about English misfits.

The only problem is that *Repo Man*'s story line is about as loose as a Funkadelic narrative. Alex Cox might have fashioned a less erratic story if he'd given Otto more definite ideas, goals, or biases.

After all, L.A. punks, even the make-good kind who become rock-and-roll capitalists, are not as innocuous as Otto. (At times Estevez makes him as much of an innocent, wide-eyed gaper as his father, Martin Sheen, was in *Apocalypse Now*.)

With a more responsive hero, like the pornography pilferer in Ian Dury's "Razzle in My Pocket," no one would mistake *Repo Man* for just an inconsequential joyride through modern American freakdom.

*Repo Man* is a classic contemporary farce, further ahead and more in touch than the year's other films: seldom is it not funny, and its humor is wanton and anarchic in a way that seems appropriate to what it shows as an endemic lunatic fringe.

This could seem disreputable to some, because *Repo Man*'s social-chaos, technology-crazed humor is psychically close to what most people dread as our shame or ruin. Even the generic food joke is not distanced (made jokey-trite) as *Saturday Night Live*–era cultural jokes have been. It's a joke that gets scary the more it appears.

When he deals with emblematic American disappointment—the re-possessed automobile—among proles and crackpots, Cox's sense of humor uncaps the anxieties that official society and bourgeois comedy bottle up.

Most recent comedies (*Ghostbusters, Trading Places, Best Defense, Risky Business*) use a joke or clever remark to abet a phony, contrived situation. Alex Cox gives us straight lines that are edged to satirize the situations (onscreen and off) that we usually take for granted and don't question.

When Bud warns Otto off Communism and Christianity, the inflection points up the craziness of received ideas taken as faith.

Clearly, Alex Cox understands the culture very well. Even the little movie parodies that fill out this one big parody are deeply funny: There's an outrageous, boomeranging joke about a punk who thinks to go straight just before meeting a noisy, gutteral fate that both evokes and ridicules the entire tradition of Hollywood sanctimony. *Repo Man* sees American madness from the inside out.

*The City Sun*
July 25, 1984

# LOOKING AT OURSELVES

M OST FILMMAKERS have to contrive an adventure; Billy Woodberry is automatically at the center of one.

As a Black independent producer, director, and editor, the thirty-six-year-old Woodberry—whose film, *Bless Their Little Hearts,* begins a two-week run December 12 [1984] at the Film Forum—had to secure funds, make creative decisions, and still break new ground.

Like it or not, the latter is a contemporary Black filmmaker's natural burden. The task of creating a new world on screen becomes an inherent obligation when depicting the experience of working-class Black Americans. What this lifestyle—usually overlooked by the movies—requires is at least equal to the demands of creative fantasy that, for instance, the ballyhoo for *Dune* describes for director David Lynch.

Yet, a serious-minded Black filmmaker must also convey his/her subject with force, credibility, and, above all, interest.

From its very first frames, *Bless Their Little Hearts* is dominated by this imperative. It's as if an offscreen voice were whispering entreaties into the ears of Woodberry and his screenwriter, Charles Burnett.

Set in Watts, the film shows how Charlie Banks (Nate Hardman), a young father and husband, becomes disoriented from his life and family when a stretch of unemployment goes long-term. This primal working-class dilemma has an unexpected, almost documentary, plainness in Woodberry's treatment. Banks hangs out with other unemployed friends. He submits to the idle man's temptations of sex and sloth but does all of it undramatically.

The *story* of a Charlie Banks seems not to be Woodberry's interest or concern. Instead, his sensibility picks out the minutiae of habitat—the dripping water faucets, broken oven doors, cramped quarters of the apartment Charlie lives in with his wife (Kaycee Moore) and three kids— along with certain telling behavioral details: the tone of conversations between Charlie and his friends, the wife and hers.

Through these unhyped details, *Bless Their Little Hearts* (like such Black independent films as Spike Lee's *We Do Heads* and Charles Burnett's own *My Brother's Wedding*) may be providing a basic picture of Black American life that other mainstream movies don't offer but might one day build upon.

While watching this film, one realizes that a good part of Woodberry's endeavor involved starting from scratch and finding a tone and a look to effectively convey his characters' lifestyles. In choosing a method between documentary and the stylization of theater, a filmmaker is always faced with the possibility of everything going wrong and the hope that some of his decisions will be right. That's truly adventurous, truly scary.

In addition, Woodberry's filmmaking has to address the biggest problem of the seventies' Blaxploitation movement—its failure to create a strongly suggestive Black movie world. The exploiters never achieved an abstract sense of character or even a sense of life one could believe immediately or in one's dreams. None came up with an image that sticks.

Here, Woodberry takes a chance on presenting Black characters who don't seem to be onscreen as a gimmick, but who are autonomous; whose actions and personalities explain themselves rather than fit a plot function like Fred Williamson's various avengers or Eddie Murphy in *Best Defense.*

The most exciting developments in movie history—like Griffith's, Renoir's, Godard's, and Altman's—have occurred this way: when filmmakers could not rely on established conventions of character or story representation and so changed our way of seeing by discovering their own.

The simplicity of Woodberry's style, his editing and camera placement (in which you can practically feel the pieces being put together), recalls the look of classic humanist trailblazers like the first half of *Open City* and Satyajit Ray's *Pather Panchali.* There is revealed an interest in the humanity of a tribe—seen in the compositions of a young boy's face stiff with fear, or an engaged couple's smiling radiance—that links Woodberry with those movements.

As with Ray, one senses a certain purity of feeling and expression in Woodberry's work. Although not enough to transcend the primitive austerity of his technique, his priorities at least seem to be uncorrupted by Hollywood standard practice. The adventure of this movie is Woodberry's obvious search for the best way to go, the best way to carry the Black filmmaker's burden.

*Bless Their Little Hearts* succeeds when it places that burden on its actors. The economic devastation that hits Charlie Banks and nearly destroys his family eventually builds to a confrontation scene between Charlie and his wife, who feels cheated and humiliated by his weakened initiative and his infidelities. The actors convey the truth of this situation more clearly than does Burnett's script or Woodberry's passive-observer, Cassavetes-style direction.

Nate Hardman maintains Charlie's stubborn egotism, while Kaycee Moore superbly shows the wife's frustration. Her performance, unfolding the wife's compassion in a way that loosens her control, letting the anger pour out in aggressive contradiction and overwhelming the woman herself, is a marvel of unselfconscious acting by which the work of such current divas as Meryl Streep in *Falling in Love* and Hanna Schygulla in *A Love in Germany* withers in comparison.

The surprise of this remarkable scene is that the husband's emotions are less intelligible than the wife's, even though he has been the film's focus.

It is, of course, difficult to sympathize with Charlie's dejection, especially when Burnett's script neglects an explicitly political perspective. But this problem may be more a matter of the filmmaker not testing the protagonist's view, accepting more of Charlie than even his wife does.

Perhaps a Black woman director would be more likely to rise above this problem. But like Woodberry, she'd have to confront it first.

*The City Sun*
December 5, 1984

# TELLING IT ON
# THE MOUNTAIN

*"That the movie star is an 'escape' personality indicates one of the irreducible dangers to which the moviegoer is exposed: the danger of surrendering to the corroboration of one's fantasies as they are thrown back from the screen."*

—JAMES BALDWIN

REJECTION OR ACCEPTANCE? Because the biggest hoodwink this century was effected by film moguls who coded their (our) dreams in WASP-face, that question most disturbs the daydreams of Blacks since discovering and asserting their minority status. Director Stan Lathan crystallizes this dilemma in his 1984 film of James Baldwin's *Go Tell It on the Mountain,* when a Black boy from Harlem goes to the movies. The feature he sees is *Of Human Bondage,* right? But it's the scene where Leslie Howard tells Bette Davis, "I love that music, whenever I hear it I think of you. How pale you are. How strange. How cold." The masochistic dialogue becomes a clever, oblique expression of Baldwin's bitterness about the deprivation Black viewers have suffered from Hollywood (stated at length in his 1975 essay "The Devil Finds Work"). But the evidence of the scene complicates Baldwin's rant.

Lathan intercuts those glowing 1934 images with shots of the young boy—as entranced by them as we are. This creates a surge of conflicting emotions that eventually conveys a shrewd sense of a moviegoer's fantasy. By counterposing cinema's allure and remoteness, the film queers Hollywood's practice of myth and eroticism (largely white) and subtly criticizes its affront to Black audiences.

Lathan, a thirteen-year veteran of TV series from "Sesame Street" to "Cagney and Lacey" and director of the Moms Mabley film *Amazing Grace,* and last year's *Beat Street,* brought his sharpest instincts as a Black journeyman—familiar with the processes of Hollywood but never a part of its inner circle—to bear on the dialectics of this scene. Lathan makes the spellbinding apparition of a young, blond Bette Davis flirting at *you* over a glass of champagne seem looser than reality and positively dreamy. Lathan borrows, illuminates, and subverts this image in order to expose the aesthetic, erotic, and political mysteries that cloud the distance between reel and real life, Hollywood and its public. He isn't afraid to admit that movies have overwhelmed ethnic and experiential differences to capture and mark Black people's imagination. More deeply imagined than the whole of *The Purple Rose of Cairo,* this one scene transforms *Go Tell It on the Mountain* from the story of a Depression-era Black boy's struggle to make sense of his personal heritage into a key statement on Black filmmakers' difficult, awestruck efforts to join the general discourse of American films.

Only a Black person as committed to filmmaking as Lathan would connect these two endeavors and articulate how they converge. This was also the important assumption of the Whitney Museum's major early-summer film series "Recording Blackness: the Visual Rhetoric of Black Independent Film." Yale professor James A. Snead, the series' curator, applied structuralist theory and scholarship to advance an understanding of the current, apparently vague movement to create a serious, authentic Black film culture. Snead's monograph described Black independent filmmakers "revising visual codes surrounding Black skin on screen and in the public realm," and identified as *new* a project Black filmmakers have been engaged in for decades. The only thing new may be the resonance between the segregated race cinema of the twenties and thirties and the work of contemporary Black filmmakers, still struggling to gain screen time.

Ironically, while *Go Tell It on the Mountain* zeroes in on a rarely stated emotional truth (the thirties setting and its production outside the commercial mainstream for PBS's "American Playhouse" conveniently locates and defines the Black filmmaking impulse), the actual progression of Black filmmaking pulls away from achieving that ideal. Unlike Black pop musicians, who proceed from an established cultural advantage, Black filmmakers (through industry and financial restrictions) begin virtually from scratch, working outside the industry as indentured mavericks, perforce against that very Hollywood tradition that entices them.

The longing to create and sustain a Black cinema still exists, as suggested by Steven Spielberg's filming of Alice Walker's *The Color Purple*—an odd historical precedent if ever there was one—yet the fact proves as elusive as ever. It was ten years before Richard Wright could mount a production of his own *Native Son* in 1951 (doomed by an inept, renegade production), and thirty-two years for any filmmaker to adapt a

Baldwin novel. What Spielberg comes up with could change movies forever—instituting the full-scale unstinted treatment of the Black experience, replete with the dream-provoking ethos of a technically proficient big-screen production. But short of such a miracle, the most difficult work addressing the longing for Black films belongs to Black independent filmmakers immediately involved with the challenge to accept or reject Hollywood. It's a cultural imperative.

At the moment, no Black filmmaker could conscionably command the apparatus of light, carefree films like *Desperately Seeking Susan* or *Blood Simple,* because such escapist forms only involve a portion of their imaginations or of what they know about the world. This is also true for whites, but a Black Susan Seidelman or Joel Coen would be politically indefensible. Realizing their work is more than a matter of shading genres, contemporary Black filmmakers can't use the m.o. of race movies, even though they are impelled by the same interests in personalized myth. In the seventies, filmmakers Warrington Hudlin and William Greaves proclaimed their artistic independence through choice of subject, technique, and format (as did William Miles working in documentary). They chose to stand apart from directors of the old separatist, stigmatized race movies and from the newer *Uptown Saturday Night, Fast Forward, The Last Dragon, Mahogany,* and *Lady Sings the Blues* generation of films that did not betray rage at Hollywood's indifference to everything they are.

Experiencing this disaffection teaches a hard lesson: that although Blacks and whites have shared the myths of Hollywood—dreaming at the same icons and projecting fantasies into a common pool—it has been an anomalous activity and a deeply superficial relationship. The critic Julie Burchill recently ridiculed a "beige" tendency in popular music that refused "to recognize any difference between the interests of Black and white—just to dance, to feel good." Black independents habitually avoid simply restyling Hollywood genres, or making chocolate edifices (like *Beverly Hills Cop*) that repeat the usual Hollywood deception of inoculating the public against its history and ignoring a portion of the population by segregating it. Their cautiousness grows out of the American independent movement that produced John Cassavetes's *Shadows* (1960), Michael Roemer and Robert Young's *Nothing but a Man* (1964), Larry Peerce's *One Potato, Two Potato* (1964), Shirley Clarke's *The Cool World* (1964), and Herbert Danska's *Sweet Love, Bitter* (1967), which attempted the first politically informed Black screen characterizations.

The disillusionment and rejection of Hollywood implicit in those earnest depictions of the other America achieved its most explicit articulation in Melvin Van Peebles's 1971 *Sweet Sweetback's Baadasssss Song.*

Through ineptitude and anger Van Peebles assaulted the white bourgeois filmgoing experience with two significant results: alerting the industry that the Black film audience was a thriving, lucrative market (thus Blaxploitation) and encouraging the Black filmmakers in the margins of TV production, theater, and university film courses to approach a politically conscious and now responsive Black audience.

Van Peebles understood—better than Baldwin—the value and liberating thrill of having your fantasies enlarged and electrified ("corroborated") onscreen. Van Peebles played directly to the Black audience's urge to escape (through the uniquely cinematic pleasure of interwoven movement, music, and fantasy), because he sensed how powerfully film could instill ideas and even, through escape, corroborate one's real-life sense of self-worth. He was after a better understanding of the angry, oppressed man's dreams. As Baldwin's literature expressed the truth of his generation, it would change later consciousness about race, heritage, and art and bestow a different, intensified, mythological need—unlike that answered by movies of previous generations. It is a natural effect of pop culture that creates a need for immediacy in art, to have our feelings and experiences defined as singular or timely.

What the stargazing boy in *Go Tell It on the Mountain* felt, Van Peebles also felt, to the point that he knew Black people were missing something by not being allowed to dream of themselves. Ossie Davis's *Cotton Comes to Harlem, Gordon's War,* and *Countdown at Kusini* demonstrate an awareness of this, but Van Peebles acted on it with an unholy vengeance. *Sweetback* is actually a lousy movie, but it has a rampaging spirit—absent in a film directed by Michael Schultz or Sidney Poitier—that carried it all the way to memorable.

Van Peebles never made good on his threat to radically introduce a vital Black screen fantasy world or a Black film ideology, but by linking the political motivations that grew out of the civil rights movement with the autonomy of American independent film, he helped create a new hermeneutics, a new paradigm for alternative Black cinema. And this is the model still in use whenever there is a basic difference between independent Black films and the old race movies or what's being done in Hollywood.

The neo-realist plots about quotidian events, the alternatingly naturalistic/theatrical acting, and the cinema verité technique used in films like Charles Burnett's *Killer of Sheep* and *My Brother's Wedding,* or Bill Woodberry's *Bless Their Little Hearts* rough out an aesthetic determined by the filmmaker's realization that the classical filmmaking style, which developed synchronistically with the generic myths of Hollywood, never included a realistic or truthful appreciation of Black American experience. (The object, David Bordwell has noted, was "a fundamental emotional appeal that transcends class and nation.") Black independents go back to the basics to recognize their response mechanism and discover their creative resources instead of following Hollywood's lead.

In Henry Miller's *Death of a Dunbar Girl* (1977), a two-character power struggle between a vaudevillian mother and her middle-class daughter, the heated discussion about caste resembles the resentment-and-spite bouts of Bergman's *Autumn Sonata* but with the spare visual style of *After the Rehearsal.* The film is almost didactic in its concentration on the issues (putting the polemic foot first), but its reliance on monologue, close-ups, and brief flashbacks to illustrate the women's histories is a deliberate refutation of conventional narrative. Miller perceives narrative as a weapon once used against Black people, and so to be avoided. Snead recognized this skepticism as a response to formula, noting, "Plot seems to limit Blacks' freedom, based as it is upon a sense of general social possibility." Consequently, Black independents move away from authoritative conventions of popular culture.

This is apparent in two recent videotapes presented in the Whitney series: *Color,* directed by Warrington Hudlin and written by Denise Oliver, explores obsession with white beauty standards, and Mary Neema Barnette's *Sky Captain* focuses on a lonely, parentless teenager's need to escape. Structured around two long-take inversions of the Calvin Klein Confession ads, *Color* reviews the period of self-hate predating "Black Is Beautiful," symbolized by a prominently featured poster of Diana Ross and the Supremes, while *Sky Captain* uses a figure in a reggae band as its protagonist's most empathic concept of the proper artistic mode for Blacks. The Supremes represent a past measure of progress and success of mostly nostalgic value now; their style and manner compromised, like race movies, with the dominant ideology and white entertainment forms. By contrast, reggae's politics are overt and intransigent.

And so is Charles Lane's 1977 *A Place in Time,* a short, Afro-style, Chaplinesque silent that parodies the notion of the struggling independent artist's moral superiority. It self-consciously presents a Black street artist ignoring signs of poverty and desperation in his community yet seeking a rapprochement with other Black artists. The film's open-end plot (Where will the artist get his inspiration? How will he make his art?) puts surprising emphasis on the larger issue of Black independents working to arrive at an expressive language.

Alile Sharon Larkin's *A Different Image* shows the progression toward a cohesive development of subject and technique, but the story of a young Black woman's sexual independence (the freedom to have a platonic friendship with a man) loses its equilibrium as Larkin's feminist issue fights the more immediate romantic drama. As a technician, Larkin refrains from exploring the sensual, aesthetic values of the story that first compel a viewer's attention; this confuses Larkin's desire to transcend existing filmmaking modes with the complications of sexual involvement itself. The lead characters are conceived in naturalistic terms, their behavior motile and plausible beyond the denigrating shorthand of caricature that Oscar Micheaux employed. But Larkin comes short of letting her very good instincts play dramatically, and instead grips her subject with a journalist's tenacity that Steinem or Brownmiller would easily approve. Her politics are rigorous, but she fails to break into sensuality or the basic pleasure of narrative.

*A Dream Is What You Wake Up From*, a semi-documentary, encapsulates the divided interests that prevent even the most perspicacious Black filmmakers from taking that next step. Using a "good" and "bad" marriage to outline the social and economic pressures wearing down the Black family structure, co-directors Larry Bullard and Carolyn W. Johnson never connect the two social strata observed or investigate a common machismo in the two troubled marriages. This convoluted attempt at enlightenment is most interesting when the characters withdraw from their dilemma in a girl-talk session or all-male rap. But it's also static. Compiling these scenes doesn't produce a complete picture of a social phenomenon so much as strain toward a totality of Black experience by its all-inclusive display of language, attitude, and situation. In both *A Different Image* and *A Dream*, the logic and documentation are sound, but there's an obvious yearning for an interpretation of these ideas—for art— that remains unfulfilled.

Regrettably, this kind of filmmaking doesn't build a mass audience, and Black filmmakers already have trouble reaching the public through the limited venues of the Harlem Studio Museum, the Newark Black Film Festival, and various PBS formats. (During the thirties, at least, there were upwards of 600 theaters in the race-movie circuit nationwide.) Gearing their work for these alternative outlets shows an audience concept that is just diverse enough to describe a potential, sizable market of political, parochial, and aesthetic-minded tastes. It also suggests the filmmakers' unconscious faith that their disparate efforts might all converge into a commercial movement where Black film artists can hold their own.

These independents, who may simply be too good, too smart for their chosen careers, have reached a point that requires a specific recoding of love, humor, pain, and anger—emotions that decades of Black caricature have obscured or rendered unrecognizable. Because Black experience has never been transformed into an acceptable movie myth, there's an unease inside even the most radically styled independent films about how to frame and present action. The distortions of the old race entertainments aren't reliable guides. If such industry B productions as *Anna Lucasta*, *The Jackie Robinson Story*, *Go, Man, Go!*, *Carmen Jones*, and *Putney Swope* constitute the major Black film heritage, then the independents understandably have no foundation to build upon.

How Black characters might be presented in a politically correct, emotionally resonant situation depends on the filmmaker's mythic or visionary sense of his subject. That's what the boy's trek to the movies symbolizes in *Go Tell It on the Mountain*. Like the hero of Delmore Schwartz's *In Dreams Begin Responsibility,* he stands in the same relationship to the movies as he does to the commanding characters of his parents (Paul Winfield and Olivia Cole in fine, persuasive performances), who have richer dimensions through their fount of memories, which weave in and out of the story. *Mountain* pinpoints the importance of myth and of heritage as an enlivening, troubling, emotional buttress. Lathan controls this material, exploiting effects of memory and filmic representation, and ultimately works the system of Black film financing to more significant effect than any filmmaker in years. But he only gets close to greatness.

The embarrassments made in race movies and the insults instituted in Hollywood's past (*Green Pastures*) and practiced in the present (*Weird Science, St. Elmo's Fire,* and *Volunteers*) have made it necessary for Black filmmakers to reinvent the wheel. Foregrounding pertinent themes, as in *A Dream Is What You Wake Up From,* or overtly manipulating stylistic tropes, as in *Sky Captain* or *Color,* is the filmmaker's attempt at political integrity. It's an art-film answer to a junk-movie hunger. Above all, it's a means of conquering the magic and mystery of movies from the inside out.

*Film Comment*
September 1985

# KIDPIX

W E HAVE SUFFERED James Dean's petulance as the symbol of confused youth for so long that the icon has become a muse. Every
American teenager inherits a mantle of gum-popping, cigarette-
puffing, ass-grabbing saintliness. And as little as this has to do with the truth
of how any of us grew up, it's what filmmakers defer to, keeping faith with a
legacy of arch, superficial, beach-party, sock-hop, street-gang conventions.
One can justifiably deplore so many recent films made for and about
teenagers primarily because they also seem to be made by teenagers—the
smarmy, insensitive, humorless kids you longed to graduate from high
school just to get away from. And did, until you went back to the movies.

Apparently some men and women never grow up to reject the half
truths and falsehoods on which they were raised (beautiful girls are
shallow; bookish girls are sweet) or the updated clichés that now infatuate
them (rebellion itself is a virtue). They just make films about it. As each
of these films shows a young person's first step toward sex and/or wisdom,
there emerges a pattern of American male fantasy securely linked with
Hollywood convention. By regurgitating stock ideas about adolescence,
each teen movie sets the stage for the genre's next fiasco.

If we accept or identify with the ideas in most teen films, it's only
marginally or through other movies. Teenagers themselves don't use
movies for truth or realism. That's why John Hughes's confessional
comedy *The Breakfast Club* is so obviously, miserably fake—the characters don't even talk like teenagers. (And who ever heard of Saturday
detention?) Hughes makes candid and inane what teens only accept or
admit through the stylization of song lyrics or of other movies, like
*Splendor in the Grass, American Graffiti,* or *St. Elmo's Fire,* that answer
their needs for escape and self-gratification with idealized portraits of
themselves. James Dean's embodiment of the yearning, dissatisfied attitude of youth plus the sea change of fifties rock music predicted this
narcissism and solipsism. By now, the process of wooing the teenage
audience by mythicizing it is so deep and complex a part of the production
and function of youth culture that movies can transcend it only when using

a star personality consonant in age and attitude with contemporary youth. Not the Warner Brothers contract youth of the sixties–Troy Donahue, Connie Stevens, Suzanne Pleshette, Diane McBain, or those spurious kids from *Fame,* but the more searching John Travolta in *Saturday Night Fever,* vulnerable Debra Winger in *Urban Cowboy,* and confident Eddie Murphy in *Beverly Hills Cop* (except that Murphy has yet to make his age an important aspect of his character).

Rock music allows us to keep better track of the emotional currents in youth culture even through changes as diverse as those represented by the Beatles, the Sex Pistols, and currently the Smiths, who bring an astounding sophistication to the totems of youth, specifically emphasizing the spoiling, agonizing effects of the sexual revolution on youthful inexperience. At the movies, though, the reflective narrative of experience and coming of age, generally referred to as *bildungsroman* in literature, has taken on the kinetic, slangy influence and mystification of rock music (*Repo Man, D. C. Cab*). Both fiction and documentary filmmakers highlight the *feel* of the protagonist's experiences, creating the coarse, unctuous nonreflective genre we know so well.

Consider the Boy Movies, as Francis Coppola's *The Outsiders* and *Rumble Fish* have come to be known, and the recent documentaries *Seventeen* by Jeff Kreines and Joel DeMott and *Streetwise* by Martin Bell, Mary Ellen Mark, and Cheryl McCall. All cover similar territory: young people in trouble or at its edge, aimless dreamers and malcontents moving between recklessness and semi-responsibility. But only *Seventeen* snaps the fever of youth glorification in which filmmakers gawk and swoon before the altar of youth. Its steady fascination with the daily life of high school students in Muncie, Indiana, eventually exposes the average filmmaker's tendency toward gaudy and tawdry teenage escapades–a fault *Streetwise* commits through its terrible condescension toward the kids who live on the streets of Seattle.

In searching out the truth about these mini-vagabonds, *Streetwise* twists and strains past pity, past outrage, to sideshow delectation and awe. When a kid shown roller-skating through an abandoned building is trailed by a camera on wheels, it destroys any balance between documenting fact and judging it. That rolling camera, used to convey the zest of the kid's experience, also slyly validates it as an act and a sensation of freedom. The urge to fantasize about adolescence (especially troubled adolescence) is apparently stronger than the filmmaker's memory or rational thought on the subject.

The artsy and Arbus-like pictorial compositions in *Streetwise* are just an f-stop away from the conspicuous flamboyance of *The Outsiders* and *Rumble Fish.* Coppola's Boy Movies were like a fever dream of adolescence conjured from pop culture's accumulated romanticizing of youth (homaging *Rebel Without a Cause, The Boy with Green Hair, A Summer Place,* etc.) more than from actual experience, so the gaffes there were more noticeable than in the "factual" *Streetwise*. The latter separates sense from sentiment no better than Coppola does, though the filmmakers had more reason to (*Streetwise* is based on a 1983 *Life* magazine article). *Streetwise*'s opening, with a boy diving off a bridge saying, "I like to fly but I hate having to come back to the fucking world," begs a tragic romanticism (the other side of carefree silliness) that many people find irresistible about adolescence.

The current run of teenage films misperceives the traumatic first encounter with the facts of life. Their only conviction comes from continuing the nearly invincible tradition of teen heartbreak and hilarity (no midrange), where Cyndi Lauper singing "Girls Just Wanna Have Fun" (and inspiring one more rip-off) is merely a dialogue with David Bowie singing "Life is pop of the cherry, when you're a boy." Most teen films (*Valley Girl, Spring Break, Just One of the Guys, Fraternity Vacation, The Wild Life,* and the two hundred others just like them that opened last week) work as a trite verification of those lyrics. Yet if you ever responded to such records, you may understand their sentimental power and see how the adolescent period and style of life are both bound to and distorted by pop's economic and cultural structures that dazzle, seduce, and exploit adolescence.

Filmmakers have only recently rivaled this standard practice of the music biz. George Lucas may have started it all with *American Graffiti*. When he recently told a *Rolling Stone* interviewer, "I'm not interested in making movies that can't be understood by five-year-olds," the meaning and instruction were so unambiguous that his pop-guru status (ever pinching the pulse of the nation) has legitimized the preoccupation with juvenilia and childish points of view in our films. Now, not even a great filmmaker like Coppola approaches a youthful subject with mature detachment.

But perhaps Coppola's film-nut folly was not merely obtuse. His blunders raised the stakes—and should have raised awareness—of what teen movies mean and could possibly be. The rightness in the badness of Coppola's Boy Movies is their resemblance to the jet streams of teenage poetry, like that propelling Bruce Springsteen's most emotional album, *Born to Run* (itself an amalgam of youth myths). The frolics of Pony Boy, Soda Pop, Motorcycle Boy, Rusty James, and their friends were absurdly grandiose, but when backed by the swirling guitar chords of Van Morrison's "Gloria" or seen through the iridescent expressionism of Stephen H. Burum's black-and-white photography, it all felt right—way back there in the corners of your heart and mind that always knew teenage movies were a crock but thrilled to the souped-up vitalism anyway. At once stirring and embarrassing, the Boy Movies failed not because of stylistic excess but from total lack of irony. Coppola didn't carry the stylization far enough to the giddy limits where one sees reality transcended by pop or fantasy run up against reality—as when a good rock musician laughs at the emotion tearing him apart, realizing the adolescent's refusal to take things too seriously, a callow, sometimes very charming cynicism.

Amy Heckerling's *Fast Times at Ridgemont High* accomplishes this in the wet-dream/daydream Judge Reinhold has of Phoebe Cates at the swimming pool, but in Coppola's *Rumble Fish* only the floating hallucination came close. What might have saved Coppola was a greater, probably satirical distance between his vision of boyhood and that of the novel's author, S. E. Hinton. More is needed to indicate the sources of teenage hero worship than highlighting Matt Dillon's flesh and swagger. Coppola bought into the process without exposing or clarifying it. Like Noel Black's recent Boy Movie, *Mischief, The Outsiders* treated a boy's attraction to his tenderhearted brothers and buddies as a rite of ecstasy, and thus threw the whole issue of teen heroism into the shadows of latent homosexuality, keeping the attitudes romantic but obscure. Coppola accepted the presumed sensitivity and fatal beauty of adolescence—"Don't shoot him, he's just a kid!"—the way less hysterical and less artistic movies also present a sentimental, fantasy-derived view of growing up. (Exaggeration may be inherent to the subject, like tall tales told in homeroom Monday mornings.) Unaware that innocent clichés are still clichés, Coppola in *Rumble Fish* tried pumping them up into existential profundities. He missed the crucial paradox of teen culture that while it is banal, there is a precious, unpredictable spark to be drawn from it. Sentimentally, Coppola took Hinton's solemn schoolgirl crush as a reliable measure of the appeal of youth. His vision softened when it should have sharpened.

But we should not forget our thrilled anticipation of Coppola's diptych, which is as significant as our eventual disappointment. It was hoped that Coppola would find, in all that youth material, a perfectly complimentary film language to address his concern with camaraderie and generational inheritance. After all, what have his experiments with form been but a (too) serious response to the changed aesthetics of the children of Marx, Coca-Cola, and Betamax? Since *Apocalypse Now,* Coppola has been trying to make opera out of pop the way his Godfather films made opera of pulp. His legato sensibility may have been wrong for this, but his instincts, like Richard Lester's in *A Hard Day's Night,* were profound.

The visual style of *The Outsiders* and *Rumble Fish,* like the sturm-und-dragstrip moodiness of *Reckless* and the neon graphic intensity of

*Tuff Turf* (shot by Willy Kurant, who also photographed the greatest youth film of all, Jean-Luc Godard's *Masculine-Feminine*) collectively presents an iconography (night, lights, wheels) appropriate to the mythology of adolescence—a trash classicism as basic to movies about youth as the Bo Diddley beat is to primal rock 'n' roll. The look of these films denotes a wily, inchoate ambition to put onscreen rock 'n' roll's vivacity plus the richness and resonance of the best of that music's emotional specificity.

Anchored to pop sound tracks, these teen films try to match the expressive authenticity of the music that sells so well and means so much. This commercial piggybacking of industries could not have been guessed at forty years ago, when MGM collected an Oscar "for depicting the American way of life in the Andy Hardy series of films." Contemporary youth culture is a terrain of comic, horrific experience best defined by rock works as astute and authentic as Stevie Wonder's "Living for the City" and Rod Stewart's "Every Picture Tells a Story"—aural bildungsromans no serious or alert filmmaker can ignore. The dichotomy represented by the Wonder-Stewart songs is more political-sexual than Black-white; Martin Scorsese's *Mean Streets* and *Who's That Knocking at My Door* (despite their racist streak) compliment "Living for the City's" critique of social circumstance even better than the Black-aimed, Lucas-derived *Cooley High* directed by Michael Schultz. Scorsese's coming-of-age films are special and authentic primarily because their form is so strongly shaped by rock sensibility; the tone, structure, and pulse of his pictures feel right, while most youth films are just formula sitcoms with acne.

Brian DePalma has tuned in to the youth-cult wavelength since his second feature, the 1968 draft-dodging comedy *Greetings*. Since then he has perfected a mode of expression so in sync with new-generation attitudes and tastes that his films *Carrie* and *The Fury* are the best fictional films yet to be made in this county explicitly about teenagers. Told in a style of rock 'n' roll, sci-fi hyperbole, these pictures are the genuine article, expressing from the inside the full range of adolescent sexual fear and desire. (Sex is not just Carrie's power, it is the source of her anxiety and confusion; it's also the area where the boy-girl psychic twins in *The Fury* are treacherously exploited by the adult world.) DePalma's depiction of youth has entered mass consciousness as surely as has Michael Jackson's *Thriller,* primarily because of his films' panache and metaphorical cunning.

Peter Bogdanovich's *Mask* suggests a related method of treating adolescent sexuality; when viewed in the context of other films about troubled youth, Bogdanovich's biography of the grotesquely deformed Rocky Dennis seems a companion piece to the summer's other pubescent allegory, Neil Jordan's *The Company of Wolves*. When Rocky falls in love at summer camp, Bogdanovich even works in his own Beauty and the Beast passage to address teenage sexuality. This trail was already knowingly blazed by DePalma in his rock musical *Phantom of the Paradise;* Bogdanovich's tantrum over the Springsteen songs excised from *Mask* primarily indicates his awareness of how he might have explored teenage trauma more effectively through rock 'n' roll. The Hank Williams tunes and fifties TV jingles that reverberate through *The Last Picture Show,* in fact, displayed Bogdanovich's sensitivity to the popular music of young people as a key to their spiritual lives.

For *Mask* Bogdanovich seems to have wanted to replace standard tear jerking with a new sentimentality—the ambiguous emotionality of tough yet lachrymose pop. Despite its factual basis, *Mask* indeed has a pop, sixties youth cult concept, in which outsiders, eccentrics, and misfits make a community together, presided over by the original rock madonna, Cher. The consistent normality of Eric Stolz's performance as Rocky is the near-perfect male counterpoint to *Carrie*—a feat that John Carpenter had everything but the talent to bring about in *Christine.* In the scenes of Rocky's conversation with the young prostitute and his practical demonstration of color to his blind girlfriend, *Mask* has the smartest, classiest treatment of first sex and innocent sensuality since Louis Malle's *Murmur of the Heart.*

Rocky's aspirations outside his circumstances, his quiet but persistent eagerness for romance and social acceptance, are ideally rendered through Anna Hamilton Phelan's shrewd but unemphatic script. The film's box-office success may result from the simplicity of its adolescent story; even its tangential episode with the boy's mother and her own father gives an unforced understanding of the bonds between generations, the complex of parent-child relationships sustained by love as well as disappointment, an issue completely muffed in *Rumble Fish.*

Rocky's disfigurement represents the ignorance and awkwardness of adolescence. The monstrousness of this pure-hearted creature also relieves the filmmakers of the dumb obligation to portray the American kid as an admirable hell raiser. Instead, they concentrate on the aspect of American adolescence that our moviemakers always screw up: making the ordinariness of teenage desire interesting and plausible. The most obvious yet most affecting scene in the film has a distorted fun-house mirror reveal the average boy hidden within Rocky's deformity. It's a startling scene even though you know it's coming, maybe because the scene is also a metaphor for the distortion wrought by teen movies in general.

Only Floyd Mutrux's *Aloha Bobby and Rose* and Walter Hill's *The Warriors* have treated the phenomenon of cultural hegemony that adolescents experience. The kids don't realize the extent to which their thoughts and aspirations are affected by the mass media, but the films imply benighted truth. *Phantom of the Paradise,* Mutrux's *American Hot Wax,* set in the fifties, Hill's future-past *Streets of Fire,* and Robert Zemeckis and Bob Gale's *I Wanna Hold Your Hand* all had the rare perception of how teenagers aided in creating their own Moloch. But the later, contemporary process of industry co-optation—repeated, for example, during the advents of psychedelic, punk, and rap music—occurs so fast (in *Streets of Fire* it is elided) that most people and most movies only catch the result.

The trap that pop culture has become for young people—feeding each new generation an inflated sense of its own vulnerability, ingenuousness, and superiority—is most apparent in the infernal movie conceits of Steven Spielberg, the only filmmaker in the world whose undeniable talent springs from a childish, total immersion in pop culture. Spielberg's rise to prominence parallels the desensitization of American movies. His *E.T.* is arguably the movie of the era for perfecting a child's autistic denial of sex and society into a state of fantastic bliss. Spielberg has mastered movie craft and the emotional archetypes of pop culture almost as a refuge, the way asocial children lock themselves away in comic books, records, and TV. Neil Jordan's *The Company of Wolves* explored this syndrome (It's *E.T.,* as imagined by D. H. Lawrence), while Spielberg continues the justification of it in *The Goonies,* directed by hack Richard Donner.

This treasure hunt–chase film is like the Mickey Mouse Club's old *Spin and Marty* series made epic and interminable. A group of kiddie misfits about to lose their neighborhood to the expansion of a local country club hunt for pirate loot to save their turf. It's not such a wonderful formula anymore. The seven kids are bratty rejects obviously conceived to draw both sympathy and derision (a commercial two-punch: the boys are spunky, the girls squeal, and the Chinese token is told to use the back door). The hunt is a pretext, as are the smart-ass castration jokes, of standard adolescent fear. Essentially, *Goonies* offers a hermetic, movie-fixated pursuit of a childish fantasy life refuting the real world. Only a Hollywood apologist or naive Freudian would consider this grub wonderful, or even edible (Oedipal?).

There's a more conscious dilemma being worked out similar to the cynical youth baiting of more serious films like *Birdy, Falcon and the Snowman,* and *St. Elmo's Fire* that pretend to penetrate the secrets of youth. Here's the count:

*The Goonies* quest begins when their leader waves goodbye to his museum-curator father taking down the American flag—a portentous show of humiliation that the kids bike speedily by.

In *St. Elmo's Fire,* Demi Moore's character, close to suicide, confesses the pain of her father's rejection.

The boys in *Birdy* are physical and mental victims of their parents' hostility (by extension, Vietnam).

*Falcon and the Snowman* shrewdly twists Christopher Boyce and Daulton Lee's espionage travesty into an indictment of American parents and The System.

Aware of their sacrifice, the kids in these films pay the costs of the past two decades' political horrors. Like Demi Moore in *St. Elmo's,* Matthew Modine in *Birdy,* the Goonies who escape to vacuous thrills and exploits, and Daulton Lee, who (Schlesinger's film says) read spy novels between acts of treason, we too may wish to retreat. Consistent here is a willful political denial that the other, more jocose teen movies present as the privilege of youth. But even here politics are flip.

*St. Elmo's Fire* often mentions the current generation's fluctuating, money-based political alliances, yet it specifies everything but their shift from Left to Right (this group is more Jean Negulesco than Mary McCarthy). *Birdy* sings the old Vietnam blues — with violin strings and Peter Pan wire. And though *Falcon and the Snowman* detailed its protagonist's behavior, there was no effort to understand the sincerity of a rash political act. *Goonies* author Christopher Columbus contributes bigoted asides to the ethnic characters, a passing mention of "the hostage crisis" and "Iranian terrorists" (which can't possibly be funny to kids), and arrives at this speech: "Goonies never say die! The next time you see the sky it'll be over another town, the next time you take a test it'll be in another school. Our parents have to do what's right for them, it's their time up there. This is our time!" That's coy but it has the whiff of cold war paranoia, of political conservatism so vague it's actually apathetic.

*Goonies* isn't a *Red Dawn* youth recruitment movie, but like most teenage films it's an invitation to ignore history and recent politics by indulging the kids' hedonistic preoccupations of finding gold, getting laid, or going to the movies. By hooking the Goonies into their parents' dreams — but only those suburban materialist cliché dreams — the film lacks the sense and satisfying resolution of a personal lesson learned, or of a dream hard-won like that danced out at the end of *Purple Rain.*

Having no idea of what a modern teenager dreams, Spielberg is obsessed with curating the junk dreams of Old Hollywood. But maybe he's waking up; *Goonies'* only moment of truth (the discovery of gold, attainment of dreams) brings the kids face to face with death and decay. The desperation and emptiness that sneak through then can't be shaken by the film's happy ending. We have glimpsed the sad inanity of Spielberg applying his wizardly instincts to perpetuating shallow teenage escapism.

The nonstop jokiness and tiresome Rube Goldberg mechanics indicate a paucity of imagination, a dismal spirit, and a determined frivolity.

That's the trap: Movies about young people's dreams that lack inspiration, and our most exuberant young filmmaker can't resist it. Spielberg reenergizes children's farce and restages elaborate chases without rethinking them. When the punks hot-wired rock music, there was a passionate sense of purpose: to define their place in society, to make art relevant, to respond to past icons and past rhythms instead of reiterating them. They screamed "No future!" as an alarm, hoping to secure a future. Boy Movies offer a stultifying surfeit of entertainment, but from *Falcon and the Snowman* to *The Breakfast Club* to *The Goonies* (all titles are interchangeable), the films embody post–baby boom comfort and entropy. This is what the celebrated film generation has come to: a nonironic way of saying "No future."

*Seventeen* avoids this fate-worse-than-Van Halen by moving away from every commonplace of the Boy Movies, providing a fresh, resonant image of American adolescence. Originally produced as a two-hour segment of Peter Davis's PBS series "Middletown", *Seventeen* was rejected for airing as unsuitable. It effects a revision of those experiences we let the media disguise and take from us. The two-person, male-female crew of Kreines and DeMott center on a seventeen-year-old white girl, Lynne Massie, in her interactions with Black and white teenagers at Southside High School in Muncie. The subject is teenage truculence and the transitory, ironic alliances made between sexual and racial opposites.

What Lynne goes through is like the greatest Debra Winger role Debra Winger never played. First seen seated next to a tough, cow-jawed schoolmate, Lynne has a placidity that rivets one's attention; then her sly flirtation with the Black boys in her coed Home Ec class reveals her wit, her softness, her radiance. As Lynne's interracial romances develop, along the typical teenage course of infatuation to resentment, matters get complicated simultaneously by the racial enmity of the Black girls, who resent Lynne and make threatening phone calls to her home, and by the unidentified whites who burn a cross on her parents' lawn. Through these conflicts we see Lynne toughen as she puts down her adversaries; then we see her ebullient personality darken and close down as she defies her parents and restricts her dating to a group of racist white boys. The filmmakers never question Lynne (she and her friends do all the talking), but they never look away either, so *Seventeen* has a more complex interest than would an "objective" journalistic probe into race conflicts in Muncie.

This is a wonderful film for the precise way it captures the unruly, native wit of teenagers (a far different thing from what *Porky's* and TV shows like "Happy Days" or "Room 222" presented). Essentially rude and combative, teenage humor has a shocking, blunt honesty and cruelty. Working with the swiftest, most astute camera control (a back-mounted videocam that gave a sense of participation, if at the cost of occasionally arriving onpoint after an action has just occurred) and directorial sense I've seen in documentary, DeMott and Kreines catch high school experience by conveying its tempo. Robert Altman's revelation during the seventies came from restructuring genres, so that the naturalistic rhythms of events could tell a more truthful story. Similarly, the brilliance of *Seventeen*'s classroom scenes derives from the liveliness and intrigue of the space between events of the sort Altman emphasized: a gesture made behind a teacher's back; the preoccupied indifference a kid feigns before the person speaking to him, by weighing the words then tossing off the burden with a joke or a smile. DeMott and Kreines catch unguarded views of these kids' deepest feelings; for instance, when a boy in love with Lynne listens to her romantic problems with another boy, his own reserve becomes touching.

The filmmakers' organic approach—traveling with the action—gives *Seventeen* a fascinating, almost dramatic grip. At its best, the film shows a lost paradise of American youth and innocence that's closer to ignorance. This essential hard fact eludes most filmmakers. The girlish enthusiasm Lynne expresses for the boys she dates, when alone with DeMott, is, at last, an American equivalent to the Miss 19 Consumer Product interviewee in *Masculine-Feminine*. Lynne's zigzagging emotional momentum carries the right note of experimentation and uncertainty, more characteristic of adolescence than sexual hunger.

Most Boy Movies working with (and out of)masculine bravado portray the variety of teenage anxieties disproportionately, putting sex first. The teen films that are not completely worthless are distinguished by something different: Matt Dillon's first innocent thrall with capitalism in *The Flamingo Kid;* Matthew Modine's mind/body split between sport and the science of sex in *Vision Quest;* Molly Ringwald's and Anthony Michael Hall's sappy-selfish longing for affection in *Sixteen Candles.*

These are the most convincing and affecting teenagers recent American feature films have yet presented. Their personalities are wonderfully, recognizably unmolded; such bogus, loathsome teens as Melissa Gilbert in *Sylvester* or Tom Cruise, in either *Risky Business* or *All the Right Moves,* are figures concocted to validate some filmmaker's personal vainglory. Lynne Massie and friends also believably fumble in their relationships, shucking off false innocence on the way to adulthood, independence, and claiming their social roles—regrettably, it seems, as homegrown racial and sexual bigots. "Unless society changes they'll still be doing what they were doing when we filmed," says DeMott. "Floating back and forth between two different worlds—worlds of boys and girls, worlds of Black and white."

This tragedy gets no sentimental embellishment from DeMott and Kreines, even when it would seem obvious. *Seventeen*'s instances of standardized grief—the pregnancy of one kid, the death of another in a car accident—and the teacher's nonplussed "I-should-give-you-a-lecture" demand that we rethink the poignancy of fleeting youth. We must look at that part of our lives with toughness, and this is exactly the challenge *Seventeen* posed to PBS. The film's sense of balance is apparent in a playful scene between two white girls and a Black boy who rank on each other while keeping their heads down, focused on their papers. The joshing treads the thin line of hostility that the words cross before the kids themselves do. The scene is painful and embarrassing, because the kids don't realize they've blundered across the line until it's too late. The words—the only words they know—demean all three of them.

In its observance of teen preoccupation with swearing, dope smoking, drinking until ugly drunk, and stupid interracial romance (stupid only in everyone's refusal to understand what they're doing), *Seventeen* is better than realistic. It's moral, it presents teenagers in a racial, political context more meaningful than just sex–drugs–rock 'n' roll. It allows them the respectful nonjudgmental distance of each viewer's discovery.

By contrast, *Streetwise* fixes its meanings in pseudo-candid street scenes and voice-over narration by the principals that allows self-dramatization that the filmmakers never question. The street urchins of Seattle (on the other side of the tracks from Matthew Modine in *Vision Quest*) are self-promoting con artists who shouldn't be given their own final, phony words. "I never miss my mom and dad, they're part of my past," one twelve-year-old boy says with a pop singer's fake melancholy. The eulogy spoken at a young suicide's funeral—"He's free, he's never been that way before"—sounds like another melodramatic lie waiting for bombastic rock accompaniment (paging Jim Steinman).

*Streetwise* is an essay on freedom of choice in which the choice is celebrated—"The open road USA is for me," says one kid—then made pathetic, as if the kids who leave home never got a fair shake. *Seventeen* disavows the placating notion of a fair shake; it presents its kids feeling out their moral and social positions, perceiving (as *Streetwise* and most of the Boy Movies do not) every kid's individual significance, making them a part of this country, not special cases or problems. "We're the future, your future!" the Sex Pistols snarled at the beginning of the punk movement.

More lenient and lax than a juvenile court judge, *Streetwise* falls for the kids' reasoning that the street is their extended home and their cronies their extended family (who also eventually abuse them). There's no framework of an institution (school or natural home) to keep what the kids say about themselves in check, no attempt by the filmmakers to keep them honest. The kids' speeches overwhelm any notion of objectivity. When an older boy tells a kid why he can't beg on the street himself (" 'Cause I don't have a face like yours"), or a girl accuses a friend of dying his hair, we know these children are clever, if not exactly smart. But these remarkable flashes—and others involving a young pimp's shy confrontation with his mother and grandmother, and a kid's jail visit to his convict daddy—take another direction from the film's predictable exposé of the demimonde.

A question of personal responsibility hovers over the scenes of fourteen-year-old prostitutes and kiddie panhandlers, but *Streetwise*'s treatment is closer to the cheap thrills of last year's *Angel* (honor student by day, hooker by night) than, say, Godard's *My Life to Live*. The film mixes shocked sensationalism with social-worker piety, just as the crassest entertainments have always done, using juvenile delinquency as an opportunity to indulge a hypocritical interest in adversity and fat-cat condescension to the poor, the underprivileged, and the young. Penelope Spheeris pioneered this modern scam of journalistic slumming in *The Decline of Western Civilization,* where interviews with outré Los Angeles punks were designed to assail a viewer's complacency about youth while exciting curiosity about freaks and desperadoes. Safety pins, vomit, and leather weren't what made the film interesting; its dirt and depravity were made stylish by the participants' youth. There was fascination in seeing bitterness unconnected to experience and terror (or unique discomfort) in seeing rage, young.

The bubble-gum angst of *The Breakfast Club* (a.k.a. *National Lampoon's Persona*) means to trade on this sort of anomaly merely as *Streetwise* does when it fails to even consider and contrast the middle-aged street bums to the kids. The filmmakers don't realize how far they get from exploring the street kids' problems and end up just recording their young, desperate glamour. We're supposed to be moved when Tiny, the child hooker, is left alone in a juvenile home and cries (a tough cookie crumbles), yet the film ends with her as Angel—fancily dressed, spunky, and ready for the night's adventures.

The film's English director, Martin Bell, says this ending simply reflected the shooting schedule, which ended at Halloween. (New title: *Streetmasks!*) He also seemed surprised that when the finished film was shown to the kids and their families, "the families say it's how it is, the kids see it as a home movie."

Of course. It's been the practice for years for filmmakers to depict adolescence according to the jolly, ribbon-tied recollection of how one wanted it to be. There's a box-office prize for presenting idealized adolescence and a critical prize, too. Many reviewers have acclaimed the chic "humanism" of *Streetwise* as if it were revealing reportage, but their ignorance only reflects the filmmaker's shamelessness. Today, reviewers recall the Studebaker reminiscences of *American Graffiti* with more affection than the superior *Last Picture Show,* obviously preferring a recreation of adolescence that harkens to stereotypes of youth. Our contemporary-set Boy Movies perform the same process without the bother of period detail, as if to prove that what people have sentimentalized in other generations of adolescents is true about *all* generations.

Despite directors Martha Coolidge (*Valley Girl*) and Amy Heckerling making their marks in this field (Heckerling's *Ridgemont High* being a high-water mark), the majority of adolescent movies constitute a white-boyish perspective, with phallocentric, blonde-chasing the point of most of the pictures. The strangest image in the whole bunch occurs in *Vision Quest,* in which superjock Frank Jasper walks up the football stadium steps, bearing a phallic weight across his shoulders, an Atlas of juvenile obsessions as worthy of psychoanalytic exegesis as the battering ram in the famous structuralist interpretation of *Young Mr. Lincoln.*

The whole complicated mess of this genre indicts the odious effect of pop culture speaking to millions on an easy, assimilable level. When the kids in *Seventeen* use a radio dedication to honor their dead friend, pop culture seems remote from the choices young people have to live with. An idiot might reflect that perhaps pop best serves its purpose as an escape valve, a conduit of emotion, or as fluff. But the fact of the scene (human emotions that dwarf a wimpy Top-10 hit) strongly suggests that something could help these kids in their life decisions, that the eighties pop arts could be something other than trivial, could be worthy of what they feel.

In this way *Seventeen* sets the record straight. Junk movies can be as guilty as rock 'n' roll in making people think that their personal lives have a simple interpretation or can be sufficiently contained in someone else's prefab mold merely because they have shared pop culture's palliative discourse. The shitstorm of Boy Movies are all crafted from reminiscence as much as reduction, and combined into romance. This does a disservice to every kid who feels misunderstood and every adult who, recalling his own adolescence, feels misunderstood, too.

*Film Comment*
August 1985

# RETHINKING HOLLYWOOD ARCHETYPES

*THE COLOR PURPLE* was the best movie of 1985 – and the strangest. Steven Spielberg adapts Alice Walker's popular tear-jerking novel with gleeful effervescence. He doesn't pretend to identify with the sorrowful story of Southern Black women's struggle in the first third of this century: we might be intrinsically skeptical if he did. Instead, Spielberg shows the same simple, optimistic, childlike perspective of his other films. He brings out the feminist fairy-tale essence of Walker's novel, more than ever confounding and expanding one's view of pop art.

Spielberg's movie recalls a pop tradition so vast it includes D. W. Griffith silents, Lana Turner soap operas, Picasso sculptures, Ntozake Shange plays, rhythm-and-blues and gospel records, Charles Dickens serials, faux naif Black musicals, liberal-social melodramas, and John Ford westerns. The film constantly shifts moods and effects and suggests other movies as Spielberg recreates Walker's fiction out of his own pop-culture syntheses.

Arguably this is the only measure of life that he knows, thus it's also an honest approach. Such a synthesis happens to bring Hollywood further up to date on feminist and racial issues than the critical establishment may be ready to admit or accept. For better or worse, *The Color Purple* is a genuine state-of-pop-consciousness movie. Its deft, undeniably effective emotional displays amid frequent, heavy-handed manipulations force a viewer to understand the artifice of which movie fiction is made and the visual, poetic codes from which Black people and Black experiences have been almost permanently segregated but that Spielberg now restores.

Because of Walker's feminist preoccupation that places racial discrimination second to the oppression of women, the filmmakers (including Dutch screenwriter Menno Meyjes) don't get hung up on the same old fairness bug that prescribed all previous movies about Blacks. Watching this film is like returning to your own reflection in a mirror— you don't notice what others may see, you recognize traits distinctly familiar to yourself, perhaps marveling at their form and substance.

The Color Purple feels like the first insider's movie about Black Americans to come out of Hollywood because the characters aren't defined by their relation to the white world or created through a white artist's sympathetic condescension. These are new Black archetypes; as fictional creations they are so free of political justification that the whole issue of "correctness" is zapped. The actors are simply wonderful to behold (in part because of Spielberg and cinematographer Allen Daviau's determined prettiness). Here, at last, is a vivid panoply of Black faces, well lighted and without exoticism, treated as natural screen images just as white faces always have been.

Because of Spielberg's famous sci-fi benevolence, you could call this "loving the alien" (he automatically transcends those do-good racial allegories The Brother from Another Planet and Enemy Mine). He has made the real advance of treating Black people (characters) as any other. Spielberg's consciousness here is so heightened, it's giddy; he floats above the earthbound particulars that snag other filmmakers who emphasize conventional Black dialects and ghetto atmosphere. Like Walker, who freely accepted these things (she knew that Black and Southern didn't always mean impoverished), he works to convey a spiritual, emotional quality instead.

Not only have reviewers who have compared The Color Purple to Disney's Song of the South misunderstood Spielberg's ingenuousness, they've read it wrong. The film's characters are not carefree, inhuman, or dimensionless. The struggle toward self-respect by the protagonist Celie may be predetermined, but it is neither shallow nor simplistic. Spielberg and Meyjes string together the most telling events of Celie's sojourn: from her submissive self-deception (Celie's advising a man to beat his wife may be the most succinct, multileveled illustration of Uncle Tomism on film) to her developing wiles in a round of pathetic-comic-ironic-then-defiant servant scenes. Each increment of her emotional climb is fleet and dramatically potent.

Profundity has only possessed Spielberg in relation to toys (E.T., Close Encounters, or the climax of The Sugarland Express, where a teddy bear bounces along a road). He's shown amazing depth in ways other "mature" filmmakers could not, such as the moment in Sugarland that wove a man's despair into a few stolen seconds of a Road Runner cartoon. Spielberg's snappy, head-on visual style is risky and arch for drama. It's what always kept people from taking him seriously, and *The Color Purple* often veers into the stylized hyperbole of Frank Tashlin farces and Byron Haskin adventure films.

But this cartoon sensibility is not subtle enough for the few scenes of Black-white interaction—as when Miss Milly (Dana Ivey), a victim of white male supremacy, vents her helplessness in paranoid hysterics. Yet the problem may actually be that Ivey, an expert stage comedienne (*Driving Miss Daisy*), lacks the emotional resonance of the Black actors. But it is nonsense to complain about Spielberg's facility. The precision of any one scene, such as a young widow admitting that her husband died "on top of me," packs an ideological wallop greater than Jill Clayburgh's whole bra-burning career.

The most common dispute with the film regards Spielberg working in broad inappropriate slapstick for fear of alienating his audience. This has invited a backlash long brewing since such loud, blunt, even racist Spielberg productions as *Gremlins*, *Indiana Jones and the Temple of Doom*, and *Goonies*. It's unfortunate that this rancor has erupted with *The Color Purple*, because this film should redeem Spielberg's "genius." His instincts for the entertaining effect here transform Hollywood's entire racist legacy.

Racism in Hollywood films was usually subtle and select—the industry regularly chose not to give fictional validation to the Black experience or to include it only when comically expedient. Post–World War II filmmakers were stumped by the need for revision, and in the civil rights era it was necessary for filmmakers to depict Black characters solely in terms of social transition. The filmmakers could not relax their view, and audiences have been tense ever since. Today the only Black performer regularly involved in recognizable moral dilemmas is a human cartoon (Mr. T.); Broadway maintains the minstrel-show façade of Black life through pastiche shows like *Sophisticated Ladies*, *Ain't Misbehavin'*, *Grind*, and *Dreamgirls*, and the highest-rated TV show in the land is Bill Cosby's pallid Black retread of "Make Room for Daddy". In this context the need for large-scale Black mythical figures—a distilled essence of human experience in black—is greater than ever before.

The first half hour of *The Color Purple* forms the basis of Spielberg's vision of childhood desire and euphoria—a precious but genuine humanist link—and it's miraculous: in a series of classic vignettes Celie is sexually abused by her "Pa," gives birth to two children who are taken from her, and is married off to Mr. (Danny Glover), who finally separates her from her sister Nettie (Akosua Busia). As the young Celie, Desreta Jackson gives the most lucid, affecting child performance since Henry Thomas in *E.T.* She has the emotional transparency of legendary film actresses and, when she is paired with pert, doll-like Busia, the two recall Lillian and Dorothy Gish in *Orphans in the Storm*, D. W. Griffith's 1922 epic about two lost sisters reunited after the French Revolution. Spielberg stages the scenes of Celie and Nettie's separation with a raw, mythic power equal to Griffith's. And if his audacity has the old master, who also directed the Ku Klux Klan romance, *Birth of a Nation*, spinning in his racist grave, it's just! This is the birth of effective Black screen fantasy—not a story of Black people who behave like whites or who finally inherit the kingdom of heaven, as in Marc Connelly's scandalous yet popular insult, *Green Pastures* (1936). It's a vision of Black life that answers strictly emotional imperatives and is the first since King Vidor's unjustly neglected *Hallelujah!* in 1929.

Spielberg's art fills in the gap that has existed between the invention of film fiction and acceptable Black screen portraiture. The narrative here is heroically simple because, as the film's Griffith and Dickens parallels suggest, the political implications don't need to be spelled out; we can intuit them, and in the remarkable teaching scene between Celie and Nettie, Spielberg adds his own sweet structuralist-linguistic flourishes.

Whoopi Goldberg as the adult Celie brings a crucial shrewdness to the film, acting out the character's secret intelligence and at the same time a demonstration of the Black survivalist's bag of tricks. Her childlike playfulness makes the performance more than clever. When Celie blooms under the loving attention of the bisexual blues singer Shug (Margaret Avery), her joyfulness betrays a perfect emotional empathy between actress and director. There is no movie scene this decade better performed and directed than the discovery and reading of letters between Celie and Shug.

The actors carry us through Spielberg's Black remake of pop and movie history—from Shug's Bessie Smith–style dress and singing to the politicization of the Big Mama myth by Oprah Winfrey as Sofia. It also places Walker's tale properly in the tradition of popular women's fiction. We see how *The Color Purple* answers the specific needs of modern women to shape their own triumphant fantasies, as once provided by the books of Edna Ferber and Fannie Hurst and not just For Colored Girls . . . either. In *The Color Purple* one feels a continuity between such early feminist-race relations classics as Ferber's *Show Boat* and Hurst's *Imitation of Life* that also provided the staples of Hollywood melodramas about women who struggled free of dependency on men.

Spielberg somehow manages both the exuberance of *Show Boat* and the emotional punch of *Imitation of Life*; *The Color Purple* should prove as endurably enjoyable as both.

The film fails in one aspect only: It doesn't sufficiently rectify Walker's hatred of men. Spielberg almost gets out of this because Danny Glover—who suddenly and terrifically has become the most important Black male actor since Poitier—has a charming, intelligent presence that enriches the hard-hearted character of Mr., but the script neglects his turnabout. It's stupid to take this as a critique of Black men in particular; the scenes between Glover and Adolph Caesar as his father and Willard Pugh as his son construct a system of oppression that explains machismo as tradition outside race. Anything more would have significantly changed the material, which was conceived in terms of how women sustain each other—exaggerated to the point of idealizing sisterhood as lesbianism (and at the other end projecting machismo into incestuous rape). Spielberg isn't up to rethinking these kinds of literary tricks. He tries expanding himself by crosscutting between Celie in Georgia and her sister in Africa; Shug at the juke joint and her father in church. He does a technically superb shuffle and condensation of various ideological and plot information but not much more (Quincy Jones's overripe score blends themes more effectively).

All this means is that there are limits to Spielberg's artistry and that it's on ground that no other mainstream filmmaker has finessed or even dared. There's much to think about, to feel, much that matters in *The Color Purple*. It's a flawed movie but possibly a great one because it's so vital.

*The City Sun*
January 15, 1986

# BEHIND THE
# BURNT CORK

W_ILLIAMS_ & W_ALKER_, the two-man musical at the American Place Theatre, investigates history and then makes it.

The songs and vaudeville routines of now-legendary Black singer-comic Bert Williams have been assembled and structured by Vincent D. Smith, who recently wrote and performed a show called *Nobody: An Evening with Bert Williams*. Here Smith leaps beyond mere musical biography and that peculiar Broadway variant in which a dead artist's work is exploited as a platform for a rising young performer. Instead, *Williams & Walker,* starring *Dreamgirls* alumni Ben Harney and Vondie Curtis-Hall, offers the stage equivalent to a literary critical biography.

Smith uses Bert Williams's turn-of-the-century experience with minstrel shows and the ethical arguments of W.E.B. Du Bois and Booker T. Washington to formulate an understanding of the aesthetics of Black performance art.

The plot centers on Williams's debut in the Ziegfeld Follies as the first Black man ever to appear in a "legitimate" Broadway revue. The elation of having "made it" is, of course, the springboard for reminiscence, and the play circles back through the events leading up to this moment of triumph. Like Williams, playwright Smith has to rethink showbiz sentimentality; the subject chosen forces him to do so.

The setup is that the Ziegfeld Follies, representing the pinnacle of the American entertainment world, offers Williams dubious acceptance in which he thinks he has ascended to performing his art, as he always dreamed of doing, without concession to the stereotypes of the mass audience's racist expectations. The punchline is that he is existentially typecast in the coon-show tradition.

Florenz Ziegfeld's command that Williams perform on Broadway in blackface—or not at all—crystallizes the crippling, discouraging frustrations that plague all Black performers. Smith is not shocked by this act of bigotry; it's not even a dramatic highlight of the play. Rather, he uses the fact as a hard, governing principle by which he charts Williams's road from rags to riches. The horror of Williams's existential typecasting is rightly projected into a vision of existential heartbreak. The concept is consistent with Williams's extremely lachrymose repertoire but classes it up.

The tear-jerking saga *Lady Sings the Blues*, the rhetorical, bombastic *Ma Rainey's Black Bottom*, and even the new Richard Pryor film *Jo Jo Dancer Your Life Is Calling* all failed to suggest the universality of what individual performers go through. They lacked the saving grace of Smith's perception of the irony in show business.

Portraying a shuffling Black buffoon, a "pathetic character with real feeling," became Williams's trademark. Smith sees Williams's act as art rendered through tortured self-mockery and his stage routines as a passion. Denied the opportunity to expand that clown's act as Charles Chaplin did meant Williams's every performance was loaded with power-ful amounts of resentment, ambition, and cathartic release. Smith takes Williams seriously, if abstractly, and goes for a statement on the Black performer's schizophrenia. The inclusion of George Walker, Williams' partner, who taught the naive kid from Antigua the tricks of survival on the road and of a successful (accepted) Black stage manner, contrasts innocence with experience, reticence with eagerness, rigor with adapt-ability, and stiffness with hip.

As Ben Harney plays Williams and Vondie Curtis-Hall plays Walker, the contrast appears as differences between performers who think too much and those who think just enough to get by. Their arguments represent Williams's own warring conscience; their rehearsals are dia-logues on practicality. Together they articulate what otherwise would be locked in solitude about Williams. The point is that fate put Williams in the spotlight, but no matter how individual his response to the situation, he lived out the dilemma of an entire race (well, species, too).

Onstage and off, Williams presented himself as a response to the then current admonition "Anywhere you see a Negro in America, there's your drama." According to Smith, Williams justified his Follies Blackface appearance, saying, "It's my decision, not preference." This statement of will carries the shame, anger, and pride of one trapped in lifelong debasement. By tracing Williams's story from the West Indies to Stanford University to work in a circus and then in minstrel shows, Smith reveals a phase in Black social progress in the late nineteenth century rarely encountered in stage or film drama. This includes the passing on of narrative and performing traditions and the crucial transition in style (that has virtually been lost to modern audiences) of how white minstrel shows took off from "coon musicals." The exaggeration then became standard, and Black performers like Williams ended up imitating whites imitating Blacks.

This confusion afflicts us today. The value of *Williams & Walker* is that it digs beneath the outrages that some Black performers dare to perpetrate against their own people. The issue is so inflammatory that the play's major weakness—Smith's reluctance to flesh out Williams's story with dramatic incident—probably results from the effort to keep the investigation abstract and thematic. (For instance, the characters' wives are only phantoms during a cakewalk, leaving the women's side of the dilemma to Bessie Smith, Ma Rainey legend.) Shauneille Perry's staging is astringently simple, keeping the two-piece band on the side and Williams and Walker up front in the symbolic black-and-white setting.

Simplicity allows Harney and Curtis-Hall to perform without blackface. They're seen *underneath* the burnt cork, making their performer's impulses the play's dramatic substance. Harney's strong point is singing; Curtis-Hall's is dancing. Both actors admirably show the shrewdness and craft of creating a performance even when it's that of chicken thieves, camp meetings, and razor fights. (It's clever of Harney to use a sly, Robert Guillaume–type pomposity for Williams's speaking voice.) Their skills are so plain and purely enjoyable that you're forced to reconsider and reject the kind of Black drag routine Ben Vereen does, as on a recent TV show where he flagellated himself through a version of "Try a Little Tenderness."

Bert Williams's singular effort to find integrity as a performer is what, for Smith, makes him an ideal, classic figure. It seems the playwright's own fantasy that Williams is eager to play Hamlet, but it is the playwright's genius to make us understand that Williams found his Hamlet (more exactly his *I Pagliacci*) while performing in blackface.

The songs Williams made famous (and wrote the music for)— "Nobody," "Constantly," and "I'd Rather Have Nothin' All of the Time Than Somethin' for a Little While"—have social significance in their titles and genuine force in their tempo and in the way they are performed here. Harney uses his modern Black actor's skepticism and intelligence as a key to Williams's psyche. This tells us that Williams is too smart to settle for the corniness of blackface (Curtis-Hall's slickness also explains Walker's lifestyle: it's what he gladly does to stave off hunger). Harney's role makes a modernist connection—it's what we want to believe—and the songs allow him to transcend it.

His weary sound during "Constantly," a song about isolation and loneliness, gives the tune's sentiment a stronger, more frightening context than usual. I don't know that Bert Williams ever sang with Harney's suffering or utter negation, but it must have occurred to him during moments of exhaustion or pride. That seems to be the secret behind his lilting, rag-era ballads. There's room for revised interpretation within these songs, room for confession and protest.

Smith, Harney, and musical director Ron Metcalf find the range that makes fully emotional articulation possible. The old comedy routines can't be transformed (they're stretched to breaking point), but the musical performances here are so rich they turn blackface conventions inside out.

*Williams & Walker* doesn't make Bert Williams into a quiet radical but something more ambiguous. When he thinks over his past and reiterates "I offer no excuses, but sometimes I wonder," it is the theater's view of the Black performer that is radicalized and, I hope, changed forever.

*The City Sun*
June 4, 1986

# PRINCE LAYS A LUST EGG

*U*NDER THE *CHERRY MOON* never recovers from the first shot of Prince wearing a skullcap with beaded fringe; or a later sight of him bathing in a tub full of flower petals; or subsequent, ill-considered scenes in which he does not sing or dance. This black-and-white fantasy about a Riviera-based American gigolo learning the meaning of true love reveals what little credibility, if not experience, lies beneath Prince's scandalous sexual ethos.

Christopher Tracy, the lead character, rags and exploits women but is essentially his own most ardent lover. That is, Christopher Tracy is Prince when he remembers to hew to the script as written and keep a straight face. After the semi-autobiographical *Purple Rain* and the media blitz that followed, Prince's personality lost its mystery and fascination. (We saw that he was just another ambitious young man but more musical than most.) Neither this script (by Becky Johnston) nor the scraps of music on the sound track make sense of his idiosyncrasies or justify the incongruousness of his consciously effeminate appearance and macho behavior. It's literally a dumb show, saying nothing. (The soundtrack album *Parade* is a different matter: ecstatic musical riffs and political/sexual topics flow into one another with almost cinematic ease.)

We're meant to enjoy Prince's vanity on this European vacation, but he's way out there on his own privately hip course playing a narcissistic martyr. Before the credits a white female's voice says "Christopher Tracy lived for all women but died for one," yet the fantasy is so self-involved that Christopher is not only a sexist prig, he is also the least interesting Black character to be portrayed on the screen in the post–civil rights era.

Prince, with as much freedom as the film industry could grant, has chosen to ignore all the complication and challenge that mere mortals experience and express the invulnerable autonomy of a man who lives like a star. *Purple Rain* dramatized the controversial world he was part of, but this is *his* shadowy universe, with the dim glow of a "cherry moon" (actually Michael Ballhaus's drab, gray cinematography) providing a personal equivalent to rose-colored glasses. Taking over the direction of this film from video ace Mary Lambert (she gets a creative consultant credit: I'd guess for the opening sequence, the film's only dramatically conceived footage), Prince reserves eroticism for the upwardly mobile spectacle of high life on the Mediterranean.

It is impossible not to see this as a confirmation of self into the international scene, sharing the playground of the white elite. It's *Mahogany Part 2* but with the ghetto left far behind. (Christopher and his partner Tricky, played by Jerome Benton, have a sentimental, *Midnight Cowboy*-type longing for Miami Beach.)

In this conception the woman Christopher dies for (and is resurrected, like Christ, to love) has to embody the ideas that a Black sexual con man would lust for: riches and clout. As Mary Sharon, the sought-after heiress, Kristin Scott-Thomas is another of Prince's bicultural sex objects: a Black woman trapped in a white girl's body. Tricky gets one, too. In fact, the only undesirable woman in the film is — pointedly — dark-skinned. Like Apollonia in *Purple Rain,* Mary Sharon has the stereotypical ethnic woman's urge to party, but her special appeal is shown to be that she looks "untainted."

This is odious but commercial as hell: It balances the cast for white viewers and allows Prince's Black fans (teens especially) to indulge that age-old movie habit of projecting their fantasy selves onto an inapposite but representative figure. *Cherry Moon* continues the racist deprivation of Hollywood love stories that made such projecting necessary.

In 1962 Martin Ritt paired Paul Newman and Joanne Woodward with Sidney Poitier and Diahann Carroll in *Paris Blues* to combat the all-white inequities of movie sex. But there's no indication that Prince, who had the foresight to integrate the race and gender of his band, The Revolution, is nearly so shrewd about integrating the conventions of movie coupling. He mounts Scott-Thomas with noticeable vigor (to the tune of "Kiss"), but his courtship is telltale Uncle Tomism.

Christopher-in-Love is Prince's diminutive version of a swaggering buck, and his idea of charming the white heiress is to make fun of the Black dialect pronunciation of "record store." Does Prince laugh as hard when reading the lyric sheets for "I Would Die 4 U" (sic) or "Anotherloverholenyohead" (sic)?

What Prince knows about the thrill of r&b-flavored rock 'n' roll has not translated to his work with movie genre here. Something close to the excitement of his singing can be heard in the rhythm and vocal inflections of his exchanges with Jerome Benton, but the dialogue stinks. It expresses little more than pimp ideology, laying lust eggs for the trinkets of Hollywood bedroom farce and the European jet set.

This would have been groundbreaking—a radicalization of such Continental film classics as *Trouble in Paradise* or *To Catch a Thief*—had Prince confronted the racial antagonism and difficulty that all interracial lovers face, thus questioning the glib assumptions of Hollywood convention. His dubious fantasizing demands the corrective balance of the hard truths that Blacks learn when passing through white society. But if Prince is going to falsify his own experience, what good is his presence in movies? The story in *Under the Cherry Moon* is an expatriate's dream, but it suggests the self-hatred of a man longing to escape himself and his heritage.

*The City Sun*
June 23, 1986

# THE STATE OF GRACE

DON'T FORGET Grace Jones is a Black woman; she hasn't. Her new album, *Inside Story* (Manhattan Records), amounts to a serious, partly autobiographical artistic statement. Jones's songs (cowritten with Bruce Wooley) solidify what has long seemed a flighty, insubstantial persona through ten idiosyncratic expressions/observations of life in the fast lane, or at least the supermarket lane of contemporary pop culture— that's where the thirty-ish Jamaican native acquired some social leverage by making a commodity of herself.

Jones pursued careers as a model, singer, and celebrity with equally suspicious notoriety. By the time her movie career began in 1984, with *Conan the Destroyer,* followed by freaky assignments in *A View to a Kill* (1985) and *Vamp* (1986), the spectacle of Jones's upward mobility seemed desperate, unwholesome, wishy-washy. Even the several good records she made in collaboration with the legendary Sly and Robbie specialized in a remote exoticism. (*Nightclubbing,* in 1981, hybridized reggae, disco, and art rock, winning the critics' poll of England's *New Musical Express* as Best Album of the Year.)

The insufficiency of all that twilight hipness must have encouraged the clear, direct pop attack of *Inside Story.* Its beauty and fun come from another artistic hybrid of Jones's personal history and her increasing musical skills. This album conveys a coherent sensibility and sketches out an intellect—things one never associated with Jones before. Starting with the first single, "I'm Not Perfect," Jones's earthy casualness and obdurate chic are no longer strategic defenses; they provide the tone and perspective through which the ideas on the record are conveyed. That song's rejoinder, "but I'm perfect for you," could be a personal or a general statement; either way, it demonstrates a witty self-acceptance. Jones can now define her ego because after three not-so-hot movies and more than a decade in the limelight, she finally understands it and how to present it effectively.

*Inside Story*'s concept has a lot in common with Prince's *Parade,* the soundtrack to *Under the Cherry Moon,* which, incidentally, was the best

America pop album of last year. Having disgraced himself onscreen in *Cherry Moon,* Prince, working in the medium he knew best, then shaped the album cinematically with impressionist segues and his toughest soul compositions, most of which had not made it to the screen. *Parade* was a triumph despite the terrible movie it represented; *Inside Story* is a launching pad and star vehicle with meanings, form, and pleasure that knowingly counter and makes up for all the poor movies Grace Jones has hidden in. And *Inside Story* is a triumph, too. Jones finds ideal expressiveness through producer Nile Rodgers. They broaden one's idea of what constitutes an authentic Black musical expression by commanding a variety of musical styles with an inherent soulfulness. (Because the record's attitude is Black, it can flirt with other ethnic forms and is successful in the end simply because it's good.)

Jones's method of declaiming over a beat has developed confidence and genuine style. She now breathes and inflects like a *singer,* going beyond the laconic songspeak of Marlene Dietrich that once sufficed for her disco-era demimonde. Jones's sultry manner on *Inside Story* (she drops Nina Simone's name intentionally) goes mellow or clipped to affect and satirize the ever-shifting pretenses of modern sophistication.

Rodgers's group Chic created the definitive mocking sound one hears on *Inside Story,* but that group's most accomplished album, *Take It Off* (1981), flopped, probably because the public could not attach a face to its Black urbane testimonies. (The characters in *Take It Off* make the characters in *She's Gotta Have It* seem like hicks.) With *Inside Story* Jones touches on those middle-class roots—urban soul is the album's moral base—but this is essentially a penthouse in a treetop vision of the hip world.

Jones, here, looks down at the high life she was aspiring to and reflects on its tangled motives and arbitrary priorities. She's not moralistically detached, just rueful. That irony fuels "Hollywood Liar," the album's wittiest tune, which draws parallels between pimps and social climbers. Jones does an audacious French rap that includes herself in the criticism, but her short, instinctive homage to the old "Hollywood Swingin' " by Kool and the Gang is stylish enough to exempt her—she's a fly-girl after all.

Such cool female irony links *Inside Story* to such female manifestoes as Donna Summer's *Bad Girls* and Janet Jackson's *Control,* but this is a smarter record than both of them, and more fascinating in Jones's application of her own self-consciousness. The cuts "Chan Goes to Shanghai" (the latest innovation for producer Rodgers, who polishes a kind of Asian disco lament) and "Victor Should Have Been a Jazz Musician" (a rumination on Black career regrets) help to populate the hip, sparse Jones world and irrigate it with mercy and sympathy.

Jones's ego comes plain in the song "Barefoot in Beverly Hills," the album's strongest, most compelling cut. This apologia for a flashy, infamous lifestyle ("Scary but Fun" a later song suggests) measures Jones's distance from/attachment to the Black working class but with the kind of honesty rarely admitted during a performer's prime. As she sings "I can walk on glass, I can walk on grass, I can walk on you name it," you sense the elation and omnipotence of stardom. Yet the arrogance, and an ironic choral backing, work to make the singer human. Then there's a sobering verse:

> *For thirteen years I walked that beat*
> *There's a callus developed under my feet*
> *What you call a callus*
> *Is an immunity to heat.*

Survival this succinctly rationalized answers curiosity that stars like Eddie Murphy, Richard Pryor, Barbra Streisand, Robert Redford are content to let remain, and it puts Jones in the heady company of an urbane social commentator like Dorothy Parker ("One Perfect Rose") and the heartbroken bitterness of the Caribbean-born writer Jean Rhys ("Mannequin"). A Black female artist certainly has a right to this kind of glamour and pith—especially if it's true to her particular experience and lifestyle. (Diana Ross dresses up, but Grace Jones has style.) Jones's lyrics sometimes fall short of a songwriter's roundedness, often repeating instead of rhyming words, but in wit and snap much of this album is as memorable and quotable as the best of Parker and Rhys: "Unfortunately you're my neighbor/ But certainly not for long" or "I didn't think Chan had a family/ I grew accustomed to his sympathy/ Chan held on to his mystery."

The language is oblique, but the meanings are down-to-earth and accessible. "White Collar Crime" starts from a reference to either Victor Hugo's *Les Misérables* or *Sounder* but shows as much social awareness and outrage at injustice as anything by current rap groups concerned with "the money/power game" that preoccupies Black peoples' struggles. That game is perhaps second only to an erotic/spiritual struggle, and Jones tackles that in the title tune, a personal tribute to her brother whose disillusionment with the Church makes her question (a bit loftily) the source and meaning of art. (The "inside story" is the Jones family story, reminiscent of the sex and religion tension in James Baldwin's *Just Above My Head*.)

*Inside Story* relates prime facets of the Black experience but from unexpected perspectives that bring surprise and diversity, humor and richness to the task.

*The City Sun*
January 14, 1987

# CLASS CLOWNS

N O ONE EVER ASKS Woody Allen for a deeper accounting of his Jewishness; the needling voice and profile seem enough. And until *Radio Days*, that was all. His new film has a fully expressed ethnic consciousness similar to Robert Townsend's *Hollywood Shuffle*. The prevailing truth in each film is the disproportionate importance pop culture has in the imaginative life of the ethnic working class: pop provides contrasting images of escape, then defines the utopia to be dreamed for.

The onscreen representation of each man (Allen narrating as himself and impersonated by a child; Townsend starring as the struggling actor Bobby Taylor) is poised in transition, uncertain and dumbstruck at the possibility of growing up and participating in show business at last. Allen edits across the social barrier between white Manhattan and Jewish Brooklyn as if it were just ethereal. Townsend drives back and forth between Watts and Westwood, intentionally maneuvering between cultures. For Allen, it's a question of putting his Jewish world and white WASP dreams together. Townsend reifies the question of race vs. fantasy into an issue of moral responsibility and ethnic pride.

Neither film shows any difference between working-class Jewish life in forties Rockaway and working-class Black life in eighties Los Angeles that truly matters in the context of showbiz aspiration. The American media-controlling dream is the same for both: Movies seem to reward hard work with luxury — an industry illusion sustained by its own manufacture of rich, flickering images. Woody Allen's near-mastery of this form in *Radio Days* is the very twinkle in the eye of Robert Townsend, whose quirky, energetic *Hollywood Shuffle* is the happiest writer-director-actor debut since Allen's *Take the Money and Run* in 1969.

These comics-turned-filmmakers have their eyes on a particularly bourgeois prize: joining and affecting the mainstream in social fact and artistic practice. The two films mythicize pop culture (radio, movies, TV) as the grail of American mass acceptance. For certain ethnic groups the mass arts (and sports) are the first step on a political, self-determining sojourn. Showbiz represents a high social plateau and realm of power – a belief reflected in Allen's skeptical, bemused recreation of radio game shows and Townsend's of TV detective dramas. The filmmakers' obsessive concern with what, essentially, is trivia is changed by the tension dramatized between the appeal of pop culture and the ethnic ethics it covertly assaults.

Allen's and Townsend's loose-narrative, episodic films are galvanizing displays of each man's psychic attachment to the cultural forms he parodies, backed by a scrutiny of the related social climes of New York broadcasting and Los Angeles film production. In working out the dilemma of upward mobility, they find that cultural assimilation is not compatible with their backgrounds, or else requires a sacrifice in self-esteem and so is an impossibility.

These are the secret truths of American entertainment. Allen's comic reminiscence and Townsend's docucomedy develop the ideas beyond typical, superficial ethnicity, as found in films by those giants of self-deprecation Neil Simon and Eddie Murphy. *Brighton Beach Memoirs* and *The Golden Child* are inflated with the egotism of successful men who don't look back; they have the cold irrelevance of blind ascension into the mainstream, confessing nothing except a belief in the luxury and not the hard work. That showbiz mainstream and that luxury are what *Radio Days* and *Hollywood Shuffle* examine at a distance, and from the position of ethnic self-acceptance. The perspective itself is not warm or successful; these films work because they show the arbitrariness of pop affirmations. There's no pretense, as in *Hannah and Her Sisters,* about the experience Allen is capable of authentically delineating or the WASP lifestyle that infatuates yet eludes him. Allen's return to what he knows is a moral and artistic breakthrough; it is an imperative of the sort that enlivens *Hollywood Shuffle* and gives its refusal of Black success at any price (Eddie Murphy style) a bracing sophistication.

How many people have accepted Woody Allen's high-cult posturing as a way of ratifying their own climb out of a ghetto mentality? The fact that *Radio Days* is the first good movie Woody Allen has made since *Annie Hall* (1977) and his only sign of artistic growth in ten years has been obscured from the public – and possibly from Allen himself – by the mass media's tendency to absorb popular artists and absolve them of any ethnic significance. The reviewer who called *Hannah and Her Sisters* "the best movie ever made about the Jewish longing for assimilation" got it wrong. The movie actually was *symptomatic* of that longing. Allen's sycophantic pandering to WASP pretenses was confused with the honest expression of same.

Becoming the establishment pet stunted Allen's special viewpoint and outsider's acerbity; his daring admissions of ego and insecurity became smug and defensive. As his films took on literary European affectations, his instincts seemed overwhelmed by the process of assimilation. Allen's serious phase—*Interiors, Manhattan, Stardust Memories, A Midsummer Night's Sex Comedy, Zelig, Broadway Danny Rose, Purple Rose of Cairo*, and *Hannah*—seemed totally facetious when not simply embarrassing. This infelicitous output offered no sign of personal knowledge or emotion. It was as if Allen made a gentleman's agreement to avoid being Jewish or, as a last resort, to satirize and patronize it. That accounts for the myth of "class" that surrounds Allen's movies; they were WASPier than films by the WASP, John Avildsen.

Bergman and Fellini became touchstones for Allen, who wanted to make serious non-Jewish art so badly that in remaking *Fanny and Alexander* as *Hannah*, he misinterpreted Bergman's view of the Jew: an outsider and purveyor of magic who saves the WASP hero; Allen turned Bergman's Jew into the death-plagued insider whose infertility is cured by the WASP family! Perhaps working through that perversity allowed Allen to come back to his roots in *Radio Days*. He keeps the Jewish and WASP worlds separate, alternating memory with fantasy. *Amarcord* is the obvious model, but this rigorous memoir is more like Fellini's earlier *I Vitelloni*, where social observation held emotionalism in check, resulting in an unusual purity of feeling.

*Radio Days* itself is like radio, the medium that brings the magical and the mundane together—most memorably in the sequence of the entire nation alert and breathless during a crisis broadcast. The control Allen has developed with pace and active frame composition seems a benefit of finally discovering his reason for making movies. He understands his relation to the WASP world through a nostalgic but not nebulous reconsideration of its media-sanctioned allure. Having owned up to what formed him, Allen accomplishes his most vibrant, sensuous filmmaking, contrasting dark, intimate scenes with glowing, spacious ones—the womb vs. the world—and his humor is felt in both areas.

With the homey/urbane dialectic of *Radio Days*, where ethnic foundations are regarded as respectfully as cosmopolitan expansion, Allen's film career recalls the progression Leslie Fiedler observed in his 1959 essay "The Jew in the American Novel:"

Long before the Jewish novelist existed in America, at any rate, the Jewish character had been invented, and had frozen into the anti-Jewish stereotype. Indeed, one of the problems of the practicing Jewish-American novelist arises form his need to create his protagonists not only out of the life he knows, but *against* the literature on which he, and his readers, have been nurtured. In order to become a novelist, the American

Jew must learn a language (learn it not as his teachers teach it, but as he speaks it with his own stubborn tongue) more complex than a mere lexicon of American words. He must assimilate a traditional vocabulary of images and symbols, changing even as he approaches it—must use it against the grain as it were, to create a compelling counter-image of the Jew, still somehow authentically American.

The failure to do this until *Radio Days* has held Allen back (it may also be what holds him in analysis). Like Rob Reiner in *Stand By Me,* Allen was worshiping at someone else's shrine, promoting ersatz truths. And millions of people agreeing with its fake sentimentality didn't make it less hollow or offensive. Is there anything more ersatz than the Gershwinated opening of *Manhattan,* with its luxe patriotism extolling an idea of a New York that everyone knows does not exist?

Allen's indulgence of such popular romance was a self-denying act, proving his comic's insecurity. (He was as much a climber as was Gershwin.) In *Take the Money and Run,* his too-humble, self-effacing Jewishness—seen in the way Virgil Starkwell's parents wore Groucho masks to shield their identities or Allen turned into a rabbi behind bars—recalled Fiedler's admonition: "Neither a Jew becoming an American . . . nor an American who was a Jew; he communicates in the nonlanguage of anticulture [and] becomes his own stereotype." Who can deny Allen's unique typecasting ("intellectual comic"; "not as vulgar as Mel Brooks"; "the American Ingmar Bergman") as anything but an anomaly? He even used the insidious joke "I wouldn't want to belong to any club that would have me as a member" merely to make credible the Jewish intellectual's delusion that successful competition with the white world makes one an accepted part of it.

With regret, Fiedler noted how "the perfection of the movies [could seal] that victory." But the art of *Radio Days* cracks it. Mia Farrow and Dianne Wiest are no longer bogus sisters, but as Aunt Bea and radio gossip Sally White they are reflections of a common urban female plight, fondly observed. These are the fairest female characters Allen has devised since Annie Hall and are surprisingly, perfectly embodied; this time the actresses aren't pretending to be Everywoman according to Allen's Keaton-smitten WASP idealization. They're also among the few Allen characters who don't talk just like him.

*Radio Days* has a large, splendid cast of *characters,* split into the ways Allen knows them best: the Jews in intimacy, the white celebrities in awe. The simplicity of this method is so right that the film resonates, it's suffused with love. Neil Simon's self-love in *Brighton Beach Memoirs* must account for the casting of WASP pros Blythe Danner and Judith Ivey as a bogus pair of adult sisters in a crowded Jewish home—a shocking attempt at ethnic upgrading that reduces these actresses to shtupping the audience with shtick. Simon has gone further than Allen in passing off Jewish sensibility as "the norm"; he now seems unable to give any behavior its correct value or to wrest human experience from the mechanics of gag writing and plot clichés.

Unlike *Radio Days, Brighton Beach Memoirs* wraps itself in its sugary satisfaction with the good old days. Simon wants to commemorate his past without seeking to understand it. His alter ego, Eugene, seems most ridiculous when he and his brother have a *Long Day's Journey*–type fight with all the unpleasantness resolved; this is O'Neill for idiots. The poignancy of *Radio Days* comes from the intimate suggestion (and brave realization) that the passing of Allen's youth was also his loss of identity. Instead of saying the past was better, like the cheap nostalgia of *Stand By Me* and *Brighton Beach Memoirs*, Allen ruefully admires the ethnic, nonorthodox, left-leaning past that countered his formation by pop. Or maybe he's just saying goodbye to it.

Robert Townsend starts out with the consciousness that Woody Allen has only just acquired. Black artists never enjoyed the ascension/acceptance delusion of Jewish artists, whose institutional camaraderie insulated them from having to know better, as it also protected them from injury. (Which explains why Richard Pryor's memoir, *JoJo Dancer,* is a more tough-minded, if less accomplished film than *Radio Days.*) Townsend embraces the identity he couldn't shunt anyway, and this gives him a skeptical attitude toward the mass-media representation of Blacks that his onscreen character covets. Townsend's debut resembles the scattershot improvisation and comic-intelligence-preening through-a-low-budget of *Take the Money and Run,* but he undercuts denigrating ethnic stereotypes. He makes a Sam Spade character into Sam Ace, where Allen toadied up to them, turning the Jewish street hustler's advice in the title into a comic criminal code. Virgil Starkwell was both a derisive and evasive creation. The hustling dance that Townsend's Bobby Taylor must do to get TV or film work in contemporary Hollywood squarely addresses assimilation and its discontents.

Once a stand-up comedian, Townsend chafes at the fact of ethnic stereotypes his Jewish colleagues often accept; he doesn't share their sense of ironic projection (which is what built Hollywood), where identity is submerged in other characterizations and your responses are detached. This detachment, the source of most media clichés and inauthenticity, has consigned ethnic groups to buffoonery or villainy on screen. Jewish filmmakers rarely subvert it even for themselves, which doesn't mean they are above swallowing and believing stereotype; just that they are reluctant to deny it—because a film like *Hannah,* which depicts a vulgar Jewish household with dirty walls, or *Down and Out in Beverly Hills,* which shows a nouveau riche Jewish home as a dream palace, flatters Jews' sense of personal improvement.

*Hollywood Shuffle* is a renegade production as casual in tone as *Kentucky Fried Movie,* but it offers a shrewd look at Hollywood's benighted attitudes and nonthinking. The parody of producer/casting directors shows Townsend's sharp skill for recognizable caricature. And satires of TV programming, like "Sneaking in the Movies" and "Death of a Breakdancer," are fresh enough to prick the preconceptions otherwise unexplored in the current movie scene—the pomposity of critics, the complacency with which exploitation movies are regarded. All this, coming through Townsend's passion about ethnic stereotyping, makes *Hollywood Shuffle* a rare ethical satire. It drives home the point of cultural and racial misperception that most people ignored in *Soul Man.* (No fault of the filmmakers themselves; *Soul Man,* a more ethics-minded cross-dressing film than *Tootsie,* was, perhaps, not distanced or skillful enough to relax people's anxieties about race. Not a very good film, it still made points and touched nerves as we like to think only good films will.)

Townsend extends his satire over a large field, responding humorously and irreverently to a long exposure to movie and TV junk food—the diet Hollywood directs at Blacks. Unlike Allen, Townsend is perforce part of a cynical, disenfranchised audience, so he's justifiably caustic about the range of media influences. His sensibility as a Black American has been offended, overlooked by the mainstream, or circumscribed and preconceived in Blaxploitation. Accepting neither—showing jive as just a new shuffle—Townsend's satire epitomizes the same revisionist energy Fiedler cited at the birth of the Jewish-American novel. He shows a need to be true to the experience he knows and to create *against* certain lies that have stood uncorrected, unchallenged, without balance.

Yet Townsend's fascination with pop culture is not embittered with disillusionment. He savages *Mandingo, Roots,* even *Rambo* as jovially as playwright George C. Wolfe's *The Colored Museum* satirizes *A Raisin in the Sun* and *For Colored Girls. . . .* Interestingly, like Wolfe, Townsend is too smart to continue the facile dismissals of *The Color Purple.* But he accurately catches the confusion that has stirred around it (climaxing in a protest scene that also plays out Bobby Taylor's private and professional paranoia). Ossie Davis has said that controversies like *The Color Purple* will continue until Black artists get the power to make their own movies. Townsend's modern insight recognizes power even in images like *The Color Purple.* He cherishes media representation, as Woody Allen does, for the formation of his aesthetic sense. That's what inspires *Hollywood*

*Shuffle,* just as we know that the radio/Rockaway juxtapositions Allen recreates are what inspired *Radio Days.*

At this point in his film career and ethnic consciousness, Townsend doesn't afford himself the luxury of reflection, basking in his awe of Hollywood. Yet his reflexive instincts give *Hollywood Shuffle* its edge, defusing pimp and junkie stereotypes by comically exaggerating them or using new-to-movie vernacular and street humor. He digs at ethnic clichés to avoid the Groucho-mask compounding Woody Allen used in *Take the Money and Run;* that film accepted the established contrivances of Jewish comedians as their spiritual essence, and for Allen this was as much intellectual pretense as ethnic naiveté. Townsend won't accept a previous standard of "advancement"; *Hollywood Shuffle* means to change Black movie history. He even keeps Eddie Murphy, the grueling Groucho of his day, on the hook, covering all bases so that there's no chance of leaving his people as figures to be laughed at.

The richness of *Radio Days* shows what Allen's films have lacked. He had seized the freedom to create without questioning it—without earning it—and so made a lot of funny movies but few that matter. A Black filmmaker can take nothing for granted. That, at least, gives Townsend an intellectual advantage. Unable to assume that making movies will automatically raise him in society, or speak well for his people, Townsend is forced to follow the modernist practices that have occasioned the best movies of the past thirty years. His spoofs reexamine conventional filmic representation and rethink his relationship to pop. The remarkable scene of Bobby playing a movie junkie to his kid brother, or Allen's father, aunt, and uncle turning a radio broadcast of "Copacabana" into a song and dance act, charts a period, its illusions and its down-home reality.

These are the richest moments in recent movies. This doesn't mean that Robert Townsend and Woody Allen should only make movies about their own ethnic types, but for complexity and meaning it's the best place to start—or to start all over again.

*Film Comment*
March, 1987

# D'ARBY MAKES POP AWESOME AGAIN

A T THE RISK of spoiling one of the artist's surprises, I want to describe the high point of *Introducing the Hardline According to Terence Trent D'Arby* (Columbia). Side Two closes with the twenty-five-year-old singer's a cappella rendition of own song "As Yet Untitled." It's written after the plaintive style of Billie Holiday's "Strange Fruit" and sung with a similar jazzy dislocation and weariness. The difference is the setting: South Africa in dark, unsettled days before liberation and self-rule. "No grave shall hold my body down / This land is still my home," the singer moans. Then D'Arby clears his throat and in his own fey speaking voice says, "Meanwhile, on the other side of the world . . ." and busts out with a full-hearted arrangement of The Temptations' "Who's Loving You."

The contrast is a kick in the head. Within these two songs D'Arby has encapsulated the complete emotional range of the Black African experience in the Western empire. If you've ever loved a record by a Black artist, you've got to hear this moment; you've got to own up to it. The juxtaposition of African/American, native/exile, politics/romance makes clear sense of the South African struggle, but it also brings a similar political consciousness to bear upon Black achievement in this country. D'Arby helps one to understand Motown and r&b better than before as the cultural expression of a people's new identity—as a poignant, perhaps illusory, belief in the promises of the new world (and the sixties Great Society). These ideas are still at the heart of any love song a Black American sings, so it's right that D'Arby in his two-part triumph be defiant and ardent with equal intensity.

The D'Arby debut album carries a heavy cultural weight with great ease and travels a long historical distance briskly and movingly. This may be the most self-conscious record ever made by a Black man, and so its absolute sincerity and authenticity are a wondrous surprise and relief.

Possessing a softly abrasive, growly voice that, in this age of rap, can be heard as the Rosetta Stone of soul signing, D'Arby recalls Sam Cooke, Al Green, Otis Redding, Wilson Pickett, Joe Tex, Eddie Kendricks, and even a little Sylvester, Prince, Michael Jackson, and many, many others. He's a cultural tape loop playing back to us what those familiar vocal stylings first meant. D'Arby points out both the passion and calculation that were behind them. This postmodernist approach stems from D'Arby's sense of alienation. Born in New Jersey, he spent army time in Europe and became a boxer and then an expatriate Anglophile. His methods are British art-rock methods—that is, American styles reconstructed as a flattering, imitative artifice. Having renamed himself in honor of the British Isles, D'Arby obviously left America only to rediscover it in his heart and most profoundly in his very Black voice. White singers like Rod Stewart and George Michael who tried to make music like this had no spiritual or political context to back it up. But D'Arby has an extra immeasurable essence. It may be patriotic but it's most certainly ethnic, conveying a richness, warmth, and joy that Stewart and Michael only allude to. He uses the exhortation "Dig it!" throughout the album, much as Bruce Springsteen uses the term "Mister" on his, but there's a greater musical vigor and honesty in D'Arby's favorite punctuation. It's anachronistic, but he brings it back in style.

And that's D'Arby's mission: to achieve a rapprochement with soul but always with the knowledge of its art value: its musical sophistication and linguistic significance. Like many young people born during or after the soul heyday, D'Arby slips into those stylings easily, as a shtick. But the great pleasure of his debut is that he avoids cheapening that style by constantly pointing it out as an affectation. If D'Arby has genius—and the purity of his songs "Let's Go Forward" and "Sign Your Name Across My Heart" says he does—it's that he means what he begins as put-on. Listen to how he interpolates the traditional "Wade in the Water" on "Seven More Days"; he further transforms the classic soul transformations of gospel into a new pop archetype.

It's easy to see why D'Arby went abroad to put his eccentricity to effect: no American record label would take a chance on a artsy Black male who looks like Jody Watley. Commercial r&b in the United States insists on a cloned conventionality. (Vandross, O'Neal, Ingram, Freddie Jackson, Oran Juice Jones, Jeffrey Osborne). D'Arby, a platinum-selling chart topper in England, makes good on the sensibility of effete, often effeminate, Black males who carry the complete works of Diana Ross, Donna Summer, Natalie Cole, Dionne Warwick, Gloria Gaynor, and Jennifer Holliday in their hearts. This kind of vocal historicism seems aberrant because it sounds androgynous. D'Arby's huskier tones slip the knot and tap into that special reservoir of musical knowledge and feeling. A great deal of it is gospel-derived, and his album is full of biblical allusions and Father references revised for skeptical, contemporary political listening. ("I'll Never Turn My Back on You," "If You All Get to Heaven.")

The gospel fervor of D'Arby's art-soul shows in his horn arrangements but mainly in his vocal virtuosity. He whoops and shouts constantly, a little like the sisters in church. It's a way of elevating himself into the ecstatic state his neo-r&b constructions demand. His happy urgency puts across the confused love story of "If You Let Me Stay," and "Wishing Well (A Tone Poem)" is, simply, a masterpiece. Between rhyming "riverboat gambler" with "midnight rambler," he dares a sassy, erotic laugh. The laugh implies, "I know that you know where I got this from, and we both know just how perfect it is."

In concert at the Ritz, D'Arby's artifice invited skepticism, but he go-go-danced right by it. Reversing custom, he had two white male backup singers, The Bojangles (schooled in faultless doo-wop and Pentecostal call-and-response). He paid sufficient homage to his masters: Wilson Pickett, Sam Cooke, Smokey Robinson. His remarkable encore was a medley of Rolling Stones songs ("Under My Thumb," "Jumpin' Jack Flash," "Street Fighting Man") done as Mick Jagger, the West's foremost r&b appropriator, probably only dreamed of them—as a gospel stomp. This feat brought the transatlantic, cross-fertilizing of Black art in Western culture full circle. Terence Trent D'Arby makes pop music awesome again.

*The City Sun*
November 4, 1987

# TO BE YOUNG, GIFTED AND WACK

WHITNEY HOUSTON offers affirmation—but of what? Her embodiment of youth, beauty, and talent in the video for her new single "I Wanna Dance with Somebody (Who Loves Me)" makes you want to shout, "Yes!" in response to the song's initial suggestion and to the image of a young Black woman's adoration by the pop media.

The video, directed by Brian Grant, who also did Whitney's "How Will I Know?" video, combines an occasion for celebration with the processes of commercial manipulation. And it works. Whitney wears multicolored, spangly glitz like a crown, but her princess's ebullience is as frightening as it is joyful. One's pride in her success is confounded by the evidence of sellout that this video shows success to mean. She's young, gifted, and wack.

After the multiplatinum success of her debut album, Whitney's second LP clings to a similar formula but without the surprise of unexpected, still-emerging glory that her singing represented.

The extreme disappointment of the new *Whitney* LP is that Arista Records is using the singer as a money machine. The album completely ignores Houston's expressive potentiality. Fitted into songs as atrocious as "Love Is a Contact Sport," and "Didn't We Almost Have It All?," Houston sings as impersonally as a machine. As I listened, I remembered hearing this same sound before—years ago—as a child riding on my first big-office-building elevator. I realized that the advent of Whitney Houston represented the most complete, successful aspiration toward Muzak that a Black female singer has ever achieved.

It was embarrassing during the 1960s when Diana Ross's envy of Barbra Streisand became so obsessive that she and the Supremes recorded an album of *Funny Girl* songs. Houston has reached a plateau of similar middle-class acceptance without the acknowledgment or imitation of previous models. And that seemed a positive sign—even when she hit number one on the charts singing a straight-faced version of "The Great-est Love of All." We had laughed at that song during the seventies as a mawkish ode to self-involvement, not dreaming it would ever be taken seriously. But last year we laughed again—nervously—because Houston seemed to be using it as a theme song for her own aggressive ambition.

The second album from Whitney Houston should have been more than a retailer's event. If she had any artistic interests, surely this was the moment to explore them—even a little. But there's no evidence here that there is any type of music Houston is suited to or prefers (again her gospel potency is left off the record). It could all be just noise to her, because she sings with the same tuneful indifference on each cut.

With her voice and her visibility, Houston could command the pop field almost the way the Beatles did. Instead she has become the pinup girl for youthful professionalism. A new product, not an innovator.

"I Wanna Dance with Somebody" is an undistinguished song, and as a record it's a totally flat, insincere aural experience. It would be negligible without a video to support it, but used as the soundtrack for the Brian Grant piece, it gains amazing resonance. The producer, Narada Michael Walden (he takes an official credit as having "loved" the album into being), is good at constructing upbeat anthems. He supplies a forum for Houston's generalized yearning and exhortations. This energetic naiveté and callow buoyancy turns out to be their specialty. The French film-maker Jean-Luc Godard referred to sixties youth as "the children of Marx and Coca-Cola." Whitney and Narada represent the aesthetics of the children of King and Coca-Cola; they combine the social advances and visibility of the civil rights era with pure commercialism, and they exult in it.

The serious or personal meaning that one misses in Whitney Houston's singing may only indicate that she hasn't yet found a meaning to express or a personality to be true to. In the new video she finesses the smiles, shimmies, poses, and gestures of an adept but vacuous photographer's model. If you should flip TV channels to this video in between news broadcasts, it would come off as a facetious, yet misleading, portrayal of the hope and vivacity young Black Americans feel.

The video plays out the essence of Houston's showbiz triumph. There's a segue from black-and-white footage of her in concert and backstage to a festive, full-color imagining of her own euphoria. In this dream state, however, Houston takes on a new appearance: in long, curly blond tresses (familiar from her first Coke commercial) she becomes a happy pop vixen who makes white men weak in the knees. Even Donnie Simpson on BET's "Video Soul" program says that this is the best Whitney's ever looked—a distressing confession that makes one hope

Whitney intends the song and video as an ironic comment on her celebrity and on the show-business trap that lies before her.

Somehow, not even Mama Cissy Houston or cousin Dionne Warwick seem to have advised her on how to pursue an artist's calling, to sing with some kind of emotional ethnic consciousness. The soullessness of her new album suggests that Whitney must have gotten instruction from Gerry Cooney on Self-Humiliation for Fun and Profit by Representing the Great White Hope (i.e., for another bleached Black vocalist).

So far Whitney Houston stymies the pride we want to have in her. It's plain that Arista Records and its exec Clive Davis have only scratched the surface of her skills—and they've exploited this without allowing her any roots exploration. Whitney's remarkable video ability could, possibly, improve all of the slack material on her album, but it's doubtful if any could be as suggestive as this one. "I Wanna Dance With Somebody" is a song and video of shallow but scary depth.

*The City Sun*
July 8, 1987

# RUN-DMC:
# JEST TO THRILL

SELF-CONSCIOUS JUNK like *Tougher Than Leather* can be more enjoyable than "serious" movies that one grows to disrespect throughout the ordeal of watching them. Rick Rubin, co-owner of Rush Artists Management and Def Jam Records and a producer on Run-DMC and Public Enemy albums, approaches his film directing and screenwriting debut with such lively, low-down expectations that finally getting the film done (and an audience into the theater) is a triumph.

Rubin has made a grungy spectacle that seems renegade, ridiculous, and refreshing. *Tougher Than Leather* proves that anyone can make a movie—specifically, that the lifestyles and fantasies of Black kids, easily transferred to pop music, can also be brought to the screen. More exactly, Rubin shows that the image created by a music act's manager and record label can reflect either supportive or exploitative interests.

In *Tougher Than Leather* the three members of Run-DMC, Joseph Simmons, Darryl McDaniels, and their DJ, Jason Mizell, play themselves as rap artists and as fantasy figures of strong Black male unity. As a cynical twist of the Beatles's *Help* plot, the group is endangered but this time—as a jaundiced view of the music biz—the enemy is their own record company kingpin. Rubin lets art imitate life by playing this part himself. The unexpected admission of racist or pecuniary motives gives the movie real mystery—a much stranger, and stronger, element than suspense.

*Tougher Than Leather* refuses the glamorous, slick, prettified style of rock promos through the use of unashamedly crude compositions and editing (every shot ends with a fade-out). It also builds an image of Run-DMC that is not altogether flattering. The aggression and pettiness of postadolescent machismo are made as obvious as the energetic bluster of the young men who profess it. The movie indulges some gross behavior by Run-DMC (especially toward women), but the indulgence includes a sense of self-mockery (at one point they're even mistaken for Hasidim).

Probably nothing in the recorded works of Run-DMC has the submerged impact of Mizell's fresh-out-of-jail account of an erotic nightmare. His tale is outrageously funny on the surface, but what it suggests psychologically, and his friends' stunned response to it, is also funny. These dudes' egos will stretch a mile (even sag) before they break an inch. That's what "tougher than leather" means: a prophylactic sense of pride.

Run-DMC adopts an urban gangster's code not like the ironic Public Enemy (whose actual logo is white) but with a juvenile enthusiasm. The movie would be fraudulent and offensive if it suggested that this point of view was anything other than fancifulness. Rubin and co-screenwriter Rick Menello shrewdly parallel the jive-macho plots of Blaxploitation movies like *Dolemite, Three the Hard Way*, and *Sweet Jesus Preacher Man*. This is not a tony legacy, but such films do represent the myths of certain class-bound dreamers. *Tougher Than Leather*'s plot is as codified and traditional as what one sees in a western (like the current miserable *Young Guns*), but the settings and atmosphere are resonant of Black urban experience—if not the real deprivation, then certainly the genuine desperation.

It's the pressured youth's will to fantasy that makes this movie kick. A perfect companion piece to last year's *Straight to Hell, Tougher Than Leather* remakes a familiar genre in terms of the raucous, would-be subversive subcultures that embraced it. Rick Rubin shows nothing like Alex Cox's visual finesse in *Straight to Hell,* but few filmmakers have equaled Rubin's unblinking pleasure in the faces and voices, the beauty and wit of Black street kids. Rubin's sensibility opens the screen up to some of the most potent All-American comedy since *Repo Man.*

There's rich social and generational conflict when an older hood says, "A Black man who wants the big money has no choice," and Mizell answers, "A *man* always has a choice." That's two self-righteous attitudes colliding in a Hollywood echo chamber. This reduction admits all the effect that any rap group bravado can ever have. It's modernist pessimism or honesty (take your pick), and one can better understand the importance of rap because of it.

"The movies are gonna make me a big star, cuz I can play the part so well" is a line from "Act Naturally," the country-and-western song that accompanies a Run-DMC barroom brawl. "I always wanted to do this," Run says before ending the scene by smashing the wall mirror. Similarly, Run-DMC and Rick Rubin smash up the urban gangster genre in order to fulfill their own showbiz ambitions. They justify themselves in set pieces like Mizell's "This Little Piggy" scene or the uncanny pathos-comedy about the group's roadie Runny Ray that mirrors their real world with absolute authenticity.

*Tougher Than Leather* is full of the paradoxes that are true to hiphop—the "new" cultural form that is, of course, indebted to the preexisting culture it superficially opposes. This is an anti-Hollywood genre film that thrives on our appreciation of Hollywood tropes. It also teases suspicion about Run-DMC's autonomy by making light of their manipulation by the crime-based record industry. (Rubin hastily signs the white rap act the Beastie Boys, claiming "Nobody wants to watch ten niggers play basketball.") Perhaps that's a tougher subject for a less defensive and less amiable movie.

*The City Sun*
September 27, 1987

# UNDERSTANDING MICHAEL JACKSON

MICHAEL JACKSON's new face stares right at you from the cover of his album *Bad* (Epic), looking lost and accusatory. In the Martin Scorsese music film for the single "Bad," it has even frightened grown children who screamed their outrage in the international press. But Michael's face may be outside the legitimate realm of music and film criticism. As he says on "The Way You Make Me Feel," the album's most infectious cut, "Ain't nobody's business 'cept mine and my baby."

Only the intimates of Jackson's life have a right to complain—or be surprised—at the physiological changes he has made of himself. The skin lightening, eye widening, nose sharpening, chin clefting, plus hair weave and processing are mad-scientist variations on the ethnic grooming and image creation that have long been part of the Black performer's under-stood contract with the white-controlled world of show business.

Most artists submit to it to some degree. Jackson's only gone the Jewish entertainer's nose-job ritual—known as the "Hollywood circumcision"—several organs better.

Almost a hundred years after minstrel shows, Jackson has engineered the ultimate critique/reversal of the blackface tradition. His plastic surgery answers the exploitation and humiliation that have always loomed ambiguously before Black performers who were ready to give the marketplace the face or hairstyle it demanded.

Jackson has speculated on the possibility of becoming the perfect model entertainer. He has cribbed notions of showbiz decorum from that most desperate integrationist, Diana Ross—specifically in terms of music and vocal nuance. But another important touchstone has been the pencil-thin, art-deco stylization of Fred Astaire in movement and dance. As a recombinant showbiz entity Michael Jackson has surpassed both of them. He's the assimilation ideal made flesh; showbiz excellence evolved into lightning-quick speed and efficiency.

Jackson's development, his growing up in public, matters to so many people because he makes the processes of cultural exploitation so plain. From his beginnings as a tinytot James Brown to his current eccentricity as the owner of a hyperbaric chamber and exotic menagerie, he has followed the steps of previous entertainers—becoming an icon for millions, then seeking a personal refuge for his own sensitive/fantasy needs. But the imperatives set before Jackson, structuring his maturation, are to be an artist, an individual, and a Black person. That's one obligation more than Elvis Presley or the Beatles had to deal with. And being Black is more complicated than the other goals.

Racial identity impinges on every move Jackson makes. So it's too simple and insensitive to say that he's trying to be white. His new face is just a manifestation of the compromises he's forced into as private and public person; as a naive young man in an industry of predatory cunning; and as a powerful Black cultural presence skeptically admitted into a largely white hierarchy.

Michael Jackson has become the social and ethnic anomaly he was raised to be. Having achieved with *Thriller* (1982) the greatest success of any performer in two decades (over 40 million sold, ushering in the music video age), Jackson has fashioned himself into what the Western world has ordained: an androgynous, uniracial creature of presumably limitless appeal. His acceptance of this role may certainly indicate a weak ethnic and political foundation (a moral slackening for which his parents should weep). But it's not simply the psychopathology people are eager to cite. The *Bad* album shows that Jackson is in control of his various projections. The success of his art is that he expresses his dilemma well enough for us to understand his neurosis in a larger sense.

Think of Michael Jackson's new face as the Portrait of Dorian Gray for a modern, racially stressed culture. Yet the evidence of brainwashing, self-denial (rather than self-hatred), and willed infantilism denotes more than a Black person's horror story—consider the pop-star-turned-grotesque examples of Judy Garland, Elvis Presley, Keith Richards, et al.

In a 1973 song, "Frankenstein," the protopunk group The New York Dolls sang about a new generation of mutant teenagers whose only response to the contradictory, threatening-and-pampering society they were born into was to become outrageous reflections of its soullessness and technological progress—Frankenstein monsters embodying both a warped hedonism and a moralistic tension. Michael Jackson gave this pop myth a new, Black reading in the song "Thriller," and its music video directed by John Landis. Jackson's career as a young-adult solo artist has proved most original only through such paranoid expressions as the songs "Thriller," "Billie Jean," "Beat It," and the new "Dirty Diana" and

"Smooth Criminal." These songs project a curious terror about sexual relationships but principally a mistrust of personal interaction. The music is an outlet for the dislocated feelings that a superstar teenager, raised to be a nice boy, has no other place to express.

Jackson distills his emotions into a representational showbiz form. That means making records that in style and content link up with the mainstream traditions of Black crossover-sixties pop performers (hence Quincy Jones as producer and Stevie Wonder and Paul McCartney as both influences and guest artists). This makes *Off the Wall* Jackson's most satisfying and consistent display of a Black musical aesthetic and conventional sexuality.

*Thriller* and *Bad* are mixed bags—uneven in quality with alternating authentic and synthetic formulations about either romance ("P.Y.T.," "Liberian Girl") or social consciousness ("Wanna Be Starting Something," "Man in the Mirror"). None of these albums has the fierce idiosyncrasy of Prince's work. The mainstream embraced *Thriller* over Prince's superior *1999* precisely because of Jackson's more muted r&b. It's naive to award Jackson the triumph of *Thriller*—as some Black critics have—without acknowledging the racial sacrifice it entailed. One was impossible without the other.

Jackson obviously knows this as well as his strengths—there is no singer more confidently individual than he—but conquering the world as he has means playing for high stakes. *Bad* is Jackson's acknowledgment of the guises and performances he has mastered in order to be successful.

*Bad*—the Scorsese-Jackson film televised on Labor Day—eclipsed the new movie season. For good reason it was all anyone talked about, but the talk was all wrong. Michael's grisly appearance was so shocking that Richard Price's racist screenplay and Scorsese's remote stereotype characterization of the supporting roles were ignored in favor of whipping Michael. The current anti-Jackson backlash stems directly from his alarming countenance, which disturbed people's easy preconceptions about Black performers and their ethnic integrity. Jackson's ascension via *Thriller* was no big deal because *Thriller* was not a great (just okay) album. But the film *Bad,* by emphasizing Michael's iconography, galvanizes the artist and his inchoate themes. It makes Jackson's socioaesthetic phenomenon a big deal.

The film is this year's most ideologically complex: Scorsese brings proficient craft to Jackson's old-fashioned (*West Side Story*-derived) fantasy about gangs. Out of touch with the reality of Black urban youth, Jackson, as Darryl, a prep school student home for holidays, acts out his distance. It's primarily emotional, because Darryl's "normal" life is preoccupied with winning friends and influencing people in the white world. "How many people you got proud of you?" a Latino schoolmate asks him, trading confidences. Both of them move through the white world strategically, deliberately.

This other-world experience has made Darryl an alien at home, but he is not alienated or insulated from the problems that confront home-boys. A smart Black screenwriter would have known to show cops or whites mistaking Darryl for a hood despite his upward mobility. Price doesn't root Darryl's moral dilemma in his racial identity, and this throws the whole film slightly off. Darryl seems to be Jackson's condescending moral example to the Black kids he was always different from (like Sidney Poitier's impertinent preaching in the films *Fast Forward* and *A Piece of the Action*).

But in fact Darryl is Jackson's attempt at solidarity. He brings the Edmund Perry story to the world by identifying with it. He sees himself as facing the same choices as other young Black men but is able (lucky) to make his decision through art.

There are differences between this and the actual Edmund Perry story. Jackson, Scorsese, and Price pull back from the complexities of the real tragedy, substituting Michael's own particular paranoid preoccupations with masculinity, home, and Blackness. But there's sufficient grimness to the entire seventeen-minute film to keep the circumstances of young Black men who are trapped between ghettoized straits and the indifferent white world and its victimizing perceptions from seeming frivolous. Jackson's/Darryl's song-and-dance championship is shown as his way of beating his destiny in the hostile white world. It's a completely serious, but *stylized,* musical film.

In *Bad* Jackson's face stands as evidence of the physical and emotional price he has paid to be where he is. We fool ourselves to think that Jackson could have gotten there without a heavy cost.

In the *Los Angeles Times* magazine playwright Charles Fuller (*A Soldier's Story*) said, "The use of language to overturn established values is a very positive statement. It seems that the way Michael is using it (the word 'bad') as in 'wonderful,' as in 'great,' and also as in 'tough,' 'very brave,' 'courageous,' 'gallant,' is very positive." But Fuller leaves out that it's also, plainly, vernacular; it's Jackson's statement to the Black audience that "in my way I've won." L.L. Cool J's juvenile attempt to swipe this victory by recording history's first before-the-fact answer record, "I'm Bad," failed to capsize Jackson's onslaught because he limited himself to the usual, stereotyped meaning of the word "bad."

L.L. Cool J hadn't yet learned what Jackson surely knows (or intuits) about the fickleness of the media, who overinflated Jackson and now vigorously ridicule him for believing their blandishments. It's an old racist story—a Jim Crow irony. So when Jackson uses the word "bad" he gives it layers of emotion and shrewdness about how Black people perceive themselves, their talent, and the white world surrounding them. He accepts their success—now on his own terms, now in our tongue. Jackson is richly aided in this by Quincy Jones's background and vocal arrangements, which evoke the Black music styles that anticipated Jackson's preeminence.

The singing and dancing in the film are phenomenal—similar to those in *Beat It* and Janet Jackson's *Nasty* videos but more astonishingly acrobatic and mimetic. At times Jackson's restructured face is perfect for his atomic Tin Man movements. The wit of Jackson fondling himself as he dances registers a self-evident ghetto code (or should Iceberg Slim and Malcolm X rise from their graves to explain it?). Jackson uses the Black musician's ethnic eccentricities, as in transforming the phrase "come on" to "sha-moan." He realizes a non-English, sensuous expression. Even though he has made his stage face permanent, this linguistic confidence is his artistic basis.

Jackson's appearance demonstrates the existential nature of being a Black artist in America. After spending a whole life in the limelight, living in quotation marks, Jackson had their evidence surgically tattooed. It's the blatancy of this act—Jackson's foolish but telling honesty—that's scary.

The substance of the album *Bad* proves there's still beauty and wonder in his singing and music. And when Jackson reprises the line "The whole world has to answer right now," his megalomania becomes a strange political challenge. Right or wrong, no one else could dare it.

*The City Sun*
October 28, 1987

# RHYMIN' REASON

*HYME PAYS* is the best Black literature anyone put on vinyl last year. It's rapper-composer goes by the name Ice-T. He's a Newark, New Jersey, native relocated to Los Angeles who thus approaches street music with a distanced perspective. It's part envy of the crude authenticity of East Coast rap and partly a challenge to it. Ice-T performs like an actor playing a role that is all soliloquies, and each one is jivy, slangy, and profane.

Beginning with a "Twilight Zone" introduction, the ten cuts on *Rhyme Pays* (Sire) are long narratives depicting street life, partying, and male bravado. Ice-T's character is always a tough gangster and ladies' man (the album jacket shows him in his gold-chain open-car element). He is pointedly not a role model, and by that particular, truculent diffidence, he illustrates the wrong choices a young Black man can make.

This is a sly—easily misunderstood—game, even though Ice-T is the most eloquent, vivid, self-conscious representative of badness and chill that rap has produced. Adult listeners may only observe that Ice-T plays his role to the hilt and with such flair that young listeners might dangerously yearn to imitate him (like the teens of the early seventies who took cues from Ron O'Neal in *Superfly*, who Ice-T physically resembles).

But that reaction only takes Ice-T at half his worth. As rap's devil's advocate, Ice-T explores the mentality of a sociopathic rebel. His songs are drenched in Iceberg Slim and *Soul on Ice* and shaped by a recognition of the venality in the social structures that oppress young Black men. He articulates the most cynical attitude heard in pop music since the punk movement.

Because American teenagers (Black and white) are so susceptible to the blandishments of youth-oriented pop culture and so easily seduced by the national dream of success, they do not theorize anarchy as the English punks did. Ice-T, who is secretive about his age but looks and writes twice the maturity of L.L. Cool J., expresses the Black American teen's social ambivalence with special insight. He understands it as upwardly mobile dissatisfaction. His persona is the underclass mirror image of the yuppie;

his self-centered, pleasure-seeking way of life is a reflection of the values taught and the possibilities immediately at hand.

The centerpiece of *Rhyme Pays* is the two-part narrative "6 in the Morning" — a Black underclass compression of *Less Than Zero*, and *Bright Lights, Big City* but less sentimental and better written than either — in which Ice-T narrates his release from jail after a one-year stint.

He rediscovers a limited freedom of the ghetto while looking for action (crime or sex) among his old male friends and women. The song conveys a restless desperation (symbolized by a plane flight east, where nothing changes) that is shared by everyone Ice-T meets. "6 in the Morning" demonstrates the high-strung, furtive activity of characters who are more anxious than night people.

These types sense the inverted priorities, the surreal, existential truth of the world that is only exposed in the after-hours dark and predawn nakedness. It's the revelation of those giddily exhausted exiles who are awake and busy while society's superego sleeps.

This is the vision of a man and a people who have no trust or place in the straight middle-class white world. Everyone in "6 in the Morning" is brought to a decisive moment where "they didn't know what hit them/ didn't have time to ask." Or:

> *Didn't know what happened*
> *Didn't take time to ask*
> *Cops woulda shot them on sight*
> *They wouldn'ta took time to ask*
> *Didn't know who they were*
> *No one had time to ask.*

These lines suggest the nihilistic heat of ghetto living, but the last also evokes a self-immolating resentment. Ice-T's lower-depths realism is also, of course, a description of pain — even in the party songs "Make It Funky," "409," and "Sex." The value of Ice-T's art is that the truth of his descriptions is so precise and so convincingly enunciated that social critique is inseparable from emotional detail. These things aren't in balance; they persist in spite of each other as in the real world — that's the paradox of an oppressed people's endurance. Ice-T does justice to this awesome and awful truth.

Vocally, Ice-T is less bodacious than his New York counterparts, and this is to the benefit of his lengthy, conversational tales. His literary style demands a subtler delivery and reception. He often uses snide, curling intonations like Slick Rick's on "La Di-Da-Dee," which are very effective against Afrikan Islam's spare but primal production. Islam understands the aural space necessary for a storyteller's voice, but he also has a strong, steady, danceable sense of rhythm.

Ice-T's talking book is the first rap album I've heard that I thought might have an even richer meaning for the parents of kids who buy it. His emphasis on sex is outrageous (with unacceptable elements of misogyny and homophobia). But just as his scandalous tongue recalls the revulsion older generations felt for books like Iceberg Slim's *Pimp,* one may be reminded that the reason we were so anxious to read *Pimp* in junior high school was that we knew the dirty life described in it was happening somewhere. As teens the possibilities titillated us; as adults the actuality made us sad and angry.

Working similarly controversial territory, Ice-T shows a more authentic (personal?) pursuit than the political didacticism that many East Coast rappers think is necessary to make their music significant. Ice T's profanity on "I Love Ladies" and "Sex" acts out a macho manifesto so completely that a mature listener will recognize its emotional limits while appreciating its exactitude intellectually or for obvious political agitation. Ice-T takes street culture at face value but has the artist's sensitivity and understanding to see *into* it.

His raps "Squeeze the Trigger" and "Pimpin' Ain't Easy (Somebody Gotta Do It)" are far from exploitation, cheap thrills, or bad examples. It's like street gospel and equal to the vision of Marvin Gaye's *What's Going' On?,* even though you'll never hear Ice-T on the Top 40.

The B-side of his newest twelve-inch single for "Pimpin' Ain't Easy" is a recently recorded takeoff on Michael Jackson, "Our Most Requested Record," in which Ice-T covets Jackson's command of the airwaves and the popular imagination but with the manic exuberance of one who knows that he'll never get it and so rants anyway because he still believes in his own significance.

Ice-T's rap is characterized by what it includes (money, sex, violence) and what it excludes (spirituality). The richness of his rap is that he fully understands the selection he has made.

*The City Sun*
January 6, 1988

# TURN IT UP

THE LATEST Public Enemy single "Bring the Noise" (Def Jam) is part of the soundtrack for the movie *Less Than Zero*. It has less than zero to do with that film's fashion show of white California decadence, but its misplacement is perfect. The strength of the record is that it doesn't—yet—have a place to belong.

On last year's debut album, *Yo! Bum Rush the Show,* Public Enemy presumed to give a voice to the anger of modern Black youth. "Bring the Noise" (not on the album) makes the more audacious effort of searching out a place for that voice, which (the quaking, abrasive sound of the record suggests) will be ANYWHERE IT WANTS. Public Enemy's rappers Chuck D and Flavor Flave specifically designate the radio as a forum, but "Bring the Noise" is not just a literal proposition. It turns "Noise" into a euphemism for revolution, and this prospect redeems Public Enemy. The group shows a purpose and justification by giving their anger direction.

Public Enemy's on-vinyl dynamism combines the slickest, most emotive, and edgy styles of m.c.-ing and scratching. They are poised to be the very best in the field. In England, where the rock press is less racist than in the United States, *New Musical Express* just named *Yo! Bum Rush the Show* the best pop album of 1987. Distanced observers might not have shared the unease I felt with the album. It first sounded disingenuous—like a presentation of rowdy spite, belligerence without ethics, all problem and no solution. I may have been mistaken; Public Enemy was/is in the process of evolving a language of dissent that today's youth can call their own.

The transcendent nature of gospel and the ameliorative functions of the blues have, possibly, forestalled the expression of anger in most Black popular music. The form is seldom practiced, or used, for polemic. But it's the direct expression of rage—minus sarcasm—that makes *Yo! Bum Rush the Show* so powerful and disquieting. This art does not internalize the rappers' concern with race, politics, and sex as things to ponder. Rather, it uses violence as the raw tendency of its young expostulators. The loud, assertive album is both a warning and an act of protest. Listening to the record was like taking a pin out of a grenade and holding it to one's chest: the anger in it was close, palpable—and it felt self-destructive.

Zeroing in on the most common offenses Black Americans experience—police harassment, sexual betrayal, the daily air of suspicion, futility, frustration, and slow death by poverty and drugs—Public Enemy forsook the goodtime affirmations of most rap and pop music. But it took "Bring the Noise" to convince me that their intentional denial of pleasure was also a political challenge. Public Enemy achieves pop culture's most alarming dual pronouncement (of identity and circumstance) since punk: When Chuck D yells "time to blow Black" on "Timebomb," he means both an assertion of racial pride and a nihilistic threat (c.f. "Paint It Black" by the early, not-nice Rolling Stones).

This combination of instinctive and intellectualized anger was unsettling. Public Enemy's aim to awaken rap listeners to the serious hostility of the white world seemed too sophisticated—useless as anything but an effect. (Repeated across the bottom of the album jacket are the words "the government's responsible"—a facile, cute ploy but not half so clever as Ice-T sampling dialogue from a Charles Bronson movie to inform *his* listeners: "Has it ever occurred to you that the President might be the one who wants you dead?")

Now, on "Bring the Noise" Chuck D (Charles Ridenhour), Flavor Flav (William Drayton), their co-writer Hank Shocklee, and co-producer Bill Stephney all solder their own extreme political and aesthetic self-consciousness to the basic unformulated restlessness of their young Black audience. Their ideas are as applicable to everyday living.

*Yo! Bum Rush the Show* is the best-produced rap album to date, yet nothing on it is as eminently danceable as "Bring the Noise" ("Rightstarter" comes close). This new record is more agit-funk than agitprop. It gives Public Enemy's harshest feelings a place to go. The indicator points toward the dance floor and the radio playlists that chart the music industry. Thus the stress is on action and change. With lines like "Farrakhan's a prophet who I think you ought to listen to," their raps aren't mere rantings but a politicized avant-garde idiom created from the ideological exchange of Black knowledge (Chuck D's confident pitchman's voice) and Black innocence (Flavor Flav's pure street roughness).

The teacher-pupil structure of Public Enemy's raps also illustrates the group's relationship to its audience. "Bring the Noise" is an open classroom in which the lesson is: acquiring a sociocultural goal and learning to achieve it. Ever serious, Public Enemy is moving beyond the victim status of its name. They are as didactic as their audience needs them to be, and so both parties gain selfhood with each rpm. Their best, angriest work is to come.

*The City Sun*
January 20, 1988

# A REDISCOVERY OF THE OBVIOUS

THE JUBA DANCE that closes the first act of *Joe Turner's Come and Gone* is the play's most interesting moment: The extended family of characters from the Black working class of 1911 Pittsburgh relax into a song after a Sunday dinner in the play's boardinghouse setting. This turns into a startling, rhythmic celebration in which we suddenly see that they are *African*. For all their American preoccupations with livelihood and survival, the old world lingers in their blood, their energy, their unconscious.

This point is too didactic, but it sets up the play's climax: The singing and dancing common folk are joined by an outsider—Herald Loomis, dressed in black, who has dragged his ten-year-old daughter around the country looking for his estranged wife.

Loomis, a resident in the boardinghouse posing as a church deacon, stomps his feet and immediately elevates the juba dance several metaphysical notches. He's possessed by the devil of white religion, seen here as a ruse designed to keep Black people content with their oppression. Loomis shivers, keels under, spasms and convulses. The juba dance shakes up something primal inside him, and we watch the pure African spirit fighting for dominion over the Black American's mind and body.

Delroy Lindo plays Loomis as a large-scale myth—which gives him an advantage over the other cast members, who act the play's other pedestrian scenes in a boring, drawn-out manner. Lindo/Loomis stands in a separate, stylized realm of self-conscious theatrical poetry that the playwright August Wilson doesn't utilize enough but relies on.

*Joe Turner's Come and Gone* is stretched between realistic and fantastic discourses. Wilson takes his literary summation of the Afro-American religious experience as a proven anthropological fact. He plays to the need for roots and cultural reenlightenment more so than to the psychological truth of Black religious confusion. It's a thesis play in the cumbersome disguise of a historical recreation. (Director Lloyd Richards's staging brings back the Victorian-era frieze.)

The result: mundane drama—the daily routine of Seth and Bertha Holly running their boardinghouse, the interactions and flirtations of the various tenants—grinds on slowly, portentously. Wilson is too aware of the value that will be placed on the dramatizing of the Black working class to be bothered with making it interesting.

On the other hand, Wilson's depiction of how African religion and voodoo thrive at the periphery or lie hidden in the center of the twentieth century's new urban Black lifestyles is unavoidably intriguing. He doesn't bother detailing this most controversial proposition; such playwright's fiat is effective, but it's also superficial. Stage magic can't substitute a sensible religious dialogue.

When Loomis finally meets up with his ex-wife—an evangelist named Martha Pentecost—the schema that opposes male/female, Black/white, African/Christian is too neat. Wilson seems satisfied with the obviousness of Difference. He fails to push his examination to a radical point of total agnosticism or dismissal. Both Loomis and Martha Pentecost might have something to say on the issue of faith but this interests Wilson the least.

One day we will be glad that August Wilson's body of work has emerged and gained significance in the contemporary theatrical mainstream. He at least puts some measure of Black thought into general consciousness. But now, dealing with his decade-by-decade chronicle of Black American experience as each play opens, is unsatisfying. *Joe Turner,* like *Ma Rainey's Black Bottom* and *Fences,* feels incomplete, tentative, a lone piece of a jigsaw puzzle.

Of the three Wilson plays to reach Broadway so far, *Fences* has the best writing and *Ma Rainey* the best structure, but *Joe Turner* is the most resonant, even though it is also the most severely flawed.

The ultimate Wilson character would probably be a preacher (male or female) who speaks out about the difficulty of earthly existence and then thinks or talks or sings his/her way through to an intellectualization of it that saves his/her psyche. *Joe Turner* gets close to achieving the Wilson ideal through Loomis, but Wilson, despite a couple of years of workshop honing, buries Loomis among the unextraordinary characters. This play does not go as far as it could. It needs to be galvanized by a full portrayal of Loomis (Lindo certainly seems up to the task). Between Loomis and the boardinghouse actors (who seem to be doing an unfunny episode of *Sanford & Son*), the whole play seems like a sketch for ideas to be concentrated on in later work.

Wilson, whose writing expresses a skeptical regard for all the means Blacks have found to make their American sojourn bearable, here seems to be advocating a neo-Garvey realization. This is distinct from actually finding a soul connection with Africa. The juba dance itself is symbolic only.

Bynum Walker, the play's conjure man–visionary, who coaxes Loomis through his psychic seizure, warns that the white man "wants your song, he wants to learn how to sing it." That's Wilson's explanation of racist exploitation, but it's also close to a sentimentalization: If all Black people need is their own song to sing, slavery and oppression wouldn't matter (it never stopped them from singing). Wilson doesn't discover the tune that keeps Black people sane—or prove whether anything does. He confuses the degradation of racist society with the complexities of sex and religion, but he never constructs a clear understanding of how one can affect the other.

Wilson's implied syllogism—that Joe Turner (the dread figure from the blues) equals Mr. Charlie equals the Black Christian's Mr. Jesus—is facile. An existential vision of how Black people choose to live gets diminished by this smug pseudo-profundity. Wilson's suggestion that Black people need to exorcise themselves of white religion is not news. It's an ideological coup worthy of 1911.

*The City Sun*
April 6, 1988

# VERNON REID'S FEAR OF MUSIC

V ERNON REID may have the best haircut in the city, but his head has been turned around by the racist ideas that prevail in the thinking about rock music. Reid's band, Living Colour, a Black four-man unit, narrows the definition of rock 'n' roll. Most people who think of rock as any popular music with a strong beat use a hazy definition that implies the influence of African rhythms on American music (as well as the primal insistence of other ethnic rhythms that are present in modern musical modes). Instead of working toward the plurality of popular music, Living Colour follows the strictest—whitest—ideas of what rock music should be. It's a challenging, but not exciting, idea.

Reid's electric guitar sustains a wild, blaring sound, using distortion for visceral impact. Drummer William Calhoun pounds out a mechanical fury, and bass player Muzz Skillings backs it up, often provoking the funk meters that occasionally take over. Lead vocalist Corey Glover yells on top of it all; he has an r&b singer's pitch but a rocker's displaced energy, screaming for the sound of it and not for any particular meaning.

None of this white rock stylization distinguishes Living Colour from a novelty act like the Beastie Boys, The Average White Band or Wild Cherry, whose 1975 hit, "Play That Funk Music, White Boy," enunciated a racial joke here reversed by Living Colour's lite-metal raveups. And since Reid & Co. don't come up with a new sound (as did Chuck Berry, Sly & The Family Stone, Jimi Hendrix, or Chic), their oddness is all that's left.

From Reid's springy crewcut that suggests upright (or uptight) dread-locks to the Anglican spelling of the band's name, everything about Living Colour seems deliberate and self-consciously political. Their debut album, *Vivid* (Epic), contains a theme song that asks and answers, "What's your favorite color, baby? Living color!" This is a neo-Black band. That means it's racially assertive yet insistent about proving its awareness of white culture. It's a highly intellectual, New York position, as opposed to the West Coast neo-Blackness of a group like Fishbone, who assume the right to appropriate American-British-Caribbean culture without much fuss but with a lot more humor and style. (Fishbone's Christmas 1987 EP, *It's a Wonderful Life,* is worth searching for and treasuring.)

The problem is, in claiming the right to "play that rocky music, Black boy," Living Colour deny themselves the freedom and esprit that lead to such advanced musical hybrids as Hendrix, Chic, or Prince.

The idea of Black musicians imitating white music seems radical only in theory. As Living Colour put it into practice, it is embarrassingly commercial and desperate. However, this cynicism in Living Colour's experiment is actually an expression of the Black middle class's multiethnic ambivalence. Reid is trying to make sense of his understandable admiration for bands like the Rolling Stones, Led Zeppelin, Roxy Music, and early Talking Heads. *Vivid* includes a cover version of "Memories Can't Wait" from the Heads' *Fear of Music* album. It seems Reid has made a political fetish of white rock as a result of the guilty pleasure it's given him.

Reid's fear of music is expressed defensively in hard-rock anthems like "Cult of Personality," "Desperate People," and "Glamour Boys" (the last one a fusion of success anxiety and homophobia). His pastiche compositions swing even the issue-oriented songs like "Open Letter to a Landlord" and "Which Way to America?" away from a Black listenership whose only criterion for pop music is: Does it have a groove? (The attendance at the band's recent Ritz concert was predominantly white.) If the Black audience's traditional disregard for hard rock was a matter of taste, Reid's broadened, integrated taste now reclaims rock as a matter of winning the acceptance and approval of the white rock establishment. (Who else would refuse Reid, or care?)

Reid has twisted himself into a nonaesthetic, unartistic position. The music on *Vivid* is not insincere, just seriously inauthentic. The mistake of trying to prove that anyone can play hard rock by then playing only a specific racial genre of it inappropriately suggests the band's cultural limitations: As a rock band, Living Colour can't compete with a group like Cheap Trick, whose 1978 *Heaven Tonight* and 1979 *Live at Budokan* are metal masterpieces. But the wonder of such albums isn't racial; it comes from the musicians extending their creativity, discovering unimagined yet perfect expressions of their feelings and experiences. This includes the osmosis of Afro-American ideas and music. The borrowing is so natural that the eight accelerating bass notes on Cheap Trick's "On the Radio" might be called All-American soul (via Chuck Berry, of course).

Obviously, Reid wants to attack the legendary example of white artists exploiting Black music for their own means. But as a rock fan he can't wholly disapprove of that history. It's a fact of what rock 'n' roll is—a great transformation, like it or not. Reid's counterattack—expropriating white rock—has no payoff and no sound of its own. In fact, it inadvertently shows that Black people get nothing out of the racial exchange of rock. It's a nonreciprocal process. Only one song, "Funny Vibe," hints at Reid's originality as an electric son of Ornette. (He may be the first jazz rocker with a true commitment to rock.) Elsewhere on the album, the imitation of white rock idioms belittles Reid's talent and intelligence.

Living Colour signals a new phase in Black artists' dealing with white domination. The trick here is to accept white styles of music and dress without regard to the meanings they carry. Living Colour wants to deny the exclusivity of what is obviously "white." The question is: Are they pioneers? Cultural devolution was a concept already marketed and mocked by Devo. It isn't clear whether Living Colour's efforts advance the independence of Black artists. I'm afraid they can only succeed by failing.

*The City Sun*
May 18, 1988

# SCHIZOGENIUS

"**D**ETROIT—WHAT'S HAPPENING?" Prince sings, slyly inserting the question into the middle of the song "Dance On" on his new album *Lovesexy*. The callout doesn't salute a region of fans or possible record buyers the way Martha and the Vandellas did in "Dancin' in the Street." Prince cites the recent moral, political, and fiscal devastation of Detroit (hometown of his mentor and current major influence, George Clinton) as an example of the political agendas that have failed for Black people. As with "2 Nigs United for West Compton," a jazz track from Prince's bootleg *The Black Album*, Prince now expresses a sinuous political awareness and alarm.

This is speaking Black in the tradition of Clinton and James Brown, who created pertinent funk. Prince's musical/political instincts have sharpened, but they have also split his consciousness into the intellectual formations of *Lovesexy* and the emotionality of *The Black Album*. These two collections of songs represent the most elaborate explication of funk aesthetics and politics any artist has ever attempted. Their contradictions are startling, but the expressiveness of each is amazing. A comprehensive investigation is in order.

*Lovesexy* is Prince's most lunatic vision. It's the album he decided to give an official release instead of *The Black Album*, seemingly because it told the message burning inside him. The title "Lovesexy" combines ideas of spiritual and physical ecstasy—an extension of the Au Pairs' description of lust: "It's not real / It's emotional, it's mystical / A fever seizing my body and mind."

On *Lovesexy* Prince works out nine extrapolations on the notion of sex as salvation. He embraces carnality as part of a heretical manifesto. "Nothing's forbidden, nothing's taboo," he sings on "When 2 R In Love" (the one song carried over from *The Black Album*). The psychedelic/ flower-child whimsies of *Around the World in a Day* get full sybaritic development. Prince seems out to shame those who called George Michael's *Faith* "a white Prince album," but he stretches so far in spiritual conceptualizing that the idea of sin gets displaced, reserved for social misdeeds.

Prince didn't drop his band, The Revolution, for nothing. On *Lovesexy* he abandons all thought of social and political change, directing his attention inward to the struggle for one's mortal soul. However, this ponderous idea is not stated ponderously. Prince's backup band (seen in the superb film *Sign O the Times*) sustains lively and lengthy percussive jams. Each song is denoted by rhythmic beats, clarion horns, and waves of overheard conversations and sound effects. The record is *vivid,* Prince's most accomplished and refined work as a producer.

If *Lovesexy* were not so obviously serious and well made one could dismiss its message as downright ludicrous—or at least ridiculously personal. Only during the spark of an orgasmic moment does one think sex is everything. Prince's porno-religion—theology based on the Big O—could only make sense as a metaphor for paradise.

The opening song, "Eye No," is Prince's own update of Clinton's "Bop Gun"—the 1977 funk treatise on the Black experience where the chorus repeated the line "We got to get over the hump," and Clinton's Brides of Funkenstein sang, "On guard! Defend Yourself!" But Prince uses the same meter for a mystic praise "Hundalasiliah." He has reversed the meanings of seventies funk: Dance is no longer the step toward liberation Clinton prophesied. Prince, in the song "Dance On," sees it as man's procession toward oblivion.

This new version of "Sign O the Times" 's catalogue of urban disasters is where Prince's musical expression of the Black psyche falters. The social nightmares he observes in 1980s American racism and fascism and the despair he feels are betrayed by his own baroque sexual beatitudes. This marvelous-sounding record seems to advocate sex as a glorified anesthetic. This, essentially, gives in to social disaster through a foolish, brazen flirtation with decadence.

*Lovesexy* leaves out the motivation for Prince's retreat into orgy—and the reasons he weighs heaven against hell—but winds up with a solution that straddles both precepts. Since Prince is here a would-be libertine, sexual inhibitions are strong in his consciousness; they can't be gainsaid. *Lovesexy* represents a sinner's willed ecstasy. Starting with "Alphabet St.," the album's song sequence is didactic, spelling things out through Prince's need to convince himself that certain indulgences are allowable or positive. But even the urgent confessional "Anna Stesia" flakes out before convincingly depicting the kind of purgatory in which sex might well seem a cure-all. That song's personal sense of everyday living is just a hint of the dissatisfaction Prince feels. Its anguish is theoretical. Prince has made great leaps in the articulation of his philosophy but he's dropped some figures in his moralistic algebra. A few hot numbers straight from perdition are what *Lovesexy* needs to hit greatness.

What's missing is all on *The Black Album*. As it turns out, that title has a double meaning: first as an audacious funk-music answer to the Beatles' 1968 LP unofficially known as *The White Album*. Second, as a description of ghetto hell and disco inferno. The songs on *The Black Album* make none of Prince's usual commercial concessions (innovations) to mainstream taste. A collection of eight hard dance, rap, and jazz-funk tunes, it was created without thought of crossover. Its appeal might be genetic; it certainly depends on a kind of musical acculturation as much as the Beatles' *White Album* does.

*The Black Album* is full of outrageous language and rowdy scenarios linked to Black American folk culture—the culture that music and records primarily disseminate and propel. There's perfect beauty in Prince's decision to not release the record, just let it slip into the "underground" to be bought and transferred in bootleg versions. The sound quality of my "fifth-generation" tape often suggests a party heard next door or a tune blaring from a street kid's beat box. This way *The Black Album* has a kind of rebel authenticity, free of the usual marketing conceits. It can be enjoyed as private gossip.

This honesty saves Prince from foundering in the hazy metaphysics of *Lovesexy*. It's as if these songs were not meant for white ears. The music is the Blackest (that is, the most soul- and funk-based) of Prince's career. Although the bootleg sound is dense and clamorous, it depicts a resonant and vivacious lifestyle. Casual exhortations are blended in with colloquial lyrics, creating a constant, exhilarating verbal tumult.

> *Prince: What are you doing here, in this house of ill repute?*
> *Cat Glover: Ah, honey, I'm scared of you!*

The songs feature the kind of scenes from Black life that were attempted between songs in the *Sign O the Times* movie but are here edging into raw verisimilitude. "Bob George" and "Dead on It" might be Prince's most powerful recordings. Both songs explore Black expression: the latter celebrating rap styles for their fresh fluency, the former a satire of profane Black bravado.

"Bob George" is a linguistic triumph in which the vulgarisms of the underclass go uncensored but are, in fact, brandished. Prince distorts his voice into a hoarse *ghetto-profundo* to portray a man incensed over his woman's new clothes and probable inconstancy. It's Prince's best acting ever, including a swipe at himself ("That skinny motherfucker with the *high* voice!"). This characterization of an embarrassing stereotype is plainly a loving recreation. "Put on that wig I bought ya," macho Prince instructs. "Duh reddish-brown one." It's classic Negro folklore and spectacularly, satirically, authentic to the styles of Rufus Thomas, Joe Tex, Pigmeat Markham, and Redd Foxx: "This is your conscience, motherfucker!"

The life in this record both riles Prince and thrills him. Behavior on the level of gut existence and stunning intuitive responses makes a young middle-class Black man like Prince ambivalent. As on last year's hilarious "Adore," Prince objectifies Blackness as few Black artists ever have. Instead of using words and speech that are naturally a reflection of a social circumstance, this griot Prince points up the strength of Black oral and musical traditions.

"Grind" and "Cindy C" are furious party numbers (the latter has a machine-gun rap by Sheila E.) that convey a desperately pursued heaven-on-earth. Sex and dancing seen not as salvation but (as most dance musicians understand it) as respite and recreation rejects the shibboleths that inform the ethnic shame behind *Lovesexy's* "higher" vision. The final cut on *The Black Album* has Prince admit, "I just hate to see an erection go to waste / I'm just rock hard in a funky place," which is as exact a statement of common-man survival (and as funny) as "got to get over the hump."

*The Black Album* and *Lovesexy* are as schizophrenic as an artist can be and still command great emotive power. The pie-in-the-sky funk of *Lovesexy* is a smokescreen for the filthy ethnicity of *The Black Album*. A masterpiece has been cracked in two by Prince's confusion over the issues of salvation and survival. He's somewhat redeemed by the overall assertion of Black (common) vernacular as classical expression. The nude cover of *Lovesexy* teases the idea of total artistic revelation. You have to hear both these albums to know how bravely and wonderfully Prince can do it.

*The City Sun*
June 8, 1988

# WHO'S COMING OUT OF AFRICA? THE MAN WHO LOST HIS ROOTS!

THIS SCENE FROM *Coming to America* should make the Eddie Murphy menace plain to everyone:

As Akeem, prince of the mythical nation Zamunda, Murphy comes to America to find a wife. He can't meet a suitable woman in bars or discos, so he goes to a Black awareness rally. In a union hall with a banner across the stage proclaiming BLACK AWARENESS RALLY, we are shown a tacky little beauty contest with women in bikinis vying for a prize. The coronation theme song is sung by an effeminate Black male crooner named Randy Watson (also played by Murphy) and his backup band Sexual Chocolate.

The Black awareness rally is the film's comic centerpiece. Of course there's nothing wrong with a satire of small-time local beauty pageants (it was done well in Michael Ritchie's *Smile;* done far less well in Milos Forman's *The Fireman's Ball*). Indeed, it is the kind of thing Redd Foxx did on "Sanford & Son." But Foxx, an artist from another generation and a different social-political perspective than Murphy's, might have called the contest what it is: A "Miss Sepia Queen" or "Miss Brown Sugar" pageant. Foxx wouldn't have called it a "Black Awareness Rally." He wouldn't have confused a political meeting with a sex show—either inadvertently or for ridicule.

For Eddie Murphy the very idea of Black politics or the political expression of Black pride is absurd. It's not a notion he recognizes; partying and sex are all, but not as signs of life. This scene reactivates the racist stereotype that Black people are so shiftless and trivial that their idea of "awareness" is a jive-time show.

*Coming to America* is not satire with the point (like the last scene in *School Daze*) that the Black community has to get its act together. The film is simply making fun of Black life—not like "Sanford & Son," which was a stylized burlesque of eccentrics. Murphy pretends to bring to pop culture insider details of Black experience: manners and dialects that he dredges up with specious authority, always falsifying or excluding their socio-economic, psychological contexts.

Black politics, Black consciousness, has never figured in the plots of Murphy's movies, but his comic's acumen uses the idea of Black awareness in order to seem truly *Black,* up to date. Actually, *Coming to America* is a betrayal of every instance of politics, history, sex, and ethnic culture Black people have ever known.

The rally scene is not only a racist conceit but sexist, too. Doubly sexist. The contestants are all light-skinned women (which in the film's scheme means they're desirable—all the unappealing or rapacious women are dark-skinned). Implicit in the mating ritual of *Coming to America* and the woman Akeem falls in love with are old "colorist" ideas about sex and chauvinist ideas about virginity. And the caricature of Randy Watson, who is part Little Richard, part Rick James, sets up a rationalization of Black homophobia. The rally audience's hostility toward Watson is a shrewdly twisted rebuke of just the kind of outrageous, flamboyant performers Apollo-type audiences will cheer. But Watson is another of Murphy's favorite targets—a gay man—and this sequence allows Murphy to hang with the "real" boys and express his contempt.

In the Africa sequences Murphy gets to display more of the roots hatred that characterized his Umfufu routine in *Raw.* Akeem and his manservant Semmi (played by Arsenio Hall) wear comic exaggerations of the ropes of gold chain favored by rappers. Murphy seeks the favor of the hiphop audience by giving that culture's most conspicuous, tasteless fashions a pseudo-historical/cultural legacy. (Like the least-enlightened rappers, Murphy's just in it for the money.)

With this kind of immediate access to the fantasies of Black kids, Murphy could have used the premise of *Coming to America* to enlighten cultural consciousness. Not surprisingly, there is no semblance of the politics that operate in actual Black African nations; no contrasts between the lifestyles of Blacks who govern themselves and those who are part of an oppressive, white-dominated system. The shadow of the slave trade never darkens Murphy's transatlantic concept. (He probably thinks "Middle Passage" refers to flatulence.)

In this ahistorical, anticultural movie, Murphy presents a fantasy vision of Africa. He says that he "wanted to make Africa look beautiful. You usually see people in the woods covered with flies and shit!" But didn't Murphy at least see *Out of Africa*? Instead of doing research that might reveal the natural communal, spiritual beauty of the place, Murphy rejects those possibilities and has constructed Zamunda as a combination of Henri Rousseau and Walt Disney.

Obviously, attending an Eddie Murphy movie is nothing like attending a Black awareness rally. There's ethnic self-loathing and humiliation throughout *Coming to America*. Murphy's consciousness is the kind that is completely detached from political action. He's a casualty, I would guess, of that period of arrested social advancement for Black people—the aftershock of the civil rights movement—the 1970s. In that period the predominant Black cultural figure was not a politician or demonstrator but the superficially, stereotypically ethnic icons of Blaxploitation movies and television sitcoms. As part of the TV generation, Murphy doesn't connect being Black with social injustice or political struggle. For him Black life is all vaudeville, so he restages the horrible joke from *Outrageous Fortune* of Harlem as a big lot for auto rip-offs, and when Murphy himself steals a sequence from *School Daze* (where a series of women address the camera), it is debased, drained of Spike Lee's erotic fascination into a mere routine.

Take this ignorance and insensitivity and add it to Murphy's undeniable talent for mimicry, his comic timing and wit, and what you get is a showbiz atrocity. As a showbiz kid, Murphy has adopted the "Black consciousness" of white ideology: Murphy sees and comments upon Black people, life, and experience in ways and terms that the mainstream readily understands and that, I fear, make Black people tolerable to whites so that they won't be surprised by Blacks and won't have to fear them or respect them.

Unlike Richard Pryor, Murphy does not make humor about how we are all foolish, ambitious, shy, neurotic, horny, greedy, and human. He confirms how Black people really are the stereotypes their enemies have always claimed. This may be New Age Blackness, which accepts denigration by others. After all, one does not make movies that gross an average of $75 million (in the United States alone) by appealing only to the interests of a minority audience.

The crazy thing about Murphy's success is that he sees nothing wrong with his jokes because he considers his popularity a certification of his humor's merit and truth. His wealth is a sign of "advancement," and probably for Murphy this means that any figure of Blackness he gets people to laugh at—shamelessly or not—seems a good, positive thing.

I recently fantasized a conversation I might have with Eddie Murphy. I asked him about the ad for *Coming to America*, which shows him in a boastful, triumphant smile. "This being 1988, the era of Goetz, Brawley, Howard Beach, and Michael Dukakis, why are you so happy?" I asked. And Murphy responded—with the fairness I allow everyone in my dreams—"Because I'm RICH!"

This made me think there are two identities artists can have in a profit motive culture—rich and poor—and these are material-related indicators of power and lack, comfort and discomfort. It's fair to say that the Black artists who are most significant in film this decade are Murphy and Spike Lee. In terms of obvious commitment and identity, these two men conveniently represent the pole between which pop artists must, if subliminally, position themselves. Rich, powerful, comfortable Murphy; relatively poor, powerless, uncomfortable Lee.

Both men make films that express their positions; Murphy makes complacent comedies, Lee makes probing satires. The difference is based in opposing approaches to life and to the conditions under which Black people live in America. Racism isn't as real for Eddie Murphy as it is for Lee; its import is never seriously considered by Murphy. Even at this year's serious Academy Awards, when he made a short, arrogant speech about the Academy's neglect of Black performers, he took a piddling stand and padded his supposed "anger" in a joke. The result was that nobody took him seriously. His misbehavior was just another wrinkle in a gremlin-plagued evening, one more poorly thought-out gesture in a deplorable career.

*The City Sun*
July 6, 1988

# WOMEN ON THE VERGE

EDRO ALMODÓVAR essays the war between men and women without the usual we-versus-them biases. His new film, *Women on the Verge of a Nervous Breakdown,* attacks the stereotypes that sex farce is based on by presenting its female characters as psychedelic myths. The exasperation of the passive sex role is stylized into the actions of a group of contemporary Spanish women trying to cope. Almodóvar presents their desperation playfully, but seriously.

Pepa, an actress, is the carnival's center. As played by the Spanish actress Carmen Maura, Pepa has the comic aplomb of Carol Burnett and the sexual, emotional agility of Jeanne Moreau. Pepa's hassled attempt to contact her elusive lover Ivan gives an alternative, skeptical look at Don Juan. Ivan is mostly embodied as a voice on Pepa's answering machine. He keeps leaving instructions and false endearments—their power to beguile lessens as Pepa's anger increases.

Her wised-up shrewdness is the assumption Almodóvar himself begins with. He rejects the acquiescence assigned to women as part of their femininity: Pepa resists, her friend Candela (Maria Barranco) worries, Ivan's former lover Lucia (Julieta Serrano) is slowly cracking, his newest paramour Paulina (Kiti Manver) is hostile to all comers, and Marisa (Rossy DePalma), the fiancée of Ivan's kissing-freak son (Antonio Banderas), eases the tensions of her frustration by psychically discovering sexual fulfillment.

The plot that interlocks these women bears an intentionally buoyant, cartoon-colored resemblance to the artificial world of the romantic comedies and women's fashion magazines from the fifties and sixties—key examples of modern romantic style. Almodóvar's point is to indulge the glamour once given to women as part of their adoration (and subjugation) but to activate them as individuals. Almodóvar's approach is camp, particularly evocative of such prefeminist films as *The Women* (1939) and *Gentlemen Prefer Blondes* (1953). But Almodóvar's camp liberates. He's clear about the surfaces of dress, makeup, and decor that please and the emotions, the struggles behind them.

The fantasies of "women's movies," often demeaned as the preoccupation of housewives and gay men, gain unexpected, startling humor and strength from Almodóvar. *Women on the Verge* translates an understanding of sexual strategy and emotional game playing. *The Women* and *Gentlemen Prefer Blondes* weren't far from drag acts in the first place. But Almodóvar's film is joyful rather than coy—a distinctly modern advantage due to his contemporary gay awareness that links the sensibilities of men and women. It's a new and crucial element for romantic comedy.

"You can never understand what goes on in a man's head," Pepa sighs, reversing an age-old adage. Almodóvar divines the battle of the sexes with a comic specificity. He sees through gender division to something essential, the playing out of roles that are only gender-assigned by social custom. He admits the universality of romance and sex, but he understands and separates love from victimization.

This truth is not imparted as a lesson, it's simply the basis on which the farcical story depends. You have to understand Almodóvar's point to believe his plot. To enjoy his film—and it's easily the most richly entertaining film this year—is to understand his point, deep down.

*Women on the Verge* is a triumph for this Spanish filmmaker who has mostly worked in the semi-underground or in the obscurity of the art-film circuit. Almodóvar's interest in romantic obsession takes on an imperial detachment and wisdom here. It's a different pleasure from his two previous films: *Law of Desire,* a gay male *Fatal Attraction* but funny and smart, and *Matador,* an update of *Duel in the Sun*'s love-it-to-death theme with the abstract, lurid sexiness of DePalma's movies.

It may seem that *Women on the Verge,* the first Almodóvar film without homosexuality, is his sellout to the mainstream, but as the work of the most sophisticated European filmmaker to make his mark in the United States in this decade, this latest film—his most visually accomplished—actually illustrates an outsider's command of the language and form that has proverbially dominated and oppressed him.

Almodóvar's own obsession with movie styles and genres makes this film tantamount to a lover's conquest. He's made the sex comedy that George Cukor, Marilyn Monroe, Billy Wilder, and many others might have made had they freed themselves of sexism. That means *Women on the Verge of a Nervous Breakdown* is not just a very funny movie but a very subtle political coup.

*The City Sun*
December 7, 1988

# CLASSICAL TWISTS

THE SINGERS AND MUSICIANS in *The Gospel at Colonus* have Broadway under siege. Through their triumphant talent the entire apparatus of the musical theater and white-controlled cultural institutions and traditions is put in perspective.

This was probably the subconscious intention of the collaborating team of Lee Breuer (writer-director) and Bob Telson (composer), who first produced *Gospel at Colonus* in 1984 at the Brooklyn Academy of Music's Next Wave festival. Their basic idea was to synthesize white European and African-American cultural forms simply for a contrast that would reveal similar themes and equivalent merit.

In its current Broadway presentations (after several years of world tours and a PBS broadcast production), the show's structure sticks to that plan: An undefined assembly of Black gospel worshipers give a sermon-song-and-testimony rendering of Sophocles' *Oedipus at Colonus* (the story of Oedipus the King's exile and death). Greek drama and Black Christianity don't exactly mirror each other, so the setup has no particular point or reason until the Institutional Radio Choir and Jevetta Steele sing the first song ("Live Where You Can") and their voices become a reason, a justification, for the cast's and the audience's presence.

The performers here are legendary—including J. J. Farley and the Soul Stirrers, the gospel quintet that first introduced Sam Cooke to the stage in the 1950s, and Clarence Fountain and the Five Blind Boys of Alabama, themselves institutions of the gospel circuit. There's also the marvelous family group, the J. D. Steele Singers, with star soloist Jevetta and such superb individual performers as singer-guitarist Sam Butler Jr. and the actor Morgan Freeman. As the interlocutor, Freeman seems left out of the joke that the singers all know about subverting the European superstructure (he has no song), but he's not left out of the celebratory mood. He's carried along by the sheer force of the singers' and musicians' talent.

The most dogmatic criticism of the show (in the *Times,* of all places) complained that Breuer and Telson force the Black performers to "worship at the shrine of white culture." This ignores the ideas behind the show's structure and disregards the obvious fact that the performers—some of whose appearance should be a celebrated event comparable to the second coming of Garbo—overwhelm the show's premise.

Certainly Breuer and Telson's structure does not fully, flexibly, account for this explosion of energy, but its possibility is anticipated in the show's concept. The performers' integrity makes an obvious fact of the American musical theater's segregation of this country's richest musical culture. The songs (with Telson's secular lyrics) are experiments in gospel that analyze the art and craft of the form—Stephen Sondheim has been canonized for less significant and more pretentious efforts.

No such analysis seems to interest Black musical theater conceptualizers like Maurice Hines or Vernel Bagneris (the skeptical view of religion August Wilson provides in *Joe Turner* is typical). Here, the incongruousness of the Greek drama and Black gospel adds irony to both practices. *The Gospel at Colonus* bears scrutiny as a demonstration of the theatrics of gospel music.

Clarence Fountain is a natural and glorious show-off, Sam Butler Jr.'s "Stop, Do Not Go On," and Willie Rogers's Al Green–ish interpretation of "Eternal Sleep," and the Soul Stirrers' Sam Cooke–style "Now Let the Weeping Cease" are the sort of objectified turns that imply their meanings and development—just as Morgan Freeman's and Isabell Monk's recitations of poetic text demonstrate certain oratorical traditions. But a performance as incandescent as Jevetta Steele's "How Shall I See You Through My Tears" and her second-act mourning, plus the Institutional Radio Choir's gospel fervor throughout is still part of the most mystifying art American culture can claim. Even Carolyn Johnson-White's pyrotechnic solo on "Lift Him Up" eludes our full understanding. This could all just be the genius of the performers, but it isn't merely whooping and hollering; it shows skill and purpose that beg for modernist understanding, especially in this secular context.

Perhaps Broadway is the wrong place for this sort of exploration. White theatergoers may be content to marvel at how "great" Black performers are, lumping a Jevetta Steele in with a Ben Vereen. And some Black patrons may, reasonably, be distressed at the lack of theology. (A woman who shouted "Sang, boys, sang!" during the show later commented, "They didn't talk about Jesus!")

Still, what better place or time to put on a show that challenges the undiscriminating acceptance of Black performance art?

Essentially, *The Gospel at Colonus* is an avant-garde endeavor. Unlike a racist production such as *Green Pastures* in the 1930s, which poked fun at the Black misinterpretation of religion, this show combines Greek and Black catharsis to claim equal greatness and equal legitimacy.

Breuer's cyclorama staging does this superbly, particularly in the "Lift Him Up" climax, where the Oedipus figures, The Five Blind Boys, rise up from the grave seated around a piano in a blaze of white light.

That's great theater. It also confers artistic interest upon a form of Black expression that these days is not in the greatest repute even among Black people. *The Gospel at Colonus* might have been reshaped to reflect the African-American mythos, but this lack (or restraint) might work well for Black people who don't go to church any more. And yet gospel as an art thrives.

David Henry Hwang's *M. Butterfly* also laid modernist siege to Broadway. Hwang, who wrote *FOB* and *The Dancer and the Railroad,* here rewrites Puccini's opera *Madame Butterfly.* Militantly, he reinterprets that sentimental love tragedy about an Asian woman who sacrifices her life for a white man as a symptom of "the West's belief that the East wants to be dominated." That's what a spy and female impersonator (B. D. Wong) says to a French diplomat (John Lithgow) who is part of France's Indochina mess in the early sixties. Political history is used to counter the art that promotes racist ideology.

Hwang's Vietnam-era cynicism is facile, but his attack on art totems like *Madame Butterfly* is invigorating. He criticizes it as "rape mentality" and works out his theories of supremacist politics in a wild plot about sexual betrayal, gender confusion, and espionage. It's never quite believable or moving, but in back of it all is a serious proposition advancing the Peking Opera as the ideal legitimate Asian cultural form. As opposed to *The Gospel at Colonus, M. Butterfly* rejects all Europe-flattering art. Even an idea this simple seems shocking on Broadway, and Eiko Ishioka's remarkable red-and-white set is a great swirling space in which smart ideas can circulate and fly. Its simplicity keeps speaking—the perfect correlative to Hwang's bold revisionist impulse. It should inspire someone to take an ideological torch to *Porgy and Bess.*

*The City Sun*
September 13, 1988

# NATION TIME

"I WAS INNOCENT because I'm militant," Chuck D says during "Black Steel in the Hour of Chaos," perhaps the greatest moment of Public Enemy's new album, *It Takes a Nation of Millions to Hold Us Back* (Def Jam). The song is a remarkable narrative of a political prisoner's uprising—the psychology of an oppressed man's defiance is described through the vivid, exciting details of a prison outbreak. The song is a fully alive, fire-breathing metaphor.

*Nation* itself is a major event in the politicization of the current generation of Black youth. It gives immediacy to the outrage and misery of Black kids through constantly erupting political rhetoric. Chuck D and Flavor Flav rap bitterly about American racism and, as a response, adopt Muslim self-improvement principles and evolution theories, Black Panther militance, and Malcolm X's determinism. Each cut is conceived and performed as a power salute, but this busy sound (culled from pieces of music and cultural history and masterfully produced by the team of Hank Shocklee, Carl Ryder, Bill Stephney, and Rick Rubin) has a visceral effect that makes the album much more than a symbolic gesture. It raises defiance to a level of pure, witty aggression.

The virtuosity one hears in the record comes from Public Enemy's aesthetic and political confidence. They reject the systematic processes and agendas of the middle-class civil rights movement. But in discarding the tactical failures and weaknesses of the past twenty years of Black social struggle (like it was just wet, useless firecrackers), Public Enemy's ballsiness seems both proud and naive.

Public Enemy's grown-up talk about Armageddon and revolution doesn't disguise their ingenuous bluster. Flavor Flav's "Yeaahh, boyyee" intros urge young Black men to be strong, but there's no sensible, practical outline toward this (or toward maturity). This album is unique—a triumph of innocent righteousness. It's the best example I know of the cynical, paranoid wisdom a Black child can (and must) absorb and develop out of the atmosphere of a hostile, racist society. ("My people are being persecuted!" cries Flavor Flav.)

Nothing this charged-up and serious has been put on vinyl since the great days of British punk. But the preternatural skepticism, the instinctive attack, of Public Enemy is a little different. The chaotic splendor of supermixed jams like "Night of the Living Baseheads" or "Terminator X to the Edge of Panic" convey a modern consciousness under so much psychic pressure and media overload that it can't devise a sensible social program. The songs are a creation of shocked but beat-smart reflexes.

When former Sex Pistol John Lydon's new group, Public Image Ltd., performed an anti-apartheid (and anti-British terrorism) song in 1986, he sang, "Anger is an energy!" Public Enemy's emergence the following year gave a Black American demonstration of that thesis while, naturally, altering it to fit their needs. Anger is a *style* to Public Enemy, and their perfection of it distinguishes them from other rap groups. It also separates them from typical politicians—although I have no idea what their ultimate political effect will be. Making records is a safe way to blow off steam from being harassed and deprived by white America. Evoking the Black politics and history that pop music usually denies its young audience (and that Black kids may be totally unaware of) is thrilling. But will listeners ever put Public Enemy's style into action?

The fantasy of action that Public Enemy ignites is the group's most powerful weapon (after its dance groove). Their syncopated anger overrides the message of Black self-determination ("Louder Than a Bomb" has rhythms so tight they defy one not to move). *Nation* takes the agitation and euphoria of last year's "Bring the Noise" and sustains it—with sonic, musical, rhetorical variations—throughout.

Oppression in "Black Steel" is told with the vivid realism of Ice-T's own masterpiece, "6 in the Morning," but as Chuck D unfolds this epic story, the dramatic scenario turns surreal. The "52 brothers bruised, battered and scarred, but hard" he describes march toward a death or liberation that is almost a spiritual vision, like Al Green's "Take Me to the River." After "Black Steel" the album's hectoring masculinity gets wearisome but the multisource sound constructs—a magnificent transformation of the decade's artiest pop music experiments, such as *My Life in the Bush of Ghosts*—just keep jumping.

Agitation, not uplift, is the point. "Your general subject, love, is minimal / It's sex for profit," Chuck D says on "Caught, Can We Get a Witness," a kind of manifesto of the group's strategies. Chuck D rejects the love song as one of the many methods used by pop culture (and Black radio) to keep Black people from considering their social positions and rising up.

This narrow view of pop is both a strength and limitation. It motivates Public Enemy to create the most explosively, openly political music in the history of American rock 'n' roll, but it also deprives their music of the emotional complexity of great political rock. (I missed a line as rich as this from a 1978 tune: "I fought with my twin / That enemy within / 'til both of us fell by the way.") English punks merged with the defiance of reggae to establish a form of rock agitprop that was often the smartest modern music one could ever hope to experience. The punks sang great negations of the status quo, but they also dealt with political imperatives *and* humanity. They understood that revolutions are made by people who needed to dance, make love, and *re*think things.

"Party for Your Right to Fight," the last cut on *Nation,* reclaims the legitimacy of rap as an authentic Black American form of expression after the form had been swiped, polished, and then trashed by the Beastie Boys hit, "Fight for Your Right to Party." It's the most didactic moment on an album, full of rhetorical flourishes, but this is the least convincing of them. When Chuck D says, "Ain't nothing but a party y'all," he doesn't sound like a lot of fun. For the first time he sounds insensate and literal.

Irony had become the operative form for political pop when the Gang of Four sang "I Love a Man in a Uniform," but Public Enemy rejects irony and subtlety as effete, evasive forms and speaks directly. The group's bluntness (which seems to underestimate the audience's ability to think or process complex ideas and experiences) may be related to the threatened masculinity that often surfaces here in ungracious ways.

Emotional complexity should now be Public Enemy's immediate goal. They've transcended the problem of radio's indifference (the funny, growly "Don't Believe the Hype" is both irresistible and unavoidable). Having excited the ears of all who will listen, they ought to aim for heads and hearts next.

*The City Sun*
July 27, 1988

# ON SPENCER WILLIAMS

SPENCER WILLIAMS'S FILMS were curious examples of 1940s pop culture—low-budget efforts geared to the movie hunger of the nonmainstream Black audiences. They have survived obscure status and come back to haunt us. The Whitney Museum's recent two-week retrospective of Williams's work (curated by Colorado College's Adrienne Lanier Seward) presented a narrative form and an emotional quality that may seem antiquated, even bizarre, today.

*The Blood of Jesus* (1941) and *Go Down, Death* (1944) are modern parables. In each, religion is the template used for setting out and exploring Black American life in the mid-twentieth century. These films ignore the white-dominated society that existed beyond Southern Black communities. A network of churches, juke joints and the private homes of Williams's characters conveys a specific Black cultural temper and atmosphere. Classic, out-of-time images like a riverbank baptism or a gospel procession down a dusty road are part of an ideally imagined and realized milieu that affords a vision uncomplicated by industrialization or the urban politics of crime and poverty that usually seem to define Black experience.

There's documentary value to be appreciated here, such as a view of a church matron's satin ribbon imprinted "Rising Star of San Antonio, Texas," plus the view of houses and of dance and singing styles that Williams captured while putting his little plots on film. This originality stems from Williams's authenticity. Despite his career in the thirties as a dialogue coach at Paramount Pictures (surely a devil's-advocate position) or his later stint as Andy in the 1950s TV series "Amos 'n' Andy," Williams's commitment to Black naturalism—as opposed to Hollywood's conventional depiction of Black life—distinguished his movies and gave them a unique style.

It's difficult to know just how serious one should take Williams's films. We have to judge his specialization by its usefulness to the intended audience that preceded us and its possible current relevance.

These films would be mere dated artifacts if not for Williams's casual spiritual/worldly split. He preserves the psychic (religious) ambiance that's all but gone from late-twentieth-century Black American living.

In outline, *The Blood of Jesus* (about a woman's salvation and her shiftless husband's contrition) and *Go Down, Death* (about a just preacher and a devout follower triumphing over a scheming evildoer) are no more than folktales. However, Williams's close attention to the spiritual yearning of his characters transforms the simplistic plots.

"Come down into this vale of sorrow," a woman prays; the high-note vibrato of her supplication makes a remarkable impression. So does the fiery clarity in a preacher's eyes. Williams catches the exact sound, look, the sensuality of Black religious experience. This gives his movies an integrity beyond their flat acting and meager technique—the crude sound recording and patched-in music, plus public-domain footage used to illustrate his characters' hysterical presentiments of hell or ecstatic visions of paradise.

Williams's primitive technique distances his films from the similar spiritual studies made, in the same era, by European giants Robert Bresson and Carl Dreyer, but no other American filmmaker I know of went as far into spiritual exploration (until Scorsese).

The recurring image in Williams's film is of genuflection and supplication, heads raised and eyes cast up in worship. These acts seem a weirdly intensified illustration of past Black struggle—and not merely pious but ambiguous, too. What does it mean when the heroine is shot while praying and the bullet goes through her into the picture of Christ? Is it cynicism that makes Williams intercut a portrait of Christ with an apparition of a devout widow's husband?

The subjugation to religion is a troubled subtheme of these movies. It's as if Williams was pandering to a general consensus he didn't truly believe in but knew would pay his rent, or that he was too uncertain about to entirely dismiss. "Churches are monuments of the human race," an angel says in *The Blood of Jesus,* narrating a montage of various Black church architecture (which, thirty-seven years later, Alan Parker would put the torch to in *Mississippi Burning*). The angel's odd statement is key to how Williams connects the place of religion in Black life: the ideology that, for a long time, adhered the race, making it a philosophical community.

There's an ultramodern (1980s) element in the tension Williams draws between secular and religious living by dramatizing the capitulation/resistance to Christianity. Throughout *The Blood of Jesus* the religious totems onscreen progress from a tender chromo to a harsh sketch to an imposing crucifix. Williams seems fully aware of this. He may have been a crude artist but not a naive one. By taking Black life and religion seriously, he was able to portray its strengths and paradoxes.

Williams's great subject is religion—which one can now see as a powerful allegory for his profession as a screen artist. The institutions of filmmaking (Hollywood) influence Williams's ideas and methods as much as the institution of the church. Deciding whether he was genuflecting or pioneering may be an issue of faith.

*The City Sun*
January 18, 1989

# HOLLYWOOD BURNING

GENE HACKMAN IS US—that's the meaning behind the great reviews accorded *Mississippi Burning* and particularly the raves that white critics gave Hackman as FBI Agent Anderson. He walks through the movie wearing an idiotic, out-of-place grin that eases some viewers into the film's uncomfortable premise of mid-1960s social upheaval. Charting the civil rights movement down South and simulating the Chaney-Goodman-Schwerner murders is potentially disturbing—Hackman's award-winning performance works as a palliative.

Agent Anderson stands for decency and "normalcy," unlike the uptight, officious, hotheaded Northern agent played by Willem Dafoe. This latter agent, Ward, is cold and intellectual; Anderson is old-fashioned, warm, full of feeling, civilized and chivalrous with an infallible sense of what's right. You got it: he's unreal. But by his friendly, homey actions, audiences are meant to identify with him; Anderson/Hackman is a self-described Southerner with a raised consciousness. He sees the light of brotherhood, of peaceful coexistence among races—a dramatic strategy that somehow makes the film not seem like preaching to the converted.

Actually, something insidious is happening here. *Mississippi Burning* makes a superficial assumption of the audience's liberalism (not their radicalism or sophistication—those are the effete, ineffectual traits of Dafoe's Ward). The basic appeal made by director Alan Parker, who personally rewrote Chris Geralmo's original screenplay, is to the audience's own sense of superiority to the past—specifically to the American movie audience's mass identity as white.

Such *Time* magazine statements that Hackman here "caps a brilliant career" and that he has "America's face" make plain what the film covertly suggests: that Anderson is a symbolic fantasy of the white lawbringer and that the nobility he embodies is represented by an "American" face. That, of course, being a white face.

The shameless reviewers who praised *Mississippi Burning* and/or Hackman—and nearly all of them did—wrote their reviews in tacit agreement with the filmmaker's distortion of history and the recasting of who spearheaded the civil rights movement. These reviewers—who are, let's face it, white—automatically accepted the film's presumptions because in Hackman's ("America's") face they recognize their own. It's the film critics' version of the "We're all white here" line in *The Great Gatsby.*

Hackman never got such glowing notices when he played multidimensional, unique personalities emphasizing individuality or class distinctions. But as agent Anderson he embodies a late-Reagan-era dream of idealized authority, and the most effective action he takes is the old pulp-movie tactic of assaulting a villain's private parts. A sure audience grabber. This performance (it's too shallow to call a characterization) only works if one accepts the film's odious subtext—that might, authority, beauty, and truth are white virtues. This would not be possible if the film encouraged viewers to see themselves in the Black Southerners who historically must oppose racist whites.

This is the underlying thought that unifies even liberal and conservative admirers of the film. They—we—all have been educated subtly to this way of thinking through textbooks, comic books, newspapers, TV shows, and movies. Our white-centered pop culture is, thus, not consciously racist but subliminally so. It is racist in practice and in fact.

The problem of *Mississippi Burning* goes beyond twisting the truth and purposely misrepresenting the past—certain distortions are often allowable in the name of dramatic necessity. But consider that Hollywood has always assumed a political right in its exercise of poetic license. (See any western that turns native Americans into villains, even the recent TV miniseries "Lonesome Dove.") The confused motives show up in Parker's press kit statement: "Our film cannot be the definitive film of the Black civil rights struggle. Our heroes are still white. And in truth the film would probably never have been made if they weren't. This is a reflection of our society, not the film industry."

This makes one want to propose a chicken-or-the-egg conundrum to Parker. He hides his own creative cowardice and political bigotry behind imagined social constraints that he willingly sets for himself. What a lie he tells. But by separating society from the film industry and assigning blame, Parker shows himself intellectually ill-equipped to make any socially based drama. He doesn't see the connection between a society and its cultural institutions. He refuses to understand how the film industry reflects and reinforces social conventions.

Parker insults the public's intelligence when he denies it the opportunity to observe the truth. *Mississippi Burning* avoids portraying the reality of the civil rights movement, whether the self-determining efforts of Black people, the humane fraternity of whites who joined in, or the difficulty of encouraging and securing governmental support. All of this was lucidly presented in Henry Hampton's stirring documentary series "Eyes on the Prize."

Parker chooses fantasy as a deliberate denial of truth. His fantasy obverts the causes of equality and understanding. Parker fulfills an essential Hollywood agenda to promote the empowered, profitable (i.e., lucrative) point of view. Society can—and does—take facts of Black achievement and celebrate or ignore them at will, whatever's easier. Commercial movies routinely excuse people from having to discern the complex or paradoxical truths of America's multiracial social history. Hollywood only disrespects history by turning it into what the film's producer, Fred Zollo, callously admits is only "a thriller."

This is how "socially conscious" filmmaking gets perverted into brainwashing, mass control. Every lie in *Mississippi Burning,* such as the final shot of a civil rights worker's desecrated gravestone that reads "1964—Not Forgotten," builds a warped, deceptive mirror maze. The way public sentiment is reflected by the base intentions of the money-minded filmmakers misremembers 1964. That final, contrived image contains both pious and craven interests and thus is false and exploitative.

When Agent Anderson finally rises in anger and strikes out against the Klan, his action has no basis in the moral objection to racism; he's simply avenging his sweetheart. It's symbolic retribution that safely tames and displaces any humanist indignation the audience might feel. This gimmick shrewdly substitutes sincerity with effect. That explains why gullible reviewers have called the film "dazzling" or "intense" or "exciting." They're only responding to the crudest Hollywood formula and mistaking Pavlovian response for moral revulsion.

"Enjoying" *Mississippi Burning* this way is its own dubious reward. The filmmakers' disregard for the political issues is subsumed in its momentum, in its "craft," in the "glory" of Hackman's star turn. All of this has the undeniable result of promoting white heroism. Parker doesn't risk giving an attractive, adult Black person any purpose or much screen time. Like the recent *Everybody's All-American, Mississippi Burning* is a civil rights movie that sustains Hollywood's segregation.

There's a principle that needs stating and defending here: The 1960s struggle for civil rights extended to equal representation in media, including popular culture—that is, movies. When liberal white filmmakers felt the urge of this imperative, the screen opened up to Black faces – Poitier's in *A Patch of Blue, Pressure Point, The Slender Thread*; Ivan Dixon and Abbey Lincoln in *Nothing but a Man;* Bernie Hamilton in *One Potato, Two Potato;* Sammy Davis Jr. in *A Man Called Adam*; Ossie Davis and Ruby Dee in *Gone Are the Days*. These films confronted the issues of race and civil rights.

Those filmmakers were not, at the time, content with simply letting audiences identify with white actors and white characters. Parker's refusal to even consider a Black protagonist negates *Mississippi Burning*'s most pious pretenses. Yet this has helped the film to critical and commercial success in an age of racial subterfuge and liberal recession. Parker can portray white Southern racists as ignorant, inbred mutants, allowing any self-respecting viewers to easily distance themselves from such bad behavior, but his portrayal of Blacks as suffering, helpless, and literally childlike allows for convenient patronizing.

There shouldn't be anything intrinsically wrong with the art that a society manufactures for its own entertainment or enlightenment. Movies are of interest as one of the ways a nation talks back to itself, offering encouragement, approval, or debate. But lately this discourse has been corrupted, thwarted by insincerity and racist greed; the profit motive has produced forms of cultural double talk in which filmmakers pick ideas out of the air, out of the headlines or history books, and then trivialize their significance.

*Mississippi Burning* is but the most transparent of recent examples of Hollywood duplicity – of power talking back to itself but never in self-critical, challenging ways. To put this simply, the whites who control the movie industry have no interest in letting go of their sovereignty or questioning it or sharing it. Movies committed to social progress don't get made because they might reflect on the inequities of the industry itself; that's a cynical view of what I am sure is an unconscious process. But anyone who has gone to movies regularly these past two decades must realize that there's some mysterious (unrecognized) force behind Hollywood's persistent narrative conventions.

In Parker's film, the makeshift FBI headquarters in an abandoned movie theater (where the agents don't even run newsreels or watch TV coverage of the Southern debacle) epitomizes this tradition. Hollywood filmmaking style has been stubbornly ethnocentric – that is, white-centered. Onscreen, America's face is always white, even as the complexion of the American masses has pluralized, diversified, rainbowed. Hackman's face in *Mississippi Burning* is like the face of Scorsese's Jesus – it's the only moral complexion, accurate or not, that people in power will tolerate or even contemplate after having enjoyed hundreds, even thousands, of years of privilege.

Clinging to its self-promoting, white-dominated conventions, "glamorous" dreams from the unenlightened past (some call it Hollywood's Golden Age or the Age of Innocence, better the Age of Ignorance), most of today's filmmakers seem morally incapable of bringing civil rights or racial equality to their filmmaking (*Tequila Sunrise, Working Girl,* etc.).

The problem for all of us is developing a less egocentric response to cinema. The transference of identity that people of color have always had to make at the movies is just the kind of theoretical, hypothetical leap of faith, pledge of fellow feeling that Hollywood filmmakers now refuse to return.

That is why I have phrased many of the ideas here in blunt racial terms. I don't mean to indict the personal point of view that fimmakers and audiences who happen to be white are born with, but to clarify and, I hope, discredit the automatic complicity so many people have with Hollywood films. As *Mississippi Burning* proves, these assumptions result in the most fallacious, meretricious, and factitious popular art. Gene Hackman is not us. He hasn't got America's face, and even *Mississippi Burning*'s title is a lie. It's Hollywood that's burning: a pathetic institution consuming itself in flames of greed and racist vanity.

*The City Sun*
March 8, 1989

# GOOD GOLLY, MISS MOLLY

"**B**ÊTE NOIRE!" a boy screams at his mother in *The Forbidden City*. This arch assertion, as spoken by a Black boy, is also a double entendre and that changes it from a bitter, woman-hating rant to a twisted statement of bitter compassion.

In this astonishing theater piece, at the Public Theater, playwright Bill Gunn essayed the coming-of-age play so late in life (he died April 5 [1989] at age fifty-nine) and so late in theater history that he often drops the basic, naturalistic sense of the genre in favor of vision and passion. Structure is less important than what Gunn had to say.

The literal, Depression-era events that lead to a teenage boy's confrontation with his intimidating parents are given hyperbolic, surreal description. Timid, effeminate Nick Jr. (portrayed by Akili Prince) begins the play crouched in the dark, hugging himself. It's through his extreme sensitivity that the domineering members of his family are viewed: the forceful, flamboyant mother, Miss Molly (Gloria Foster), and the fond but distant father, Nick Sr. (Frankie R. Faison). There's also the ghost of a dead brother who haunts Nick Jr.'s imagination, embodying his psychic connection to the barely understood fears and regrets of his parents.

Gunn's acute sense of the ridiculous was first evident in the sharp, satirical script he wrote for the 1970 film *The Landlord*. It also dictated the hallucinogenic form of *Ganja and Hess*, the rarely seen 1972 horror movie he wrote and directed. Those films, about black-white social confusion and the complications of African heritage and Christianity, perceive deep troubles that few modern artists have thought through clearly in their work or in life. Gunn's tendency to give familiar shape to his demons invites an immediate, facile understanding and then offers a tangle of psychological obsession in a sardonic tone—as in the radical climax of *The Forbidden City*.

Literal-minded people who dismissed *Ganja and Hess* as an occult thriller will likely scoff at *The Forbidden City* as a tiresome Black amalgam of *Dark at the Top of the Stairs*, *The Glass Menagerie* and *Member of the Wedding*. But it was Gunn's awareness of these preexisting works that caused him to choose their style. Their distance from details of Black experience caused him to then push their similarities—their extremes of guilt, gothic domesticity, and internalized emotions.

Miss Molly lacks only the "Good Golly" in front of her name. She's an Oedipal monster, a Black version of the Gorgon mothers in post-World War II Freudian drama, and Gunn characterizes her with the same awe and repulsion and amusement. He's animating an effigy that he loves too deeply to burn. But Gunn's difference from Tennessee Williams and William Inge—his predecessors in this style—may be an especially Black difference: He empathizes with Miss Molly out of the hostility and social frustration they both share as Black people.

This is a mother-son connection deeper than Oedipus. It reflects the psychological wounds of political struggle that white playwrights after Sophocles—and especially after Freud—felt it unnecessary to emphasize. A special, ethnic (and feminist?) view of the world gives Gunn an additional layer of identity that binds him to Miss Molly where age and gender might otherwise encourage his detachment from her. Instead, he has written the largest, richest Black female role in American drama (certainly since *The Amen Corner*) and Gloria Foster, drawing upon her extraordinary emotional force and her experience performing the classics, scales the character for myth.

After losing her first son to racist doctors in the South, Miss Molly takes neurotic pride in her Northern (Philadelphia) life as a woman with a working husband and house during the Depression. Her lofty, conceited manner shields a hurt and panicky response to racism. Trapped between a cynical view of the white world, the Black condition, and the assimilationist urge, she is a beautiful terror to the males in her home—a figure to please and to cower before.

Gunn trades the obdurate, bovine suffering Black mother of stereotype for one with glamorous, melodramatic contours; his taste for camp saves the character from being maudlin. Her sass ("Between Greta Garbo and *Vanity Fair* I haven't been the same since") balances the humility she shows to a group of itinerant workers who beg for food. She has the mother wit to read the needs of these hungry men who spout Paul Laurence Dunbar. Miss Molly doesn't join their recitation (she later shows a shared knowledge), but she can express their circumstances in the plain, hard language of experience. She comprises the antagonisms in the male-female debate that have arisen since *The Color Purple.*

It's the submerged pain and the buried poetry inside this tough, pragmatic woman that dismay Nick Jr. She judges him "a disappointment," warns him, "Gumption seldom does colored men any good, it most likely gets you killed." While suffering her cruelty, Nick Jr. is startled by her jaded wisdom.

Gunn makes this looming figure of racial and sexual conflicts account for too much—much more than the offspring's inversion as proposed by those fifties playwrights. But this larger-than-life character also thoughtfully redresses the hard face Black men sometimes see in their women. Describing an acquaintance, Miss Molly says, "She hid her true self for so long she forgot where she put it. . . . Her children got her rage." It's almost self-description.

Most significantly Miss Molly, who rations her love to spare herself grief, is a Black tragic muse. She mirrors the Black male's anxious, desperate soul. White critics have not understood this, and Black audiences may find the mother-son relationship controversial. But it was clear in the *Ganja and Hess* monologue that Bill Gunn himself acted out with strange desperation, that his Black consciousness was turbulent. In fact, it was unsettling. His desire to explode the horror-film and memory-play genres might be linked to his inability to assume a received Black identity. Gunn questioned the sense of Black pride that is usually set in codes of Black heterosexual machismo; neither could he accept the clichés of neater dramatists and lesser artists. Greatness—expressions of poetry and pain—burst through the tackiest devices of *The Forbidden City.* It helps that the faultless cast, under Joe Papp's direction, hits the right note on every rich, confidently written line, because this is actually less a play than one man's self-revealing romantic gesture—it's Gunn's unorthodox attempt to define the psychological complexities behind Black art.

Nick Jr., on the threshold of the world, needs to express the history and unruly impulses that he inherited and that compelled him to write. Each successive generation of Black people knows the hardships, dilemmas, and expediences differently, although the enormity of their struggle remains the same. Miss Molly's and Nick Sr.'s knowledge of lynching and harassment are like phantoms to Nick Jr., with his agenda of literary aspirations and sexual freedom. He's oppressed by a history that he doesn't fully understand but that can possibly forearm him. Yet he's swayed by the same irresistible, middle-class (movie-inspired) dreams as his mother. He senses Miss Molly's bête noire in himself.

Gunn takes a lot of dares here (one theatrical coup is an adulterous "primal scene" staged in a morgue-like setting). The riskiest and most devastating is Nick Jr.'s final scene. Akili Prince does the hebephrenic monologue with amazing precision. The boy's confession plays back and confuses the mother's hysteria and the father's masculine rectitude in childish parody. He lies, fantasizes, hallucinates—bugging out with ghostly sarcasm. This ending catches the comic-pathos of typical family neurosis and goes on to something much more shocking and sad.

On the basis of *The Forbidden City* Bill Gunn should be remembered as the most fearless Black artist of his time. His efforts in film and theater were little known compared to unquestionable historic achievements such as "The Cosby Show." But where a well-adjusted mainstream artist like Cosby works to keep us sane, the scary, beautiful *Forbidden City* tells us why there is a need to.

*The City Sun*
April 19, 1989

# KEEPING UP WITH THE JONESES

*When the legend becomes fact, print the legend.*

Dᴇ IVINERS OF POPULAR CULTURE who once celebrated Steven Spielberg for his ingenious extension of the Hollywood film tradition ("A new generation's Howard Hawks") have deserted him when he needs them most. Spielberg's last three films—*The Color Purple, Empire of the Sun*, and *Indiana Jones and the Last Crusade*—are transitional landmarks in Hollywood's ethos. They attempt to expand the cultural awareness of commercial films, struggling with generic form while improving their political implication. This is nothing less than Hollywood *glasnost*, but reviewers expect aesthetic reform and cultural revision to come from Young Turk independents outside the official institution, or to be neatly differentiated by an acceptable passage of time—such as the generations that separate John Ford's sagebrush sentimentality from Sam Peckinpah's anti-Hollywood revisionism.

In *The Last Crusade*, Spielberg repudiates the very genre conventions and moral infractions he himself perpetrated in the two previous films of this George Lucas–produced series. It was the thinnest material Spielberg worked on since *Jaws*. Complaints that this final, third installment lacks zest disregard the extraordinary enhancement Spielberg has effected. In place of the melodramatic Freudian suggestions that Irving Kershner used to spike the pulpy *The Empire Strikes Back*, Spielberg makes a clean, funny, close-to-structuralist analysis of narrative practice. Insight about myth, not speed, is now the series' point.

The sensational timing and stunt work in the second of the Indiana Jones trilogy, *Temple of Doom*, could not be praised as anything but a dispassionate exercise of craft; the increased speed and smoothness were at the expense of sensible, responsible cultural expression. It was an infantile jamboree. But there's no need to tolerate that misused virtuosity when films like *A Chinese Ghost Story* can, miracle by miracle, step on *Temple of Doom*'s feats, while offering an authentic picture of a foreign culture. *The Last Crusade* redresses the issues of culture and imperialism that Spielberg and Lucas previously ignored. This film doesn't need to be paced any faster, because, now, everything that happens around Indiana Jones is something to think about. The mind races along with the heart.

This improvement is, doubtlessly, more instinctual than calculated, yet it's also a rare sign of folk-pop development in Hollywood. Spielberg's extraordinary mastery of formula and of structural tropes seems, on its own, to tend toward cultural inclusion, a global egalitarianism—the opposite of "classical" Hollywood's aesthetics. Back then, the perfection of escapist forms was a systemic social reflex, an expression of the country's political ideology. Films like *Gunga Din, Lives of a Bengal Lancer, Beau Geste, Drums Along the Mohawk,* and *The Four Feathers* (and countless others) roused motor responses at the same time that they sanctioned belief in white superiority and Western imperialism.

After *E.T.,* the era's great popular film, Spielberg tackled two "minority" projects: *The Color Purple,* where he adapted Black American iconography to the Hollywood fantasy styles previously reserved for white fiction; and *Empire of the Sun,* where he showed absolute empathy for both the Chinese and Japanese positions in World War II. (It was, perhaps, less Sino-sympathy than Sony savvy.) These creative experiences must have sensitized Spielberg to the different, third-world readings that a nonwhite viewer might give to Hollywood genre films— consideration that never occurred to old moguls who simply wanted to conquer world markets. The nationalist and racist biases in Hollywood cinema are appalling if viewed intelligently today. The entire history of Hollywood fantasy reveals its corruption in the persistence of white male heroism and Western domination. Yes, Spielberg should have known better when he began the Indiana Jones series, but the general enthusiasm for *Temple of Doom*'s overwhelming kinetics and shoddy anthropology also proved that most critics neither knew better nor cared.

*The Last Crusade*'s full-color, wide-screen shots of Monument Valley in the opening sequence are brilliantly clever revisionism: the setting, familiar from John Ford westerns, is the *locus classicus* of American cinema's solipsism. Spielberg sums up the process of patriotic indoctrination with a joke: the figures we see commanding this locale are a horseback Boy Scout troop. The point: American action in the primeval West is, essentially, child's play. But movies that are proud of their national and racial biases are not kid's stuff, they're dangerous. *The Last Crusade* is knowingly constructed with allusions to the self-aggrandizing parochialism of the adventure film genre. There's a satirical element in seeing white male American derring-do writ so large. It becomes simultaneously tumid, neurotic, and comic. But unlike *Temple of Doom* and parts of *Raiders of the Lost Ark,* it's never insulting or oppressive.

Instead of presenting the opening sequence (with River Phoenix playing the teenage Indy) as a prologue, Spielberg compresses this antecedent information into the main story. Manipulating narrativity this way is the prerogative of a famous showman—he's tweaking the audience's awareness of storytelling, stoking the engine of his plot. The locomotive set piece is a metaphor for narrative momentum, a visceral anecdote economically and humorously explaining the origins of Indy's mythic characteristics—his scarred chin, his fear of snakes, his dexterity with a bullwhip, and his trademark fedora. (Spielberg audaciously casts Richard Young, an actor who resembles himself and Harrison Ford, as Indy's amoral alternative role model.) This western-cum-circus-train sequence gives Indy his first quotable dialogue of the trilogy—"That belongs in a museum!" The phrase describes his motives and tenacity, but it also reverberates as a statement of western acquisitiveness, as applicable to the Elgin Marbles as to the pretend goodies—the Cross of Coronado and the Holy Grail—fought over in the film.

Linking American adventure movies to the Crusades shows a shrewd understanding of what adventure movies are designed to do culturally and politically. They're ideological war machines.

This makes good on the Joseph Campbell influence that Lucas botched in his *Star Wars* trilogy and in the little-people-as-the-third-world-making-their-own-history in *Willow.* The allusions to the big-screen history of the American West are connected to the Middle East pursuit of the Holy Grail by way of pre-Renaissance Italy. The global/historical sleight of hand is pure philological wit. We see the Grail as an artifact that, like westerns and adventure movies, confers beauty, power, and divinity upon its owner. These historical referents in the Menno Meyjes–Jeffrey Boam script expose the fascist, quasi-religious fervor that's been a part of the American adventure film from D. W. Griffith's *The Birth of a Nation* and John Ford's *The Iron Horse* to *Out of Africa* and *Mississippi Burning.*

Spielberg's formal expertise makes *The Last Crusade*—a beautiful title, unlike *Temple of Doom,* which suggests an amusement park ride—into one of the most sophisticated adventure films ever made: its parts snap together with precise, dry cunning. It's the wised-up razzmatazz of an adult playing within the acceptable boundaries of world politics and subverts the globetrotter caprice that the Indy series revives. Finally, in *The Last Crusade*, the interplay between Indy's boyish spirit and (his father's) scholarly, political rectitude dramatizes the creative impulse threading its way through this era of dwindling western superiority. One response is to make a lovely but wan little myth study like Caleb Deschanel's smart revision of Daniel Defoe, *Crusoe*. Spielberg's recent cinema, however, remains boldly fantastic while adjusting to global realities; his transitional films confront and rewrite historical fiction.

"Movies and TV programs like *The Jewel in the Crown* and *A Passage to India* are what I call 'Easterns,' " Hanif Kureishi once told me, citing the European counterpart to the historical inaccuracies and political conceits of American westerns. Kureishi was disgusted at the imperialist arrogance that only recognizes third-world cultures as things "that belong in a museum" for the first world's delectation. *The Last Crusade* is in agreement: as Indy maniacally reaches for the Holy Grail, his archaeologist father cautions, "Let it go."

That advice, morally inspired, is also politically enlightened. And it gains significance coming from Sean Connery, who, fourteen years ago, in his best performance, as Danny Dravat in John Huston's *The Man Who Would Be King*, acted out the racist-colonialist vanity of the British empire—the cultural tradition Indiana Jones inherited, via James Bond. Of course, Huston's film updated Rudyard Kipling by making it a working-class fantasy trapped inside the psychology of colonialism. Ultimately, the movie failed to break completely away from it. Spielberg distances himself by riding the genre into the sunset. He's not looking for a *Tequila Sunrise*, the sour, decadent renewal of Hollywood's past.

This "letting go" upsets people who want to believe in John Wayne and the raj and in the fast deployment of film technique without political consciousness. When the once "liberal" *Village Voice* recently printed film reviewer Georgia Brown's blithe admission of her antipathy to and impatience with films about people of color, it's clear that our film culture is mired in barely understood racism. Brown instead glossed over *The Last Crusade*'s political themes to make knee-jerk accusations of sexism—the only ethical issue most white critics seem to care about.

The most audacious moment in *The Last Crusade* deals impudently with the significance of history and myth: carrying his father's diary, Indy comes face-to-face with Adolf Hitler in the middle of a Nazi bookburning rally. Hitler—a media star and he knows it—autographs the diary rather than burning it. By inscribing the text that Indy has been using— almost religiously—as a reverent guide for survival, Hitler puts his mark on a historical record. This scene is worthy of E. L. Doctorow's *Ragtime*: Hitler's graffito intrudes on a subjective text; his existence is a type of uncomfortable truth that must be dealt with in all our personal versions of history. The anti-Spielberg critics are all little Hitlers—cinema burners—who don't want movies to tell the truth. Realizing how moviegoers turn legend into "fact," Spielberg will no longer simply film the legend people want to believe, because history is more complicated than movie myths allow.

Regarding the sexist charges: Unlike *Raiders'* Karen Allen or *Temple of Doom*'s Kate Capshaw, Alison Doody's Elsa is the series' first female who is not helplessly feminine. In the larger historical framework her "villainy" is as ambiguous as Indy's "heroism." They're psychopolitical peers. The comic use of Nazis surpasses Ernst Lubitsch's in *To Be or Not to Be*. It's historically apt for Indy to say "I hate those guys" matter-of-factly; the film eschews sentimentality on this subject, too, yet shows prescience (with the benefit of hindsight) in a closeup of an indestructible Nazi insignia. That shot forecasts the next probable development and final solution of the Indiana Jones saga: the War, which was only entertaining in the movies.

Born a Jew and consecrated a filmmaker who's taken on the task of entertaining the world, Spielberg has to maneuver between a personal political agenda and a respect for both Christian and non-Jewish, American and international cultures. Few men in the history of Hollywood have attempted this honestly. Spielberg closes off a racist film form with *The Last Crusade*, because today no one can conscientiously make movies the way they used to.

*Film Comment*
July 1989

# REBIRTH OF A NATION

D*O THE RIGHT THING* opens with a funny, erotic sequence in which a woman of color (Rosie Perez) asserts both the integrity of boxing and dancing in time to Public Enemy's rap song "Fight the Power." Pugilistic, political funk sums up the style of Spike Lee's film. His boldest, most accomplished moviemaking yet, it drives home the cultural and political awareness that his first two films (*She's Gotta Have It* and *School Daze*) only suggested. *Do the Right Thing*'s view of a Black New York neighborhood on the hottest day of the year counters most mainstream ideas about America and movies

Light on its feet, the movie dances among an assortment of characters in a one-block area of Brooklyn's Bedford-Stuyvesant. Young adults, kids, old folks, working people, and idlers all express their dissatisfaction and heat-aggravated temper in a contrapuntal dialogue that makes this movie, like Public Enemy's music, an artful arrangement of cultural fragments. It, too, spars with the complacency of pop tradition in which Black politics or viewpoints never mattered. This charming, dreamlike film means business.

*Do the Right Thing* is going to trouble people raised on Hollywood's specious idolatry of American democracy. The movie's sentimental style ironically embraces social distress in a more realistic, cautionary way. This is the torpor and tension of 1980s America that *Rain Man, Broadcast News,* and most other Hollywood films that glorify the white middle class avoid showing. Lee himself plays Mookie, who works as a delivery boy for the Italian pizzeria on his block. Sal (Danny Aiello) runs the place as he has for years, along with his two sons, the angry Pino (John Turturro) and cool, timid Vito (Richard Edson). On his rounds, Mookie moves among the block's types: a benign drunk called Da Mayor (Ossie Davis), the nosy-neighbor Mother Sister (Ruby Dee), a quartet of frisky teens, Korean grocers, Latin boys, and a trio of out-of-work men (Paul

Benjamin, Robin Harris, and Frankie Faison), whose joshing routines under a sun umbrella in front of a bright red wall work as a soulful Greek chorus.

Lee's own affectionate bemusement weaves these characters together. Even the bickering between Mookie and Tina, his Latin girlfriend (Perez), who berates him for not visiting their baby, seems rapturously intimate. Lee's structure may be schematic, but no filmmaker since Robert Altman has shown such a profound knack for American vernacular. The modulations between harsh, seductive and just plain social talk seem effortless. One sequence shows off this gift in a montage of Black, Italian, Latin, and Jewish epithets. Lee uses language—the sound of urban unease—to intensify his story's social dynamics.

Radio is the key to *Do the Right Thing*'s brilliance. The movie has a high-frequency style jolting with bursts of music, color, humor, and serious ideas. Lee breaks with Hollywood narrative convention and takes his tone from the populist mode of airwave entertainment. That's perfect for a film about urban African-American life. Lee is able to monitor the collective unconscious of Bed-Stuy through Mister Señor Lovedaddy (Sam Jackson), DJ for WELOVE radio station. Spinning r&b platters and broadcasting verbal reports, the DJ comments on twenty-four hours of Black life. More could be made of this device, but it effectively constructs the film in flowing, start-stop rhythms that match the flux of radio—the only mass-communication medium that has been open to Black people. Through this, Lee picks up signals that are remote to established white filmmaking practice. And unlike the casual radio-derived structures of *American Graffiti* and *Radio Days*, *Do the Right Thing* is tuned in to the ongoing primacy of pop experience. Its person-on-the-street multiplicity suggests the surreal dissonance of dial spinning. The relation to African oral tradition is obvious, but more important is the implication that in post-sixties America, Black people (and Asians and Latinos)—who may be isolated by age, sex, and taste—are still under the sway of a common cultural wave.

The film's emotional undercurrent, represented by persistent pop music motifs, is brand new for American movies. There's more vitality and warmth here than in a typical lament for the downtrodden. Lee brings to cinema the impudent integrity of hiphop. Unlike mainstream (read white) social tracts about America's class system from *Dead End* (1937) to *Saturday Night Fever* (1977), *Do the Right Thing* doesn't condescend to working-class culture. Lee may borrow the unified time frame and basic setting of the tenement plays and folk dramas from earlier eras, but the action he stages and the dialogue he writes are new-jack, thrilling.

"Fight the Power" is heard throughout the film as the theme song of Radio Raheem (Bill Nunn), a towering young Black man who paces Bed-Stuy carrying a formidably huge beat box. "You don't like Public Enemy?" he asks the jivy hothead Buggin' Out (Giancarlo Esposito). Public Enemy's no-half-measures rap screeds define the intensity of young Black male discontent. The group's propulsive, keening sound collages give the taciturn Raheem eloquence. In one of *Do the Right Thing*'s moments of startling wit, Raheem faces the camera and does a *Night of the Hunter*-style recitation on "love" and "hate" and the battle between good and evil. The scene suggests Travis Bickle as a Gentle Giant and would-be poet and fondly evokes the pent-up inarticulateness of underclass youth. As Mookie, Lee himself acts out the charming, hilarious response to Raheem's speech. Mookie, the film's central figure, knows psychic torment when he sees it—even if he doesn't understand it yet—and like Spike Lee, he respects it.

By fetishizing Raheem's beat box, Lee honors the medium that expands the indigenous musical expressions of America's different ethnic groups. This, clearly, is a criticism of the monopoly that other, more socially mobile ethnic groups have made of movies, television, and the print media. It is Buggin' Out's fury over the domineering photographs of Italian movie stars in Sal's Pizzeria ("How come there ain't no Black people on your wall of pride!") that turns the day's events to tragedy. When Sal smashes Raheem's radio—the kid's preeminent means of articulation—all hell breaks loose.

*Do the Right Thing* is an antiracist taboo buster. Instead of moralizing about races living together in peace—the "official" made-for-TV-movie manner used whenever Hollywood feels like exploiting the problem—it broadcasts the aggrieved exasperations of racism's Black and white victims. Lee doesn't vent gaseous indignation about the confrontation between radio Raheem and Sal. He makes the ideologies at war frighteningly clear; good and bad intentions fly up and land indistinguishably. In the aftermath, when Mookie speaks up to Sal, the scene's matter-of-fact sorrow is honestly and authentically ambiguous. It's the true mood of America's disenfranchised and dispossessed. This appalling, funny exchange in front of the burned-down, gutted ruins of Sal's shop may suggest homegrown, political Beckett, but its stylistic peculiarity has a different intent—a thorough rejection of the false optimism in mainstream entertainment.

Like the best rap and punk music of the past decade, *Do the Right Thing* makes personal behavior inseparable from politics. When Mookie notices that his pretty career-girl sister, Jade (Joie Lee), brings out a schoolboy courtliness in Sal, the sexual tension is released in a sibling debate in front of a blaring graffito: "Tawana Told The Truth." New York City's recent racial controversies (such as the Tawana Brawley affair, Howard Beach, and the police killing of Michael Griffiths) are here turned into folklore that's meant to be argued about.

Lee doesn't preach, but he indicates – spectacularly. That flirtation scene between Sal and Jade is watched by a resentful Mookie and Pino in teasing slow motion. Lee uses a Martin Scorsese trope here, as well as in Radio Raheem's showdown with a group of Puerto Ricans and in Buggin' Out's pitched argument with a gentrifying white yuppie (John Savage). His animated camera style builds on the most important things Lee could have learned from his New York colleague: that movies should be culturally specific and that style should serve audience awareness.

Scorsese's Italian-American trilogy – *Who's That Knocking at My Door?*, *Mean Streets*, and *Raging Bull* – brought new elements to American filmmaking: determinedly ethnic, those movies went fearlessly into the hellishness of their characters' particular racial and sexual biases. Until Spike Lee, such raw emotional milieu has been the province of white filmmakers. Even that sequence sampling assorted racial slurs recalls the classroom face-off between Black and white teens in Philip Kaufman's *The Wanderers*.

Lately, white filmmakers like Kaufman have abandoned American subjects for the safe, ersatz sophistication of "European" political movies like *The Unbearable Lightness of Being*. That leaves a Black artist like Lee to fill the gap and correct the balance.

Black America's pluralism is more affectionately and smartly depicted in *Do the Right Thing* than in *School Daze,* and the *Rashomon* structure of *She's Gotta Have It* is replaced by an agitprop fancifulness much like Jean-Luc Godard's eye-popping sixties political comedies (*Made in U.S.A , A Woman Is a Woman*). All this proves that Lee is on his way to commanding a many-faceted, expressive technique that will answer both the creative and the political imperatives that he refuses to separate. With cinematographer Ernest Dickerson he refashions a ghetto location into a gold-toned, ordered universe of fractious democracy. This small-scale Gotham is actually a greater achievement than Tim Burton and Anton Furst's *Batman* setting; its look emanates from the fundamental modern American experience of territory and dislocation – the personal sense of home that one views with a global awareness of economic and political inequity.

Lee understands this well enough to treat the film's climax as a social uprising, not a riot. Mookie and his community react to police brutality and the general state of frustration by attacking the institution that pathetically symbolizes their deprivation. Sal, the person, is not their target. There's order in Lee's survey of social chaos. Ending with the philosophies of Martin Luther King Jr. and Malcolm X echoing in sweet, bitter counterpoint, *Do the Right Thing* speaks to today's racial crisis as a matter of individual conscience. Daringly, and with lots of wit and style, it uses the aggregate boiling tempers of New York to portray the state of the nation.

*L.A. Weekly*
July 7, 1989

# THE WRATH OF MADONNA VS. POP-GOSPEL

G OSPEL CHOIRS can be seen as an expression of unity. Every voice is lifted in song; deep, personal yearnings are joined together, and the individual is endowed with the strength of masses.

This political aspect is not separate from the spiritual profundity of the gospel choral songform. The emotive power of gospel choirs suggests something divine — something transfigured — even in secular contexts like the new version of "Lean on Me" (Warner Bros.) recorded by Thelma Houston and The Winans for the Morgan Freeman movie. There's an object lesson in salvation-by-community in the way Houston takes heart in the tune and sings her dormant career momentarily back to life, egged on by the uplifting harmonic support of The Winans.

This is part of the knowledge that African-American singers take with them when they trade in their choir robes for a record contract and a "Soul Train" appearance. White pop producers understand the value of this sensibility and will exploit it even to the point of nightmare, like the scene in *Rattle and Hum* where U2 coerces New Voices of Freedom into doing the fake gospel "I Still Haven't Found What I'm Looking For."

Madonna's "Like a Prayer" is the latest white pop record to employ a Black gospel choir (The Andrae Crouch Singers). On first hearing, before the song's pop craft kicks in, the Crouch choir's participation seems hypocritical. Are they lending their spirituality to the service of a shameless hedonist? Most Black gospel-turned-pop singers exhibit the same blithe attitude toward their soulful art as expressed in Prince's 12-inch gospel version of "I Wish You Heaven" when he says, "Take this beat, I don't mind / Got many others and it's so fine": They sing pop without thinking.

Clinton Utterbach and the Praisers sing with such dignified gospel pomp on their album *Sing a New Song* (Lection/Polygram) that the sound of an auditorium full of applause that ends the first cut, "Lord, We Invite You Here," is a stirring surprise. Is it live or artificial? The sound of rote response or spontaneous joy that's turned down in the mix?

This rectitude on *Sing a New Song* is a curious strategy. There's no getting down in Utterbach's conception of "upper room," but as he conducts his Praisers to trim, precise, full-throated exultation, the restraint becomes admirable. This is gospel in the face of pop gospel. Some of the horn charts (as on "Hallelujah") and the guitar picking (on "The Name of the Lord") show the influence of pop, but basically these arrangements walk a straight and narrow path.

The album is fast and listenable in ways that suggest Utterbach and the Praisers have found an economical access to religious celebration. The súreness of the stately rhythms very steadily proves moving, like horizontal conveyors in airports.

Redeeming Love Christian Center in Nanuet, New York, is home to the Praisers and the church where Utterbach is pastor. They don't sound like dynamized urban-storefront worshipers or southern tent-revival zealots, yet there's enough bottom in the vocal harmonies to distinguish them from "P.T.L. Show" white gospel.

Utterbach, a preacher-singer-composer, seems to direct his interest toward achieving a distinction from current pop gospel. His strict, middle-class harmonies are explained in his spoken introduction to "Sing a New Song": "The word of God tells us that in the Old Testament, when the singers and instrumentalists came together and they were of one accord, the spirit of God came in and the priests couldn't stand to minister." This title tune is a church person's version of "Get Back," an admonition to keep gospel pure of the vernacular excesses that commonly result from secular uses.

There's no fiery Vanessa Bell-Armstrong–type of shouting here – and such songs as "No One Like You," which sounds uncomfortably like Kenny Rogers's "We've Got Tonight," could use some – yet there's a genuine less-is-more beauty to "Come, Lord Jesus" and "We Approach Your Throne." From the latter, the lyric "We leave our carnal minds at your feet" tells much of what's going on in this record. Utterbach cuts the provocative keyboard cadenza just at the point the whole song should erupt into dance and carrying on. This is no *Lovesexy;* the separation between flesh and spirit is fundamental to Utterbach's method. The result, on record at least, is noncorporeal, which makes the effort toward salvation seem a matter of will rather than a struggle between flesh and spirit. "Sinners" may have trouble with this approach, but Utterbach has not made a proselytizing record, it's one of evangelical tact. The sheep don't mingle with the goats.

Patty Holley, a California-based actress, emblemizes the gospel-versus-pop dilemma in the way she pantomimes the Sandra Crouch vocal lines in the *Like a Prayer* video. Holley plays a dual part of angelic avatar and choir singer demonstrating the redemptive qualities of African-American gospel music. In the dream sequence she displays the phenomenal erotic ecstasy of Black religion. Holley is the first actress since Nina Mae MacKinney in King Vidor's 1931 *Hallelujah!* to act out this paradox of flesh and spirit in a mainstream film. In the modern age we've gotten used to observing this split in the form that Ray Charles and especially Aretha Franklin perfected in their performance of church-based, love-suffering songs.

Holley's remarkable video performance connotes both the sexual and religious ramifications of Black gospel. By miming a voice, she acts out how Black gospel precepts have extended into secular, political action and ideology.

That's the starting point of the video Mary Lambert has directed for the Madonna song. The record itself describes a Saint Theresa–like commingling of sensual and spiritual feeling. With the record's success at the top of the singles chart, it has also been taken as an expression of female sexual power controlling male passion through fellatio. Yet the concept that Lambert worked out with Madonna is more audacious and sensible than that.

*Like a Prayer* puts across complex and controversial ideas with simple clarity and an insistent, infectious dance rhythm. It uses the beat of the song to propel its mixture of religion, sex, and race. None of these ideas are new in Lambert's work. *Like a Prayer* recalls various visual tropes and pop codes that Lambert has used—such as the choir in her "Higher and Higher" Arrow Shirts commercial; the ethnic-religious tie of *La Isla Bonita;* the modernist use of a proscenium in *Nasty* for Janet Jackson; the consciousness of Black music icons in Chris Isaak's *Dancin'.*

All this pop background is at work in the way Lambert compresses action within five minutes. Our general familiarity with pop icons is put into witty, abstract context: Madonna witnesses a woman being attacked on the street by a group of white thugs. When a Black man (played by the actor Leon, from *Women of Brewster Place*) helps the injured woman, a police car pulls up and the man is arrested for the crime. Running away, in fear and shame, Madonna comes upon a church. Inside, she approaches a statue of a Black saint (Saint Martin de Porres?) on an altar behind a wrought-iron gate, and the resemblance to the Black man whose arrest she witnessed causes a moral frisson; it invokes a sense of Christian love and duty.

In her spiritual agony/reverie Madonna is overwhelmed by entreaties from a Black gospel choir. The film goes into high gear as the chorus builds and violent images of social turmoil alternate with visions of interracial sensuality. These encourage Madonna to act on her social and religious responsibility and report the Black man's false arrest. In 1989 that's a radical act.

*Like a Prayer* is the most exciting film (short or feature length) made in America in several years. With its race-and-sex nexus, it puts the two most volatile themes in our culture in the center of public mind. But the poetry of its music-video structure makes it aesthetically daring and inventive. Lambert's expertise is an interesting recent example of the ingenuity of music video. Her film doesn't simply illustrate the song's lyrics (or recreate actual social history like the Edmund Perry story that inspired the Martin Scorsese–Michael Jackson *Bad*); Lambert creates a story from the social and emotional subtext of the song's musical structure.

Madonna's association with Black music styles, which peaked in her collaboration with Stephen Bray on "Into the Groove," has long sought a transcendent emotional release. The visceral urge of African rhythm is the basis for her trademark physical abandon—she's a lousy dancer, as her videos from *Lucky Star* to *Dress You Up* proved, but in *Like a Prayer* her gauche-Black moves have an ingenuousness. Her will to be one with Black music becomes a charming physical fact.

This changes the nature of a white exploiting Black culture through naive sincerity. The moment that Holley steps out of the choir stand, when she and Madonna exchange hot looks of sisterhood, reifies this often notorious cultural exchange. It is "sanctified" in Holley's anointing Madonna, a dramatic gesture that solidifies Black-white solidarity through religion and sex. This is much more fascinating than the Black-white communion of the Foreigner video *I Want to Know What Love Is*, where Blackness is viewed stereotypically, if not condescendingly. Members of the New Jersey Mass Choir were simply toilers and extollers. Their lives took a back seat to the trysting of a white yuppie couple.

"I Want to Know What Love Is" is a fine pop recording, but there's nothing new or subversive in its borrowing of Black gospel. There's a psychic depth and sociological awareness to Madonna and co-composer Patrick Leonard's borrowing. If the obviousness of Madonna's commercial calculation makes you doubt that, Lambert's video convinces through the force of art. Lambert says she and Madonna work together on video concepts, but when Lambert talks about the controversy over *Like a Prayer* her personal objectives become apparent.

"We wanted to say something about racism" explains Lambert, a native of Arkansas who studied at the Rhode Island School of Design. "I think a lot of the religious controversy is just racism in disguise."

Among the many radical ideas in the video is the close, sensual embrace of Madonna and Leon, where dark and light lips meet. Lambert says, "People are offended, but we wanted to make the idea of interracial love a real point—love in the fullest sense of the word." The racial shock is based in a religious precept. "We wanted to let the hero be a saint and a person, a fellow human being and a lover," Lambert says. The video's imagery represents a certain polytheism. The exterior of the church looks like one of the Protestant edifices from *Mississippi Burning*, but the interior suggests Latin Catholic atmosphere. Lambert's idea was "to represent religion in details, not overall accuracy; to convey different aspects of spirituality."

Lambert insists, "It's not intended to be profane. There's a deep sense of the sacred." The video uses religion, she says, as a way of "letting saints step down off the altar and become a part of your life. You know, 'If you can talk it, you should walk it.' "

This ethical challenge is the point of *Like a Prayer*'s most striking device: In the midst of her emotional torment Madonna is shown singing the song's bridge on a field of burning crosses. "It's an ecstatic vision," Lambert says. "A cautionary symbol. The burning cross is a symbol older than the Ku Klux Klan. Saints had it. It's a symbol of the wrath of God."

Lambert has expropriated an image befouled by racism and won back its original, moral meaning as a scourge of iniquity. It's a scene of absolute moral authority and female sexual aggression; the complexity is just plain thrilling. Martin Scorsese's *The Last Temptation of Christ* cannot touch *Like a Prayer* for cultural revision or innovative technique.

This amazing pop-gospel parable avoids piety every second. It ends with a curtain coming down on Madonna's effort to get the unjustly arrested Black man released from jail. The self-conscious theatricality certifies the video as an expression of hopeful enlightenment. *Like a Prayer* extends a white appreciation of Black culture to a recognition of the contradictory social attitudes—and social structures like church and jails—that are used to oppress Black people and women. Lambert and Madonna bear their burning cross through to the other side of cultural patronization.

# A METAPHYSICAL MOVIE MUSICAL

E LLA FITZGERALD'S RENDITION of "Taking a Chance on Love" underscores a remarkable sequence in *Distant Voices, Still Lives*. A group
of children watch their mother sit precariously on a window ledge as
she scrubs the grimy glass. "Please, Mommy, don't fall," one child begs.
In a sudden time shift, the mother is shown being beaten by her husband.
Then, bruised and sobbing, she continues her housecleaning chores and
her movements keep time with Fitzgerald's singing.

Director-writer Terence Davies lets Fitzgerald's record fill out his
characters' unconscious. It expresses in one sweet, melodic phrase all of
their highest, most sincere feelings and aspirations, while their rough,
risky lives mock their dreams. Davies's counterpoint gives this stark
depiction of white English working-class life true poignancy. The unflinching revelation of pain makes a great film out of Davies's concentration on our fascination with popular music.

*Distant Voices, Still Lives* recalls Davies's own family history in
Liverpool in the forties and fifties in a mosaic of vignettes and memory
flashes. He envisions dark, realistic despair and bright, pop-culture hope
as the essence of modern existence. That's not too lofty a description.
Davies realizes the way people grasp their positions in life and wrestle to
control their emotions and destinies.

Davies distills autobiography into extreme visual and musical stylization. He shuffles drama, music, and different periods of his decade-long
family chronicle—not simply for contrast but for the direct, emotional
intensity of hotly remembered grief and fondly recalled joy. These essences
of family life rank with the greatest that have ever been created—Welles's
*The Magnificent Ambersons* and O'Neill's *Long Day's Journey Into Night*.
He finds a common denominator in the eerie intimacy of family life, in
which the structure of domestic relationships becomes transparent and the
vulnerability of the individuals is both revealed and shared.

Women carry the songs in this powerfully metaphysical movie musical. There's a feminist basis in Davies's scrapbook-jukebox reminiscence that pays special attention to suffering under cruel patriarchy. *Distant Voices, Still Lives* is structured around the subtle, circumspect subversions practiced by oppressed groups—women, specifically, but by extension, gays, the working class, and so on. "Innocuous" pop songs and conventional social rituals like public sing-alongs and moviegoing make up the special moments that are seized by the mother and sisters in Davies's recreated family to vent their usually suppressed feelings.

Fitzgerald's "Taking a Chance on Love" is one of the few professional, prerecorded singing performances used by Davies, who finds profundity in the "untrained" singing voices of his characters. This "live" singing gives a different insight than the Herbert Ross–Dennis Potter film *Pennies from Heaven*, which only—but brilliantly—showed the imprint of pop culture on the subconscious. Davies reflects on pop culture more critically. The distance he maintains from the glossy, slick escapism of professional pop fantasy objectifies its powerful sway and marks it as placebo.

Unlike Ross and Potter, Davies is mindful of the sociological fact of pop communication. His demonstrations of this are amazing: a group of dissatisfied white housewives sing "Brown Skin Girl, Stay Home and Mind Baby (I killed nobody but me husband)"; a Catholic woman toasts her mother singing "My Yiddishe Mama." Davies shows the uses that can be made of pop from disparate cultures. Seen this way, pop-music communication is an explicitly political phenomenon. But Davies never neglects the emotional basis; it comes through powerfully in the scene where Angela Walsh as the youngest sister defies her marital subjugation in a full-throated performance of "I Want to Be Around to Pick Up the Pieces (when she breaks your heart like you broke mine)." It's the most psychologically vivid, emotionally vibrant movie scene this year. Through the humane effort of singing, this film conveys great purity of feeling.

Davies's musical numbers are a culture and several generations away from my own experience, yet they have a raw potency like African-American storefront gospel. This is the only movie musical I know to capture the basic cultural function of song without swamping it in excessive production furbelows. The astringency of Davies's method—the dogged presentation of one solemn episode after another—makes this film a tough watch. Many of the greatest filmmakers have lacked a gift for buoyancy (Ozu, Dreyer, Visconti, Bresson), yet Davies accomplishes what the best movie art seeks to do. Each formally conceived sequence expresses an idea in an image: A child shown singing to herself in a doorway suspends the character—a whole life—in time; the late-night leave-taking of the family from the local pub surrounds them all with mortality; a son's pitiful view of his mother's toil and his subsequent wedding day, on which he grieves for his father, summarize his inheritance. The resonance of these images and ideas ties together the terror of family life and the isolation of aesthetic experience in a way that is truthful and overwhelming.

*Distant Voices, Still Lives* takes place pre–rock 'n' roll, so the pop music–mass audience relationship it details is different. It's debatable that so much misery would thrive in an era of aggressive protest music, but the fact remains, the majority of pop experience always comprises romantic fantasy. Davies pays tribute to pop's power while shaking up, diversifying its meanings. Two years ago Todd Haynes's *Superstar: The Karen Carpenter Story* subverted pop vapidity by dramatizing real-life tragedy in absurd pop form (he used Barbie dolls as characters). Haynes's trivializing technique was deceptive—he caught the irony of Karen Carpenter's art and life with merciless cunning. Davies's sense of pop life has a little more heart, yet it's too disturbing to mistake for Vincente Minnelli jollity. If he never makes another film as strong as this one, Davies ranks in the vanguard of radical pop sensibility.

*The City Sun*
August 30, 1989

# LIVING IN
# METAPHOR

"**C**OULD THIS BE ME, immersed in funk so deep?" the late Philippe
Wynne found himself wondering on Funkadelic's "(not just)
Knee Deep." Ten years later, sampled as the key riff of De
La Soul's "Me Myself and I," the original song is a hit all over again, and
Wynne's Hamletesque funk soliloquy shows unsuspected, prescient depth.

De La Soul's debut album, *3 Feet High and Rising* (Tommy Boy), is an
epic about the young-adult African-American male's state of mind. It's a
political record in the sense that the three group members (stage names
Pace Master Mase, Trugoy the Dov, and Posdnuos) find the social meaning
in Wynne's exclamation: "Me Myself and I" is as unpretentiously philosophical as "Knee Deep." Immersed in the rhythmic flux of life at the end of
the eighties, these ex-kids from Amityville are figuring out who they are in
this world: I Rap Therefore I Am. (That's musical politics inherited from
Charles Mingus's composition *Me, Myself, an Eye*.)

In decentered African-American life (i.e., outside the church), the
search for identity and stability throws the seeker back upon himself, in
need of a moral guidepost. Gospel is perhaps the only form of American
music not sampled or alluded to on *3 Feet High and Rising;* instead De La
Soul has a secular belief system, turning this album into a virtual concor-
dance of pop-music history. Digital links are made to "Rockin' It," Michael
Jackson, Public Enemy, Hall & Oates, M. C. Lyte, and dozens of other
totems. De La Soul fractures and rebuilds pop culture as a way of talking
about this world, like the children of Huey Newton and George Clinton:
The group is far out but they keep their feet on the ground.

De La Soul's wacky names (Trugoy is "yogurt" backwards), their
convoluted jargon ("dialect drug" as one song describes it), and suburban
b-boy couture first mistakenly were identified as a new hippie style. But the
group's social significance is closer to the heart of Everyghetto: Their style
is a showbiz gimmick like Funkadelic's sci-fi funk, reminding us that since

Bert Williams's 'minstrelsy,' Black pop has shown the amplitude to be sincere about the crucial issues of sex and politics even while posturing. (On *Uncle Jam Wants You*, Funkadelic's long-playing dance tracks are lubriciously erotic, and Clinton himself assumes the famous Huey Newton pose on the cover.) De La Soul chooses to live in the metaphors of pop culture and illustrate the absurdity of the present Black condition. This funny, self-mocking album is more than a joke.

If the pop allusions on *3 Feet High and Rising* seem too calculated to term "genius," like Clinton's inspired creations, let's qualify the term: Call it "boy-genius" as in Orson Welles, whose legendary 1930s radio broadcasts are evoked in the album's structure. It's a trivia quiz show freely associated with the hiphop mindset, but the themes (or categories) explored are weird, tangential, and authentic. A recent study found that "Blacks spend 1.4 hours watching television for every hour spent by the rest of the population." That's largely kids, for sure, and *3 Feet High and Rising* is a surprisingly thorough illumination of their escapist culture. Once oriented to De La Soul, one can interpret their comically arch, almost autistic withdrawal from the real world as a shrewd comment on the nature of middle-class information access and pop stimuli—not merely a pathological symptom.

Each delightfully obscure cut (produced by Prince Paul of Stetsasonic) is a challenge to think and to dance, and it all comes together on "Tread Water," where the group's measured rapping shows them keeping time consciously, politically:

> *Sony Walkmen keep us walkin'*
> *De La Soul can help you breathe*
> *When you tread water*

It was a while before I realized that De La Soul wasn't just redefining a figure of speech (as "dope" now means "good" and "stupid" now means "excellent") but were using vernacular to make a political observation on social conditions. The verses in "Tread Water" recount an Aesop's fable as a parable for Black perseverance. In "Tread Water," De La Soul perceives the eighties as an era of political stasis (for Blacks); they wrap skepticism in humor rather than defeat.

De La Soul plays deliberately naive, but they aren't kids and their nursery rhymes aren't trivial. "I can stick my hand in my air," Posdnuos says, commanding as much of the universe as any offspring of the disenfranchised can. That line—from the song "I Can Do Anything (Delacratic),"—recalls the "I Am Responsible" monologue of Jean-Luc Godard's *My Life to Live*. Though said with whimsy, De La Soul's message is also a sober statement of freedom. And individuality. "My Buddy" confirms it, going all the way through homoeroticism and autoeroticism to do so. Is there another song like it in the whole history of pop music?

*3 Feet High and Rising* shows De La Soul resisting the encroachment of waste and conformity. Their name means "from the soul" as in distanced from the clichés of Black pop. Ironically, their nerdy, out-of-fashion approach is also "from the soul"—a heartfelt legacy from pop music's innovators. They invoke the entirety of pop (from Steely Dan to Liberace), while more pretentious artists do covers of "What's Goin' On"; De La soul intends the references to signify all that they've heard and what they feel about their immersion in the funk of contemporary living. While not faking a political answer, their originality is a heroic political example.

De La Soul's language on a song like "Say No Go" and "Potholes in My Lawn" suggests a hiphop Esperanto. Their endless verbal creativity demonstrates the proverbial Black (subcultural) ability to invent rich, vital slang. There's a simple-and-complex purity to the wonderful "Say No Go"—an anticrack song that shuffles you between rhythms and moral decisions. It's what De La Soul calls a skit, and nothing so smoothly brilliant shows up on the new Beastie Boys album *Paul's Boutique* (Capitol).

When De La Soul says, "Listen to the inner sound, y'all," the sentiment isn't new but it's fairly courageous in the macho context of hiphop's herd (posse) mentality. If Black rappers want all young men to be strong, the Beastie Boys want all young men to be jerks. There's a bigger issue to be addressed here about white privilege as a mass-media disease. But right now it's important to recognize De La Soul in counterdistinction to the Beastie Boys and other rap. In *3 Feet High and Rising* brilliance is writ large; De La Soul should not be relegated to the fine print of "official" pop history.

*The City Sun*
September 20, 1989

# FROM BURKINA FASO WITH ART

EWS OF A FILM from Burkina Faso like Idrissa Ouedraogo's *Yaaba*
probably excites African Americans much less than the announcement of a new mind-numbing Sylvester Stallone epic. The cultural
gap that explains this is wider and scarier than the Middle Passage.
Hollywood movies corrupt audiences into expecting formulaic plots and
blatantly obvious technique. The devices used to make American films
into efficient export products that appeal across language barriers have
backfired on us, encouraging illiteracy and insensitivity. The noise, the
garish sex, the senseless violence, all excite the crudest instincts and, over
time, create jaded, debased senses.

Keenen Ivory Wayans wasn't sharp enough to account for this in his
Blaxploitation parody *I'mo Git You Sucka*. He treated the coarsening
effect of Hollywood's contemptuous style as a boon to African-American
well-being. Even comedian Rudy Ray Moore knew better than that when,
back in the seventies, his films *Dolemite* and *The Human Tornado* turned
Blaxploitation films ass-up, making the most of the slim opportunity to
show some distinctive Black American jive and effrontery. In the trash
pile, Moore found something organic and authentic, whereas Wayans
busied himself polishing tin.

As a result of Hollywood's corrupting influence, Black moviegoers
have an especially hard time determining types of entertainment that are
authentic to their lifestyles, organic to their culture, or edifying to their
existence. The quotation that opens Public Enemy's "Night of the Living
Baseheads" is appropriate: "Have you forgotten that once we were
brought here we were robbed of our name, robbed of our language? We
lost our religion, our culture, our God; and by the way many of us act,
we've even lost our minds."

The lack of interest African Americans have in African films is
explained partly by the estrangement effected by colonialism (slavery)

and the indifference of America's Eurocentric film culture. But Hollywood also has given American viewers a jaded palette. Even an African import filled with dazzling derring-do like *Yeelen* would seem wan to those thrilled by *Die Hard* or *Lethal Weapon*.

Filmmakers like Ouedraogo, Souleymane Cisse, Ousmane Sembene, Ecare Desiré, and others also are burdened by this problem. They must break through the hardened perceptions of action-film fans even in their own countries, where the long arm of Hollywood sometimes interferes. It's a poignant dilemma. These pioneering filmmakers train in Europe, but their serious interests lead them to study art films rather than popular hits. When they return home to forge their own national cinemas, their attempts to translate indigenous art forms into movie terms often come out strained in ways that seem inept to us.

The integrity of their method can be maddening—like using calculus to reinvent the wheel—but *Yaaba* is a good sign that the conscientiousness of African filmmakers can pay off with pure artistry. Ouedraogo's simplicity and the extreme effectiveness of his means also may point the way toward saving the souls of the heathenish filmgoers Hollywood has spawned.

*Yaaba*'s gentle tone demands a little patience, like adjusting to the longer forms of Nigerian pop music. The audience that shows this sophistication is the audience that is ready to bridge the oceanic gap between Africa and North America and discover the other sources of their "American" cultural heritage.

Ouedraogo's tale of a prepubescent boy's awakening to the complex of character types in his home on the outskirts of Ouagadougou is like the numerous folktale bildungsromans seen mostly coming from Eastern Europe, like *If I Had a Gun*, *When Father Was Away on Business*, and *My Little Village*. But Ouedraogo avoids quaintness. He follows wily little Bila (Noufou Ouedraogo) and his demure cousin Nopoko (Roukietou Barry) through the steps toward their future lives together. He shows the kind of deft simplicity of Satyajit Ray's *Pather Panchali*—the artlessness that people mistook for primitivism.

It's gradually apparent that Ouedraogo has organized his action and various shots perfectly to portray the casual life cycle that is revealed when Bila and the villagers face a small but intense crisis. Ouedraogo shows a dramatist's instinct and an artist's lyricism. There's not a bland, *National Geographic* moment. Each image, photographed by Matthias Kalin, is charged with fable. The establishing shot of Bila and Nopoko pouring water on Nopoko's mother's grave has a primal elegance. With Yaaba (Fatimata Sanga) standing in the background, the graceful harmony of the scene says that these people and their habits rise from the earth and will return to it. The tone is spiritual, not anthropological. Bila, Nopoko, and Yaaba share a charmingly contentious relationship. They're discovering the eternal laws that we observe. And Ouedraogo keeps our observation dramatic and sensual. Bila's coming of age is his awakening to the roles of women—his attraction to Nopoko, the balance of power between his parents, and the fascination with which he honors Yaaba, the aged woman the villagers have cast out as a witch.

Tall, balding, and slack-breasted, Sanga's Yaaba, a leather-covered skeleton, is a striking figure of female wisdom and mystery. The human lesson she teaches Bila is sobering rather than sanctimonious. Yaaba's demonstration of virtue and paradox recalls another stern, solitary female figure, Hilda Carlsberg, in Carl Dreyer's 1924 silent classic, *The Parson's Widow.* Either a film student like Ouedraogo is well acquainted with that film or else patterns of human behavior in Scandinavia also hold true in Africa.

*Yaaba* makes both connections seem wondrously probable. Certainly Ouedraogo's anecdotal style communicates with an eloquence comparable to Dreyer's. The opening and closing shots that conceptualize an African sense of destiny are the most plangent images in any movie this year.

*The City Sun*
October 18, 1989

# MICHELLE SHOCKED

VEN BEFORE *The Fabulous Baker Boys*, Michelle Pfeiffer had been
the object of film reviewers' adoration. She seemed to inspire the
most shameless declarations of sexual preference, whether or not it
was germane to the roles she played and, most remarkably, as if the
appreciation of her beauty were universal and indisputable.

*Baker Boys* has brought this insanity to a head. One could shrug off
Pfeiffer's acclaim in *Married to the Mob* (where she was neither convincingly likable nor convincingly Italian), and her victim role in *Dangerous
Liaisons* (an inadequate performance of a sympathetic role that anyone—
saint, whore, CPA, or canine—would have done to equal effect). But
starting with *Tequila Sunrise,* the critical confusion of her California
cheerleader's essence with acting became problematic. Plainly, Pfeiffer's
praise is racist—that is, it's for her blond whiteness (say, a classy version
of Ellen Barkin or Daryl Hannah).

Now, following her appearance in *Baker Boys,* Pfeiffer is being
called both a great actress and a great singer. It's the movie equivalent of
the Elvis phenomenon, in which the white press is so thrilled with a
version of itself that they promote it out of proportion to its worth.

The fact is, *Baker Boys* falls flat precisely because Pfeiffer lacks both
the humor and the singing ability to put across this white romantic fantasy
of sex and show business. In the plot, about a team of brother musicians,
Frank and Jack (Beau and Jeff Bridges), who make their living playing at
motor inn lounges and cheap nightclubs, Pfeiffer is the feminine element
who disturbs the uneasy camaraderie of male bonding. A sexual catalyst,
she makes the Baker brothers understand their unhealthy dependence
upon each other. But the film's writer-director, Steve (*Racing with
the Moon*) Kloves, is shy of investigating masculine defensiveness.
The Bakers are utter clichés. Frank is dull and business-minded; Jack
is a cynical would-be artist wasting his gifts on drinking, smoking,
and womanizing.

Kloves doesn't animate or innovate a new, modernist romanticism as
seen in the chic, attitudinizing, lovelorn characters of Alan Rudolph's

marvelous *Choose Me* or *Trouble in Mind*. Like the latter film, *Baker Boys* is set primarily in Seattle, but Kloves can't make imaginative use of what Rudolph characterized as "Rain City." *Baker Boys* is a drab rehash of old-fashioned romance. Kloves, significantly, uses Pfeiffer as a goddess by nature. Her stage performance scenes and the "toughness" of her character (a former "escort" whose natural musical ability helps boost the Baker Boys' faltering careers) make sense only as references to past backstage musical gimmicks and the all-pervasive charm of Hollywood deities. But if one does not buy into the WASP whimsy or shiksa worship, if one has another idea of "desirability" or of romance, Pfeiffer's casting, and her praise, seem fraudulent.

To paraphrase Robert DoQui to Gwen Welles in *Nashville:* Pfeiffer *can't sing*. It's impossible to believe her rescue effect on the Baker brothers' careers. This fundamentally dishonest film doesn't even acknowledge its crassest impulse—that its plot hinges on Pfeiffer's white sexuality. When she does an uninspired, barely sustained, and poorly choreographed version of "Makin' Whoopee" or "Ten Cents a Dance," the onscreen audience reacts to her brazen sexual come-on, not to the "power" of her singing.

It's okay for Hollywood filmmakers like Kloves and his producer, Sydney Pollack, to be big-screen pimps, selling poontang (it's part of a long-practiced tradition). But to pretend that this film is something else—a meditation on contemporary malaise or the poignancy of pop art—is offensive.

One easily can see through the lies of *Baker Boys* to the white exclusivity and segregation that have helped loosen Hollywood's hold on at least a part of the national consciousness. Filmmakers like Kloves and Pollack still are refusing to let people of color in on the national fantasy trip—and reviewers all are going along with their racism.

In the current social climate *Baker Boys* would have made a great movie fantasy—the kind of film *Cotton Club* or *Tap* was supposed to be—only with the right, talented actors. Would the filmmakers have had to look hard to cast this story Black? Lonette McKee, a proven, radiant film presence—a vivid, sensual actress who really can sing—could have hooked into our sanity and unleashed our fantasies. Pfeiffer's substitution for the kind of talent the role requires is a rebuke to our common sense. It says: *Only a white woman will do*. This racially cautious way of making popular fiction—according to the literal methods of Hollywood's past—is stagnant, decadent. Was it naiveté that made Hollywood think only white people could be interesting on film? Or something more pernicious—a continuation of Western art's legacy that, in fact, denies the democratic potential of a mass medium like movies?

Whites no longer can stand as the only embodiment of our culture's artistic values or literary (cinematic) themes. One of the reasons watching music videos has been so rewarding this decade is it's the only motion picture medium in which people of color consistently are allowed to be witty, glamorous, and fantastic.

It isn't Pfeiffer's fault that she's become an icon of white supremacy, but when does this problem stop? In *Scarface,* she was stunningly effective as Elvira, a third-world gangster's idea of a prestige possession (the idea August Darnell satirizes with Kid Creole's Coconuts). DePalma exposed the unpleasant truth of this idea, but *Baker Boys* wants us all supplicating on Tony Montana's level, pathetically unenlightened about our subjugation (through the media) to the persuasion of white ideas and idols. Even Madison Avenue is more responsible about the ideas and products it sells: after the social revolutions of the fifties and sixties, advertisers court buyers through flattery. In the eighties, Hollywood has the tacky arrogance to still foist off its ideas of white superiority knowing people will buy them out of habit. *Tequila Sunrise* was regressive in its determination to address the social phenomenon of eighties drug culture through the metaphors of attractive white protagonists. That's as much a social sickness as drugs.

Pop glamour needn't be defined by white skin, blond hair, and blue eyes any longer. It's a joke to see Pfeiffer described as "stunning," "incendiary," "thrilling" in the year of Neneh Cherry's hot, cosmopolitan, and *musical* music video debut. *Baker Boys* might have worked—trite melodrama and all—if we could believe in the performers. Kloves resorts to forties mnemonics to make his big lie; he even revives the old canard of a soulful white jazz musician. Jeff Bridges grimaces when he performs in a Black jazz club to show that he *feels* the music, and, of course, the Blacks who hear him (including Albert Hall, a *Trouble in Mind* refugee) are impressed.

I'm not impressed. Movie fantasy is not harmless when it is this conceited and mendacious. It's in the oppressive glorification of white drama and white beauty that so much social depression (the sense of inferiority people can't put their finger on) begins. Nonwhites get nothing substantive from this picture, and the whites who praise it and flock to it just add one more layer of dishonesty to their political cocoon.

Hollywood used to be better than this. When Rita Hayworth did the famous mock striptease to "Put the Blame on Mame" in the 1946 *Gilda,* the filmmakers knew how to contextualize her sexiness, and they dubbed her singing to preserve the fabulous illusion. *Baker Boys* tells us to worship Pfeiffer simply because she's there; the only possible value we can place on her is the value we place on her sociopolitical being—her whiteness. Hayworth's Gilda and Pfeiffer's own Elvira in *Scarface* understood their sexual exploitation in the underworld class wars and they fought against it—warning us. But in *Baker Boys,* Pfeiffer's character is reduced to race, sex, ego, and greed and, in true Reagan-Bush spirit, is justified as such. Her character's name—Susie Diamond—is the most hilariously venal moniker since Whoopi Goldberg, but one suspects Kloves is catering to, rather than commenting on, ethnic conceit. Susie Pfeiffer is an ideological tool of the race that rules Hollywood. *Baker Boys* is a white exploitation movie.

*The City Sun*
October 25, 1989

# MISS DAISY'S MORAL ANACHRONISMS

A S A STAGE PLAY *Driving Miss Daisy* was an acceptable little acting
exercise that also made an interesting point about the irony of
master-servant roles being played out in the American South between two "minority" types—an old Jewish woman and an elderly Black
man. By transferring this sentimental sketch to film as a realistic chronicle of a platonic friendship, the delicate minor work becomes specious,
distasteful, and offensive.

Bruce Beresford's genteel, picturesque direction turns Alfred Uhry's
theaterpiece into a sentimental reverie on racism and classism as benign
social circumstances. The film longs for the period when Black people
knew their "correct" place as servants to whites; when Jews didn't have to
think about committing the political sins they abhor in others.

Making this film was not a progressive thing to do; its critical acclaim is
sad evidence of the backward social sense that is typical of current American
movie culture. *Driving Miss Daisy* gives the nonthreatening treatment of
U.S. race relations that people who hated *Do the Right Thing* longed for.

The kindliness of this story—"how a retired handyman, Hoke Col-
burn (Morgan Freeman), becomes the chauffeur for an aging schoolteacher, Daisy Werthan (Jessica Tandy), but first has to win her affection"—doesn't work in the "opened-up," realistic setting.

The real world that is lavishly presented in the film's period recreation (set in Georgia from 1947 to the early 1970s) imposes a political
perception. This is not satisfied by such details as a movie marquee
advertising *Gentleman's Agreement*, or the sound of Martin Luther King
Jr. (offscreen) delivering a speech. Hoke and Miss Daisy are unrealistic,
cartoon figures—moral anachronisms.

And if one compares them to the master-servant characters of even
such 1947 films as *Intruder in the Dust* and *The Reckless Moment*, *Driving
Miss Daisy* still falls short of conveying the different worlds and world

views that conceivably would mix as Hoke and Miss Daisy chatter on their road to nowhere.

Even forty years ago Hollywood filmmakers seemed to have a better grasp of the distance between races. *Driving Miss Daisy* suggests that the common sense of class and race perception needs to be learned all over again.

Beresford and Uhry's greatest failure is in keeping the characters stiff and one-dimensional. There is no room for subtlety in these characterizations—the roles have so many feints and so much circumspect behavior written into them that the actors cannot portray anything subversive or "deep." The only way to improve these roles for film is to reconceive them and bring the clash of temperaments to the fore.

Unable to add a note of militant truth that might challenge Uhry and Beresford's sweet-natured conception, Morgan Freeman seems stuck in superficiality. It isn't a bad performance, but Freeman is suckered into reenacting a stage triumphant while forfeiting the control of the audience that originally gave the play its only justification. One could sense political forthrightness in watching Freeman match tempers with his white co-star. In a spare, abstract setting *Driving Miss Daisy* offered an egalitarian, theatrical coup.

Now that the control of the drama is taken away from the actors, the play only illustrates the complacency of Hollywood's dominant ideology. Uhry's title no longer has (vague) political resonance, it is just literal, banal. And with the status quo on Miss Daisy's side, the film becomes a showcase for her crochets and punctiliousness, thus an opportunity for the actress Jessica Tandy to dominate through her usual combination of opacity and skill that only occasionally gives a superficial role the breath of life.

Still, nothing said or done in *Driving Miss Daisy* causes one to question an unequal social situation. It's a breeding ground for horribly condescending attitudes, such as that in the *New Yorker*'s description of the maid's (Esther Rolle) death and funeral scene featuring a gospel choir: "It must be worth dying to have singing like that." This movie is comforting for whites who feel that their own pleasure and convenience is the reason Black folks exist.

*The City Sun*
January 10, 1990

# JUST SAY NO TO THE WHITE GIRL

Tony Brown owes an apology to America for the abomination known as *The White Girl*, but can he ever forgive himself for putting the final kibosh on a once exemplary journalism career? Brown's original "Black Journal" TV series pioneered a serious African-American perspective on contemporary news events. In the early seventies his electronic journalism was the equivalent of footnotes that are more interesting than the text they annotate.

It seems as if so many years spent as network marginalia bred a terrible impatience and envy, so Brown dismantled his essayistic format and sought the center-stage focus of Oprah Winfrey and Phil Donahue. His own stewardship became more important than the subject of individual shows. Coiffed, powdered, and armed with a microphone, Brown now leads audience members and guest panelists into making "proper' statements.

This monomania concerning Black propriety results in the peculiar dogmatism of *The White Girl*, Brown's vanity production. Brown combines an antidrug preachment with his own Hollywood calling card. But it's not a documentary survey of the modern drug-and-racism crisis; Brown throws out his practical experience and attempts to make the Black fiction film to end them all. Thank God that he doesn't.

Instead of shaming Hollywood, Brown embarrasses every person who wants to see people of color portrayed onscreen with beauty and credibility.

As a technical exercise, *The White Girl* is execrable and its ideas are frighteningly reactionary. Producer-writer-director Brown uses Barbie and Ken doll protagonists Kim (Troy Beyer) and Bobby (Taimak) as "typical" African-American youths amid the dangers of the drug age. But the kids-in-trouble theme isn't enough; Brown dishes up allegories about class-and-color prejudice that eventually play havoc with his essential interest in providing positive role-model images.

Kim is a product of the Black bourgeoisie whose parents send her to a state university rather than one of the well-known Black colleges. With her poor foundation, lack of racial pride, Kim succumbs to cocaine—"the white girl"—an addiction that replicates her fondness for Caucasian men and styles. Pure Bobby tries to rescue her through an aerobics regimen and a lesson in loving one's own kind, but trouble interrupts.

That's Kim's new roommate, Vanessa (Teresa Farley), a careerist who wears blue contact lenses and uses drugs and sex as means to escape oppression and enter the white business world (TV journalism). Kim is soon seduced and then threatened further by a Black pimp and pusher (O. L. Duke).

Brown's idea of drama goes back to the simplistic moral schemes of early silent movies—Good Girl/Bad Girl, Heroic Action/Irredeemable Vice. This does nothing to impress the true nature of contemporary experience, whether young-adult peer pressure or culture lust. Instead of heeding this cautionary tale, most people will laugh at it. The rollicking audience I saw *The White Girl* with was calling for Brown's head, their screams echo in the gap between Brown's pitiful idea of cinema and their own imaginative expectations.

Cecil B. DeMille, Hollywood's most fabulous moralist, was also shameful in the way he preached Christian ethics but took care to include attention-grabbing dollops of sex and violence between the lessons. Brown possesses nothing like C.B.'s skill, but his holier-than-thou stance is a neck-in-noose match for any TV evangelist. So is his neck-in-noose hypocrisy.

Despite the film's suggestions about proper behavior, it panders to the audience's sleaziest interests. The camera focuses on Beyer's rear; Farley regularly flashes thigh at her fellow actors. To illustrate the depravity of drug culture, Brown builds several sequences to a peak of ribaldry: Orgies, gay trysts, even pedophilia are boldly introduced, then timidly evaded. That's not "taste"; it's cheap titillation.

Brown's puritanical point-making is at odds with the reasons people go to the movies. The pleasures of sensuality, of vicarious experience and dreams-made-real, keep viewers excited about the film medium. They don't go to be teased—it might even be argued that C. B. DeMille knew the value of honest catharsis. Brown wouldn't risk an effective sex scene or even a sequence confronting a junkie's indulgence or a gangster's thrill, as in *Drugstore Cowboy* or *Tougher Than Leather*. Even if he had the talent to bring off such scenes, his moralistic temperament would censor them.

*The White Girl* was conceived without any regard for the imaginative power of art. Brown's mode is didactic—and ridiculous. His idea of entertaining the audience is to offer sideshow exploitation. When the college's Black Student Union holds an anti-apartheid rally, a master of ceremonies introduces "sisters who fight apartheid with beauty." That's a tacky fashion show reminiscent of the Black Pride Show in *Coming to America*. Brown follows this with a tribute to Black male prelaw and premed students who step out of full-length fur coats to strut the runway in bikini briefs.

This sequence destroys Brown's own credibility in two ways: By treating sex as a diversion, he degrades the onscreen idea of life. The first close-ups on the runway are of light-skinned women—darker women are seen only in long shot. *The White Girl* revives the trashiest aspects of Oscar Micheaux's cinema, which foolishly sought to compete with Hollywood by imitating its racist precepts. Beyer and Taimak could pass for white in many parts of America. There's no escaping that Brown's movie-fed ideas of beauty, purity, and goodness have a white model; his love duo is as bourgie, scrubbed, and high-yellow as possible. Despite one dark-skinned female token, Brown's strongest "Black" statement is casting the ebon O. L. Duke as the Draculalike pimp.

In codes like the above, *The White Girl* proves that it is as much a part of the traditional ways of making white, middle-class, conservative movies as anything with Tom Cruise or Michelle Pfeiffer. If *The White Girl* had a bit of style or humor, it wouldn't look out of place among a group of seventies blaxploitation films. Brown has not risen above those cartoonish depictions. His white characters are foolish or evil (the opening sequence shows a group of white coeds in a red convertible speeding down a highway while taking drugs; they have nothing to do with the rest of the film). His female characters are shallow and gullible (as Kim and Vanessa get high, they inevitably acquire lesbian habits).

When Brown means to emphasize a point, he uses such devices as intercutting shots of someone in a Halloween devil's mask, an antidrug public service announcement or a scene from . . . "The Tony Brown Show" (featuring former comedian, ex-addict George Kirby reciting a poem about King Heroin).

This worthless movie proclaims itself "the first buy-freedom" film production. That means that for a year Brown was able to use Black organizations as a captive test market—*The White Girl* could be rented for benefit showings at special (inflated) prices. The money that people thought was supporting independent filmmaking was going to underwrite Brown's folly.

It's been at least a year now that people have known what a disaster *The White Girl* is. But criticism was withheld out of good-heartedness. Well, that ends here because the sensibility of a sexist, racist, and fascist movie like this is no good for anyone. If too many people see *The White Girl*, it could set the cause of independent filmmaking back a century. Tony Brown has turned an art form into a racket.

*The City Sun*
February 21, 1990

# IDEOLOGY ON THE WATERFRONT

T'S FITTING THAT most reviewers were repulsed by *Last Exit to Brooklyn*. This film version of the Hubert Selby Jr. novel defies the sentimentality of most Hollywood product that people now, automatically, take to be the proper tone for movies.

There's a great deal of emotion in screenwriter Desmond Nakano's scrupulous, action-packed adaptation. He's written a political melodrama full of incidents so rich that every character's personal turmoil is intricately related to the social context that the film evokes. This atmosphere is primarily the achievement of German director Uli Edel and his cinematographer Stefan Czapsky. These Europeans eschew nostalgia for the period setting (1952, the Red Hook section of Brooklyn) and treat the era expressionistically. It's the dark ages showing the white American working class's unconsciousness.

Racism is barely a subtext here; the filmmakers depict other social pathologies in which these Italian and Irish proles victimize and suffer among one another. Harry Black (Stephen Lang), the union steward overseeing a strike at a waterfront factory, discovers his true sexuality; Tralala (Jennifer Jason Leigh), the neighborhood tramp, finds unexpected sensitivity within herself; Big Joe (Burt Young) arranges a shotgun wedding for his pregnant teenage daughter (Ricki Lake).

*On the Waterfront*, the archetypal blue-collar melodrama from 1954, didn't have a similar realistic range of characters. As a mainstream Hollywood production, it looked away from aspects of social corruption that couldn't simply be resolved according to official morality. (*Waterfront* offered great acting and a typically hypocritical bourgeois view of human relations and politics.) In *Last Exit to Brooklyn*, the hellishness of urban ignorance and poverty is fully acknowledged, but the film's depth — and its surprising emotional effect — results from a simultaneous, full-out acceptance of human failure. All of the trapped characters have problems or idiosyncrasies that make them sociological grotesques, but Nakano, Edel, and the actors withhold judgment (or dismissal). This grim-looking movie makes its characters' desperation poignant. It reveals the human value in "distasteful" people. That's a rare feat in movies; most reviewers prefer to ratify the humanity of comfortable middle-class characters like those in *Crimes and Misdemeanors* or *sex, lies, and videotape.*

The scene where Harry stops and stares at Georgette (Alexis Arquette), an effeminate homosexual, is the film's first complex moment. His attraction to Georgette disorients him; unaware of his own instincts, Harry sees Georgette as a mocking, fun-house mirror reflection. Later, Georgette's flirtatious groveling after the ex-con Vinnie (Peter Dobson) and his crew of tough neighborhood boys connects with an earlier scene of Harry joining the boys in their macho rituals. These parallel scenes reverberate off each other as part of the film's strategy. They reveal how each character's behavior reflects a dominant social idea: Harry acts butch for the same reason Georgette idolizes a bunch of he-man clowns. Their emotional lives are oppressed by codes of masculinity that are unnatural to them.

This becomes the stuff of high pathos and tragedy in a great scene where Georgette's illusions are stripped away before his mother and brother and in the sequence of Harry's virgin gay affair with Regina (Zette). These events tie together sex, family, and economics but without the usual dramatized sentimentality; each aspect of the characters' lives is shown to be ideologically determined. It's the plain, comic horror of people living under social forces they don't understand that marks *Last Exit to Brooklyn* as a particularly modern vision.

It's also an alternative political vision, as was *Do the Right Thing.* But where Spike Lee's ideology was primarily (and legitimately) racial, Edel and Nakano work more purely politically, and so with much more specificity about how sex and economics affect our personal lives. In the mid-seventies, Rainer Werner Fassbinder was interested in adding this political consciousness to the melodrama tradition. The politics of sex and race were unavoidable in Fassbinder's *Fear Eats the Soul/Ali* (an update of Douglas Sirk's 1952 Hollywood weepie, *All That Heaven Allows*) and in *The Merchant of Four Seasons, Mother Kusters Goes to Heaven,* and *Fox and His Friends.*

But where Fassbinder's outsider, radical view was proudly alienated (and coldly obvious), Edel and Nakano successfully have Americanized it. They understand how to evoke honest sentiment; its proper, balanced use can increase one's sympathy for even outrageous characters. Visually, *Last Exit to Brooklyn* combines Fassbinder's harshness with Edward Hopper's desolate realism. It's also a precarious, thematic balance that is probably the only sensible way to render Selby's material; by now, the sexual underworld has become the familiar twin peaks of prime-time television and tabloid newspapers.

*Last Exit to Brooklyn* treats the complexity of urban life in the style of an epic so that large-scale issues are given ritualistic, dramatic space — the spectacular strikebreaking scene that may be the best in an American film since *Intolerance,* and the wedding party that suggests a berserk parody of *The Godfather.* Most amazing is when a personal crisis takes on dramatic scale: Harry's denouement is the film's one lapse of taste (it goes bogusly timid), but Tralala's nightmarish disenchantment is a triumph of expressionist filmmaking. Tralala's brazen sexuality is humanized by her emotional confusion; when her heart is hurt, she disguises her hostility by a self-destructive act — taking on a bar full of men. Jennifer Jason Leigh has always explored, fearlessly, the sexuality of her characters; in this film and in *Miami Blues,* her uncanny balance of coarseness and naiveté makes her the actress of the year so far.

The pain of Tralala's humiliation suffuses the film; it's a moving treatment of lives that are so benighted that people, estranged from their own deepest feelings, only realize it in the middle of trouble. When the strike ends and Big Joe and the neighborhood guys go back to work, the men are happy to resume their dehumanizing cycle.

It's worth repeating how Stephen Lang, in the film's press kit, summed up the film's presentation of character: "Harry is an assembly-line man made with a defect. How can it not break your heart?"

*The City Sun*
May 16, 1990

# VOGUE

I N LAST YEAR'S *Like a Prayer* video, Madonna led the pop world into political consciousness, but this year her latest single seems like a double cross. "Vogue" continues the borrowing from Black culture that was at the core of the *Like a Prayer* video's treatise on religion and racism. But instead of acknowledging her sources and blowing the whistle on racist beauty standards, Madonna celebrates the biases of the fashion system. "Vogue" is her first despotic recording.

Sure enough the video—a glossy, black-and-white fashion show—has the appropriate uniracial, unisex iconography, but there's no subversive edge. Every Black, Latino, androgynous image is imprisoned in a sultry, glamorous affectation—Madonna and her voguers are vamping for class approval. The video is a demonstration of the process by which the middle class usurps the energies of oppressed subcultures. (Last year's Malcolm McLaren video *Deep In Vogue* avoided this offense through stroboscopic silhouettes of vogue champ Willie Ninja authenticating McLaren's artsy hybrid.)

Madonna's only irony this time is in her first-rate imitation of house—yet the propulsive rhythm (co-written and produced by Shep Pettibone) relentlessly pushes voguing toward the mainstream's domination.

When that happens, history gets rewritten for the worse. Check out Madonna's "Vogue" rap: "Greta Garbo and Monroe / Dietrich and DiMaggio . . . Gene Kelly, Fred Astaire / Ginger Rogers danced on air . . . Marlon Brando, Jimmy Dean / On the cover of a magazine."

These all-white icons may be Madonna's way of keying in on underground fantasies as white fixated, but there's no suggestion that this is a racial pathology; she merely regresses to Warhol's all-white politics. To make "Vogue" a song of liberation, Madonna needed to show the subculture's special knowledge, integrity, and heritage. A better litany would salute: Diana Ross, Little Richard / Jean Shrimpton and Esquerita / Beverly Johnson, Iman, too / Iris Chacon and Vida Blue. . . . Well, he's as camp as DiMaggio.

*The City Sun*
June 13, 1990

# DOPPEL-GÄNGERBANGER: RAP'S LOSS OF REASON

WELCOME TO THE Chuck D cartoon show. As one of the producers, writers, and performers on *AmeriKKKa's Most Wanted* (Ruthless/Priority)—the solo debut album by former N.W.A. member Ice Cube—Chuck D has helped fashion an exaggerated, absurd version of the politically committed rap artist that he epitomizes in Public Enemy.

Ice Cube's ten cuts use broad strokes and apoplexy to portray the wild conditions of African-American life. Calling himself "The Nigga Ya Love to Hate" [sic], Ice Cube shows off the ferocious language and hostile behavior that Public Enemy outclasses. The point of his hard-core epithets and impudent swaggering is to represent the desperate Black underclass whom polite society is trying to sweep under the carpet. They're the "niggas" who embarrass the Black bourgeoisie, yet, in Ice Cube's view, they speak the ugly truth about life in America. But this album, I think, is an embarrassment to hiphop.

Last year's N.W.A. album, *Straight Outta Compton,* began: "You are about to witness the strength of street knowledge." It's easy to see how a middle-class young man like Chuck D could fall for that boast (most white rock critics did, too), because in rap nothing is as exciting, honest, or raw as street credibility. In the constant battle against white racism and indifference, Chuck D may feel that his savviest rhymes and most sophisticated logic are not effective enough, and so he admires the way a group like N.W.A. seems to cut through pretense.

But N.W.A.'s ability to offend isn't the same thing as powerful expression. (In high school shop class a blackboard motto warned: "Profanity is the product of a small mind trying to express itself forcefully.") As N.W.A.'s principal songwriter and accomplished cuss-meister, Ice Cube depended on a listener's guilt or condescension to gain effect; one had to accept the ignorance and debasement of Compton, California's Black population (standing in for the U.S. total), in order to find truth in N.W.A.'s raps.

Like Truffaut or DePalma illogically admiring Hitchcock, Chuck D invests N.W.A. with his own seriousness. And though Chuck D has given Ice Cube a deeper, more polished soundscape than N.W.A. ever dreamed of, he can't make him his equal—only his psychotic double, his doppelgänger, at best.

The outrageousness that Ice Cube brings from N.W.A. is still, essentially, caricature. The name N.W.A. stood for—Niggas With Attitude—is a less creative moniker than Public Enemy, just as the band's gangster image had less social purpose than PE's neo-militancy.

Ice Cube poses as a rank criminal with a scowl on his face, which perverts the "innocence" of Chuck D's average young Black man trapped in white society's gun sights. On cuts like "Turn Off the Radio," "Endangered Species," and "The Drive By," he limits himself to the sociopathic ways of "rebellion," out of sync with human rights or Black nationalism or Afrocentricity.

It's the absence of positivity—the rejection of meaning—that makes Ice Cube a belligerent parody of Chuck D. When they come together on "Endangered Species," their rap styles clash like wood to flesh and blood: Ice Cube's voice is clenched and monotonous, but Chuck D's rapid-fire syllables produce heat and drama when he says, "The color of my clothes match the one on my face as they wonder what's under my waist."

That line combines the eroticism and violence of racial fear in a style that makes Chuck D an artist to reckon with; Ice Cube simply goes along with the track's rattling turmoil. "Endangered Species" is subtitled "Tales from the Darkside," yet Ice Cube lacks a genuine tragic vision and voice. He's piddling and small-time—a political atrocity. And for that reason he and N.W.A. will be no more than a footnote in the larger story of rap.

Ice Cube presents a rap alternative that's even more confused than Public Enemy's mix of showbiz and politics. On N.W.A.'s "Gangsta, Gangsta"—an easy appeal to the rebel-worship mentality of traditional (white) rock—the chorus chanted, "It's not about a salary; it's all about reality." Kids who liked that song hadn't lived long enough to know that it made the oldest, most venal statement in the book—pandering to audience taste while appearing to do the opposite.

N.W.A. celebrated the nihilism of Los Angeles ghetto life, but the group misrepresented the sociological truth behind gangbanging: that Black youth who grew up in the midst of deprivation don't want revolution; they want capitalism. N.W.A. contrived anarchy because it was a profitable gimmick.

This seemed like show biz as usual until the white rock press took up N.W.A.'s cause and turned the group into an absolute obscenity. The song "F--- Tha Police" brought N.W.A. to the attention of law-enforcement officials wherever the group toured; last fall an FBI spokesman sent an advisory notice to the group's record company. The white press spilled the beans of this alphabet soup, invidiously championing N.W.A. as a censorship issue while ignoring the song's derangement of Black people's needs.

"F--- Tha Police" is as wack as the S1W's toy Uzis—a travesty of Black activism that disgraces both the Black Panthers and the sixties slogan "Off the Pigs." That movement and idea once meant something that the hard-core extreme of rap now trivializes. White reviewers who, last year, criticized Public Enemy while defending N.W.A. apparently like to see Black performers (clowns) whose every gesture ultimately proves predictable and insignificant.

It's in this pernicious climate that Chuck D has made his misalliance with Ice Cube. They're united in their political disorientation. Note the Ku Klux Klan allusion in the album's title; it has no resonance on the record itself, which offers a vision of America without political reasoning. It's a showcase for the degradations that amuse Ice Cube—pregnant girlfriends, drive-by shootings, robberies—but appall Chuck D. The result is a musically vivid political standoff: Black expression without progress.

At age twenty, Ice Cube—real name, Oshea Jackson—has a stunted worldview. He shows his naiveté on "A Gansta' Fairytale," where, as a reprobate Slick Rick, he proceeds to "tell the kids how the story should go." He demystifies nursery rhymes, pretending to educate a child by poisoning the child's innocence. This autobiographical cut is no joke; the same thing obviously happened to Ice Cube—as it does to most Black American youth.

However, the cynical education that's gained from early street knowledge (and no guidance) leads to the moral idiocy of *AmeriKKKa's Most Wanted*. It's the same thing that helps devastate the quality of Black urban life. And the tough, supple, beautifully spare sound that Chuck D and The Bomb Squad provide for Ice Cube can't redeem the shame of it.

Most of the trouble can be found in Ice Cube's favored noun, "nigga," with which he accepts the white world's lowest expectations and spreads the despondency to his brothers. He never uses the term ironically – only the negative connotations apply.

This mindless disrespect is a recent occurrence in Black culture, not a brave admission of the rap generation. When you hear that word on this record (or from schoolkids on the street), it sounds like a cry of the lost. These kids don't know who they are or what to esteem in themselves.

It follows that the anger in Ice Cube's raps is pointless. "Once Upon a Time in the Projects" has insipid moralism about crack houses; "Who's the Mack?" embodies the album's only complex view (that everyone in this system is a pimp); and "The Bomb" is an ego rap in which Ice Cube boasts, "I control your mind like Hitler."

Incredibly, Ice Cube has no concept of fascism; aggression and vengeance are the motives that rule his world. This pathology seems authentic in "The Drive By," a soap opera track where intimate Black voices convey the horror of Black-on-Black violence. But this rapper lacks the brainpower and the narrative logic to play out the scene's ghetto pain (the kind of detail that distinguishes Ice-T). Instead, Ice Cube jumps to a news report to show (as in "Turn Off the Radio") the white world's insensitivity, as if that's what matters. It doesn't justify Blacks' bad behavior to show simply that white people hate them for it. He's unaware that in-group animosity stems from self-hatred.

"Rollin' wit the Lench Mob" proposes an answer to Black self-destruction: rapping. But Ice Cube's line "I do the right thing / I do the wrong thing / It only matters how much bacon you bring" is pathetic. He plain misses the brilliant ambiguity of John Lydon singing, "I could be wrong / I could be right / I could be Black / I could be white" in Public Image Ltd.'s "Rise."

Most of *AmeriKKKa's Most Wanted* suggests a mind in pitiful isolation; Ice Cube seems compelled to deprecate himself and see all women as "bitches."

So the duet "It's a Man's World" promises an illuminating dialectic with eighteen-year-old female rapper Yo Yo (Yolanda Whitaker). It starts out like rap's answer to Otis Redding and Carla Thomas's "Tramp," but the hope of equality disappears into an argument between two stupid people; the young Black man treats the young Black woman like a whore and she responds in kind.

Hitler and whoredom, it's hopeless. Ice Cube should listen to Elvis Costello's *Armed Forces*.

"Don't try to apprehend him," a cop character says of Ice Cube on the album's title cut. But the problem is *comprehending* him and facing the realization that this is how low a generation has sunk. It's sad that this garbage is what Chuck D thinks we all should dance to; he carries rebel romance too far. When Hollywood established this practice in thirties gangster films, the white movie hustlers knew Cagney wasn't a hero, and their stories judged his actions out of moral necessity. The respect and validation that Chuck D shows Ice Cube (another middle-class kid carrying a big shtick) isn't from brotherly love but immaturity.

The truth is: *AmeriKKKa* doesn't afford Black youth the casual rebellion that white teens enjoy. Black youth carry an extra burden of responsibility in order to avoid society's inevitable traps, but Ice Cube exploits the animalism of the ghetto as if there were no consequences and life had no value.

Despite a few good, insolent lines ("They asked me did I like Arsenio / About as much as the bicentennial"), it's Ice Cube's ignorance that finally makes this album loathsome.

When you look at Ice Cube as he assumes the face of a Black youth in trouble, fate seems to be making a premature claim. You can hear in his voice the same clash of hormones and colloquialisms as on the street—the truculent, profane slang is shouted out to convince no one more than the kid speaking that the world has been sized up and is in for a fight. It's annoying to witness a child faking wisdom this way, yet I know that a child who has "wisdom" thrust upon him is the tragedy of our time.

*The City Sun*
June 6, 1990

# AN "OH, BLEEK" DEFENSE OF EGO

MARTIN SCORSESE is a good filmmaker for Spike Lee to model himself after: Scorsese's movies show a genuine preoccupation with the moral, racial, and sexual tensions of New York. Plus, Scorsese moves his camera like an artist possessed of fleeting insights that must be pounced upon quickly – wildly – or else are lost.

One can draw thematic parallels between Scorsese and Lee (sexual questions in *Who's That Knocking at My Door?* and *She's Gotta Have It*; musical experimentation in *New York, New York* and *School Daze*; tests of camaraderie in *Mean Streets* and Lee's new film, *Mo' Better Blues*), but there are major artistic differences, and they're a little embarrassing to point out: It's difficult to account for the creative freedom expressed by a white filmmaker like Scorsese who, along with seizing the opportunity to make art, also seizes the chance to admit weakness and doubt as if proving his sincerity and his political independence.

Black male filmmakers, however, long denied opportunity, rarely will risk confession – certainly not Lee. This insecurity turns *Mo' Better Blues* – an attempted examination of a romantic hound dog – into a psychological ruse. Lee doesn't really deal with masculine psychology, or any other kind. He shies away from exploring the anguish of Black male bluster. It's a huge irony that our most ambitious African-American filmmaker is also the most superficial.

This didn't stop *Do the Right Thing* from being a remarkable picture; it's the work Lee was probably born to do. Simply by recording aspects of American social experience that mainstream filmmakers ignore gave that movie focus and impact. Its tough but simple facts could pass for profundity (and did); the near-Brechtian, self-conscious style made up for Lee's poor narrative logic.

In *Mo' Better Blues*, Lee is stuck using unfounded Scorsese visual mannerisms. (Although the picture is so profligately stylish, it suggests the Oliver Stone brand of flashy but empty New York University filmmaking.) Unfortunately, Lee can't imitate Scorsese's substance or his internal crises, and it was Scorsese's honesty about personal conflicts of ethnicity, religion, sex, and friendship that made *Mean Streets* a great film about masculine role playing.

Lee is limited by the Black masculinity syndrome; traditional macho defensiveness about one's social standing, personal history, and sexual pride take the place of insight into *Mo' Better Blues'* characters. This paradox – or hypocrisy – makes *Mo' Better Blues* an authentic emotional document of this b-boy era. But it's frustratingly imprecise as either storytelling or character study.

Consider the names: Bleek (Denzel Washington), his women Indigo (Joie Lee), and Clarke (Cynda Williams), and his manager-friend Giant (Spike Lee). It sounds like a faux-naif bebop parody in which animated barnyard animals imitate a jazz combo. The fantasy evocation is part of Lee's political manifesto; he wants to put onscreen those obscured or ignored aspects of African-American history. His method – like his style – is half mythological, half documentary. This split consciousness indicates Lee's hyperawareness of his position as an oblique cultural commentator.

It's easy to tell from the way Bleek's mismanagement of his career as a jazz musician and his love lives with two women is further mismanaged by the filmmaker's loose attention span (more tangents here than in a fireworks display) that Lee means to cover more ground than is dramatically coherent. Ordinarily, one would admire a director who made every film as if it were his last, but Lee's all-inclusiveness tends to be trivializing – and wearying. Each character, each speech, is meant to exemplify African-American uniqueness. (It's telling that the only area where Lee displays a credible sensibility and singular voice is his Nike commercials. Maybe one day these will be anthologized like Langston Hughes's Simple tales into the definitive Spike Lee epic.) In the end Lee endorses the freshest cultural archetypes – that is, clichés.

The worst of them is the film's complacent view of male folly. Giant is Bleek's mascot, not his conscience or alter ego. He's also the runt Lee fears himself to be, while Bleek is the tall, handsome, creative stud he fantasizes about. It's funny that Washington impersonates a trumpeter (rather than, say, a fly, Gil Scott-Heron–type monologist, which is more in the actor's range of suavity) because he doesn't have to say anything, just blow hot air and – as jazz legend has it – get all the women. Washington rarely has had so little character to play; he poses cutely but blankly. Big Daddy Kane projects more sexual knowing in a three-minute video. In the upcoming *After Dark My Sweet*, Jason Patric does the most psychologically revealing sex scene since Brando's in *Last Tango in Paris*;

Washington achieves nothing comparable, because, I'd guess, Lee is too satisfied with the jazz-hound myth.

Perhaps the reason Lee avoids the psychological turmoil at the center of previous jazz dramas—such as *Sweet Love, Bitter, A Man Called Adam, 'Round Midnight* and *Bird*—is that he considers drugs and neuroses derogatory. But that's propagandistic thinking, not understanding. If Lee feels himself called to make movies, then he is needed to make credible and sympathetic films about the collapse, or missteps, of Black people. Instead, *Mo' Better Blues* degenerates into the hoariest clichés of white Hollywood: a silhouetted Bleek is shown playing alone on the Brooklyn Bridge; after humiliating himself at a failed comeback, Bleek strides out into a sentimental rainstorm, leaving behind a beautiful, white, full-length designer raincoat. Black folks don't do things like that—but that's the very folk logic that's missing from *Mo' Better Blues*.

Even though the costumes are retro-chic, the portrayal of man-woman relationships shouldn't slip back into patriarchal cliché. Lee's attempt to do the right thing by the Black male image and by the dreams of his second-rate musician father, Bill Lee (who contributes his best yet mewling, amorphous pseudo-jazz score), resorts in a bogus ode to male ego. Bleek's two-timing only lacks one of Sharazad Ali's birdbrained Blackman-Is-God defenses. Lee indulges onscreen coupling to show Black sexual mastery, but he has so little skill for dramatizing emotional affection that Bleek's return to Indigo ("Save my life!") comes across impertinent, not romantic.

Nothing about Bleek's salvation connects with the epigraph Lee chose from John Coltrane's *A Love Supreme*. Coltrane's quote, about redemption, exposes *Mo' Better Blues'* complete lack of spirituality. There was at least some sense of the ineffable in *'Round Midnight*, plus some meditation on existence in *Bird* and Gordon Parks's *Leadbelly*. Lee's script isn't focused enough to expose Bleek's soul. Worldly-spiritual ambivalence was better defined in *Mean Streets*, when the gangster-hero's girlfriend cut through his guff and reminded him that "Saint Francis didn't run numbers!"

Lee spares Bleek from the hot seat: He and Giant get beaten up together (a diversion that poorly motivates Bleek's emotional break-down), and Indigo's accusation ("You're a dog!") is, in typical Spike Lee fashion, an oblique compliment: Oh, Bleek! As in *She's Gotta Have It*, Lee is on the side of rascally caninism, not sexual equality.

The only compliment *Mo' Better Blues* deserves goes to cinematographer Ernest Dickerson, who here surpasses the heated-up tonalities of *Do the Right Thing* to do his most consistent and subtly beautiful lighting yet. The film is all surface, but Dickerson makes it a sensual, alluring surface. This is a history-making coordination of various-colored skin tones and the dark but equally colorful atmosphere of nightclubs and love nests. The picture looks extraordinarily good—and the performers look better than they act, given Lee's undisciplined melange of dramatic tones.

As The Flatbush Brothers, John and Nick Turturro are the most bizarre disruption: They're rare white faces in the film's visual scheme, reversing the racist stereotypes that Hollywood used to save for Black actors. This recalls how Scorsese's racial ambivalence has made for some of the most complex moments in modern cinema. Lee would do well to study them. But this here—well, it ain't funny, it ain't art, and it sho ain't progress.

*The City Sun*
August 1, 1990

# ALAS, L. L. COOL J'S MANNISH MASTERWORKS

L. COOL J is a mannish boy. In an interview last year, he became annoyed at my suggestion that his year away from the charts meant he was lying low, and his new album *Mama Said Knock You Out* (Def Jam/Columbia) is similarly on the defensive. The title track is a rewrite of the "I'm Bad" boast. It achieves greatness by summing up the history of masculine indoctrination. Depicting his aggression as a culturally determined reflex, James Todd Smith goes back to the beginning of what made him the rapper he is.

The title evokes a primal scene for almost every Black boy raised in an American city: when you run home crying after losing a fight and are told to go back out there and kick ass. It was the directive of many mothers (and fathers) preparing their sons to stand up to life's hassles. But we know that it also enforces a rigid belligerence that often leads to insensitivity among males who never question their assigned social roles.

L.L. and his co-producer, Marley Marl, illuminate this dilemma and satirize it with a *Popeye* cartoonlike aura of huffing and puffing machismo, underscored by the id-infant's bawling. The ironic structure even includes a consistent "sissy" reference (the kind X-Clan fail at). It recalls the great Gang of Four song, "I Love a Man in a Uniform," that traced male habits to the coercion of females, who also play a part in continuing traditional sexual and social roles. *Mama Said Knock You Out* avoids the inadvertent sexism of Spike Lee's monster mothers in *Mo' Better Blues* because here the small-mindedness—the responsibility—is felt as the young male's burden. It's what condemns youths to be mannish boys.

This partly explains why L.L.'s publicity spat with Kool Moe Dee—and lately with his more serious rival, Ice-T, in the new uncharitable cut

"To Da Break of Dawn"—centers on sexual oneupmanship. L.L.'s sense of self shows an adolescent's pride in prowess and freedom. In "To Da Break of Dawn" L.L. regresses to the callousness of "the dozens"; he seems threatened by the fearful complexity of the way rappers like Ice-T and Kool Moe Dee attempt to balance their sexual and social lives and so disses them to bolster himself. This cockfighting seems unbrotherly, except that it characterizes Black adolescent infighting too well. The question "To mature or not to mature" expresses the tension between L.L. and older rappers. It also begs the genre's future and its artistic potential.

The answers are abundant on *Mama Said Knock You Out* and last year's LP, *Walking with a Panther*—alas, both mannish masterpieces. In the four years since his 1986 debut, *Radio* (released when he was seventeen), L.L. has raised boasting to an art form. The obvious political, Afrocentric messages of progressive hiphop are not in his purview; rather, it is through dramatizing himself that L.L. has been able to describe and clarify adolescent male biases and confusions. He explicates the attitudes that most rappers take for granted.

"I'm That Type of Guy," "Jingling Baby," and "Big Ole Butt" were shockingly convincing expositions of authentic, modern male sensibilities. L.L. doesn't fake political excuses for the way Black boys try to be men, but he cannily enunciates the mental process. His most complex records show him to be psychologically closer to Ice-T and Kool Moe Dee than his artistic Oedipal complex may let him admit. But for all his bragging and macho obtuseness, L.L. has a genuine artist's instinct. That's a rare thing: 2 Live Crew don't have it but Slick Rick does; Ice Cube has only a microscopic bit, but L.L.'s acuity makes him *the one*, even if it doesn't make him perfect.

Start with the voice. Where most rappers concentrate on verbal gymnastics, L.L. masters the complex meters of his lyrics while delivering them in sly, theatrical tones: intimate-seductive ("6 Minutes of Pleasure"); cocky bellowing ("I'm Bad"); pleading ("I Need Love"); sneering ("I'm That Type of Guy"); jocular ("Milky Cereal"); cheerleading ("Farmers Blvd."); and variations on them all. The range of L.L.'s performances is as impressive as his lyrical skills. He has enriched rap's declarative mode more than any other single artist.

On "The Boomin' System"—the greatest car song in almost two decades—L.L. answers the crazy-countrified intro by Marley Marl with a Testarossa smoothness. The warmth of his voice sneaks him into your consciousness—it's the ideal way to campaign for the automobile boombox culture because it conveys the reason and the pleasure for this unique urban-bourgeois indulgence: "They don't understand why I act this way /

Pumpin' up the funky beat until the break of day / It's because I want attention when I'm drivin' by / And the girls be on my jock because my system's fly."

There's more to this than a glorification of disturbing the peace; it describes the world from which Public Enemy theorized "Bring the Noise" at the same time that it evokes the all-American car culture that Chuck Berry and then The Beach Boys laid claim to. L.L.'s vocal is winning in that same way that makes fine songs personal; he glides above Marl's thick, close, party-textured production, speaking in an unhurried companionable way. Good phrases are dropped confidentially: "Like Spoonie Gee said, my seats are soft like a bed / They recline way back so I can get real cozy." He literally busts the rhyme pattern to make an image and an emotion sink in. It's the best acting.

L.L.'s rests and elisions develop out of the routine bombardment of rap; his finesse and ambition (proclaimed by such watershed singles as "I Need Love" and "Goin' Back to Cali") are part of the way he broadens rap's scope, to make its language and discourse say more than usual. On *Walking with a Panther* he depicted the duality of pimp-think in the audacious singles "I'm That Type of Guy" and "Big Ole Butt." On the surface these were unlikable expressions of masuline hostility and sexist selfishness (toward men in the former song, toward women in the latter).

Produced by L.L. himself, these records used an insinuating mode that was dangerously misleading; one could mistake the observation of illicit or lascivious behavior for the artist's approval. But greatness lay in the way "Guy" also contained fear and dismay and "Butt" presented shame along with its smirks. L.L. didn't separate himself from the grossness of male privilege in those songs, but there's more distance in the *Mama* tracks that probably comes out of his collaboration with Marl (and even greater perspective may come from L.L. with age and experience).

It's important to note how L.L. confronts intimidation and aggression in those songs. "Guy" may be the most implacably frightening hiphop yet made – that's because it's honest (and more subtly daring than anything by N.W.A.). From a position of dominance, L.L. zeroed in on the vulnerability of young men's egos, then in "Butt" applied that same not-niceness to young women.

"Jingling Baby" was the culmination of L.L.'s uncompromised vision. Its coital dialogue transformed a rapper-fan tryst into a metaphor of L.L.'s rap-ability and career standing. His equation of sex with rapping was outrageous. He upped the stakes of how rappers regard themselves and how they prove themselves. "Jingling Baby," a formidable piece of wordplay and musical production, was a stunning, arrogant success: L.L.'s boasts came in rhythmic thrusts – such music, race, and sex similes as "Taking out suckers while the ladies pucker / And rollin' over niggers like a redneck trucker." His consciousness of racial politics matches his awareness of audience response; for proof he asks, "Let me see your earrings jingle." And the ecstatic, frankly orgasmic chorus consists of a female fan confessing about more than her earrings— "They're jingling, baby"—paced by L.L.'s one-to-one encouragement, "Yeah, go ahead, baby."

You can't deny that record was a clever, erotic piece of mainstream naughtiness (perhaps the wittiest since the heyday of the blues), but it's socially redeemed—if necessary—by L.L.'s compounded meanings and then by the spoken break, a documentary encapsulation of hiphop pillow talk. ("It's real wild to me, honey, you know what I mean? The way you be jingling. Word.") The intensity of that record was so overwhelming that L.L. and Marl slowed it down and made it more sexually egalitarian in the twelve-inch remix (also included on *Mama*). The remix marks a turning point between the single-handed, almost single-minded bravura of *Panther* and the wondrous street diversity of *Mama*.

On the remix, L.L. and Marl treat *Jingling Baby* as a historical fact— a proven turntable hit that measures the social temper of rap. They've judged its sexist effect in the real world of men and women living together (and partying together in the video). The line "Now I'm gonna do you while the party people watch" sounds friendlier in the remix—renouncing L.L.'s stud exhibitionism and placing his actions in a communal context. This does not imply that L.L. is softening, but he is, in fact, maturing along the lines of social awareness in Public Enemy's "I Can't Do Nuttin' for Ya, Man" and "Brothers Gonna Work It Out." His newly discovered identity—Uncle L. Future of the Funk—makes him a people's artist.

If that sounds boring or goody-two-shoes, remember how complex L.L. makes people's art in *Mama Said Knock You Out*. That same complexity is all over the album in dazzling numbers like the extended metaphors of "Milky Cereal," where each facetious line is more ingenious than the last. The exercise demonstrates that L.L. can address *any* issue through rap boasting, that there's no limit to the genre's expressiveness—only to individual rappers' imaginations. "Around the Way Girl," an inspired rap-r&b fusion (like last year's "Clap Your Hands" and "Jealous"), shows courtly romanticism that also suggests maturity.

How far L.L. takes his art depends on how long he can stay inspired, which probably means staying infatuated with himself. Luckily, his narcissism is transparent; he sees through himself and reveals more than the biases of a gifted fortunate boy from Queens. His emotional analyses may be naive but they're also astute. If L.L. Cool J can mature and prove that young Black men can learn to realize themselves in the world, then rap will be much more than an art form in vain or for a passing (adolescent) phase.

L.L. asks himself Muddy Waters's question of maturity, and that will indeed determine the future of the funk. Obviously, it's a future that will recall the past—specifically the type of blues that Muddy Waters, Willie Dixon, and Jimmy Reed created—as well as bring that sensibility into nineties focus. The blues artists' closeness to the African-American ways of life—the indigenous, beautiful, sometimes peculiar, self-sufficient manners and style—can be seen as an antecedent to the verisimilitude that is prized by rappers.

Artists like L.L. must, of necessity, preserve their sense of self with the same honesty and rigor with which their forebears preserved theirs. But this cultural continuity does not excuse any disregard for the changes in everyday values and African-American thinking that occurred automatically during forty years of progress and setbacks since the recordings of "Mannish Boy" and "Hoochie Coochie Man."

This means the age-old (and dubious) aspects of "manly" behavior that young men readily emulate have to be rethought and considered along with the social conditions that perpetuate those codes and make pathologies seem like virtues. All this is well within the gifts and intelligence of the young man who made *Mama Said Knock You Out*. L.L. has a line on this album about falling off the edge but not knowing where it is. That's a poet's admission of his conscience and a Black youth's expression of awareness.

*The City Sun*
September 12, 1990

# TO SLEEP
# WITH ANGER

I N *To Sleep with Anger*, filmmaker Charles Burnett offers a surrealistic comedy-drama about blood ties and spiritual heritage. His subtle portrait of the intimacy of family life sets this film apart from others you might think to compare it with. It succeeds without overwrought confrontational fireworks or becoming a survival epic like such family classics as *Long Day's Journey into Night, Sounder, The Magnificent Ambersons, or The Godfather*.

Burnett concentrates on the mysterious disintegration that occurs within a middle-class Los Angeles family with roots in the rural South when an old friend from back home, Harry Mention (Danny Glover), visits and outstays his welcome. Each calm, scrupulous image of domestic life conveys an open, dramatic space of unpredictable potential.

This anything-can-happen quality gives *To Sleep with Anger* a rare, unexpected tone of psychic suspense. It's the most subtly intense American movie since Alan Parker's 1982 *Shoot the Moon*, in which family strife escalated toward climaxes of unsettling violence. Burnett follows a similar trajectory, but his method—disarming, colloquial, and finally spooky—takes in a wider range of experience. Instead of forcing the trendy realization of the pathetic interdependency felt by people trapped within that most basic social unit, Burnett illuminates the possibilities of redemption and rehabilitation.

*To Sleep with Anger* will provide most moviegoers with their first exposure to Burnett's artistry. This film, winner of the Special Jury Prize at last winter's Sundance United States Film Festival, continues the intimate observation of family manners that Burnett created in such striking but little-seen movies as *Killer of Sheep* (1977), *My Brother's Wedding* (1984), and director Billy Woodbury's *Bless Their Little Hearts* (1982), for which Burnett was screenwriter and director of photography.

One distinguishing aspect of Burnett's domestic tales is the natural rhythm of the dialogue exchanges and the unforced presentation of everyday rituals like homecomings, group discussions, family meals. Burnett depicts these scenes with firsthand knowledge and the intimacy of real life recalled. These are the special benefits of independent filmmaking that allow a writer-director like Burnett to stick close to his own personal experience and evoke the audience's.

*To Sleep with Anger* offers the good news that Burnett's graduation to a bigger budget and a cast of nationally known actors (including Mary Alice, Carl Lumbly, Vonetta McGee, Richard Brooks, Sheryl Lee Ralph, Julius Harris, Sy Richardson, and Paul Butler) has not hardened his sensitive touch. He controls the emotional tone between mundane events and uncanny happenings masterfully. *To Sleep with Anger* moves Black independent filmmaking into the art-house realm.

Burnett's secret? He isn't afraid of profundity or complexity. He shows the riskiness that a filmmaker can learn only outside Hollywood, where the convention is to rehash stories that the public has been sold before. Burnett's story comes from the deep core of African-American folklore. He presents a world of portents that is nothing less than the culture's heritage—its shared knowledge and its superstitions put to action. Expressing this is his unforgettable opening shot: The family patriarch, Gideon (Paul Butler), sits wearily at a table while his feet and a basket of fruit resist being consumed by flames. The image is underscored by Sister Rosetta Tharpe's supernal recording of "Precious Memories."

It's the ineffableness of that scene that gives it power, and Burnett isn't so trite that he spends the rest of the movie explaining it; he uses its otherworldly resonance to set up the display of dangerous but healing forces that pit brother against brother and test the strength of a mother's devotion.

Glover's central role in *To Sleep with Anger* is as the catalyst that pushes family relationships to frightening extremes. Under the guise of friendship, Glover gradually usurps the father's position in the household once Gideon takes ill. Harry Mention's influence over Gideon's adult sons, Junior (Carl Lumbly) and Babe Brother (Richard Brooks), affects the range of their responses, from domestic responsibility to anarchic displays of temperament, which are customarily the poles of Black male behavior.

Babe Brother is tempted by the illusion of pride, independence, and freedom that Harry eerily embodies, becoming a young, surly double of Harry. Glover's Harry is on the edge of decrepitude, embodying a long-standing orneriness. Yet he seems a specter—a troubled spirit who is not evil so much as soul sick. This awful yet pitiable man has given in to bedevilment and pain earlier in his life, and his curse is that he now spreads his spiritual disease.

It is up to the women in the family to dispel Harry's bad "charm." Mary Alice's matriarchal Suzie is a practicing midwife whose laying-on of hands becomes the film's most remarkable symbol. Along with her pregnant daughter-in-law (Vonetta McGee), and a longtime family friend who casts a skeptical eye on Harry's action (Ethel Ayler), who also sings "Stand By Me" in superb voice), Suzie moves into the middle of the chaos to save the family, reestablish order, and outwit disaster. Mary Alice has perfected such roles in *Sparkle* and on the stage in *Fences* but here invests more quiet force than ever before. Burnett so skillfully coordinates the performers that this simple morality tale is transformed into a spectacle of individual and ensemble emotions.

As with any great film, the rich incidents of *To Sleep with Anger* lend themselves to numerous interpretations—not the least of which is the film's allegorical treatment of what has been called the crisis of leadership in Black America. Burnett intuitively traces this dilemma to the role of religion in contemporary life, but he carefully resists simplistic moral suasion. Burnett's restraint gives *To Sleep with Anger* a graceful balance of ominousness and optimism. He means to convey the emotional amplitude within family life visually and rhythmically—his preference over the starkly prosaic spiritual message that August Wilson evoked in his strongest play, *Joe Turner's Come and Gone*.

Burnett's humanist side wins out even though the film concentrates on spiritual matters; his view is linked to the mother wit of folklore and such "signifying monkey" tales as the trickster legend (bringing confusion to morals) that scholar Henry Louis Gates Jr. found in Black mythology from Africa to the Caribbean to South America. Burnett seems well aware of its peculiarity within the context of modern Los Angeles, and he shrewdly uses that oddness as a source of comedy and power. *To Sleep with Anger* contends with the essence of folklore. Burnett, like his characters, is involved in a struggle to understand the efficacy of African-American culture and honor the heritage that is usually taken for granted. The film's title comes from a familiar homily that advises forgiveness instead of letting grudges simmer overnight: Never go to bed angry. *To Sleep with Anger* is an existential comedy about Black people's need to love.

*Emerge*
September 1990

# ROBIN HARRIS'S VULGAR INTEGRITY

WHEN ROBIN HARRIS DIED last spring at age thirty-six, his humor seemed wild beyond his years. That's because in the Eddie Murphy era of any disgrace for a buck, ethnic humor had become the domain of opportunists: young, dumb, and full of "comedy."

The eighties spotlighted more aggressively self-deprecating Black comics than up-and-coming prizefighters: Murphy, Robert Townsend, Keenan Ivory Wayans, Whoopi Goldberg, Arsenio Hall, Damon Wayans, Marsha Warfield, Chris Rock, Michael Winslow, and others. Comedy became the new way for Black folks to beat each other to death (by broadcasting insults and stereotypes). Any fast-talking Black kid hungry to escape the ghetto of ignominy got a shot at fame by desensitizing himself, and the world, to his frustrations.

Television made this a spectator sport for the New Regression of the Reagan administration. And no wonder: This generation of Black comics was probably the first to grow up under the influence of TV and its distorted but popular images of African Americans and racial politics. Norman Lear, the entrepreneur of "Sanford and Son" and such dubious shows as "The Jeffersons," "Good Times," "Maude," "All in the Family," and "Chico and the Man," may be as seminal a figure for contemporary Black comics as Richard Pryor. Lear helped establish an alternative, self-conscious standard of ethnic identity for the public to expect and young Black comics to pursue.

But Robin Harris was the rare, real thing. By characterizing the maddening aspects of African-American lore, Harris cut close to the bone, satirizing behavior that most people were content to leave unexamined and that other comics were quick to portray in simple ridicule.

On *BéBé's* Kids (Wing/Polygram), an over-seventy-minute compilation of Harris's live stand-up routine, you can hear more than a funny show. It's a legacy to the wayward generation of Black comics who all seemed to have misunderstood Pryor and Redd Foxx's pungency. Harris started from that recognition and evolved a comedy style that drew the connection between humanity and ethnicity without making a joke of Blackness in itself.

It's necessary to concentrate on what Harris *was not*, because complex, personal responses to comedy often preclude analysis: People think funny is funny and that's enough. But without a concept of bad humor, it is impossible to distinguish good humor. (The old joke equating sex with business—"even when it's bad it's still good"—changes for ethnic comedy because its essence is political. And like politics, when ethnic comedy is bad, it's disastrous.)

Many Black comedians pander to their circumscribed audience (which is also influenced by the mainstream) and thus limit their scope to that group's biases. They purvey specious Black behavior as authentic, confusing the recognition of stereotype with truth. This leads to a basic lack of understanding about the psychological pressures and cultural traditions that create ethnic humor (Murphy and friends have no idea how much they Lear). The result is self-mocking at best, but usually downright embarrassing. This comedy without a background leaves Black people without a foundation—their lives are turned into jokes. But Harris's humor is uniquely restorative because he conveyed a vitality in Black American life, not merely extremes of behavior.

Harris's stance as the "middle-aged" Black dyspeptic allowed him to gain a true perspective on Black American folly without making the usual jive compensation of young comics that all Black American character traits are outrageous and thus proudly laughed at. That's the way ethnic comedians usually trade self-respect for success. Harris presented the normality of Black behavior—the same thing Bill Cosby does—but not about the Black bourgeoisie.

The title track that climaxes *BéBé's Kids* sums up the theme of Harris's exasperation with the current Black condition—specifically the uncontrolled violence and unchecked arrogance of the new, lost generation. Harris was too clever and sensible to moralize about love and brotherhood (although you can pick up those feelings in the veracity of his observations, the accuracy of his inflections). But it's a mistake to ignore the moral tone of a routine like "BéBé's Kids at Disneyland." The entire account portrays a mature Black man's outrage/affection; the ambivalence that other cuts show stemmed from Harris's alertness to what goes down in Compton and all over Black America. (There's insight in the names BéBé and her sister Jamika.)

Harris's showbiz position was not uprooted from reality, and that's his appeal to California's wack gangster rappers, even though they deliberately ignored his bemused scolding. On "Proud to Be from Compton?" Harris opposed the perverted patriotism of gangster rap. When an audience member heckled, "Don't talk about Compton, I'm from N.W.A.," Harris quickly shot back, "So?" He used attitude as an age-old battle tactic: "I don't give a fuck about Compton. That's where the cost of living is going up and the chance of living is going *down*."

As a comic with a sense of proportion, Harris wasn't above altering his key phrase from "BéBé's Kids at Disneyland" ("We don't die, we multiply") to scrutinize the lethal indulgences of criminal living in "Death Penalty." That's where Harris volunteers to pull the switch on the electric chair. When a criminal pleads, "I'm not going to do it no more," Harris, evoking the spirit of Pigmeat Markham's comic Judge, replied, "I know! Gotta go—gotta go!" The best part of this is the cultural understanding about ghetto traits—they may be familiar but they all are not allowed. ("In Living Color" avoids this in its obscene "Homeboy Shopping Network.")

The best part of Harris's legacy is that he evinced this understanding throughout the range of his routines with jokes that were vulgar in the best sense. This ability enabled Harris to give *House Party* its two concrete moments: His response to harassment by cops which switched the power surge of that typical American conflict—the other side of the story became the truest side. But you had to listen sharp to catch Harris's other slam: Frustrated from dealing with his bugged-out son (Kid-N-Play's Christopher Reid), Harris sighed, and said, "I never should have married that white woman."

Filling in the details of *House Party's* sketchy cartoon, Harris proved the value of a keen and authentic comic intelligence. (Actually, he confirmed the talent that his performance in *Do the Right Thing* first suggested.) His humor was based in the complexities of African-American life. In *House Party* his sly understanding and presentation of this complexity matched W. C. Fields's average, revealing curmudgeonliness in the classic *It's a Gift*. The complications that the Hudlin Brothers couldn't detail were Harris's absolute; he brought the texture of experience to a slick, superficial film even though he was neither lit nor recorded properly and illness was obviously overtaking him.

Harris's death from heart disease is almost a poetic comment on the heartbreaking cruelty of most Black comics and the lies that take over in commercial presentations of Black life. The Apollo Theatre's tribute to Harris on September 22 [1990] will show whether his colleagues learned anything from his example. Harris's vulgar integrity should haunt them all.

*The City Sun*
September 19, 1990

# BRIAN DEPALMA, POLITICAL FILMMAKER

F Brian DePalma and Spike Lee had switched the titles of their 1989 films *Casualties of War* and *Do the Right Thing*, no one would have missed their points. Each movie advanced positions on humanist-liberal politics that were completely out of fashion by the end of the Reagan decade: War is no longer judged morally, and the nation's Black underclass is blamed for its own deprivation.

Complainers (I'd rather not call them critics) also mistook DePalma's and Lee's artistic passions for frivolous philosophy and shaky aesthetics. This is less a reflection on those filmmakers' art than a comment on the contemporary cultural mood. The postmodern age seems almost counter-revolutionary in the way self-consciousness and self-reflexivity in film, music, literature, TV, and painting obscure a work's social meaning. And film critics, notorious for their love of genre exercises that take them away from the real world, stick to superficial interpretations. While this is not surprising in the case of Lee, who, being African-American, is more foreign to U.S. critics than a director from Teheran, it is a shocking fate for DePalma. The problem Lee faces by asserting a racial and therefore political consciousness in film is the same that DePalma has run into as he has pursued his artistic maturity in the past decade.

DePalma's sojourn from the Sarah Lawrence project *The Wedding Party* (1966, his first feature) to the Guber-Peters production of *Bonfire of the Vanities* took him from the fringes of independent filmmaking to the heart of the Hollywood institution. This trek also describes the most recent progress of the American cinema. The skills DePalma developed with each film evince various chronological influences: the U.S. avant-garde/independent movement (*Wotan's Wake, The Responsive Eye, The*

*Wedding Party, Dionysus in '69*), the French New Wave (*Greetings, Hi, Mom!, Get to Know Your Rabbit, Sisters, Phantom of the Paradise*), and the American renaissance of the seventies (*Obsession, Carrie, The Fury, Dressed to Kill, Home Movie, Blow Out*). All these phases of different kinds of radical filmmaking became obsolete as the industry "righted" itself (that's the best term for it) in the eighties, the decade of ruthless opportunism.

The great directors of the seventies—Altman, Coppola, Scorsese, Spielberg, and DePalma—brought their modernism into the postmodern age and faced an era of retrenchment. An incurious "sophisticated" public ignored the narrative experiments of these modern masters who, their first great works behind them, no longer felt a common creative impulse. Following the civil rights protests, Vietnam, and Watergate, American filmmakers had expressed a shared sensibility. But in the solipsistic eighties, film artists worked out an ever-private morality. The zeitgeist that runs through *Nashville, The Godfather Part II, Taxi Driver, Close Encounters of the Third Kind*, and *The Fury* was replaced by a spirit of isolated interests that resulted in *Fool for Love, The Outsiders/Rumble Fish, The Last Temptation of Christ, The Color Purple*, and *Body Double*—each one peculiarly personal.

This meant aligning their aesthetics to the business of filmmaking more than before, but in a period that no longer prized idiosyncratic dissent. Altman remained the great intransigent maverick, Spielberg transcended the fray, while Coppola and Scorsese struggled to balance independence with compromise. It is DePalma who exhibited the fascinating complexities of both radical and commercial instincts working in counterpoint, in each picture. And he did it against the odds, in spite of the worst press a major American filmmaker has ever received, culminating in the near-complete (and gleeful) derision of *Bonfire of the Vanities*.

It is high irony, since *Bonfire* is the funniest, splashiest comedy out of Hollywood since William Richert last worked. An amazing lack of cultural confidence shows in reviewers' inability to appreciate DePalma's adaptation of the Tom Wolfe novel. The same critics who resisted racial politics in *Do the Right Thing* took their measure of social conditions from Wolfe's burlesque, then complained that DePalma trifled with its seriousness. But the slickness and frivolity of DePalma's film is what's pleasurable and outrageous about it. In the face of solemn, inaccurate, bourgeois depictions of urban crisis such as the highly praised and disingenuous duds *Q&A* and *Presumed Innocent*, DePalma takes a nervy slap at the self-righteous, middle-class presumptions that come with the lavishness and privilege of a mainstream movie. Inherent in *Bonfire* is a skeptical regard of the upper-class view a film like *Crimes and Misdemeanors* accepts as a given. DePalma actually manages to hold to that skeptical stance more consistently than Wolfe did. Because of his background, DePalma has learned to thoroughly tease and investigate the politics of POV.

*Bonfire* isn't the first occasion of DePalma's politics being ignored in favor of an easy attack. Even though he made *Greetings*, the first (hell, the only) American antidraft movie (in 1968, when the idea was unfashionable—when it counted), he has instead been branded a misogynist, a pornographer, and a Neanderthal because the erotic themes in his later pictures overshadowed his political themes. DePalma isn't merely the prisoner of sex that Norman Mailer described but a victim of reactionary feminism. (He's even hounded by reviewers employed by porno magazines.) This isn't because erotic art is itself controversial—it's simply that the principles of feminist thought took stronger hold in the media and held sway even as the appeal of other counterculture, leftist politics waned.

Yet, as feminist knees jerked (and Hitchcockians mourned), De-Palma took on a series of studio assignments that proved him to be the most ingeniously political, socially aware mainstream moviemaker. Exploring various genres allowed him to address topics of popular interest in a personal, informed way. *Scarface* recounted the Cuban Marielita migration (in a style that anticipated *Godfather III*'s updating of the Borgias); *Body Double* was an addendum to *Dressed to Kill*'s study of class desire and sex attraction (territory Woody Allen fears to tread); the amoral absurdity of gangsterism in *Wise Guys* scooped *GoodFellas* (and its original title); *The Untouchables* scrutinized imperial notions of justice as an American mythology; and *Casualties of War* looked into the dark heart of sexual violence to reveal, in its essential moral horror, a persistent American nightmare.

While *Bonfire* was less successful artistically than most of these movies, it was not less intelligently conceived. Nor, as popular wisdom has it, was *Bonfire* beyond DePalma's range. The 1970 *Hi, Mom* came from a young talent of infinite range. Rated X and little seen at the time, *Hi, Mom* holds up remarkably in the age of sex, lies, and videotape; DePalma's tale of a peep-art voyeur/revolutionary (Robert De Niro doing a rough draft of Travis Bickle's anomie) seems absolutely prescient about the pervasive private uses of media and the concomitant isolation of the sexes and races. The "Be Black Baby" sequence, in which the pieties of public television are satirized, then vilified, is simply one of the great moments in American movies. It simultaneously (and with hilarious shock) explodes racial stereotypes and the conventions of TV/film perception.

*Hi, Mom* was the kind of film that could only be made outside the system. Since then, no mainstream movie has said more about race or media (Atom Egoyan, begone!). DePalma's subsequent adventures in the screen trade were experiments in narrative that conducted his youthful rebellion and didacticism into more commercial forms.

Though DePalma's skill was always striking and his politics alert, it's his sublimation of both, while emphasizing genre, that proves his recent mastery. The "Hitchcock problem" of borrowed tropes has become the basis of his most daring work: the problem of raising genre conventions and the audience's artistic awareness to the level of contemporary political awareness. "Be Black, Baby" warned about the complexity of ideology, exposing "objective" points of view as a matter of hegemony. So for DePalma it was a matter of moral necessity that *Scarface* be updated to express the experience of the nation's nonwhite underclass; that *The Untouchables* examine both the thirties gangster film and the western for the ethnic undercurrents of official law and order; and that *Casualties of War* clear away sentimentality from the Vietnam war flick.

*The Untouchables* was a super-ornate version of the gangster picture done in the grand, serious style Brian DePalma developed in *Blow Out* and *Scarface*. Although it's set in 1930 Chicago and deals with Eliot Ness and his quartet of gangbusters trying to put a stop to bootlegger and racketeer Al Capone, it is utterly modern. Legalistics cut across macho bang-bang, because what finally brought Capone down was tax evasion, not bullets. Along with his usual visual splendor, the director brought sober, filmwise insight into the gangster genre—and not by simply showing Ness's immunity to bribery or corruption. DePalma's interest is in the consciousness of a man who has to fight hard, even kill, to "do some good." The subject was not the proper federal agent's loss of innocence—such a clichéd point of identification would be inappropriate for the jaded contemporary audience—but an idealized view of the workings of society conveying Ness's crushed idealism, and our own.

Of the Hollywood movies designed to be all-out entertainment (that is, keep people satisfied with their own social circumstances), *The Untouchables* was the smartest and most challenging since *The Color Purple*; it was pop art made with great cunning. The film's *Homo urbanus* thesis was played out by De Niro as the vicious, flamboyant Italian gangster Capone, and Sean Connery as the granitic, dedicated Malone, a streetwise (Scottish-sounding) Irish cop. Between this polarity of white American immigrant aggression, Kevin Costner's quiet, officious Ness navigates a course toward propriety, reflectiveness, and middle-class family values. As an artist, DePalma avoids the Hollywood gimmick of sponsoring a prototype for the audience; he wants us less to worship The Untouchables' nobility and courage than to understand their actions as personal, fallible, human.

This decentralized heroism helped make *The Untouchables* a modern epic. DePalma's control of the ethnic subtext—the war of corruption among Italian and Irish lawbreakers and WASP law enforcers—is an extension of *Godfather II*'s revelations about the crossed social aims of the country's different ethnic groups. More effectively than Tom Wolfe or Sidney Lumet, DePalma created a spectacle of the American social system in the twentieth century: police corruption is as much a part of it as a quiet white home life or a swarthy gangster's ambition. The director replays these myths, fascinated with them as generic elements but without the condescension and moralistic judgment such scenes usually imply.

DePalma's unbiased relationship to real and cinematic history—seen in the objectified use of newspaper headlines—gave *The Untouchables* a detached viewpoint on law and human behavior. Instead of cold brutality or sentimental dramaturgy, DePalma found the key to movie thrills in the speed of editing, the clarity and deep focus of photography, the personality of actors.

Immediately in *Casualties of War*, one is struck by DePalma's memory. The first shot is 1974 on a city bus; passengers are reading newspapers emblazoned NIXON RESIGNING. This takes us back to a national moment of political shock and ambiguity. Then, as DePalma's sensibility asserts itself, the screen is flooded with an almost dreamlike flashback belonging to Eriksson (Michael J. Fox), who, now a civilian riding that San Francisco bus, is haunted by the memory of his experience in Vietnam.

This setup heads off any sentimental indulgence—*Casualties* isn't a nostalgic lament for a generation of American soldiers betrayed by their government. DePalma's context evokes the moral questioning that never stops; it connects Vietnam to Watergate and, in a scene of Eriksson being lectured to by Lieutenant Reiley, a Black commanding officer (Ving Rhames), it is connected to the civil rights movement. The consistency of this vision is part of what gives *Casualties of War* its power. DePalma's memory serves him in seeing through the war to a much larger, more serious issue than just "the horror, the horror." He enters—shares—Eriksson's nightmare as a witness to the kidnapping and rape of a Vietnamese farm girl by a squad of GIs. This opening sequence marked DePalma's most deeply serious exposition since *Blow Out*, another film about memory and, more significantly, about moral conscience—the forbidden subject of eighties movies.

The connection between *Casualties* and DePalma's other, more popular thrillers is its emphasis on psychological drama. Having specialized in portraying terrorized, paranoid states of consciousness, DePalma turned to

using his virtuosic film technique on sociological, "real world" subjects—
dissolving all form (and thus, somewhat ironically, achieving the "invisible" technique of classical Hollywood). The microtelescopic compositions,
presenting a scene close up and at the same time in detailed distance,
exemplify his directorial skill. *Casualties* doesn't have the artificial realism
or fake documentary look expected of war movies. DePalma employs a
lushness and surreal clarity that, having lent his earlier films a hallucina-
tory feeling, here impart precise Olympian vision.

The violation of the Vietnamese girl (Thuy Thu Le) is never graph-
ically shown, but the intensification, the veritable transparency, of De-
Palma's art brings those events emotionally close. We witness the atrocity
along with Eriksson, rather than just watching a glossy reenactment of
wartime tragedy. Fox is superb at showing the suffering of conscience.
His is not an easy role, because it isn't made morally superior; Eriksson
may stand in counterpoint to the war-is-hell nihilism of his troop leader
Meserve (Sean Penn), but while he refuses to take part in the rape, it is
also true that he can't bring himself to actively oppose it either. We as
viewers may be equally appalled at Meserve's racist, sexist actions, yet
we have no recourse to sharing—to being locked into—Eriksson's agony
of powerlessness.

DePalma's moral context won't let audiences brush off the ugliness of
violence. When Oliver Stone showed the lurid aftereffect of a nun's rape
and murder in *Salvador*, he wanted the frisson of quick, easy disgust;
he trusted that audiences would respond on cue—which means that
they wouldn't respond deeply. DePalma's storytelling is so perceptive that
it increases one's understanding of the events Eriksson saw, and the
torment he experienced in reporting them to the authorities and then
living with his memory of the entire ordeal. DePalma can't absolve
Eriksson's guilt over the Vietnamese girl or his fellow soldiers, but he
won't let the audience escape the burden of consciousness. The ending of
*Casualties*, which conveyed the hope for reprieve, deserved to be as
controversial as the climax of *Do the Right Thing*, because it recognized
the moral weight that is always pressed upon Americans whether they've
been to Vietnam or not.

After *Casualties of War*, DePalma was right to consider *The Bonfire
of the Vanities* lightweight. Despite Tom Wolfe's obfuscating details of
class, shame, and acrimony (which only got readers caught up in their
own fear and loathing), DePalma saw through to the book's essence—a
farce with pretensions of kinship to Fielding, Thackeray, and Dickens.
The director does what a smart reader of the book should have been able
to do: connect style to meaning. The elitism of Wolfe's choice of literary
models is worthy of Allan Bloom, and it transfers to the sympathy he

creates for his protagonist WASP bondseller Sherman McCoy, and his social decline. The novel ends with a parody of a *New York Times* editorial that sums up the entire hectic saga. But that satirical gesture still claims the very authoritative, middle-class point of view Wolfe only seemed to transcend. If there's anything the director of *Hi, Mom* is sure of, it's the tyranny of "official" narrative. He understands Wolfe's novel as a witty, pugnacious, racist, sexist diatribe; its meanness is total, but not visionary.

The genius of DePalma's adaptation is in recognizing Wolfe's subjectivity and its characteristic bourgeois "knowingness." This arrogance is taken for granted in middle-class industries like publishing and filmmaking that always (and automatically) promote a privileged class's point of view. Over the past decade DePalma the former radical has refined his subversive methods to resemble the grand style of the Hollywood tradition he aspired to—all the while aspiring to change it.

*The Bonfire of the Vanities* is DePalma's first "typical" Hollywood movie. It is cast, designed, photographed, scored, and edited to recall the big-budget bourgeois warhorses—often based on hit books—that were made in the last decadent days of the studio system: stinkers like *Youngblood Hawke, An American Dream, Justine, The Best of Everything*. DePalma's movie has that sixties–Twentieth Century Fox look of Glorified Ignorance—what sentient moviegoers of the time recognized as an American equivalent to the fascist architecture and white-telephone movies of the thirties (now with Color by DeLuxe).

Perhaps only a movie nut would connect that look to Tom Wolfe's greed-and-corruption screed, but it's a telling, sly thing to do. Instead of emphasizing the convolutions of Wolfe's narrative, DePalma uses that bygone movie style as a vehicle for critique, even emphasizing it to fire up an awareness of narrative choices. This strategy is consistent with that of his best movies—*The Fury, Blow Out*, maybe even *Carrie*—which all are, essentially, movies about watching movies. The great five-minute take that opens *Bonfire* challenges the five-minute Copacabana sequence in *GoodFellas*, but it works differently: In addition to taking in the details of experience, DePalma tests, extends, and analyzes spectatorship. Like the dizzying overhead angle that opens *The Untouchables*, *Bonfire*'s Steadicam shot is itself an essay on the use of Steadicam shots as a philosophic and artistic gesture.

While liberal critics were outraged that Wolfe's white-supremacist story was filmed at all, DePalma, the great student of movies, knew that *Bonfire*'s plot adhered to all the "classic" Hollywood pieties. Caught in the system himself, DePalma practices a personal code of ethics—he "goes Hollywood" to the point that we see clearly both the glamour and the disingenuousness of a Hollywood vision and, by extension, the whole mainstream entertainment complex.

Hoping to excite the perceptions of moviegoers, DePalma looses a variety of visual tricks, including wide-angle lenses and split-screen effects, to make plain the distorted perspectives passed off by Wolfe as honest observation. DePalma himself may be equally unfair when it comes to his treatment of the Reverend Bacon character (an opportunistic Black minister-politico whom Wolfe probably patterned after Jesse Jackson but whom DePalma explicitly models on Al Sharpton); at least he employs the method consistently throughout the movie for all the characters. The director's caricatures come from the realm of Hollywood fiction; they're not based on the trite East Coast "realism" of Lumet's *Q&A* and *Prince of the City*, or drab, earnest histories like John Sayles's *Matewan*, and *Eight Men Out*. Reviewers unfamiliar with the ironies of stylized narratives (from Sirk to Demy to Fassbinder) are biased against this method. They reject the political critique implicit in DePalma's distanced storytelling because it effectively provokes their detachment from Hollywood style — it's as troubling as being asked to disbelieve *The New York Times*.

*Bonfire* finds DePalma up against the same problem of bourgeois hegemony he bucked when he made his first films. But now, working within the system, he must express his independence through more precarious choices. *Bonfire* attempts to subvert the master while speaking the master's tongue — a risky, perhaps even dubious, gambit. In answer to the question "If you have any racial scruples at all, why make *The Bonfire of the Vanities* in the first place?," the answer is simply to challenge the authority of Wolfe's point of view, which would otherwise be legitimized by a "faithful" film version.

And that's important. (If Wolfe were a filmmaker instead of a New Journalist, his *The Right Stuff* would undoubtedly have been more NASA than Phil Kaufman.) DePalma changes the moral basis of *Bonfire*. Turning the Bronx judge into the moral voice of the film is a device owing much to the equations of screwball comedy: it's a corny device that's intended as corny — with the crucial difference that DePalma makes Judge White a Black man ("dignified" Morgan Freeman making an unconscious comment on the treacly emotions of *Driving Miss Daisy*). This small gesture of casting revisionism provides a necessary balance for a contemporary comedy about racial politics. It's frightening to imagine the number of mainstream filmmakers who wouldn't bother.

These differences enrich Wolfe's story while proving DePalma's unheralded skill with actors — especially the three white leads: Tom Hanks as Sherman McCoy; Melanie Griffith as his mistress Maria, who drives his Mercedes during the hit-and-run accident in the Bronx that triggers his downfall; and Bruce Willis as Peter Fallow, the tabloid journalist-bum who cashes in on McCoy's misfortune by manipulating New York City's mass emotions. Every departure from the book has a human charm and farcical wit: the simpatico subway ride McCoy shares with Fallow, the slapstick funeral scene between Sherman and Maria. F. Murray Abraham as District Attorney Weiss gives his best, funniest screen performance, one of many beautifully cogent cameos that include Mary Alice, Alan King, André Gregory. And the wildest dialogue doesn't come from the book ("Sherman, you know I'm a sucker for a limp dick") — it sounds like undiluted DePalma more than celebrity writer-for-hire Michael Cristofer.

If anything is missing from *Bonfire*, it's the young DePalma's savagery, the all-out assault and political liberation that marked *Hi, Mom* (Peter Fallow would have been the central figure — and a TV reporter to boot). But that's just another way DePalma could have slaked our expectations. He may have lost his anarchic streak, but he's replaced it with a humanism that subverts Wolfe's cynicism. DePalma provides the white protagonists mandated by Hollywood, but he still challenges status quo notions of heroism. Tom Hanks contributes a soulful bafflement that does more for the story's meaning than the WASP chin Wolfe dotes on. Hanks makes McCoy almost as deeply felt as the heroes of *Hi, Mom, Carrie, Blow Out,* and *Casualties of War*. Through him, the heart of *Bonfire* is now the lie McCoy learns to tell — a lie Wolfe glibly passed by.

Again, DePalma insists on the personal morality that distinguishes this later, mature phase of his career. It goes deeper than the speculative political gossip of Wolfe's roman á clef. Yes, McCoy's surrender to the vulgar circus is almost too precious a moment for the noise Wolfe stirs up. But its plainness brings the story down to earth. It leads into the audacious ending, in which Bruce Willis's dirty, cool, cocksure stride demonstrates Tom Wolfe's venal triumph, and at the same time turns the author's bile back on himself.

*Film Comment*
May 1991

# AMERICAN HAIKU

I T'LL BE 1993 before we'll see the effects of Bush's Persian Gulf War in Hollywood movies (it usually takes two years for social events to filter through the studio process), but *Home Alone* offers a beautiful coincidental reading of the social climate and political ethos behind the United States's Middle East actions.

This isn't stretching. As *Home Alone* races toward the $200-million-gross milestone (with momentum to take it far past that marker), it automatically takes on significance. More so than past blockbusters like *Top Gun, Beverly Hills Cop*, even going back as far as 1969's *The Love Bug, Home Alone* is a blockbuster in human scale. The story of a nine-year-old white boy (Macaulay Culkin) who is accidentally left home as his family flies off for a Christmas vacation in France, *Home Alone* explores an easily identifiable dilemma. Little Kevin must fend for himself, even fight off a pair of comic burglars who have staked out his home in the Chicago suburbs.

This is a David-and-Goliath story, a brat party, a mock thriller, and a sentimental holiday story—each deftly blended so that its appeal has lasted through Thanksgiving, Christmas, Hanukkah, Kwaanza, New Year's Day, Martin Luther King's Birthday, and Valentine's Day, with no end in sight. Certainly this is because *Home Alone* has what *Top Gun, Beverly Hills Cop, Flashdance*, and others lacked: charm. But it is a special, ecumenical charm that appeals to ideas about American life that just about everybody accepts as a given.

It starts with the myth of the family—large, boisterous, and bound together—and then dramatizes a child's separation. That's primal stuff, but it isn't extended into a social or historical exploration such as Spielberg gave after the moment of separation in *Empire of the Sun*. *Home Alone*—the title is practically a haiku of solipsistic isolation—keeps to the hearth as it works out a defense of privatization.

Without ever achieving a moment of Spielberg-like grace or sweetness, *Home Alone* demonstrates producer-writer John Hughes and director Chris Columbus exercising some of the basic domestic tenets of

American cultural life. The film's international appeal has not been tested, but it will be interesting to see how the rest of the world responds to this latest, rather accomplished, idealization that America has made of itself.

In fact, for some Americans *Home Alone*'s visual surface is almost as exotic as a foreign film. Kevin's three-story suburban home has the huge, comfy accoutrements of a manse from the days when American aristocracy still lived in the city (it's a post–World War II version of the mansion in *The Magnificent Ambersons*, the kind of home that, in the Midwest, has been left to ruin in what is now the inner city). *Home Alone* updates all-American luxe to the only place it possibly exists (the suburbs) and with the kind of warmth and visual splendor one associates with fable: Kevin's house has a wood-lacquer sheen not unlike the great turn-of-the-century family home in Ingmar Bergman's *Fanny and Alexander*. The bedrooms, staircases, videos, carpets, toys, and other visual signs of abundance have got to hit most American viewers like a month with the Rockefellers (not the Trumps, this decor is too tasteful and WASP).

Hughes is typically cunning in the way he accepts white American privilege yet gives it an unpretentious, knockabout treatment (the secret of his best films *Sixteen Candles, The Breakfast Club, Ferris Bueller's Day Off*, and *Planes, Trains and Automobiles*, as well as the films he scripted: *Mr. Mom* and the *National Lampoon's Vacation* series). By expertly exploiting the slapstick impact of Kevin's war with the crooks and his impudent relation to his family, Hughes and Columbus subtly uphold the normalization of affluence. The wit in their method is that the sentimental parts of the story rise to the surface with something like subtlety.

In the old days Hollywood emphasized sentimentality as part of the illusion of the country's moral unity; no doubt people believed it then, but Hughes is a perfect product of the Reagan-Bush era because he disregards whoever doesn't believe American myth. He supplies the sentiments of the few as the dream of the many. That's called hegemony, and although most people don't feel a connection between Kevin's warrior exploits (he's a four-foot Patriot missile) and the ongoing conquest of the Persian Gulf, Kevin's sense of his own righteousness is consonant with mainstream media's cant about "American interests," "liberating Kuwait," and "fighting aggression."

*Home Alone* is also significant for the way Columbus, whose depiction of white suburban ideology is a bit sweeter, less malign than Hughes's (Columbus previously directed *Adventures in Babysitting* and *Heartbreak Hotel*), is able to construct a kind of innocent atmosphere: Kevin is always a child in his behavior, especially when matching wits with salesclerks or the lonely neighborhood senior citizen, or when taunting his mother (a terse effective characterization by Catherine O'Hara). Kevin shows the heart and ingenuity of the ideal pampered American child. He's a live-action counterpart to Bart Simpson rather than a nineties male Polly-anna—that makes his soft spots all the less mushy.

It is fitting that the most emblematic American movie character so far this decade is a child. (I personally prefer Kevin's impudence to the deceit in *Pretty Woman* and the pointless conceit of *Ghost, Home Alone*'s box-office rivals.) Kevin's homefront victory is well timed with the Pentagon's current imperialist onslaught as the culminating event of the West's pop revolution: Its figurehead has always been the child, the embodiment of "posterity" and both the inspiration and target of commerce through rock 'n' roll, comic books, video games, television, and the movies.

Seeing *Home Alone* provides a laugh, a stir, and more than a clue to what American pop culture means. Capitalism's motto can be stated in a paraphrase of a current Persian Gulf joke: Honey, I Scud the Kids.

*The City Sun*
February 20, 1991

# UNDERGROUND MAN

EDDIE MURPHY got it wrong in *48 HRS.* when he waved a gun and a badge and presented himself as white America's worst nightmare. The stunt itself was a reassuring act. Millions laughed because they knew they were being kidded—not only by a fictional character but by a young performer who clearly just wanted to fit into the showbiz system by any means necessary. But Hollywood will have to break its mold to accommodate Wendell B. Harris Jr. and *Chameleon Street*, a film in limbo since winning the top prize at the United States Film Festival in Park City more than a year ago, and only now leaking into arthouse release. The virtues of Harris's debut are anathema to the current film establishment—which is probably the highest praise a critic can confer.

*Chameleon Street* is about an individual man's ambition (possibly paralleling Harris's own) that has been so thwarted and twisted, it has no means to be openly, "healthily" expressed. The hero's desires are inverted but not given up, and his psychic energy goes underground. Street the chameleon is a subversive with a proper, smiling, acceptably middle-class appearance. His "criminality" stems from his unstoppable ambition. His instincts are on the loose and unpredictable, refuting the social positions of class and race. And that makes him a truly dangerous man.

The film isn't "ahead of its time" (there's really no such thing), but it will be fascinating to see whether the network of European-centered, white-focused film reviewers, production executives, and museum curators is ready for what *Chameleon Street* represents. Wendell B. Harris has made a real work of art, short on budget but long on film savvy. And it evinces the rarest thing: a personal sensibility almost completely unrelated to the popular methods of commercial filmmaking—methods that typically seek to ingratiate a film's characters and events into audiences' goodwill.

Instead, Harris has conceived an insolent psychodrama. It's based on the real-life experiences of William Street, a Michigan con artist who passed himself off as a *Time* magazine journalist, a surgeon, a Yale grad student—each time being found out, prosecuted, and incarcerated before moving on. Harris's Street—acted by the writer-director-editor himself—is a Black man who can't be pinned down by his wife (Angela Leslie), his mistress (Amina Fakir), or the various authorities. That must be what makes his story so frightening to the guardians of film culture. (Remake rights have already been sold, but a Hollywood version—rumored to be planned for Arsenio Hall—could only be fatuous.)

Street takes personal freedom near the point of anarchy. He rejects the complacency of his brother and father, who run a burglar-alarm business (a joke on Black American self-control), and he does poker faced parodies of the professional class in each of his new jobs. His impudence implicitly assails the standards held by most people who obediently accept their assigned social roles. The supercilious wit Street uses to insult a redneck bar patron who mistakes Street's wife for a prostitute features the sting of intellectual and racial pride. This isn't the Black hostility usually seen in movies. Unlike the rage Eddie Murphy's comedy diffuses, it's smart, calculated, and it reveals, through a mounting disgust, a wily and mighty personal conviction.

One feels the same temper and drive in Harris's film craft. The verbal effusiveness and structure of symbolic anecdotes derive from French art cinema and attitudes, from the auteurist appreciation of the *Shanghai Gesture* clip to the quotes from Cocteau's *Beauty and the Beast*. Best—and riskiest—of all is Harris's sassy manipulation of such formal devices as fast-forwards and overlapping narration in the manner of vintage Godard: always an apt model, but one it takes talent to justify. Like Godard, Harris brings a unique political and cultural consciousness to the screen. Hence the packed, odd-angled compositions, and the intense close-up of the swirling brew inside a coffee cup—an homage to the famous coffee cup/universe sequence in *Two or Three Things I Know About Her*. Harris's work doesn't look like a home movie, but it doesn't look like most other movies either. His non-"imagistic" scenes avoid polished lighting to appear spontaneous, newly discovered, fresh.

The style is what early-sixties film culture accepted as avant garde; as used by a nineties African-American cinéaste, it is a daring rejection of mainstream cinema's "norm"—the style now taken to be the only style. This challenge goes very deep. *Chameleon Street* can disturb one's complacency about how society forms an individual's character, because Street's mercuriality serves as a metaphor for the randomness and arbitrariness of our social system. Each time Street gets caught and starts all over again is a reminder of the impermanence of class and social position. It's a parody of the advancement that society regards as proof of individual worth. And a Black protagonist makes that condition plain to see.

Street appears exceptional to the same degree that American society shows itself to be restricted. His extraordinary efforts stem from a barely controlled psychological distress. In the era of yuppies and buppies, this chronic overachiever is the unmistakable product of racism. (He's the skeleton in Shelby Steele's closet.) Street doesn't fight the power so much as struggle to subdue the tension he feels as an outcast, disfranchised person. Harris zooms in on the personal, intimate way African Americans suffer racism.

The scenes of Street's sexual life confound one's indifference about his plight. His misogyny is an objective correlative for his political frustration, egged on by the women who depend on him. (He shows the same macho defensiveness when a prison inmate makes advances.) There's a scene of domestic knifeplay in which the deepest fears of modern American psychosis rise to the surface. The joke that follows it wins Harris something akin to greatness; he understands that part of the absurdity of the African-American condition is best seen when its moments of dread have such close proximity to the mundane.

*Zelig*, Woody Allen's comedy about the ultimate conformist, featured Irving Howe's analysis "Zelig wanted to assimilate like crazy." But that funny line is not a definitive statement on ethnic pathology. Middle-class African Americans view these things differently from the way middle-class Jewish Americans view them. Harris offers new social insight that goes beyond assimilation and conformity and scrutinizes the exercise of social power as a need inspired by American oppression.

As a result, *Chameleon Street* is about the same anomie as *Taxi Driver*, perhaps the last pure work of American existentialism. Most reviewers failed to note that *Taxi Driver*'s link to Dostoevsky ran through Black American urban literature: the emblematic troubled men created by Ralph Ellison in *Invisible Man* and Richard Wright in *The Man Who Lived Underground*. *Chameleon Street* carries those tales from the dark side forward into nineties cinema.

All this makes *Chameleon Street* a good, troubling American movie debut. Harris respects his subject too much to close it off with homilies or solutions that would put innocuous movie culture at ease. The mystery of Street's character is as wide open as Harris's talent and potential.

*Film Comment*
May 1991

# COLE AND CLIVILLÉS MANUFACTURE DREAMS

// **F**ASHION COMES from the street," a photographer once explained
while trying to chart the source of recent trends. But the street is
what's absent from the very trendy video, *Gonna Make You Sweat
(Everybody Dance Now)*. The extravaganza that Marcus Nispel has
directed for the hit song by C + C Music Factory shifts the site of
contemporary style.

It follows the lead of M.C. Hammer's *U Can't Touch This* video, which
located style in an eternal dance space where function dictated form
(minimalist imagery plus full-cut and athletic clothes). Nispel visualizes
where-we-are-now at this moment in pop culture through images that link
emotion to fashion and dance steps. *Gonna Make You Sweat* leaves the street
behind: Its performers occupy the ethereal space of the airwaves. This
video itself takes place in the land of TV commercials and music videos,
which is to say that Nispel defines and makes visible a fabulous new
territory: It's the fantasy space that resulted from the acceptance, embrace
and exploitation of particular cultural habits—the flashy land of commerce.

*Gonna Make You Sweat* is about the very commercialization of
hiphop culture. It is not the means of commercialization (as was *U Can't
Touch This*), nor is it a critique. Nispel and C + C Music Factory celebrate
by making hiphop totems upscale. This would be unremarkable (and
lamentable) if the video did not touch on some fascinating, paradoxical
truths about the process of commercialization and the experience of
cultural co-optation. Both can be felt in the wondrous way the music
pumps up Nispel's images of luxe, and those images, in turn, are timed to
the rhythm of the music. Politics probably could tear sound and image
apart—but only if either related to the real world.

Instead, this video is a pageant displaying the great American ineffable: want. Its images describe material desire (looking good); its music describes spiritual desire (release). The voices of rapper Freedom Williams and the incomparable diva Martha Wash describe the human effort (the sweat) that must be expended toward those goals. The video's thematic elements are interlocked through a familiar method of presentation that is both arresting and seductive: Zelma Davis, a bosomy model-girl, juggles her wares, poses on a revolving pedestal while lip-synching Martha Wash's exhortations ("Work me all night!"), and for sexual balance the bespectacled rapper is intercut with images of himself without glasses showing off a taut muscularity. These transmutations are sexual stereotypes, of course, because Nispel uses the common-denominator language of advertising.

Nispel takes a specific thing—the intense euphoria of hip-house—and packages it as something for everybody. And because Nispel's guess is right (the video exudes the pleasure and expectancy of newness—the perpetual condition of advertising), he can get away with the audacity of flashing the rapper's stage name across his own eyeglasses. "FREEDOM" is a floating concept; it appears throughout the video as a reflection of what the singers and C + C Music Factory are *making* music about. It's also a password—an "Open Sesame" to riches and dreams: things.

Every time *Gonna Make You Sweat* is aired, it becomes television's most hype game show; call it "Inventory" for the chance it offers consumers to itemize possible possessions. Here's a short list:

A gold brooch
bracelets
wire hoop earrings
white sneakers
blond wig
seashell necklace
fade haircut
gold Mercedes medallion
black cap
kinte-cloth jacket
circular shades
bicycle wheel
silver finger ring
silver pump shoes
a "Paris" earring
a gold tooth
a bike

fur-trimmed hood
gabardine suit with a derby
a kufi
shrimp earrings
and a gold-suited and -gloved model holding what looks like a Gold Coin condom.

That last image connects subliminally with the frequently intercut shots of flesh and muscle; it also recalls the Paula Abdul video *The Way That You Love Me*, where she sings a kept woman's checklist of extravagant goodies. The one bold idea in Abdul's video was giving her skin the same shimmering tint as the dream images of champagne and gold jewelry. But that effect imprisoned Abdul in her own venality: Gold was used as a neutralizing color, symbolic of something considered more important than race. That's a crossover delusion that most artists of color— especially Black artists—cannot afford.

*Gonna Make You Sweat* is immediately striking because it doesn't neutralize its high-style imagery. These fresh, sexy images defy seventy years of segregated luxe in *Vogue*, in *Vanity Fair*, on Madison Avenue, and in Hollywood. Nispel is selling Black beauty; he uses the elegant extravagance of elbow-length evening gloves and windblown chiffon mixed with Black street concupiscence to demonstrate the symbiosis of crossover. The fetishistic touching of various cap brims by Black fingers shows just who is determining mainstream fashion.

The move toward the mainstream is seen as a style revolution: Blacks don't turn into whites here, but the national self-image becomes Black— enlivened by cultural forms that no longer remain underground. These are not images of middle-class striving. They're about transcendence through commercial success. If *U Can't Touch This* teases the unhip (whites) with what they cannot do, *Gonna Make You Sweat* entices Blacks with the flash and glamour they're usually denied. It shows the urge toward a sexy imperial dream status (what, in reality, never gets higher than the bourgeoisie).

This is a perfect debut video for C + C Music Factory, a corporate dance music group on CBS Records founded by the producing team, David Cole and Robert Clivillés, responsible for club hits by Seduction ("Heartbeat"), Noel ("Silent Morning"), and 2 Puerto Ricans, a Blackman, and a Dominican ("Do It Properly"). This self-proclaimed music factory consciously participates in the commodification of dance culture.

In this video they demonstrate that people of color are no longer gullible primitives eager to be exploited. Opportunity is seen as advancement. Cole and Clivillés have entered the rat race and turned it into a dance contest. Graphics in the video point out their mix of "rock & soul & funk & techno & pop" – obviously for fun and profit. It's poignant and significant that when Cole and Clivillés appear onscreen, they are seen half-standing, half-dancing, trying to keep their balance while moving in circles.

*The City Sun*
January 23, 1991

# JANET JACKSON'S BODY ELECTRIC AND BODY POLITICS

L AST YEAR, Janet Jackson took the music video crown from Madonna – a fact made clear in A&M Records' video release *The Rhythm Nation Compilation*, but especially by the sexy music video for Jackson's latest single, "Love Will Never Do (Without You)." At a time when Madonna's promiscuous image mongering has become solely representative of the collusion between mass communication and mass merchandising (she deserves a Pet Rock Economics prize for the way *Justify My Love* created a new video market), Janet Jackson saves the form with a perfectly revolutionary video art work.

*Love Will Never Do* is the second music video directed by fashion photographer Herb Ritts (he's best known for his Gap ads, and his narcissistic style is regarded as a nonracist, egalitarian answer to Bruce Weber). Ritts says, "Janet and I decided to try something innovative," and this is her most blatantly sexual video yet. Its theme is body-consciousness, demonstrated by a literal unveiling of her dècolletage and midriff.

Usually Jackson is covered up in layered tunics, the buttoned-up uniform of *Rhythm Nation* or the exercise togs of *The Pleasure Principle*. The latter emphasized her ample lower contours; she had pop's most lusted-after female rump since Jane Fonda's in *Walk on the Wild Side* – a straightforward, if localized, sexual object. Perfectly titled, *The Pleasure Principle* consolidated the mass, crossover appeal Jackson won with her 1986 album, *Control*. She affected a "good girl" and "good Negro" guise, doing wholesome aerobics while actually demonstrating a generous, healthy sexuality.

After that success, the 1989 album *Rhythm Nation* offered a battle plan for Janet Jackson to conquer the world, and this video compilation shows the imaginative, felicitous ways she has adapted herself to the emotional needs of her expanding audience (it's also no small feat that these videos help distinguish the better cuts from *Rhythm Nation*'s overlong program).

Certainly "Love Will Never Do," with its spunky call-and-response chorus and trumpet-line homage (played by the founder of A&M, Herb Alpert), is as much a pop idol's expression of gratitude to the "little people who made it all possible" as it is a personal love song. The video is fascinating for the way it transforms Jackson's facile declarations into thrilling political propositions. That Jackson usually has nothing to "say" was made clear by the pointless, martinet gestures in the *Rhythm Nation* video; since then her videos have made their meaning by producing a subtextual, anterior logic like Madonna's used to have.

*Escapade*, directed by Peter Smillie, was the first of the great videos out of *Rhythm Nation*, with Jackson parading through a small-town Caribbean carnival. The color scheme of orange, dusty brown, and early-evening blue recalls the dreamlike naturalism of Spielberg's *Always*. This cultural evocation seemed the closest a Jackson could come to a political statement. (And it said more than "Come to Jamaica!") *Escapade* has the subtle, insistent and *lively* ethnic political atmosphere that George C. Wolfe and Thulani Davis missed in their Afro-masque adaptation of Bertolt Brecht's *The Caucasian Chalk Circle*. Director Smillie brought the beat to Brecht; his folk-art premise visualized the link between the technological sounds Jimmy Jam and Terry Lewis prepared for Janet and the proverbial ways African Americans find relief from toil.

The beat resonates and the video's meanings amplify as Jackson, dancing in the street, gets closer to the esprit her Black audience demands. Out of this necessity comes the expressive freedom that Paul Simon could not access in his Capoeira-themed video for "The Obvious Child." Despite Simon's privilege and "serious" good intentions, his video remains rigid and didactic, but the r&b essence of *Escapade* opens up a colorful new world.

In Julien Temple's seven-minute *Alright*, the sound-stage slickness and bright, movie-musical hues achieve the kind of postmodern kitsch Warren Beatty (and Madonna) lacked the style to pull off in *Dick Tracy*. Instead of merely copying Hollywood history, as he did in *When I Think of You, Absolute Beginners*, and *Earth Girls are Easy*, Temple this time offers a context that allows a sociological reading of movie style: A quaint, make-believe city wakes up to the newspaper headline CAB CALLO-WAY IS COMING! and its significance is unavoidable—the Jackson psyche finds eschatology and salvation in showbiz style. Of course, the real second coming in *Alright* is Janet Jackson's Pop ascension—that's why her homages to Calloway, the Nicholas Brothers, and Cyd Charisse ironically give those legends short shrift. (Only Heavy D gets a real showcase; he links Jackson to the present, as do the voguing dancers.)

Yet there's a message here about the homeless, but it isn't patronizing. Because the theme is "Alright with me," Jackson and Temple revive the nostalgic glamour of the zoot-suit, big-band era to prove the beauty and heritage that down-and-out Blacks might cling to. For them it's escape; for Jackson it's inspiration.

At the beginning of *The Rhythm Nation Compilation*, Terry Lewis says, "Janet is just a visionary. She knows what she wants and she sees it." That's simplisitic enough to explain the dreadful videos for "Black Cat" and *Come Back to Me*. The latter is pre-Afrocentric—pre-Diana Ross, even—in its hankering for European romance and a "Latin lover," as Janet and a gaucho stroll the parks of Paris. Look closely: The visionary wears blue contact lenses.

*Come Back to Me* and *Black Cat* aren't just about Jackson's personal tastes; those videos are geared to white fans as much as *Escapade* and *Alright* target Black fans—or at least Black cultural knowledge. But there's a special, overlapping demographic that *Love Will Never Do* targets remarkably.

Not only do Ritts and his superb cinematographer Rolf Kestermann (who shot Babyface's striking *Tender Lover* video), show Jackson as sexy; she's made conspicuously feminine in the super-lush style of a camp gay icon. But Jackson's vivacity and her huge, melting smile save her from the freakishness of big dishes like Jayne Mansfield or Marilyn Monroe or even poor LaToya.

Ritts highlights Jackson's friendly, warm, still healthy sexuality. Without winking, she invites the gay members of her audience to participate in her pop celebration. That attitude is so sophisticated it makes Jackson seem adult for the first time. A female star's acceptance of her own glamour sometimes parallels her embrace of gay fans—her persona then seems enriched, humanized. For instance, Jackson now has this; Michelle Pfeiffer doesn't. When Jackson ad-libs, "What?" to her video partner in *Love Will Never Do*, it's clear that this video is a conversation in code between a female star and her male admirers. Ritts helps Jackson put the sexual and racial underground on high terrain.

Her fake eyelashes, the headband, and the blond wig are multiracial come-ons (Brigitte Bardot by way of Claudia Schiffer), but Jackson's every jiggle and sway is spectacularly womanly. No amount of skin lightening (or the muted tones of black-and-white photography) can separate her sexual identity from her racial identity—that's one of the beautiful truths of Herb Ritt's art. So Jackson's openly sexual appearance in an abstract desert setting provides the perfect juxtaposition for an erotic display of various male torsos, flexing and stretching to the beat like a nineties *Olympiad*.

*Love Will Never Do*'s most striking image—after Janet herself—is of the video's central acrobat, a bald, ink-black man whose radiant teeth gleam as he lip-syncs the chorus. He has three traits: Blackness, masculine strength, and feminine delicacy. Each is presented audaciously, politically, and joyfully.

Any semiotician will tell you that this image, stuck in the middle of so much pulchritude and anonymous earth, is, essentially, phallic. It is the balancing half of *Love Will Never Do*'s sexual content. And as the Black acrobat teeters on a white hemispherical platform, he reminds you that music videos are best about the sexual affirmation of their subjects and audiences. (This idea failed when Ritts had Madonna swim with dorsal-finned mermen in *Cherish*.) This makes *Love Will Never Do* a subtle weapon in the war against homophobia, and it's the first indication that Janet Jackson may be an artist of principle.

*The City Sun*
January 9, 1991

# ANATOMY OF
# A FLOP

*HE FIVE HEARTBEATS* deserved to fail. Its continuous slide down the box-office charts has caused cultural pundits to worry over the future of "serious," "wholesome," "positive" movies about Black people, but perhaps the reason *The Five Heartbeats* has not attracted even a large Black audience is that it is not particularly serious, wholesome, or positive.

Robert Townsend's fantasy about a 1960s male r&b group that struggles to success, suffers personal disputes, but, through several decades, hold together as family and friends is as suspicious as it is virtuous. It represents the same kind of repackaging of Black pop culture that happened in *Lady Sings the Blues* and *Sparkle* — 1970s myths that interpreted social history through dramas of musical style. But those trite, compulsively watchable movies had conventional narrative formulas that worked for the feminine romanticism of the music they featured.

As Spike Lee discovered with *Mo' Better Blues*, the musical melodrama doesn't sync with the conventions of masculine behavior. The musical performances that are meant to reveal emotion don't expose much except the filmmaker's own fondness for the image — the facade — of performance. Townsend, like Lee, has not cracked the surface of male camaraderie. It is depressing to watch even the reunion scenes in *The Five Heartbeats* — they have no heart. Friends and brothers reconcile by rote without the passion of people who ever meant what they sang with one another.

It's likely that the best approach to this story — which is basically a tale of African-American male competitiveness — would have been satire. And indeed it might have been if Townsend and co-screenwriter Keenen Ivory Wayans had conceived the project more honestly.

Instead, they cheat analysis of the 1960s era — the transitional period between cultural conformity and revolution. This is most apparent in the details of costuming and speech; in each case Townsend goes for what is cute rather than what's authentically evocative. Michael Wright as Eddie, The Five Heartbeats lead singer, and Leon as the sexy backup singer J.T. are skilled and stylish enough to carry the dandyish hauteur of 1960s slickness, but the other actors are stuck in their makeup—especially the women. Townsend's misconception is glaring in the early scenes, where Troy Beyer (yes, *The White Girl*) represents the 1960s female show-biz prototype. Beyer has the wrong look; she seems cosmeticized by nostalgia and misses the era's wild, incongruous Negroness-in-white-coiffure. (It's also strangely dismaying to see Diahann Carroll, as the wary wife of the group's manager, put back into the stultifying 1960s makeup she outgrew in *Claudine*.) These details were done correctly in *American Hot Wax* and Jonathan Kaplan's video for John Cougar Mellencamp's *R.O.C.K. in the U.S.A.*

Townsend misses an entire area of political meaning by not emphasizing the sartorial and linguistic changes that went on in r&b. It suggests that he doesn't really understand the period he's dealing with or the pertinent issues of Black adaptability. Shifts in cultural style *are* politics for sentient Black males; the change from processes to afros, Italian suits to jump suits, are keys to social mood and cultural consciousness.

The glib treatment of history in *The Five Heartbeats* suggests that instead of finding a satirical style that expressed cultural change, Townsend aimed for a *Big Chill* nostalgia—then compounded his misperception with a sappy treatise on brotherhood. That's Blackness-in-white-coiffure all over again.

It's impossible to grasp the tone of a movie so divided in its aims. *Lady Sings the Blues* and *Sparkle* went straight for heartbreak and heartwarming, but the fibrillating *Five Heartbeats* starts out with a distanced 1960s groove and tries to pass for in-group essence.

Phoniness results. It's the same kind of eager self-exploitation one senses in a bad "In Living Color" skit—the evidence of Black artists involved in too much mainstream compromise. Townsend hasn't worked out this dilemma, and giving himself the role of *The Five Heartbeats* songwriter, Duck, doesn't quite explain it, either, although one scene really clarifies the problem: The "We Haven't Finished Yet" number where Townsend is helped out of writer's block by his little sister (Tressa Thomas), who interrupts her house cleaning to improvise a song and gets carried away. The scene is so wrong and so right that even as it presents the clichés of poverty (a cramped house, scraps of brown bags used for writing paper), it obliterates them by parodying the singing-dancing myth of natural Black talent.

*The Five Heartbeats* might have been interesting if Townsend could sustain that balance of absurdity. He only comes close in a frightening scene where an insolent singer is thrashed by crooked record executive

Big Red (a powerfully malicious, gleeful performance by Hawthorn James—who's even got the right hair). *Sparkle* entertained the myth that early sixties Black artists controlled their pop careers; the Big Red sequence is a memorable, larger-than-life gothic cartoon that says otherwise. It has more edge, more reality than the rest of the movie's cuckolding and drug-addict soap opera.

Townsend isn't nearly as accomplished a technician as Oliver Stone, whose own sixties pop movie, *The Doors*, was another deserved "failure" (to date, *The Five Heartbeats* has grossed $7 million to *The Doors'* $33 million), but there's a more human scale to Townsend's film. He uses The Drifters, The Four Tops, and The Isley Brothers as prototypes, building a view of the sixties around their legend, whereas Stone took Jim Morrison at his own messianic-poet evaluation and produced an extravagant inanity. *The Doors* was a hypocrite's view of the counterculture—a Cecil B. DeMille rock movie—yet even a film as modestly ambitious as *The Five Heartbeats* is subject to similar misjudgments.

Townsend isn't as slick as he thinks he is. In a Southern tour sequence where the group experiences its first lesson in corporate racism, their humiliation is doubled by a police incident where they must prove their singing ability under duress. With false sophistication, Townsend follows that scene with a rendition of "America the Beautiful," insulting our intelligence and the group's honor. It would have been smarter, and truer, to have the group sing "America the Beautiful" to the cops. Such audacity also would have undermined the "sound of young America" complacency of *Big Chill* nostalgia. This could have been the first r&b musical with what a radio DJ once described as testicular weight.

The sign of Townsend's dishonesty is a success montage that depicts the group's achievement in terms of media coverage. He puts them on the cover of a 1966 issue of *Rolling Stone* (which didn't exist at the time) and *Esquire* (which wouldn't have dared r&b cover boys). At the end, it's hard to believe Townsend's matured characters have learned anything when the filmmaker himself knows so little.

*The City Sun*
May 15, 1991

# SPIKE LEE'S PORNOGRAFFITI

CINEMATOGRAPHER ERNEST DICKERSON understands that a movie about interracial sex ought to be largely about skin and the sensuality of hue. His deep-toned lighting for Spike Lee's interracial-sex drama *Jungle Fever* gives that movie its only artistic merit.

It should be said outright that no one before Dickerson has photographed people of color with such intelligence, imagination, or beauty — that includes Soumendu Roy's work with Indian filmmaker Satyajit Ray or even the color films of Idrissa Ouedroago, Ousmane Sembene, or Akira Kurosawa. Since *Do the Right Thing*, Dickerson has framed and lighted performers of varying skin shades so that a viewer gets a palpable delight in the human rainbow. *Mo' Better Blues* was the most sheerly beautiful-looking movie of 1990.

More than that, Dickerson's work in contemporary settings conveys an appreciation for the photogenic aspects of race politics. Even street scenes and interiors are *visualized* as opposed to merely "captured." His color patterns have been as delicate and pure as some of Sven Nykvist's lighting for Ingmar Bergman's films but without abstracting the figures from their social roots. The way Dickerson makes "a picture" of people in workplaces or domestic locations shows an important conceptualization of cinematic vision. He doesn't just remove the lens cap and adjust the focus, basing his lighting style around Caucasian skin tones, as is the norm. He has transformed the way beauty is perceived in the movies. It's an aesthetic discovery comparable to Gauguin's and Matisse's exotic paintings but minus the exoticism. He has found a whole new visual aura.

Unfortunately, *Jungle Fever*'s visual sophistication is miles ahead of its verbalized and acted-out political ideas. In a sense, Dickerson's work is far too rich for Lee's simplified demonstration of what Black and white people, men and women, don't know about each other. He's photographing real people, while Lee is using stick figures to dramatize a scene.

Something extraordinarily complicated—and morally ugly—is going on in this messed-up, shallow movie that directly parallels the problem of racism.

Despite the sensual and emotional fact of sex relationships, *Jungle Fever* is conceived as a political hypothesis. Flipper Purify (Wesley Snipes in a weak performance) is an architect who lives in Harlem with his wife and one child; he begins a sexual relationship with his secretary, Angie Tucci (Anabella Sciorra), a working-class girl from Bensonhurst. Neither is presented in emotional detail because Lee works primarily in terms of stereotypes, so Flipper is Black Man; Angie is White Woman. Their backgrounds don't define them either; the settings are points on a tribal subway map. Their relationship can be called an affair only as a matter of convenience; Lee dramatizes it as a nonstate, something between détente and warfare, where there is no communication, just impersonal commingling. Yet, Flipper and Angie's lack of emotional sync still produces serious disruption in their homes that eventually plays out Lee's implicit idea that interracial relationships cannot work.

In the 1967 film *Guess Who's Coming to Dinner?* crusading filmmaker Stanley Kramer created a liberal fantasy about the problems of integration being overcome by true love. (Kramer simplified the controversy of a Black-white marriage between Sidney Poitier and Katharine Houghton by shifting the film's concentration onto the stalwart romanticism of the white girl's parents, played by Spencer Tracy and Katharine Hepburn.) *Guess Who's Coming to Dinner?* was good-hearted, socially conscious pabulum—every bit as schematic and artificial as *Jungle Fever*. But at least its ideas were clearly organized into effective though predictable comedy.

*Jungle Fever* is rarely funny; the difference is the film's pessimistic view, which may be as apt to this era as Kramer's optimism was for the peak of the civil rights movement. Yet this doesn't mean that Lee offers greater truth or honesty than Kramer. In fact, *Jungle Fever* seems twisted and confused by its creator's cynicism. Lee makes an inexact leap from the generalities of urban racism to the personal complications of two individuals.

Lee is being artistically dishonest by pretending to illustrate an interracial relationship when he is only offering a proposition that guarantees to get the backs up of some Black and white people. *Jungle Fever* is insufficiently dramatized—the Italian Americans are as embarrassingly one-dimensional as the African Americans. The movie operates at the superficial level of an agitprop skit but one that runs over two hours and weighs in at two tons of presumptuousness. Lee thinks provocation is equal to artistic insight. It's the folly of this era of young Black artists—

just as Kramer's bleeding heart was the folly of the sixties—that Lee considers his own recalcitrance as the vanguard of social thought. But the rap group Public Enemy got a much deeper and wide-ranging consideration of miscegenation on the remarkable title track of *Fear of a Black Planet* and the song "Pollywannacracka." *Jungle Fever* is a step back from Public Enemy's landmark encapsulation of the multisided issue. Nothing in this movie matches Public Enemy's astute and emotional view of the contradictions of race pride, social advancement, and human progress. Lee fumbles miscegenation, just as he missed the colorism target in *Social Daze*.

Banality usually exposes the sentimentality of artists, but here Lee's banality reveals small-mindedness along with a small spirit. This does unfortunate damage to a great subject that should have made a great movie. How could Lee have gone through with this depressive a priori argument on the unfeasibility of interracial love when the proof of its possibility surrounds him in his father's remarriage; the domicile of his latest champion, Henry Louis Gates; in the marriage of last winter's media hero, Shelby Steele; and so many other prominent examples?

It's obvious that Lee considers himself a soothsayer, not for such members of the colonized Black middle class who indulge in Black and white sexual chess games, but for the Black and Italian underclass still trapped in dead-end parochialism where the thought of race and class mixing is abhorred. If *Jungle Fever* were a better film, it would convey the conflict of a middle-class Black artist straining to believe in the mandates of the lower class. Instead, Lee bluffs a hard-line Black-is-best ethic. Flipper and Angie's incompatibility no doubt is a metaphor for the current disbelief in integration. But as a storyteller Lee has accepted the idea's one-to-one failure without first having experimented with it. By insisting on the geographical and ideological boundaries of Black and white communities (first shown in the half-witty title sequence—a rip of *West Side Story*), Lee fails to consider the personal bridges that people build all the time and that must be the basis of even temporary liaisons. (Couldn't Flipper and Angie share favorite baseball teams, musical groups, politicians? That might have made their breakup more poignant and more puzzling.) *Jungle Fever* doesn't present a new tragic reality but a sour, ignorant preference.

Lee plays out his own hysteria and disgust by overestimating what is essentially Flipper and Angie's quickie. Every character talks like a *New York Post* headline—belligerent, impetuous, thoughtless—and Lee accepts the sensibilities of contemporary, debased New York as an accurate measure of human psychology. Like the *Post*, Lee exhibits a kind of racial prudery. He refuses to truly contemplate cross-race sexual attraction. A great provocateur would have acknowledged the thrill of racial difference or of taboo-breaking and filled the screen with transgressive lust and visual mind-fucking. There's a precedent for this in L.L. Cool J's music video *Goin Back to Cali*. As Benj DeMott discussed, white female hands lasciviously reached for L.L.'s sleek-muscled Black torso while the rapper projected a teasing-yet-steadfast impassivity. Lee seems afraid of such suggestiveness, even though his cinematographer seems fully capable of exploring the sensuality that confounds even radical Black politics. When Lee ignores this, he ignores the human scope of his story.

The subplots involving Flipper's crackhead brother, Gator (powerfully acted by Samuel L. Jackson), his religious-zealot parents (Ruby Dee and Ossie Davis), and his troubled wife (Lonette McKee) and Angie's Italian boyfriend, Paulie (John Turturro), don't make up for the horrendously mangled main theme. Even these tangents are awkward and trite — they don't substantiate the "real world" that inspired Lee's plot because Lee doesn't know how to — or even want to — evoke realism.

A superficial thinker, Lee is attracted to prototypes, then bends them to his own meaning rather than balancing or testing them with research or truth. This wasn't exactly the case in *Do the Right Thing*, but there Lee was fueled by the outrage of Howard Beach and captured it artistically. *Jungle Fever* is shamelessly dedicated to Yusuf Hawkins, but Lee has not figured out how to use the overwhelming evidence of New York racial hatred (a mock-documentary approach might have been ideal), so he resorts to his own defensive incredulity. Lee's solipsistic movie world consists of a crack-house set piece done like an Oliver Stone production number and frequent lugubrious music counterpoints. Theatrical psychodrama seems to be Lee's true style — a mode of artifice and sensationalism that might best be called Pornograffiti.

*Jungle Fever* says interracial sex can't work because integration doesn't work. Only a fool would confuse the two, and only a racist would insist on the analogy.

*The City Sun*
June 5, 1991

# MATTY RICH GOES STRAIGHT DOWN A BLIND ALLEY

T ISN'T UNTIL the very end of *Straight Out of Brooklyn* that the filmmaker Matty Rich gives any sign that he knows what he's doing. This climactic sequence shows the simultaneous deaths—in a hospital and in the streets—of the lead character's parents. These events are edited together with a quick, calibrated rhythm; the sense of inevitability suggests the remorselessness of fate.

The control, however is all Rich's. He contrives the same telepathic technique that D. W. Griffith (the first poet of cross-cutting) originated in the 1922 film *Way Down East*. The manipulation of his characters' lives is the one place in this film that Rich doesn't try to get away with "realism," and the moment works for precisely that reason. It's an unexpectedly poignant close for a film that steadily has ground down one's senses through the shambling, artless style Rich has chosen to film the story in.

The ending comes as a relief as much as a surprise. One responds to the handiwork—and the movement of mind—that is finally revealed because before the ending occurs Rich threatens to make a "virtue" of the film's primitive look and amateurish methods. His approach dangerously conforms to the mainstream (white) notion that Black artists are themselves primitive amateurs incapable of any sophisticated expression.

*Straight Out of Brooklyn*'s ending proves that Rich's ideas got onscreen through deliberateness and guile, if not very much talent. He isn't an agent of truth or wisdom, as he has been celebrated in the media (from *The New York Times* to PBS' *McNeil-Lehrer Newshour*). He's an enterprising young hustler who has moved on the advantages of the post–*Do the Right Thing* moment by offering a marketable display of young Black anger.

Set in the Red Hook section of Brooklyn—inside the housing projects' miasma of drugs, crime, and violence—this movie makes myth out of Evening News pathologies. Young Dennis (Lawrence Gilliard Jr.) is sick of his impoverishment, tired of watching his father (George T. Odom) beat on his mother (Ann D. Sanders). To lift himself out of this misery, he plans with two homeboys, Kevin (Mark Malone) and Larry (played by Rich), to rob a local drug dealer and use the money to escape. All this is laughably pathetic (Rich's imagination seems equal to the meager circumstances of his protagonist), but the way it is played out should not be misconstrued as a raw vision. In *Straight Out of Brooklyn*, Rich's vision is decidedly cooked. It's the same ol' dingy hang-ups fed to us by unoriginal sociologists—a meal prepared with condescension.

*Straight Out of Brooklyn* will appeal to those people who objected to the fantasy vision of *The Color Purple* because the lifestyle shown seemed too clean, too rich, for Southern Blacks. This movie brandishes poverty as the only truth. Rich's ideal of ghetto decor looks more like the spare decrepitude of junkies and drunks than the earnestly pieced-together living space of a struggling nuclear family. If you buy Rich's vision, even the TV series "Good Times" looks like living high on the hog. It's a measure of the changes in social consciousness that reviewers have hailed *Straight Out of Brooklyn* for "honesty" and "raw elegance" when all they're really responding to is the part of Rich's imagination that seems a perverse offshoot of "Good Times" artifice.

Rich bases his movie in the lacunae of that Norman Lear series. His camera setup in Dennis's home preserves the three-wall proscenium perspective of TV sit-coms, but his insistence on realism means this essentially artificial perspective is no more than an angle taken on what he perceives as reality. And Rich's perception is born out of the gap between Norman Lear fabrication and the anxious desire of Rich's generation to connect with the closest equivalent to a media representation of their experience. The result is a humorless version of "Good Times"; steeped in misery, relentlessly dismal, and (the nineties touch) self-righteous about it.

Something fundamentally untrustworthy emanates from *Straight Out of Brooklyn*'s plain, grim view. It is dull and moralizing more than it is recognizable. Rich is faking "slice-of-life" insight when the greatest, most profoundly moving depictions of poverty in movie fiction (Vittorio DeSica's *Shoeshine*, Luchino Visconti's *La Terra Trema*, Luis Buñuel's *Los Olvidados*, Satyajit Ray's *Pather Panchali*, Martin Ritt's *Sounder*) have been the creation of enlightened sensibilities and sophisticated craft. White critics should disabuse themselves of the idea that this film's lack of beauty portrays a sociological essence.

The fact is, Rich isn't skilled enough to convey more fully the pleasures and terrors of experience. There are no camera movements or compositions that evoke a character's feelings. Rich stays aloof from coercive narrative in a subdocumentary way. He suggests that observation has no spiritual dimension. The generic scene of the lower-class hero and his girlfriend questioning life against the skyline of the big city turns into a grim statement of purpose. Looking at the towers of Manhattan, Dennis complains to Shirley (Reana E. Drummond), "They [built New York] by steppin' on the Black man, steppin' on the Black family!" The trouble with this heartfelt expression is that it's merely sincere. Like everything else in this film, desperation overwhelms the viewer. But Rich doesn't understand that Dennis's (and perhaps his own) desperation ought to be argued, built through detail, rather than simply spoken.

Except for the final sequence, *Straight Out of Brooklyn* exists mainly in the realm of the spoken, barely in the cinematic. The white family in John Boorman's *Where the Heart Is*, who struggle to regain their middle-class affluence, played out class desire; it was seen in the details of their behavior and vivid images of their wanderings. Rich keeps Black experience at the rudimentary, prefiction level. The bitter speeches pile up like broken dishes, or the scars and knots that swell inconsistently on the mother's face. Nothing new is said, so nothing can be discovered in this movie. All that stands out are Odom's performance (he suggests Robin Harris's Dad in *House Party* without the resources of a sense of humor and so is always on the edge of disaster), and Drummond's performance (she's an around-the-way girl with a level head; her sanity and warmth are betrayed by Rich's defeatist vision and dank photography which make the semi-nude love scene both dismal and grotesque).

Rich wouldn't be the first young filmmaker to turn a love story into a disaster, yet he nearly ruins the father-son relationship but for the familiar pattern of generational frustration that a modern moviegoer cannot fail to intuit. There simply isn't enough imagination in this movie beyond the hustling it took to get it made and win over the too-easily-convinced executives at Samuel Goldwyn and American Playhouse. *Straight Out of Brooklyn* represents an a priori success for the enthusiasm it has garnered in the film industry and the media. The movie doesn't have to work or mean much, because its ultimate significance lies in the fact that a young Black man like Matty Rich was able to parlay the myth of the underprivileged, determined Black into a socially sanctioned Horatio Alger reality.

This is phenomenal. In fact, shocking. Just consider the examples of truly talented Black filmmakers that the industry has ignored or wasted— from Spencer Williams to Bill Gunn to Wendell B. Harris. Their art didn't fit the view, preferred by the mainstream, that African Americans are a permanent underclass without any self-sustaining culture or heritage. Such films as *Go Down, Moses, Ganja and Hess*, and *Chameleon Street* were enlivened by distinctive concepts, ambitious compositions, a creative richness that bolstered the human value of the distinctive stories. Nothing so organic or instinctive appears in *Straight Out of Brooklyn* until the final sequence.

Yet, Rich's final contrivance is so different from the preceding ninty-minute catastrophe that his aesthetics *and* his ethics come into question.

In this year of new young Black male film directors, the challenge is to find one who isn't already corrupted by the cheap, trite methods of Hollywood filmmaking that reduce experience to formula. That's exactly what Rich has done here but in an uncanny way. The bad sound recording, the out-of-focus compositions, the atrocious blocking that has actors' backs to the cameras, or the restaurant scene in which the sounds of eating garble the dialogue are left in, displayed like battle scars. But the savvy ending reveals these are specious badges of honor and that Rich is perpetrating an almost incredible artistic fraud.

Think about it: He eventually summons skill and discipline only to underscore the nihilism of his fantasy. The ending of *Straight Out of Brooklyn* effects patricide and matricide. It's the result of a naive young man's sentimental misunderstanding of the human crises he pretends to address. Dennis could be seen as an innocent, violently cut off from roots, heritage, and love, but even that angle frees him of responsibility and leaves the audience in a void. Dennis is hapless; Matty Rich isn't, but there's no connection between their contrasting fates. Rich is denying the truth he knows about adolescent resourcefulness. He's preaching down to Black America for white America's benefit. In the world of entertainment, that's the real sign of a Dead End Kid.

*The City Sun*
June 26, 1991

# VOICES THAT CARE— DARE

WHENEVER ANYONE SINGS the "La-da-dee, La-da-da" chorus of "Gypsy Woman (She's Homeless)," nineties isolationism gets subverted. This radical act starts with the fast shuffle of The Basement Boys' neo-Philly house production. The familiar good-time groove suggests that it's morning in America's discos. Then Crystal Waters sings her poignant character sketch, which goes from humanizing details straight into psychotic stream-of-consciousness.

The very infectiousness of the chorus suggests that this isn't a song about empathy; instead, it embraces madness. Waters may never record a track this good again, but she has achieved a pop art equivalent to saintly sacrifice by blending her emotions with the misfortune of others. In this debut (on Mercury), Waters gives up her own persona so that any piety in the song's concept virtually disappears from the aural mix.

What's left is a very simple story that, in the telling, becomes remarkably complex. Waters's singsong chorus inspires such genuine response that the song deserved its dance club popularity. It's not a distanced, ironic celebration of the collapse of the republic; it's an implacably strong expression of human will.

Civilized habits to which the "Gypsy Woman" clings, such as grooming herself in the morning ("Cuz she cares, y'all"), stand in for larger social habits—the routines people practice in the midst of chaos, in the hope for order. But Waters reports these actions in a dry, insinuating tone. Her notes are as flat as Stevie Nicks's, but she sounds as sexy as Lesley Woods, the lead singer of the Au Pairs, doing one of her sociopolitical character analyses.

And just the way a great Au Pairs record like "Diet" cut through individual social delusions ("He works the car / She the sink / She's not here to think"), "Gypsy Woman" also questions the conditions against which people numb themselves and continue to live. The combed hair and made-up face Waters describes could be the happy mask of Bush/Gulf War–era propriety. The grin is hollowed out by glossolalia: "La-da-dee, La-da-da" mocks satisfaction while longing for it.

That's what's subversive in "Gypsy Woman;" Its innate catchiness forces listeners to share a dismay that's so acute it can't be uttered in words, only in sounds—deadpan mirth. The creation of this song may have been fortuitous—like a lot of great records—but the video for "Gypsy Woman" shows that Waters understands what she had done: She performs it with the dead-eyed look of everyday insanity that you see in some mental-care outpatients. There's serious dislocation in her glare; it's impossible to laugh at her. (This formidable acting instinct could be a family trait; Crystal is a niece of the legendary Ethel Waters.)

It is because the record goes far past empathy that it is so powerful. By deliberately losing control of her tongue on the first enunciation of "La-da-dee, La-da-da," Waters creates a sound picture of helplessness as homelessness. Her chorus is inviolable; if you sing it right you can feel your sanity going under. That's the mood of 1991.

The greatness in "Gypsy Woman" makes Kirsty MacColl's "Walking Down Madison" seem relatively tame. MacColl is one of the best song-writers in the pop world, and her take on homelessness is smart, compassionate, and richly performed. From the distance of a Brit observing inequities in the American way of life she finds seductive, MacColl deals out guilt, pity, and anger. Those cards are also in her own hand, and she shows them instead of faking humility as in George Michael's "Praying for Time" or Phil Collins's "Another Day in Paradise."

But homelessness is such a timely subject that singers can't be called brave simply for singing about it. The occasion for easy pathos makes one demand more of any attempt to show sympathy from on high. It is essential to convey the social climate rather than just describe misery, and in doing that MacColl proves as psychologically precise as Waters. She begins the song:

> *Walking down Madison*
> *I swear I never had a gun*
> *No, I never shot no one*
> *I was only having fun*
> *I was philosophizing some*
> *Checking out the bums.*

The subject is not old in those lyrics, but a complicated dilemma is gradually brought to life. MacColl weighs social responsibility against her abstracting intelligence. That always has been the emotional tension of her best songs, as on last year's excellent album, *Kite*, and the 1986 single "He's on the Beach" (a lost-friendship song as amazingly potent as "Gypsy Woman" that Charisma Records should import on the next Mac-Coll release). But the topicality of homelessness somehow renders Mac-Coll's approach more schematic than effective.

MacColl's soft soprano can make sharp insights surprisingly deft:

> *From an uptown apartment*
> *To a knife on the A train*
> *It's not that far*
> *From the sharks in the penthouse*
> *To the rats in the basement*
> *It's not that far*

Still, this brilliance lacks "Gypsy Woman"'s kick; Waters's house track makes history by exposing the limits of traditional, folk-based song craft to convey modern social complexities.

It's plain that MacColl and her co-composer on "Madison," Johnny Marr, wanted another approach, because the song's structure goes beyond its Morrissey-like verses to include two rap bridges (performed by a guest artist named Aniff Cousins). But this shows more strain than street credibility. The rap has only four strong lines:

> *It's a shame to be human*
> *It's a human shame*
> *It seems we've forgotten*
> *We're one and the same*

But that merely states what "Gypsy Woman" proves. The use of rap, though well intentioned, is presumptuous. A second voice on the record only underscores MacColl's distance (she misses the empathy that made "He's on the Beach" unforgettable).

The good news is that she and Marr rediscover it on the song's Club Mix. Marr's lovely guitar figures multiply and gain rhythmic force while MacColl's lyrical strategies take advantage of aural space and, in the room for dancing, becomes a three-dimensional drama.

"Walking Down Madison"'s Club Mix is no threat to "Gypsy Woman," but there may be a lesson in this successful treatment that defines the glory of dance music as much as it characterizes the emotional imperatives of the homeless issue: It is the communal, interactive song form that does the topic justice, aesthetically. It suggests that the people's problem needs a people's art form, not an effete one, to describe it. In a crisis, artists of conscience—Black or white—can't afford to keep their distance. They have to dive in and mix it up; making room for communion and shared experience.

Both "Gypsy Woman" and the Club Mix of "Walking Down Madison" take musical risks. Waters's and MacColl's daring are marvelous demonstrations of caring.

*The City Sun*
July 3, 1991

# A MORAL METAPHOR

OVIE CULTURE finally may have caught up with Sam Fuller, America's most interesting didactic filmmaker. His 1982 film *White Dog*, about the deprogramming of a German shepherd who had been trained to attack Black people, benefits from the mainstream airing-out of racial themes popularized in movies like *Do the Right Thing*. The time may be right for filmgoers to appreciate Fuller's method of outlining social controversy in blunt, intense, provocative melodrama. *White Dog* is now having its American theatrical premiere at Film Forum after being kept out of national distribution for nearly a decade by Paramount Pictures.

Fuller's movie was effectively suppressed as a result of the mainstream culture's cumulative detachment (in movies) and distortion (on television) of racial issues during the seventies. By the time Fuller's film was ready for release, forces both within and outside the industry converged to hush up the onscreen treatment of racism.

The notorious Beverly Hills–Hollywood branch of the National Association for the Advancement of Colored People spoke against the film's showing. In April 1982, spokeswoman Collette Wood was quoted in the press: "We're against the whole thrust of the film and what it says about racism, especially with the rise of the Klan, which always occurs during bad economic times."Strangely, that was sufficient to scare Paramount into canceling its release strategy; *White Dog* showed only in Europe. Two years later, plans to broadcast it on NBC were dropped when Beverly Hills NAACP Executive Director Wilis Edwards also spoke against the film. *White Dog* eventually surfaced on the Lifetime cable network (a liberal limbo), but the damage already had been done: The industry's indifference to the film as a low-budget work with a disturbing theme and the NAACP's unfortunate (and unfounded) panic created a sad farce of good intentions.

The conclusion—liberal censorship—shouldn't be misunderstood as an early example of "political correctness." Both positions grew out of lack of communication between people concerned about race and those concerned about profit. They disregarded each other's needs and the potential for popular art to reflect and influence or effect and improve social conditions. It's doubtful that Paramount would have run scared if *White Dog* represented a large investment of money and corporate enthusiasm. As things stood, the NAACP's interference stigmatized race as a subject for public discussion and contributed to the gross regard of movies as trivial and irrelevant. It made the world safe for garbage like *Cujo*.

The secret perversity of Sam Fuller's movies—from *White Dog* on back to his fifties and sixties classics *Underworld, U.S.A., The Naked Kiss, Shock Corridor, The Crimson Kimono, Steel Helmet* and *Pick Up on South Street*—is that despite his serious intention and earnest political analyses, he never transcends his chosen pulp genres. This is part of his pop appeal and his aesthetic strangeness. The immediacy of Fuller's politics is conveyed by the punchy, terse filmmaking style.

In *White Dog*, the direct, impudent story telling charges right past the pretensions of Fuller's metaphoric conceit. Kristy McNichol plays a young Hollywood actress who, while driving through the hills, hits a stray dog. She advertises for its owner and becomes attached to the animal before discovering it has been conditioned to attack on sight any Black person. McNichol takes the dog to an animal compound called Noah's Ark run by Burl Ives and Paul Winfield. As a trainer-anthropologist, Winfield accepts the challenge to retrain the dog through a cultural experiment; his motives parallel Fuller's.

*White Dog* illustrates Fuller's desire to effect social change through the impact of movie fiction. His interviews during the film's production boastfully promised a psychologically complex character of the German shepherd. But that was just Fuller's crusading zeal trying to articulate the way he would anthropomorphize racist characteristics. Taking the idea of *White Dog* from writings by novelist Romain Gary, Fuller examined the heinous practice of how hatred is taught (to pets in Gary's nonfiction account, to people in Fuller's experience of the world).

The use of the white dog gives the film a powerfully resonant metaphor about cause-and-effect and social conditioning. Fuller's dare is more politically conscious than most movie treatments of bigotry. Think of the silly *Betrayed* in which white supremacists served each other slices of "white cake." It was a stupid detail, typical of the way Hollywood oversimplifies the complexity of cultural custom. Fuller's cartoon-editorial "realist" perspective uses an attack dog to convey cultural malevolence.

*White Dog* features the moral use of a violent idea. The NAACP's familiarity with the meretricious ways of Hollywood fiction probably caused them to suspect the film would gloat over the spectacle of Blacks being attacked by canines. Certainly the same industry that has turned Nazi war crime stories into formulaic thrillers would not shy from twisting the most traumatizing images of Black civil rights protesters under attack into cheap thrills. But Fuller is a more rigorous—and hardheaded—moralist than to sell out his moral outrage.

Much of *White Dog* criticizes the ignorant practices within Hollywood. The most visually stunning scene features McNichol and Lynne Moody as young actresses working on a rear-projection sound stage when the white dog makes its most startling attack. Fuller's subtext scrutinizes the way racist ideas are condoned and replicated unconsciously. Pets and the production of leisure-time art are presented as the agents of loose-cannon racist ideology. Fuller is harshly—if subtly—judgmental of Hollywood's tacit racism.

This may have been what offended Paramount the most. A wonderful Burl Ives scene points out a poster of R2D2 and warns, "That is the enemy." A realization about mindless, inhuman "entertainment" informs this creed, and Fuller's shrewd way of conveying this is proven by casting McNichol as the actress who becomes enlightened. When McNichol confronts the owner of the lost pet and asks if he trained the animal "to be a *white* dog," her reading is peerless.

In the early eighties, following the TV series "Family" and the movie *Little Darlings*, McNichol was an actress of genuine promise. Fuller caught her in career decline to the advantage of them both. Fuller's status as a B-movie master comes from the way he exemplified the brilliance of "cheap" filmmaking. He transgressed bourgeois Hollywood through directness, efficiency, and dynamics. (That's why he's been hailed by Godard and DePalma, who claims *Body Double* was inspired by the camera moves in *White Dog*.)

Fuller's genius for casting the perfect C-list actor also shows in Paul Winfield's performance. He gets the best line in the film ("To me Noah's Ark is a laboratory Darwin himself would go ape over"), and he beautifully illustrates a Black man's secure awareness of the difference between racial pride and moral integrity. A culturally rich moment shows Winfield witnessing the white dog's retreat—after a kill—from a church as portentously, ostentatiously white as the church memorably joked about in *Sounder*.

Winfield updates the character of Black intellectual race theorist that Sidney Poitier originated in the 1962 *Pressure Point* as a psychiatrist battling a racist psycho played by Bobby Darin. For this characterization alone, *White Dog* would be a landmark film.

In 1982, Winfield justified his role and the movie, for *Film Comment*:

I gave it a lot of hard thought. I liked that the story showed a thinking Black man, a scientist who did not react in a knee-jerk way. He was neither an all-perfect Black man nor a clown or a villain. That appealed to me. The Black consultants on the film were concerned about a lot of details. For example, my character didn't actually finish his degree at Harvard; he felt he had dropped out. He was something of a renegade which interested me, but the NAACP representative wanted us to change that. All of those concerns might be valid if you were writing an article for the NAACP journal, but they have very little to do with theater or drama.

Part of the difference between the film and journalism is that Fuller changes the ending of Gary's essay to a more ambiguous one that denies revenge as a solution to racist violence. That's smart, because there's no way to get back at the NAACP or Paramount Pictures. It is essential to let art resonate in society and let artists deal with the most disputatious ideas lest they become clouded with fear and ignorance.

Fuller is the forerunner of such tendentious filmmakers as Spike Lee and Oliver Stone, but his ten-year-old film is better than their new ones. He bites the hand that feeds him; they only bark.

*The City Sun*
July 24, 1991

# DE LA SOUL'S "IMPOSSIBLE" REVOLUTION

THE PAST FOUR YEARS in pop music have been as fertile and innovative as the most legendary eras of the sixties and seventies, but the music press that chronicles such things is typically reluctant to acknowledge the achievements of the Black artists who have set the pace for this era, specifically in hiphop. Meanwhile, the Black music audience that inspires this boom reacts—typically—with nonchalance, taking greatness in stride (letting life's struggles push the envelope of art).

Public Enemy set new standards with 1988's *It Takes a Nation of Millions to Hold Us Back*, an unexpected feat matched the next year by the equally revolutionary burst of creativity in De La Soul's *3 Feet High and Rising*. PE came back, reestablishing its prominence last year with *Fear of a Black Planet*, and that benchmark is now superseded by the new De La Soul album: *De La Soul Is Dead* (Tommy Boy). This friendly one-upmanship (remember The Beatles vs. The Rolling Stones, The Sex Pistols vs. The Clash?) is the peak of a widespread cultural ferment; it happens before a backdrop of remarkable hiphop albums—the Jungle Brothers' *Straight Out the Jungle*, L.L. Cool J's *Walking With a Panther*, Ice-T's *The Iceberg*, L.L.'s *Mama Said Knock You Out*, A Tribe Called Quest's *People's Instinctive Travels and the Paths of Rhythm*, Son of Bazerk's *Bazerk, Bazerk, Bazerk*, Ice-T's *O.G.: Original Gangster*, and countless excellent singles. The abundance should make you stand still in awe.

"Should" is the key word. But hiphop artists seldom get their due regard because their race and their age are held against their ability to create significant work; people seem reluctant to believe that an art form can be this casually revolutionized. It's this "impossible" situation that De

La Soul takes as its subject. Tickled and saddened by their surprise success and the demands of celebrity, De La Soul's three young adults take a fresh perspective on the vicissitudes of Black American life. Privilege, and imagination, have given them an insightful advantage.

De La Soul's humorous approach responds to the pressure to match the last album and outwit the fickle dictates of a public that either defies them to succeed or seeks to devour them. The strain of resentment in this album is shocking but real. Only fools or frauds portray this era as a playground of positivity and righteousness. But the Daisy Age kids aren't spacey at all; they simply confound anyone who is unprepared to relish the coexistence of joy and pain that the group bravely accepts with such, well, grandiloquence.

Most listeners easily grooved to the good vibes of "Me Myself and I" and "Buddy." But this new vision is both more intricate and more complex. Songs like "Millie Pulled a Pistol on Santa," "My Brother's a Basehead," and "Ring Ring Ring (Ha Ha Hey)" may be angry or rueful on their subjects but they are not bitter. Joy and pain interweave in scenarios that are literally fantastic and authentic, combining wild imagination with autobiography. Compared with this, the current wave of Black Hollywood films is not exciting or even interesting.

*De La Soul Is Dead* is made up of songs and endless good beats, but it smashes the concept of the pop single as a contained, distinct unit and makes it a component in a large-scale work. Not merely concept artists, De La Soul has gone from creating a hiphop dictionary to creating a hiphop encyclopedia. On this ingenious, overflowing album the narrative of the group's past two years' experience is made synonymous with the ebb and flow of America's pleasures and fears.

"Millie Pulled a Pistol on Santa" tells a story of incest and domestic violence that erupts into social horror. Deceptively cute, it gives crucial evidence of hiphop's seriousness. The narrative cuts off abruptly, just like the innocence of youth. But a portrait of human treachery and desperation has been vividly etched.

"My Brother's a Basehead" uses the trenchant melody of "Game of Love," and the hook of "Touch Me," to make real the mixed feelings of love and shame. ("Now the brother who could take any drug / Has just found the one that pulled his plug.") It's a paradox that few Black artists have the political confidence to admit. The song's coda expands the sense of betrayal with an overheard colorist insult that queries the general sense of the word "brother."

"Bitties in the BK Lounge" turns infighting into a sexual sitcom. Tracy Chapman's disrespect on the street defines Black America's complex of gender and class animosity. (A kazoo version of "Dancing Machine" also brings Michael Jackson into the debate.) This may be the best example of nonstop verbal wit since "Milky Cereal" and "Cold Lampin'" but it's wilder, heated by the emotions of a male-female argument that cuts all self-important pretenses. This one-act play is a crabs-in-the-barrel masterpiece — a wonder developed out of nothing more than a bad Burger King incident.

"Ring Ring Ring (Ha Ha Hey)" is based on the pesky requests made by strangers wanting to partake of De La Soul's success. Structured around the use of a "non-answering machine," the track conveys the group's candid detachment from the social advancement people envy. The taped voices sound needy, an aspect of Black progress the group never expected, yet the sense of imposition is as strong as the tug of responsibility.

"Talkin' Bout Hey Love," an "Ooh Child" update (and the flip side of "Bitties"), is a dramatic display that chivalry lives, but here it is defined by the girl, usually the patronized object. "Revolutionary Generation" indeed.

"Pease Porridge" turns the macho urge to prove oneself by "throwing joints" into the subject of neighborhood gossip. Layered with a spiffy, tap-dancing soft shoe, it makes a comic defense of musical style as prowess.

Each of these songs codifies the range of modern American life through a particular style of expression: rap as confession, tall tale, satire, love song, and the dozens. For each form De La Soul finds a theme that fits. Their real-life details excite, instruct, and astonish through multiple story lines about the hiphop audience (fans and nonfans) and the group itself, plus a radio show and a talking storybook format. All this makes the album difficult to grasp on cursory listens. The traditions of pop, soul, rock 'n' roll, Broadway schmaltz, house, and jazz are used with a new, intensified purpose. It's a little bewildering, but it confirms the aesthetic sea change of hiphop.

That's why the entire album is underscored by one of the seminal twelve-inches of eighties hiphop, Doug E. Fresh and Slick Rick's "The Show"/"La Dee Da Dee." De La Soul's skits really are a show, but they don't gloss over unpleasantness. De La Soul knows right from wrong; the group has no need to exhibit a psychic split. Throughout their cheerfulness, Rick's voice ("I can't be your lover") crops up at moments of stress, a sociological id. "Oodles of O's," which explicitly quotes "The Show," describes how ambiguous human relations can be in the course of living and making a living.

The ironic title of *De La Soul Is Dead* indicates how hiphop exists as an "impossible" revolution; one that the mainstream — journalists, radio programmers — resist. In numerous tracks the group suffers various indignities (Arsenio Hall, Vanilla Ice) and responds to them with sly, cutting wit. A weird, funny sound effect punctuates the album—it's one word, a name, used as an expletive with different conjugations: *CROCKER*. The reference to radio disc jockey Frankie Crocker indicts the world that ignores their efforts but that must be confronted and endured—always with a sense of humor (the vivacious "A Roller Skating Jam Called 'Saturdays'") and (in "Shwingalokate") with the swing of the spirit that used to be called soul.

*The City Sun*
August 14, 1991

# ASIAN RUT INDEED

ARLY IN HIS FIRST Madison Square Garden concert, Morrissey acknowledged where he was by doing a cover version of the New York
Dolls tune "Trash." He also seemed to be commenting on place when
he launched into one of *Kill Uncle*'s provocative tunes, "Asian Rut," a
song about racial violence. In the song's paradoxes of bravery, foolish-
ness, hatred, and pride, a white artist sympathizes with an oppressed
person of color, but he more strongly identifies himself as a person
trapped among the group of oppressors. "Asian Rut" presents Morrissey
as silent partner, who sings, "Oh, English boys, it must be wrong / Three
against one! . . . I'm just passing through here / On my way to somewhere civilized / And maybe I'll even arrive."

Frankly, I want a stronger statement than that, yet I can't argue the
sensibleness in those lines or ignore their protest and weariness. Their
effect was vividly demonstrated at MSG when a fan—an Asian youth—
climbed onto the stage and kissed Morrissey midway through the song.
Asian rut, indeed. That song—a rare expression of the shame bred by
racism—wins for Morrissey the responsibility of admiration. The Asian
kid's devotion was based in Morrissey's unusual candor and intelligence;
most kisses express ardor, but the kid's wild, determined gesture also
expressed ethical gratitude. It redefined the show.

MSG ratified the moral expressions of Morrissey's singular song
catalogue in a social situation. It made up for the isolation and marginality
in which Morrissey songs are usually experienced, and the need to affirm
the integrity of this music is what compelled the kiss and made it an
awesome, righteous political act.

To hear Morrissey's songs fill the air in a concert context (and to be in
the presence of thousands of responsive listeners) confirms the individual
sense that this is some of the most significant and moving music ever
created. Morrissey's new band thrashes out a mixture of rockabilly
rhythms and punk fervor that is regrettably unmodulated (*Kill Uncle* is
always tuneful and adroit), but it helps clear a space for Morrissey's
particular, personal ethic. Where the recordings were wittily arranged

persuasions, these live performances were more *forceful*. Songs like "Interesting Drug," "Will Never Marry," and "Last of the Famous International Playboys" retained their thrill, while others grew into their proper magnificence, especially "November Spawned a Monster"—an emotional epic about the inner life of a crippled girl. ("Sleep on and dream of love / "Cause it's the closest you will get to love.")

Instead of exploiting misfortune, Morrissey accepts it and extracts an empathetic metaphor about human difference, the miserable thrall of romance and individual dignity.

> *November spawned a monster*
> *In the shape of this child*
> *Who must remain*
> *A hostage to kindness*
> *And the wheels underneath her*
> *A symbol of where mad, mad lovers*
> *Must pause and draw the line*

The rocking, rhythmic waves that follow those lines made real drama of a poetic conceit. In the cascading thunder Morrissey chooses a whimsical outro.

> *One fine day*
> *Let it be soon*
> *She won't be rich or beautiful*
> *But she'll be walking your streets*
> *In the clothes that she went out*
> *And chose for herself*

His offhand poignancy was devastating. This *Kill Uncle* concert hit greatness again when Morrissey covered The Jam's classic "That's Entertainment" as the show's centerpiece. His pleading voice took on an ironic sound of happiness and triumph.

> *Days of speed and slow time Mondays*
> *Wake at 6 a.m. and think about your holidays*
> *Open windows and breathe in petrol*
> *Cold flat with damp on the walls*
> *Yes, that's entertainment*

Here Morrissey lets his band stretch the melody and build it into a raveup as he stepped away and circled the bass player, two guitarists, and drummer. His gaze was quizzical, lustful. As the band began to smash their instruments, Morrissey's private smile offered a sardonic realization about rock-'n'-roll rituals; he satirized extrovert abandon. The band's stunt, with its butch, dangerous appeal, still left the individual in personal crisis, which "That's Entertainment" projected into a full sociological condition.

This complex awareness comments on pop's typical irrelevance to human despair. The indifference has become an escapist institution but one that inspires Morrissey's unique, musical human rights effort.

*The City Sun*
September 3, 1991

# PARANOID LIKE ME

*RICOCHET* ARRIVES in theaters with perfect B-movie timing as a hysterical reflection of real life events. As Supreme Court nominee Clarence Thomas complains about having his reputation besmirched before TV cameras by the Senate judicial hearings, Denzel Washington can be seen on the big screen as Nick Styles, a Los Angeles assistant district attorney battling an outrageous, violent smear campaign waged against him by Earl Talbot Blake (John Lithgow), an insane, vengeful escaped convict.

Rallying his action-movie rebuttal (to be fought with the help of a boyhood friend played by Ice-T), Styles looks to his wife and says, "I am fighting for what used to be my life and you are all of it. Are you with me?" That speech evokes Thomas, but it's also pure matinee-idol stuff, and it resonates more effectively than the "save my life" line in *Mo' Better Blues* that was meant to turn Washington into a romantic icon.

Nick Styles connects more immediately to contemporary experience than did the egotistical jazzbo Bleek Gilliam. In *Ricochet*, Washington has the crazy luck to act out a paradigm of this moment in African-American life: Nick Styles is a put-upon media star, a young Black man who worked his way through law school and the police force (where, early in his career, he arrested mad killer Blake) and is headed for electoral politics under the threat of white racism—an irrational social force embodied in Blake. The always ascendant Washington is perfectly cast; the friction he faces in his own not-quite-superstar career parallels the hindrance Styles experiences.

There probably have never been as many Black media stars as now, and yet the public scrutiny and media harassment they receive neutralize the euphoria of their achievement. For almost every Black celebrity or success story, there is a media scandal that, somehow in the post-Tawana era, comes to seem more than simply the price of fame. It suggests a psychosocial nightmare in which the individual Black celebrity gets overwhelmed by white institutions and racist social forces. This—the subliminal shame of the Thomas hearings—is the reality alluded to by Nick Styles's personal turmoil.

When Blake (dubbed "a true Aryan" by his neo-Nazi prisonmates) eventually kidnaps Styles, they face off in a key, tense, arm-wrestling scene that may be as emblematic of nineties race relations as the clasp of outstretched hands in *The Defiant Ones* was for the burgeoning civil rights movement of the late fifties. Blake's psychotic obsession with Styles suggests the deep-seated animosity the Reagan administration bred in the white working class, who are envious of imagined Black preferential advantages. Race tensions in the nineties are summed up by those clenched fists.

Forgive the pun, but this affirmative-action action movie (its title warns against the hazard of white backlash) satirizes how civil rights developments have created a monstrous sociological nightmare. It's a two-man test of cultural and moral power—a folly perpetrated by the absence of political solidarity among races. Blake expedites the unleashing of conservatism's most debilitating forces—perfectly illustrated in his manipulation of Styles's various images from videotapes, live TV broadcasts, and newspaper and magazine clippings. He wants to cut up and defile Styles. At his most obsessive, Blake photocopies a picture of Styles, blowing it up until he isolates the image of Styles's eye, which inevitably turns into a void of Benday dots. That's B-movie psychosymbolism for the racial panic a white man feels when he rejects identification with a Black person and for the way white media trashes Black people.

These ideas probably should not be travestied in what is essentially a wham-bam chase flick, but the history of genre movies often has revealed complex social truths inadvertently tangled within the plotting of B movies. The freshest element in *Ricochet*, which producer Joel Silver (*48 HRS., Die Hard, Lethal Weapon*) describes as—"an anti-buddy movie," is its racial subtext. It explores two genuine American racial and cultural phenomena: the resistance some whites may feel, particularly at this moment of African-American cultural domination; the resentment some Blacks may feel at certain moments when their pop cult or political rise is disrespected. The best thing about *Ricochet* is that it is weighted on the side of change by being one of the few movies to recognize Black heroism or at least to acknowledge the existence of a Black representative of American progress.

Model citizen Styles isn't a new Sidney Poitier but a young, sexy, pumped-up version of Danny Glover's solid-but-stolid Murtagh in *Lethal Weapon*—the sop to Black action audiences here given three dimensions and Hollywood's seal of approval: glamour. Actually, Washington's powdery makeup and the loose fit of his wardrobe on his newly gymmed body are B-movie cheap, but there's a special essence in Styles's personification of contemporary Black paranoia.

*Ricochet* gets the jump on Martin Scorsese's upcoming family-menace thriller, *Cape Fear*, in the gruesome scenes of Blake violating Styles's home and the various frame-ups that include shooting Styles full of drugs or murdering his friends. Styles's various trials are a distillation of the mainstream's "Kafkaesque racism" to use the term Clarence Thomas invoked and the expressionism *Ricochet* evokes. Beset by a white antagonist only slightly more devious and relentless than, say, Joe Klein, Pete Hamill, Alfonse D'Amato, or Barry Slotnick, Styles in his perplexity makes one realize something that Tawana Brawley, Clarence Thomas, Marion Barry, and Mike Tyson have in common with Bill Cosby, Public Enemy, Leonard Jeffries, Al Sharpton, and Vanessa Williams: their justified paranoia.

With a Black protagonist undergoing the anxiety of a social period when individuals cannot determine the source of their misery except to blame a convenient, immediate other (it's what Blake does and what Styles eventually horrifically realizes), *Ricochet* feels like a classic metaphor for social distress. Instead of *Black Like Me*, it's *Paranoid Like Me*, playing out the current American existentialism.

What Clarence Thomas called "a high-tech lynching of an uppity Black" is the perfect description of Russell Mulcahy's direction. Working from a script by Steven DeSouza, Fred Dekker, and Menno (*The Color Purple*) Meyjes, Mulcahy accepts the social and racial elements but emphasizes the postmodern chaos. A brilliant music video director (Duran Duran's *Wild Boys*, Elton John's *I'm Still Standing*), Mulcahy has one of the strongest wide-screen visions since the French New Wave; he turns every shot into a pop-art panorama. His images have the frenzied vibrancy of movie clips that are all climaxes—like James Cagney's "Top of the world, Ma!" orgasm from *White Heat* that inspires the spectacular explosion climaxing this particular expression of Black Heat.

Mulcahy's other theatrical films, *Razorback* and *Highlander*, were light fun, but neither offered *Ricochet*'s political makeover of Hollywood genre. Race is what justifies this cartoonish spree, in which Mulcahy (invaluably assisted by Alan Silvestri's score) polishes every action-flick cliché into a politically charged, postmodern flourish: the amber-toned prison "sword fight," the bad guys' "Viking funeral" shot in cobalt-blue silhouette. Menno Meyjes's participation links *Ricochet* to the Hollywood racial transformation that began with *The Color Purple*. Styles fights to keep his sanity and his integrity more than to maintain the social order, as did the white heroes of action movies. The difference relates to his African-American status; he isn't just a token Black hero.

A plot development that surely derives from Meyjes hinges Styles's comeback on his ability to remember accurately how Blake humiliated him. Similarly, the crisis of every upwardly mobile Black person is rooted in his capacity to trust the memory of his degradation—that is, to understand clearly his *history*. This serious notion provides the foundation for *Ricochet*'s barely coherent story. The film is a gleaming, admirable contraption arising from truth the same way Simon Rodia's Watts Towers—the site of the film's climax—were built atop the blasted truths of the Watts riot. *Ricochet* matches the pop-art majesty of the Watts Towers.

Producer Silver's—"anti-buddy movie" designation shows the self-conscious transgression of Hollywood formula, but Silver's concentration on the Black-white racial dynamic overlooks the part of the film that revives the old formula: Styles's reconciliation with his homeboy Odessa. Ice-T makes the drug-dealing Odessa a more authentic type than the good cop he played in *New Jack City*; Odessa took a different path from the one Styles took, but they hook up for a cause that is, at least, mythically satisfying. After an audacious kamikaze scene in which Styles advises his old friend to "do the right thing," the brothers come together to combat white racism.

The best seventies exploitation films—*Cool Breeze, Cleopatra Jones*—offered this kind of allied offensive, too, but the total war game was perceived with far less intelligence. As Ice-T/Odessa raps to Blake: "You wanna find out who's really got the power / Bring your punk ass to the towers."

From rap to Hollywood to Washington, D.C., Black folks of different political stripe find themselves commonly embattled by the specter of white racism. *Ricochet*'s solution is not particularly sophisticated, but it lays out the problem in a good—rare— example of Hollywood myth used to express African-American psychological tension. (It would be stupid to think that Blake represents all whites, and captious to ignore the flirtatious racial, sexual equality Styles displays with his boss, Lindsay Wagner.)

*Ricochet* uses more radical ideas than prestigious Hollywood films such as *Presumed Innocent, Homicide, Terminator 2*, and *Backdraft*. When Styles hides his wife and children with Odessa's gang, he says, "You'll be safer with them than you are with the police." Little things like that help to change the action-movie genre from a repository of white, empowered sentiments. The film has an authentic African-American ethos, from the scene where Styles meets his wife to such details as the prominence of *Upscale* magazine. The makers of *Ricochet* are tuned in to the tenor of Black American life; they have no delusions about the system

Styles works within. He may be paranoid, yet he's a few steps ahead of Clarence Thomas.

But make no mistake, the outrageousness of *Ricochet* is why it's fun. It refuses the staid, polite, hypocritical indignation of the Thomas hearings. It's vividly perturbed as it changes the concept of "professional victim" into victor.

*The City Sun*
October 16, 1991

# NELSON GEORGE REMAKES "I'M A HO"

N OW THAT NELSON GEORGE'S personal prejudices have become a part of big-screen cultural mythology, he is more dangerous than ever before. As the co-author and associate producer of the abysmal new film *Strictly Business*, George has put the sexist, capitalist, accommodationist agenda of his writing as a journalist into fiction form.

*Strictly Business* is superficially autobiographical in its "success" story of a young buppie, Waymon (Joseph C. Phillips), at a high-stakes real estate corporation and b-boy Bobby (Tommy Davidson) of the firm's mail room. These alter egos share a typically chauvinistic American male love story, rooted not in the trials and humor of working together but in their parallel dreams of making money and, of course, their partnership in scheming on one woman, a "hostess" named Natalie (Halle Berry).

If *Strictly Business*'s premise itself seems insipid, consider that it's all you get onscreen. There isn't much of a story in the script or any substance in Kevin Hooks's TV-drab direction. The movie is a bald, unprepossessing widget – a worthless product of interest only for its demonstration of George's personal economic hypotheses at work.

With a little wit and imagination, *Strictly Business* might have been as smooth and fantastical as such (uneven) white-collar farces as *The Secret of My Success* or *How to Succeed in Business Without Really Trying*. A little intelligence, artistry – and honesty – might have brought the film to the level of *The Apprenticeship of Duddy Kravitz* or *Shampoo*. Instead, George's interest in buppie "progress" is so single-minded that combined with contemporary Hollywood's opportunistic exploitation of hiphop culture, the film's title winds up being a literal explanation of what's onscreen and how it got there. It's strictly business, not a fun time or a romance or a lesson learned but a cold, dry moneymaking transaction.

The buppie hero's tail-chasing, money-grubbing comedic exploits seem projections of the filmmaker's own psyche, since they repeat George's obsessive celebration of Black professional achievers in his articles for both *Billboard* and *The Village Voice*. George's career has profited from explaining Black culture to the white world but with none of the passion, talent, art, or love that make Black culture worth noticing. In the guise of celebrating Black artists, George the journalist went about procuring mostly positive (and condescending) white attention. (In some circles he passes for an expert.) *Strictly Business* is another of George's acts of love without love.

When Whodini sang "I'm a Ho" there was a good-time mixture of candor, humor, ego, and humility. It was an authentic hound's testimony *and priceless*. "I'm a Ho" showed that even when some Black folks cheapen themselves, they're aware of how they look and won't try to get by on the humble with a false sense of righteousness. But George's fascination with "making it" by any means necessary denies the characters he created (with co-writer Pam Gibson) a single moment as funny or revealing as Whodini's song.

*Strictly Business* pumps the same fallacious success syndrome as the awful *House Party 2*. "You wanna make a power move," slick Bobby tells dull Waymon. "You go for yours; I'm damn sure gonna go for mine!" This horribly reduces African-American culture to its most craven aspects rather than its most honest or humane. Ironically, it shows just how "I'm a Ho" has lost its confessional essence to become the predominant social ideology among Bush-era young Black professionals—the very people who now probably disdain Whodini's expression of vulgar drives. (It's the same crowd that resented *Livin' Large!*)

It's this interest in achievement instead of morality that makes *Strictly Business* offensive. Despite the number of Black folks in charge of this film's image, the characters are gross—simplistic buppies rather than simplistic domestics—not an improvement given the attendant class snobbery. Joseph C. Phillips, an alarmingly stolid actor, recalls the middle-class reserve of the bland young Fred MacMurray, while Tommy Davidson, the "In Living Color" comedian best known for his Hammer impersonation, is a slight actor for dramatic contexts. They have zero rapport, so even the film's key scene—when Bobby teaches Waymon about the fly fashions and down behavior that will get Natalie's attention—never registers as a moment of genuine communication. That cultural transference unites the poles of contemporary Black urban masculinity while hinting that it takes jive for a Black man to get over. George already played this idea in *Def by Temptation*, but there, with better actors (James Bond III and Kadeem Hardison), it worked.

Phillips and Davidson (in fact, the entire cast) are too glib to make these unfunny, half-baked roles into characters. They expose the shallow concept. It's likely George pitched Warner Bros. the idea of a Richard Pryor type teaching a Sidney Poitier type the ways of the hiphop nation. But Phillips's trite reaction to a Harlem insult from white co-workers has none of Poitier's resonant complexity, and Davidson's bright-eyed smirk is appalling and charmless. He distills Black street style to manic stereotype.

As the sex object Natalie, Halle Berry recalls the young Lena Horne. Too bad the role recalls the same self-hating early-Hollywood racial codes that Horne also had to endure. The plot conspires to unite the most bourgeois Black male with the most light-skinned Black female—the same kind of "ideal" Black couple in Oscar Micheaux's preenlightened movies.

Natalie is only a body, not a character. The brothers' business is to pimp her to each other and then to society at large when they set her up as hostess of her own dance club. It's unfair to judge from this exactly how bad an actress Berry might be, but she made a stronger impression as the cursing crack ho in *Jungle Fever*. Trouble is, in *Strictly Business* she still plays (and is treated as) a "crack ho."

All this is part of George's fantasy about Black professional advancement. In *Strictly Business* the characters are addicted to "making it." Success is a symbolic buppie drug. No one cares about art or politics. The movie pushes the idea of making money and joining big corporations because that is the social system believed in by the people who created it, including record producer Andre Harrell. As George damn sure goes for his own, he never explores the pitfalls of American capitalism that disfranchised Blacks know all too well.

It's amazing that a professional music journalist like George still can entertain the fantasy of Black showbiz triumph despite music history's multitude of Black showbiz failures for whom just opening a club or making a record was not sufficient for success or spiritual satisfaction. (This movie misses the complex themes that made GUY's album *The Future* a sensational aural version of a backstage musical, a hiphop version of *How to Succeed*. . . . )

George's disregard of history cannily exploits the naive hiphop nation that thinks signing a contract or getting a deal is all that matters. A music publicist tells me that at a sneak preview of *Strictly Business*, audiences applauded the evasive, superficial sequence of a Black cartel moving in on the white real estate business. (They swallowed the canard that business is green, not Black and white.) I was reminded of the similarly dumb sequence in *Baby Boom* at which a mostly white audience also applauded the sight of a chart with an upward-moving arrow—no details needed, just the idea of success.

And "just the idea of success" is what separates Black capitalists from what used to be called Black nationalists. George blithely has scripted a fable in which Black professionals are eager to join the white system rather than build an economic alternative of their own.

*Strictly Business* is a Black Republican date film (Clarence Thomas and Anita Hill might like it more than *Long Dong Silver*), but it's a "film" only because it was shot on celluloid. Hooks's direction provides no tone, no emotional texture; every scene plays flat and is underlighted. This is a Black careerist's version of *Pretty Woman*'s capitalist, patriarchal lie. The funniest moment is unintentional: when Hooks blurs the sex scene to focus on a burning candelabra as if it were a moment to bless with banal romanticism.

When Black folks seize the opportunity to make a movie as shallow as any by the worst white hacks, it's an occasion for disgust, not pride.

*The City Sun*
November 13, 1991

# SING-A-LONG
# CYNICISM

How can a song as immoral as "O.P.P." be so much fun? The New Jersey–based rap group Naughty by Nature (the trouble begins with their name) have made "O.P.P." the most ubiquitous infidelity song since Billy Paul's "Me and Mrs. Jones." It similarly impresses one's consciousness through a sure, catchy melody.

But while cheating songs are not original, Naughty by Nature add a disturbing new element by being precocious: "O.P.P.'s" melody is based on a piano riff from the wonderful 1970 Jackson Five song "A.B.C." They take bubble-gum pop to the No Tell Motel, a bit of culture shock that combines the issues of teen sexuality and social irresponsibility. "Me and Mrs. Jones" appealed to one's secret knowing, but "O.P.P." brashly admits social transgression; it celebrates, in youths, the urge to sin that conventionally shames adults.

It's no longer a surprise to hear young people sing about sex and romance, especially as hiphop infuses pop music with the most startling social realities. But as the group's name suggests, the accelerated "maturity" that young people experience today puts experience before understanding, so that they confuse society with nature, will with impulse. As a result, Naughty by Nature adopts the criminal charge imposed on African-American youth, accepting wrongdoing as the essence of their being. Their self-titled debut album on Tommy Boy includes several tough-nut songs ("Ghetto Bastard" and "Guard Your Grill" are as delightful and clever as "O.P.P.") that define a proudly embraced bad self-image.

Almost from the beginning of teen culture in the fifties, it has been de rigueur to celebrate a young person's challenge to authority as an expression of his/her lively human essence. As youth culture developed commercially, this idea became a kind of capitalist existentialism promoted through the code word "rebel." William T. Lhamon's *Deliberate Speed*, a recent study of post–World War II culture, lays out the social circumstances that brought about a revolution in the cultural mainstream. Lhamon cites the idea of Negro outlawry as a large part of this mainstream mythology.

Sometime during the course of pop's short history, Black experience became identified as bad rather than different—an analogue to youth experience defined as rebellious rather than suppressed. Naughty by Nature represents the way some hiphop artists have appropriated that white misconception as a way of explaining to themselves how Black youth are stigmatized in society.

The crucial mistake made in "O.P.P." is that social oppression is confused with sexual repression. That explains the lyrics' central conceit: The sophomoric acronym for Other People's Property is used here to objectify both female and male genitalia. Lead rapper Treach first sings, "It's sort of like, oh well, another way to call a cat a kitten" and "It's the longest, the loveliest, I call it the leanest, it's another five-letter word rhyming with cleanest or meanest."

Naughty by Nature's cleverness recalls the juvenile excitement of sexual discovery. Despite an adult-seeming line ("There's no time for relationships; there's just room to hit it"), the song is not a breakthrough to understanding; it's just audaciously blunt. That alone isn't enough to clear the contemporary climate of moral corruption and hypocrisy; instead, the song seems to play right into those moods, and that's what is scary.

To join Naughty by Nature's sing-along feels like giving up because the infectious track goes against one's most mature instincts for trust and honesty. This cynical ditty is about the distrust that men and women hold in common. That alone makes these Jersey boys smarter than Shahrazad Ali, Clarence Thomas, and Anita Hill put together. The best thing about the record is that it doesn't antagonize; it's a *friendly* cheating song, proving girls can be as naughty as boys.

As the emphasis of those genital descriptions suggests, "O.P.P." is based on male privilege. The question "You down with O.P.P.?" usually is answered by a male chorus (the group's two other rappers, Kaygee and Vinnie) who chant, "Yeah, you know me!" or "Every last home B." But the record becomes a community sing when a guest chorus of homegirls (including Queen Latifah and Nikki D in the video) answer the question, "All ladies!"

Women are essential to completing Naughty by Nature's neat trick of moral suasion. The breathy female moan that comes and goes in the song balances Treach's fast-paced ragamuffin rapping. It takes two to be entangled.

"O.P.P." clarifies the mutuality that isn't always apparent in the more traditional slackness of reggae. But this truth isn't exactly liberating and the illusion it gives of a generation unified in sexual duplicity is, well, dubious.

## □   *"O.P.P." POSTSCRIPT*

A friend witnessed a mugging in midtown Manhattan last week. He realized that the young man in front of him was *actually walking away* with a smaller, older man's videocamera, and his shock became complicated as the young thief turned around and winked at him.

That stomach-turning presumption of complicity is just the kind of wrongdoing "O.P.P." fails to criticize. This happy-sounding record confesses an unacceptable truth in terms that are implicitly approving. Naughty by Nature may not be to blame for all the deception, adultery, and theft that occur from now on but their record certainly contributes to the degree of heedlessness with which the pop audience perceives social and personal relationships.

The mugger's wink was a street-theater version of the line "You down with O.P.P.?" It shows the degree to which mindless celebrations of group identity can become repugnant. Naughty by Nature have to find a more substantive means of Black camaraderie. It's virtually impossible to compartmentalize one's listening experience but it is necessary to freeze out most of "O.P.P.'s" insidious message.

With maturity one realizes the human capacity for sin, but that's only a partial insight. Until Naughty by Nature tells its young audience more, they can only broadcast the old news about corrupt human nature. In the end "O.P.P." is, truly, spiritually offensive. Instead of denouncing inhumanity, it winks at it.

*The City Sun*
October 23, 1991

# THE GLOVED ONE IS NOT A CHUMP

☐ *THE OFFICIAL VERSION*

Raised in the Motown ethic of assimilate-and-accommodate, Michael Jackson means it when he preaches brotherhood in "Black or White." Integration and racial unity are indispensable tenets of his philosophy for showbiz success (partly because of the practical need for Black artists to work with white musicians, technicians, and business people, partly because Jackson, no doubt, believes in it). Jackson ain't just whistlin' Dixie, to use an old phrase—in fact, he gives racial unity a modern emphasis, adding a new, shocking sincerity to the politics of crossover.

If this isn't immediately apparent in the song "Black or White"—a very good pop tune that uses romantic expectation as the platform for addressing race hatred and race fear—the video *Black or White* makes Jackson's message clear and buoyant through quite miraculous imagery.

Perhaps because *Black or White* doesn't tell a "story" but is structured in four abstract narratives that flow together mostly on the rhythm of the tune, many people have mistaken the mix of styles for Jackson's personal confusion. Truth is, this is one of the best music videos ever made—probably the outstanding film of 1991—and in it Jackson's articulation of his own consciousness through visual and music tropes has never been more daring, as ambitious or as precise.

Even though the video's credits say "Directed by John Landis," this is significantly the work of an auteur whose image and personality dominate every frame. *Black or White* is very much a Hollywood production, filled with million-dollar savvy and showbiz panache. It is ebulliently photographed and has been ebulliently conceived. The color doesn't imitate old MGM musicals, as Janet Jackson's *Alright* does; this is a brighter, smoother palette, like Steven Spielberg's zestier productions. The slickness and vibrancy generate a cheerful mood, just as they reify a philosophy of benevolent transformation that becomes literal in the video's fourth sequence.

*Black or White*'s uplifting message is addressed to the mass audience in mainstream terms. Yes, that mostly means white, but Jackson is not turning his back on the African-American empirical. He's forgotten nothing; the opening scene that moves from a cosmic, omniscient view to a white suburban perspective reveals a strategy superior to mainstream discourse, one that intentionally manipulates it.

This is shrewd marketing but it also makes a point. Macaulay Culkin (star of *Home Alone* and Jackson's newest celebrity friend) incarnates the young, enthusiastic, impressionable white rock audience. His loud hard-rock listening irritates his father (George Wendt of TV's *Cheers*), who makes a domineering complaint as in the old *Twisted Sister* video (a routine that by now is a classic bit of rock-n-roll vaudeville). The rebellious little white kid then pushes two huge amps into the family living room, turns up the volume and blasts Dad through the roof . . . *all the way to Africa*.

That's an ideological transition, like the crosscutting between Georgia and Africa in the letters sequence of *The Color Purple*. White America's proverbial resistance to the music of savages here meets its Afrocentric heritage. It's the proper beginning of the song and Jackson's entrance here, among a group of spear-and-shield-carrying warriors in Black and white face paint doing a light-footed Watusi dance denies the resistance by embracing the heritage.

Jackson's claim to African roots is in part a universalist act, but the warrior scene also complements the performer's oddity. He fits in as a pop-culture shaman celebrating his own scarification ritual. Yet his plastic surgery effects, mandated by showbiz assimilation, seem to embody the identity of the mass audience. As much as the video's lighting style, Jackson's bright, sharp-featured face, is generic rather than specific. He's bleached for neutrality. Whether or not this is politically acceptable, it certainly wipes away any group's prior claim on Jackson or the meanings he can make in his art. And like a shaman or witch doctor he does service to the world community (dancing with an Indonesian troupe), but he stands alone.

This is music video philology. Jackson ties together the world and cultural history through pop images that come out of his own imagination and his response to media (Hollywood) archetypes. The song's persistent melody gives these fantasies an urgent pulse. Its guitar-based riff has a particular pop resonance of the Rolling Stones and their tradition of Black borrowings and cultural mixing. Thus, the video follows a subliminally predetermined itinerary back to America as Jackson leaps from the African warriors and Indonesian dancers to a sound stage filled with America's first dispossessed rhythm nation, Native Americans. This tumultuous scene uses the same modernist Western mythology as *Back to the Future III:* It travels along an anthropological space/time continuum.

Jackson's Third World tour is not about market domination; he steps out of white suburban insularity to identify with a range of cultural, musical essences. He's after something purer and better than the childish, rockist idea of pop as rebellion. Jackson knows culture is more than that, and he shows it in the video's first sublime image: a pas de deux with an Indian woman performed in the midst of highway traffic with an oil refinery in the background. The zooming cars and the graceful dancing visualize the concept of polyrhythm while the backdrop recalls the industrialization of human energy that defines the pop world. (It also recalls Spielberg's explanation for the design of the *Close Encounter* mothership; he patterned it after a refinery he observed at night in India.)

When that poignant traffic dance is covered over by a gentle snowfall, the scene shifts to onion-bulb Russian architecture, where Jackson and costumed Russians kick through a symbolic Cold War. This scene freezes, becomes a toylike relic played with by a pair of Black and white babies sitting atop a globe. But just before this saccharine image can pall, it turns apocalyptic. The screen is immolated in time to the song's hard-edged bridge and Jackson reappears walking through a wall of flames as he sings:

> *I am tired of this devil*
> *I am tired of this stuff*
> *I am tired of this business*
> *So when the goin' gets rough*

As Jackson parts the flames, images of war and misery haunt the background, but he keeps moving toward us. Finally, pushing aside a burning cross, Jackson shouts:

> *I ain't scared of your brother*
> *I ain't scared of no sheets*

This is reminiscent of the most audacious scene in Madonna's *Like a Prayer*, but Jackson displays a more defiant indignation. And coming in the midst of the video's one-world idealism, Jackson's anger has a stronger effect. (It's badder than all of Ice Cube's vaunted profanities.) This is the tough center of the entire video, it's core of strength. Yet even at his most abstract. Jackson does not lose his grip: Where Madonna and her director, Mary Lambert, sought to subvert the Ku Klux Klan's use of the burning cross and return the medieval significance of the wrath of God, Michael keeps the argument secular when he subtitutes the flames of chaos for the flame of the Statue of Liberty's torch. (The ambiguity of this doubling also reflects on the failures of American democracy.)

A melting pot segment follows where Michael joins Macaulay Culkin and a tribe of various children on a generic city stoop (as in Frank Sinatra's 1947 short film *The House I Live In*) to lip-synch the song's rap:

> *It's not about races*
> *Just places*
> *Faces*
> *Where your blood comes from*
> *Is where your space is*
> *I've seen the bright get duller*
> *I'm not gonna spend my life*
> *Being a color*

That's a rejoinder to the ideas in Public Enemy's "Fear of a Black Planet," and it's just as politically astute even if it's more personally stated. The rap shows Jackson's determination to rise above politics, but this is said in a rap (dubbed by its white author) because that desire, like rap itself, is an intrinsically political act.

The triumphant image of Jackson held aloft by the Statue of Liberty (he strikes the pose of his *Bad* video), negating Barbra Streisand's narcissism in *Funny Girl*, announces a new level of symbolism. As the image widens, Jackson is seen surrounded by the Eiffel Tower, the Sphinx, the Taj Mahal, the Acropolis, Big Ben, and other wonders of the world in a vivid fantasy collage. It's obvious that he is speaking to the world at large, but the less superficial meaning of the image shows that he is equal to these wonders: equally famous, equally legendary, equally "big."

Celebrity places Jackson beyond average human experience, as does his reconstructed face—a scientific feat that may be the eighth wonder of the world. The video's final sequence explains this while summing up the song's universal-international sentiments. It's done with the special effects technique called "morphing" popularized in movies like *Terminator 2*. But this is not just a gimmick; the meanings that are conveyed when one person's face turns into another's transcend the similar portrait surveys in New Order's 1988 video *Round & Round* and Godley & Creme's 1985 *Cry*.

At least fifteen faces are part of this miraculous metamorphosis, some faces appearing just a fraction of a second: a large Chinese man becomes a thin African woman who becomes a red-haired Celtic woman, and so on, in a multiracial, androgynous relay. The subtle physical development shown by the morphing technique combines science and nature, technology and flesh. After viewing this sequence alone, it's impossible to think of Jackson's own facial changes as anything other than an attempt at transcendent humanity. His lyric "It doesn't matter if you're Black or white" now seems prophetic. Charles Darwin should have lived to see this demonstration of electronic genetics. It is a humbling, utterly moving sight.

## ☐ *THE ORIGINAL VERSION*

After *Black or White*'s nationwide, televised premiere November 14, 1991, viewer complaints about the four-minute coda in which Jackson does a violent, sexual a cappella solo dance, convinced him to withdraw it from future broadcasts. Score one for the forces of repression.

But don't forget the significance of Jackson's original act. His solo dance forced the American public to look at the underside of its benighted racial fantasies and to recognize the unruly feelings inside its most popular entertainer. No other African-American artist has dared such a thing (certainly not on the scale of *Black or White*) and no comparably popular white artist has even tried.

It's doubtful if the most devoted Jackson fans were prepared for the coda's display of complex, raw anger. On the sound stage where the morphing sequence was shot, a panther stalks the set unnoticed by the technicians, and wanders off to a dark, misty city-street set, where the panther transforms into Jackson. Dressed in black, with white socks and arm brace, plus a black fedora, Jackson turns his early eighties robotic break moves into Kewpie doll spasms that are jerky, tense (his joints seem to have 360-degree hinges) and finally sensual.

This is a film noir version of Gene Kelly's famous *Singin' in the Rain* number, and Jackson's subversion of that cheerful archetype surely disturbed most people's notion of what show business is all about. But this coda is Michael's truth; his astonishing performance lets the world know his dissatisfaction about show business. There's no music because Jackson, who's been performing since childhood, has no tradition for the musical expression of anger. The distemper ballet is done to internal rhythms; what he can't say in words comes out as the roar of a (that's right) black panther.

When Jackson jumps on top of an automobile and smashes its windows with a crowbar, his hostility is vented against the same object that Godard used to epitomize bourgeois society twenty-three years ago in *Weekend*. Jackson follows his demolition derby with a trash-can-through-a-storefront gesture straight out of *Do the Right Thing* to underscore the social and racial terms of his resentment.

Without this animosity, *Black or White* is merely an excellent video; this bitterness makes it great, because the previous loving message is rooted in an embittered social view. The sweetest sentiments are hard-earned. It is, in fact, a visionary music video giving the full complement of Jackson's sensibility, which, twelve years after *Off the Wall*, shows he has matured into a more confident, substantial artist.

This wasn't the case in 1982, when the nice collection of pop ditties *Thriller* sold beyond expectation and made him a world-class figure. *Thriller* wasn't half as original or intense as Prince's *1999*, released the same time, and until *Black or White*, Jackson always has stood in Prince's shadow. But *Black or White* comes from Jackson's scariest depths, so there's more going on in his angry solo than in any of Prince's brazen but calculated outrages.

Fondling his groin and pinching his nipple, Jackson goes past exhibitionism into artfully rendered obsessiveness. For anyone who had him pigeonholed as a harmless eccentric eunuch, this coda says, "Not so fast! I'm an adult, I got a dick! And I'm angry."

The coda's most amazing semiotic moment is a close shot of Jackson slowly zipping up his fly. The invisible penis is what's called a "structuring absence"—the drive of the entire video represents the thrust of his ego. Until now Jackson's sexual expressions have been either conventional or inchoate but most distinctively so in songs like "Billie Jean," "Dirty Diana," or the title cut of the excellent new album *Dangerous*, which portray an adolescent's guilt and fear about his/her sexuality.

Jackson's struggle to release his sexual nature in his art went off track with the *Bad* album and video in which the leather, buckles, and hoodlum guise misrepresented his sense of himself. Even the video *The Way You Make Me Feel*, with Jackson and an L.A. gang relentlessly pursuing a leggy female until she gives in and giggles, confused sexual harassment with the role of conventional heterosexual courtship. (Or did it?)

Both videos betrayed an outsider's awkward effort to make conformist fiction—and failing ostentatiously. Such populist impulses have constrained Jackson's art as much as they have shaped it; the decision to cut out the last four minutes of *Black or White* is part of the same crowd-pleasing instinct. It also made him turn "Beat It" into a pseudo-*West Side Story* gang drama when the song's true meaning hit somewhere between

Elvis Costello's "Pump It Up" and Prince's "Little Red Corvette"—both subjective fantasies about escape through masturbation. In the coda, Jackson simulates masturbation in three dissolving images that emphasize his furious isolation. It recalls the "Beat It" line "You're playing with your life / This ain't no truth or dare!"

There may never be a day when the mainstream media encourages the serious regard of Black artists that it automatically confers on white artists. Still, Jackson's coda reduces Madonna's daring to trivial folly; his role playing is life's work. The shock of *Black or White*'s coda comes from the unmistakable evidence that Jackson wants to wreck the party everyone throws to the beat of his records.

This solo dance lets loose the frustration built up from twenty-two years of professional good behavior, a lost childhood and an estranged private life. As a critic wrote of Marlon Brando's self-revealing performance in *Last Tango in Paris*, if Michael Jackson knows this hell, why should we pretend we don't recognize it, too?

If it weren't so popular to subject Jackson to Black-fascist and homophobic backlash, people would have no trouble recognizing that the dilemma acted out in the video's coda is essential to the experience of Black public figures. Individually, Black people have to choose between personal culture and white social manner whenever they make professional moves—whether they eventually sell out or not. (And whether they admit it or not. As Jackson sings "Don't tell me that you understand / When I saw you kicking dirt in my eye.")

This is the conflict—not confusion—that *Black or White* psycho-dramatizes. Between his Watusi entrance and his black panther exit, Jackson makes it clear that he is analyzing his own condition. The equality and humanism he sings about is a fantasy and actually less solipsistic than the kind of revenge fantasy Prince concocted in "Lady Cab Driver." Jackson could not resolve his conflicts in a composition as lubricious as that, but he has learned to argue his thesis in impeccably musical phrases. In *Black or White*'s chorus, he imparts rhythmic drama to the conditional terms: "But . . . if . . . you're thinkin' about being my brother / It doesn't matter if you're Black or White."

That phrase, coming from anyone else (notoriously one of Motown's accommodationists who are forever pooh-poohing racial distinction), would be highly offensive. But the sentiment has to be taken more seriously coming from Jackson, who literally has inscribed that belief in his own flesh.

Michael's physical transformation isn't merely a game of truth or dare like the costumes put on and cast off by Madonna or David Bowie. Consider that the one identity Madonna and Bowie have never flirted with is as a racial Other. But their "probity" is more shrewd than judicious; they know the identity from which expressive freedom customarily is withheld. Silence is their ultimate taboo. But silence unleashes the part of Jackson that always was suppressed in song. He dances free of the personal, social, racial constraints that are inseparable from Jackson's Black and human experience in ways that empowered whites may never understand.

It's important that Black folks understand Jackson's physical appearance isn't anything so superficially pathetic as wanting to be white. His greatest desire — which he sang passionately in "Man in the Mirror" — is to "lift yourself" above the common, petty fetters and divisions that affect most people's lives. The degree to which he has attempted this turns the song title "Black or White" into a question about himself — a question made irrelevant by the obvious answer: "Human."

Much of this meaning may be lost if audiences are prevented from seeing the audacious coda to *Black or White*. I've gone on about it at length because the video seems, to me, to be the most significant personal gesture any American artist has made in years. At a time when movies have been mostly shabby, *Black or White* illuminates the zeitgeist. Michael Jackson has given pop culture an unforgettable jolt of seriousness.

The frantic triviality of most pop is represented by the current Hammer video *Too Legit to Quit*, but even Hammer's attempted apotheosis must reflect Michael Jackson's cultural predominance: Hammer posits a make-believe rivalry between him and Jackson and then declares himself the anointed traditionalist by personally conferring with his "godfather," James Brown. But Brown has the best line in Hammer's caprice when he warns, "The Gloved One Is Not a Chump."

*Black or White* proves that when Jackson reconciles the larger meanings of art and contemporary politics, no one else can touch him. He's already charmed the world; *Black or White* shows he has the courage to shake it up.

*The City Sun*
November 21, 1991

# WHO'S AFRAID OF DONNA SUMMER?

THE INTERRACIAL COUPLE at the center of *Servy-N-Bernice 4 Ever* (at Provincetown Playhouse) are perfectly mismatched. Servy, the young white man who talks and dresses real street, loves the young Black woman, Bernice, with whom he grew up in one of New York's Lower East Side tenements.

Now that they are entering adulthood, Servy and Bernice try to regain the idyll of their shared youth, which provided a cultural orientation that seemed to transcend racial difference. But worldly experience— which brings to bear the realities of race and class divisions—forces the couple to confront their personal feelings as sociologically determined desires.

That is, Servy realizes that for all his secondary traits and mannerisms, it's his whiteness that makes him attractive to Bernice. Bernice's moment of truth comes with the discovery that Servy's street style makes him the wrong kind of white boy for her romantic ideal.

She has moved to Boston and tried to invent a new biography for herself among the upwardly mobile middle class, but after romantic trouble, she calls Servy to the rescue.

Playwright Seth Avi Rosenfeld has devised a trap for the children of urban integration and contemporary class wars. This tragicomedy about a white boy falling for a fake Black girl and a Black girl falling for a fake white boy has absurdist classicism. If Rosenfeld had written closer to the bone (providing dialogue for Servy to explain his affinity to Black expression and Bernice to reveal her middle-class compulsions), this might have become a perfect interracial myth—an integrationist Sisyphus story.

But while he sees Servy and Bernice's dilemma clearly, he doesn't probe it very deeply. The most Rosenfeld does—and this is something noteworthy for a white American playwright—is come close to transcribing accurately Servy and Bernice as social *types*. Director Terry Kinney bases his interpretation on this achievement and gets his very good cast to put credible flesh, blood, and emotion into these types.

The supporting players, Erik King and Cynthia Nixon, are both remarkable as the best friends who emulate Servy and Bernice's relationship but without the title couple's neurotic confusion. The lead actors, Ron Eldard and Lisa Gay Hamilton, also are excellent, particularly at illustrating the erotic basis of Servy and Bernice's romantic paradox.

It's Eldard's and Hamilton's sexual presence that gives Rosenfeld's oppositions their dynamic effect. This is the key thing that was missing from Spike Lee's *Jungle Fever*. Eldard and Hamilton give a physical (sensual) counterpoint to stereotypical behavior. Hamilton's sensuality pervades Bernice's bourgie affectations, just as Eldard makes homeboy virile swagger his own.

Eldard's Servy suggests a dramatic variation on pop music's Wahlberg brothers, while Hamilton evokes the "snow queen" dilemma of a demure Tina Turner—say, Donna Summer. These are not coincidental resemblances.

Kinney sets up each sequence with pop-song cues that reflect the influence of Black music as an ecumenical, emotional soundtrack. Making Black pop a part of *Servy-N-Bernice*'s text helps illustrate the ambiguous psychology of democratic culture. It's a large part of the impetus for racial crossover, as Lynda Barry recognized in her own stage play *The Good Times Are Killing Me*.

Barry's play was a safe look at platonic, interracial relations. Rosenfeld risks dramatizing something trickier—the same crossover complications that Donna Summer brought to light in her 1979 single "Dim All the Lights." That year, Summer's bold admittance "Turn my brown body white" was as controversial as the magazine interview in which she explained her romantic preference for white men with the observation that "they smell different."

Bernice's emotional breakdown centers on a failed relationship with a man whose smell she *doesn't* like; the implication is that he is a different "kind" from Servy, to whom she still has an instinctual (aromatic) attraction.

The best writing Rosenfeld does gives play to Servy's and Bernice's inchoate instincts in their pantomimes of pop romantic idols that hark back to their innocent enjoyment of pop culture and their youthful supplication to its suggestion of unlimited, raceless romantic possibilities (although there ought to be some *Shaft* or *Superfly* in Servy's game playing).

These play-acting scenes, in which Servy and Bernice indulge each other's fantasy image of themselves, recall Edward Albee's epochal insight in *Who's Afraid of Virginia Woolf?* The symbiosis of a neurotic couple may be the quintessential modern melodrama. *Servy-N-Bernice* uses this form to investigate the kind of thinking that made Donna Summer's statements seem outrageous *and* what made those statements possible.

As Donna Summer and her co-writers-producers—Giorgio Moroder and Pete Bellotte—utilized their chosen art form, pop culture became an ideal vehicle for expressing complex personal longings. The Donna Summer team gave themselves an advantage over Rosenfeld by not assuming that the wish for emotional, racial crossover was a problem. Within the fantasy realm of pop music (disco), one could be whatever one fancied.

Beginning to articulate fantasy transformation, Summer wrote and sang "Change me bottom to top/ Don't leave even one drop." Ironically, those horrible, self-denying lines have a startling sensual conviction. But the frankness of Summer's in-the-blood despair made "Dim All the Lights" amazing to hear, even as one wished what it said wasn't real.

The song hinted at integration on a deeper level than the sociological. Summer moved into the psychology of identity crisis by accepting the out-of-body, out-of-your-head experience offered by disco culture's libertinism. Getting closer to her desire ("Do it tonight / You know the moment's so right"), Summer took the pop idea of romantic isolation (in the late seventies, typified by Teddy Pendergrass's "Close the Door" and Rod Stewart's "Tonight's the Night"). But instead of blotting out society, she retreats, calling for the obliteration of her identity and, at the same time, evoking a darkness that dissolves all distinctions. (Yet, the singer remains conscious of difference.)

"Dim All the Lights" locks on the point that pop fantasy *does not* transcend social pathology—that's also the quintessential psychological moment in *Servy-N-Bernice*. It raises the suggestion that in the modern world there can be no pure racial-ethnic identity—a reality that was gainsaid by the headlong hedonism of the disco era (and most pop). "Dim All the Lights," Summer's most revealing song, may be her most important because it opened the door on racial-social-sexual confusion, the same thing Rosenfeld attempts in his play.

The nexus of race and sex gives the play a complexity that Rosenfeld isn't able to explore fully. He leaves Servy and Bernice emotionally stranded like Albee's George and Martha, but they are only superficially destitute. Rosenfeld doesn't allow them the recognition of acceptable differences. At the end, they don't seem to really know each other; they just seem to be making do.

*The City Sun*
November 20, 1991

# SON OF BAZERK REDEFINES THE WORD

S ON OF BAZERK (Anthony Allen) presents his soulman résumé on "Are
You Wit Me?":

*Well I am the sure shock*
*The body rock*
*The earth quakin'*
*The disco shakin'*
*The bell ringin'*
*The mornin' singin'*
*The woman teasin'*
*I'm the baby makin'*
*The salt'n'pepper shakin'*
*The water walker*
*The midnight stalker*
*I'm the image for the ladies*
*I'm a sweet-talker*
*The nature riser*
*The hyp-ma-tizer*
*The sweat maker*
*The booty shaker*
*The mind blower*
*The Philly-roller*
*I'm the kid of disaster*
*No one cuts faster*
*The cut creator*
*Most definitely greater*
*Young ladies, huh*
*I'll see ya later.*

Each accomplishment is put into context by the next, even greater, feat. His meter changes as the couplets flow to fit the rise and fall of the song's breaking beats. This isn't just boasting; Bazerk's adept self-description is simultaneously proof of the very improvisatory skills implied by his testimony. Bazerk's bragging surpasses crude vanity and achieves comic heroism. The song's title asks if you understand where Bazerk is coming from, because the sense of his inflated fantasy and glorified prowess recalls a cultural mode so trashy and vivid, a listener may forget to consider that it's also *classical*.

That word still doesn't sound right for pop music, but its meaning as an established, esteemed, lasting artwork nonetheless well describes Son of Bazerk's album *Bazerk, Bazerk, Bazerk* on Hank Shocklee's custom label, S.O.U.L. (a decidedly nonclassical acronym for Sound Of Urban Listeners). *Bazerk, Bazerk, Bazerk* — one of the best things about 1991 — is classical r&b without one old-sounding, staid note, lyric, or shout. This five-vocalist combo (billed as the No-Self-Control-Band) finds and partakes of the rich treasury in Black pop, a culture that keeps revitalizing itself. These young Long Islanders are part of that continual renaissance, adding hiphop's aggresive flair and Afrocentric consciousness.

But be warned: This consciousness carries the understanding that the life force in Black culture is amoral — independent of positive, "correct" attitudes and unafraid of negative, "incorrect" ones. That's what makes a plainly rude track like "What Could Be Better, Bitch?" an unignorable, maybe great, work of art.

Son of Bazerk salutes Black pop's various styles — r&b, soul, blues, funk, reggae, and metal — moving through this history with the same creative drive that inspired each form originally. Listening to the album lets one revel in reminiscence of Stax, Motown, Gamble and Huff, Minneapolis, but these are only touchstones, sounds that evoke the images of an interchangeable cast of characters (artists) from Otis Redding, Millie Jackson, Prince, and Johnny Taylor to dozens of others. The essence, though, might be better identified away from music in the parallel mythology of raunchy comedian Rudy Ray Moore (*Dolomite*, *The Human Tornado*) and negritude poet Langston Hughes ("Tales of Simple").

Each artist assayed a particular style of common Black experience according to his own taste for the picaresque. They both celebrated the vulgar though a proud, ingenious use of vernacular skill. Bazerk's self-assessment in "Are You Wit Me?" comes from the same poetic strain as Moore's Peaty Wheatstraw epics or Hughes's on-the-block misadventures for Simple. Son of Bazerk makes the most of the main differences between those two pioneers: *the record as medium*. He combines Hughes's purely literary appreciation with Moore's wild vocal thrust.

The plain truth is that the greatest African-American art isn't on the page; it's in the air—in sonic waves and gusts of enthusiastic sass and passion. *Bazerk, Bazerk, Bazerk* is proof of this, not just a proposition. The group's passion moves between love and anger, egged on by producer-composer Shocklee's ecstatic sampling *and* live band arrangements, plus each rapper-singer's own linguisitic audacity. There's Son of Bazerk's raunchy soul-man rapping; Prince Jahwell's ragamuffin speed rap; Daddy Rawe's smooth-yet-sharp crooning; Cassandra Half-Pint's spiky, feminine accents, and Sandman's brother-man commentary.

The No-Self-Control Band's name suggests that art is in their fun—they eagerly *perform* the acculturated roles that African Americans long have subverted through personal will and radiance, changing from denigration to definition of self. Admittedly, a lot of this sociological change is wishful, but Son of Bazerk realizes that before this happens, first there is the word: Among "Are You Wit Me?"'s boasts is deliberate use of dialect—"hyp-ma-tizer." Its brilliance is not in the sense of the phonetic change but in its emotional effect—it emphasizes the word *hip* but the change from "no" to "ma" is just plain Black American English warmth. The sheer will evidenced by this change results in a hilarious, wonderful creativity; it has the bursting charge of freedom—for the person behind the art and for the listener who bears witness to his largess.

In "Are You Wit Me?" Son of Bazerk takes on all the jive characteristics the soul man has invented for himself from the beginning of Black pop—the title may even be a spiritual invocation of the ghosts of Muddy Waters, Sam Cooke, Louis Jordan, Blind Lemmon Jefferson, and others. He uses their personae-on-wax as his urtext (call it the Joe Tex).

Son of Bazerk brings these mythologies together out of the same need for beauty and cultural continuity that figured in Bertolucci's *1900* and Andre Téchine's *French Provincial*, two pop-memory movies with the subtheme of folk controlling the shape and meaning of their own history through art. The original title of Téchine's film is *Souvenir d'en France*—a pun on "Childhood Memories of France." *Bazerk, Bazerk, Bazerk* refurbishes souvenirs of Black pop in order to define an African-American essence that most hiphoppers take for granted, misconstrue, and then misrepresent.

Producer Shocklee describes the idea behind Son of Bazerk philosophically: "When you talk about Black groups, man, there's a pigeonhole of what they are expected to be. Not many Black groups are allowed, either from their own perspective or from outside peer pressure, to be pretty much anything they want to be. You have a lot of rock bands that can do and be anything; they can do whatever they want, no matter how outrageous. Well, Black bands don't have that same situation. So Bazerk is designed to go and transcend beyond all of that.

"When you look at Bazerk, you see a little seventies, a little Deee-Lite, a little hiphop, a lot of things in there. I see that group just being extreme—whatever it is, it's extreme. And that's what Bazerk is all about, and the videos and everything else follows that—those methods of extremeness. I know most people think that Bazerk means he's gonna tear up shit. No, I'm saying Bazerk is just extreme, to an extreme."

It's that lack of caution that allows Shocklee and the group to express themselves without musical limits. And their honesty (that's the significant title of the track that closes the album) prevents them from censoring their thoughts and their feelings. The strain of macho chauvinism that the group inherits from the soul man tradition continues into the bus-riding track "N-41" in which Cassandra has to bum-rush the guys in the group to do her strong, flavorful rap. She's a standard-bearer, all right, but when she's cut off (the bus reaches the group's stop), she also realistically presents where women stand in hiphop culture.

The extreme behavior evident throughout the album implies a moral perspective; the shock it produces effects its own form of criticism. This, too, is consistent with the tradition of African-American music. "Trapped Inside the Rage of Jahwell" ends with an amazing audio-verité drama of a disrupted house party in which the host threatens violence. The curiously deleted expletives don't detract from the extraordinary bluntness of his emotions. This cut accepts the full range of heated-up passion—the consequences most pop music denies. It recalls the "Bob George" track from Prince's *The Black Album* but without the embarrassment implicit in Prince's own "censorship" of that album. *Bazerk, Bazerk, Bazerk* shows the difference Afrocentricity makes: Hiphop's embrace of impolite Black culture and behavior heralds a new era of aesthetic and political consciousness.

Sex songs and violence songs no longer can be made naively. Son of Bazerk's extremism boldly proclaims funk and soul archetypes as a kind of African-American stigmata; they are signs of sensual musical ecstasy that derive from the confluence of social and cultural conditions. Note: This has nothing to do with the condescending white deifying of the Negro as social outlaw. (Neat reversal: The magnificent "One Time for the Rebel" is about Black artists who dare to create outside the blurred definitions of pop music. It's ingeniously based on the co-opted blues riff that Led Zeppelin popularized in "Whole Lotta Love" and the chorus of The Isely Brothers' "Fight The Power." This cut, which would seem to back up Black rockers Living Colour, 247-Spyz, and even Fishbone, is so powerful it actually makes those groups irrelevant.)

Son of Bazerk recognizes the contexts of Black passion and creativity; what looks like rebellion to outsiders is simply a way of life – even as it blends into sometimes antisocial behavior. This is an extremely moral view, even though it isn't at all judgmental.

"Lifestyles of the Blacks in the Brick" is a masterpiece that describes a pimp-gangster's pride and revenge with full treachery. Paced to neo-Parliament funk with background shouts and a whining guitar, the monologue is infectious; it has a recognizable meanness, desperation, and glee. Daddy Rawe comes up with one remarkable social detail after another. This is the stuff Blaxploitation movies, from *Superfly* to *New Jack City*, were after, but they lacked comparable toughness, authenticity and sense. Daddy Rawe shows all that in the splendid double entendre "So many keys around here/But ain't no locksmiths."

This is the real ghetto music – edutainment that's not pious. The songs are vivid enough both to describe life and perceive its traps.

"Lifestyles" ends with a daring account of world-is-a-ghetto blues:

> *Yo, Rich, get the back door*
> *This is it*
> *I'm about slash his throat*
> *Then throw him in a ditch*
> *His days is over as a D.A. lawyer*
> *Huh! See this ain't a nice neighborhood*
> *For ya!*
> *He tried to buy some white collar drugs*
> *Coke, crack or smack*
> *Or whatever the hell it was*
> *He had to climb the ropes of Hell's Kitchen*
> *The cop*
> *Now he's one dead cracker*
> *On the Brick city bus*
> *I put my blade in your guts*
> *'Cause you wasn't honest*
> *Now you're laying face down*
> *Bathed in blood*
> *Ho money*
> *Sho money beats no money*
> *They turn so many tricks*
> *But that's my money*
> *I keep my razor by my side*
> *'cause that's my ho*
> *And if the dough ain't right*

*Then I cut her B-12*
*Fryin' chicken for the Brick crew*
*Lifestyles of the Blacks in the Brick*

That's appalling and wonderful—a song in a wide-open moral space without the self-saving restrictions of a record like Geto Boys' "Mind Playing Tricks on Me." It's also the flip side of "Are You Wit Me?," but the question no longers needs to be asked because the suggestion of white duplicity and home cooking spring authentically from Black experience. So do the violence and sexism—all of it the legacy of countless Saturday nights.

Of course, there's no Sunday morning; the hiphop era has no concept of redemption. "Honesty," however, ends the album calling for an end to the mind games used to justify all sorts of behavioral stereotypes. It's a different kind of love song, and that's as basic and profound as a pop-music innovation can be.

*The City Sun*
December 11, 1991

# A NEW WAVE EBBS

I T LOOKS LIKE everything is in place for American film culture's most exciting display of new talent and upstart sensibilities since the seventies renaissance–only this time by African-American filmmakers. Afrocentric fervor has emerged from a politically regressive decade: There's a wellspring of musical creativity to offer inspiration; plus the support of film industry speculators. Everything is set–everything except a new school of critics who can demonstrate a feeling for non-Hollywood styles and nonwhite artists. Above all, critics who can lead public thinking and discussion about these movies toward a meaningful understanding of art and politics.

For most people who read about film–whether newspaper reviews, magazine articles, books or quarterly journals–the perspective they get is usually white. The problem is, that's never specified. So the particular experiences, politics, and biases that go into a writer's responses get mistaken for "common sense." But the history of American film criticism is an accumulation of these subjectivities. Ideology passes for essence. That explains why people can talk about "Black movies" without ever having defined "white movies," and Black artists wind up separated from the cultural mainstream.

In politics this is called segregation, in film culture it's called taste. All filmmakers share this problem but it devastates Black filmmakers–as proved by the poorly attended premiere of Wendell B. Harris's *Chameleon Street* sandwiched in between *Citizen Kane* and *Paris Is Burning* at the Film Forum. Poised–with perfect irony–between an aesthetic breakthrough and a view of a different world, *Chameleon Street* never got the attention of the counterculture audience it deserved. It fell through the racial gap that has always existed in film culture.

This is a bigger problem than Georgia Brown's hostile *Chameleon Street* review in *The Village Voice* that gave short shrift to its racial meaning. The trouble goes back further than the film's entry two years ago into the festival scene, where it was rejected by both the Museum of Modern Art's New Directors/New Films series and the Film Society of

Lincoln Center's New York Film Festival before winning the Grand Prize at the 1990 Sundance–U.S. Film Festival. This mixed reception for such a daring and witty film suggests a familiar cultural unease. Some call it racism, some white supremacy; what Richard Corliss, guesting in *Premiere*, called Eurocentrism, then boasted "guilty, friend, guilty." From his regular *Time* magazine perch, Corliss wrote last month a roundup of the independent films for select audiences currently on the art-house circuit, conspicuously omitting *Chameleon Street*.

These slights can't be ignored as just personal reactions. The indifference shown *Chameleon Street* by New York film circles is a cold, tonier version of the frantic hostility that greeted Spike Lee's *Do the Right Thing*. In both cases the guardians of film have resisted serious work by Black film artists by taking positions that confuse politics for aesthetics. Their fear has been shameless: David Denby turned editorial writer and false prophet to nix *Do the Right Thing*; Rex Reed appeared on TV urging Black kids to go see *Batman* instead, merely verbalizing what many critics had already said in print.

All these incidents are the true signs of an impoverished film culture that keeps looking to Europe and Hollywood for saviors. But Europe and Hollywood are exhausted. The future of film art must be in our cities, not our institutions. Unfortunately, critics who lack the cultural confidence to admit this are more accepting of a leftist film from Eastern Europe than a Brooklyn-based showdown. Without saying so, they insist that Black filmmakers deny their own experience and espouse the same homilies as white filmmakers. It's pre-civil-rights-era aesthetics derived, no doubt, from the delusion of film as a mass art for a unified society. But no one who made it through the eighties can reasonably think movies are still a democratic art form. That was a shaky idea even for D.W. Griffith, and for Steven Spielberg, too. *The Color Purple* (1985), Spielberg's experiment in narrativity, should have inaugurated a new era in pop film theory, inspiring critics to rethink the tropes they subconsciously associate with white/Black narratives or feminist/pre-feminist literature. Instead, reviewers conveniently dismissed *The Color Purple* as bad Disney, quickly sidestepping the racial politics of movie history that were Spielberg's real subject.

In 1985 pop critics played dumb; today there's an easier out—they can give their attention to movies like *Poison, Begotten, Paris Is Burning*—all worthy films that just happened to be made by whites but that, most important, avoid the kinds of confrontations that a racially oppressed artist might explore. The irony is that sexual oppression is easier for critics to deal with than racial oppression. It's asking a lot for a contemporary bourgeois—which every critic is—to be sympathetic toward film implicitly about class struggle, yet the least a journalist-critic can do is show some curiosity. But social politics and racial politics, which began to figure in reviews of 1960s New American Cinema have lost glamour; now sexual politics are favored on the critical tip. And it's Ishmael Reed's nightmare come to life when Wendell Harris, a very shrewd cinéaste, makes sly use of both the history of Ida B. Wells and the contemporary rhetoric of Haki Madhubuti but is vilified as misogynist by the alternative press. Feminism has become another excuse for denying racial impera- tives as a legitimate film subject. (Harris shouldn't have to pass a NOW or NAACP exam to be taken seriously. Besides, where would movie art be without the rich ambiguities of Welles and Peckinpah on sex, Griffith and Scorsese on race?)

Under the heading "There are none so blind as those who will not see," film critics come first. Their blindness—it's not metaphorical and it's harsher than disinterest—condemns even a movement of young Black filmmakers to be ghettoized. The appellation "Black film" that turns up in current trend pieces has the same categorizing limits that made James Baldwin flinch thirty years ago when he read the terms "protest fiction" and "problem fiction." Labels are for control, not description. In film culture they are a way of denying Black moviemakers any pure artistic status while defusing their visions as special pleading.

That any of this should not seem so only proves how effectively our film culture has exercised its indifference to the work of African- American artists and domestic films about people of color. No film critic has been brazen enough to rephrase Saul Bellow's "Tolstoy of the Zulus" faux pas. (At least, not yet.) But the way reviewers ballyhooed the commercial re-release of *Citizen Kane* while giving perfunctory notice of *Chameleon Street*—the most vital American movie so far this year— presents the same problem. Critics don't have to reiterate Welles's genius but they need to be alert to what is essential in the art of their times, to the way new filmmakers express ideas and imitate the perplexing or profound qualities of life.

Certainly America needs some Black film critics—not a moonlight- ing Ivy League prof with the right bloodlines, a rock-'n'-roll refugee with a credible hairdo, or even an ax-grinding freelancer but someone (this may sound radical) *who knows film*. That's never been a high priority in the media, but nothing beats it. What too often replaces knowledge is a parochialism (critics trapped in their own backyards) and hack journalists ready to buy whatever's being sold.

Reviewers don't need to be omniscient—sensitivity will do. But that's not guaranteed by race either. It's an ongoing emotional and intellectual process that can make a *Daily News* review more perceptive about *Chameleon Street* than any of the Black monthlies, or that makes *The City*

*Sun* and *The New York Times* celebrate the 1986 Brixton comedy *Black Joy* when most other reviewers in town look away, consigning a remarkable film on diaspora culture to the land Hollywood forgot. Given this record, a generation of new Black filmmakers badly needs a generation of film reviewers who are not enslaved to Hollywood orthodoxy, but who can see that or hodoxy is to blame for both the shallow melodrama of *The Five Heartbeats* and the primitive neorealism of *Straight Out of Brooklyn*. If there are filmmakers with the guts or the inspiration to put a frame around their individual view of the world, like Wendell Harris, or attempt creating their own syntax like Julie Dash with *Daughters of the Dust*, it may require a compatible critic who has a cultural headstart to accurately describe the effort. This is too crucial a period in American cultural history to be left to fools.

Ideally, this would have been a Sunday *Times* Arts and Leisure article offering a firm, reassuring report that the obvious racial segregation in film discourse was changing. But the problem isn't obvious (the same ignorance infects New York's sports media, where there are no Black columnists) and it isn't changing—not even with a new wave of Black filmmakers about to flood or fade. And exactly how this wave measures up will be determined by the attitudes, the predispositions, of those who write its immediate history.

History and provenance are at stake here, matters more serious than whether a homeboy or Arnold will provide $7.50 worth of summer's distraction. Until now, film culture, despite its populist aura, has been able to keep its hall of fame and its library of theories all white by the simple expedient of criticism that determined what is important. (Beneath the acclaim for *The Silence of the Lambs*, it whispers: *"Hallelujah!*, Spencer Williams, *Intruder in the Dust*, Sidney Poitier, *Sounder*, William Greaves, Bill Gunn, *Killer of Sheep*, *The Color Purple*, *Sign o' the Times*, *Do the Right Thing*, *Glory* and *Chameleon Street* don't really matter.")

That power to actively influence culture, from the courses taught in film schools to the queues in front of theaters, has never been entrusted to a Black person in a mainstream medium and rarely to anyone who would not defend the status quo. Museums and publishing companies guard this power dearly; it's worth more than the films themselves, because even in a postliterate world, thought and language are the foundations of culture. There's never been a real new wave that didn't bring in a new generation of critics. They have to sweep away the fossils. Pleading guilty to Eurocentrism only allows white critics to continue their antipathy toward Black artists and their favor of white artists. And that's an unpardonable offense.

*The Village Voice*
June 1991

# YOU GOTTA BELIEVE
# MARKY MARK

ARKY MARK WAHLBERG has the best definition of any white rapper—
meaning that he doesn't just have better pecs than 3rd Bass or drop
his drawers with more style than The Beastie Boys drop science,
but that he defines hiphop as a Black cultural movement. His brashness
does not distort the music's essence.

> *Alright, alright*
> *What an odd sight*
> *Here's another MC whose skin is white*
> *A white kid, a white boy*
> *With a white voice*
> *Just like The Beastie Boys and 3rd Bass*
> *Hmm. This looks like a topic for discussion*
> *To build racial tension*
> *For fussin' and cussin'*

Such honesty makes him the first white rapper to dispel derision. A
Marky Mark record and video proudly acknowledge their derivation
from Black culture. There's a paradox here: When white artists give
Black pop its proper homage, there is still a limit to how far they can take
their appreciation. This isn't determined by the artist's ability or the
audience's acceptance but by the artist's own imagination. They must be
able to borrow without losing sight of themselves as borrowers. The
secret is attitude and the attitude must be shared (as California's Latino
rappers Cypress Hill show) before any mannerism can be copied.

From the release of his initial single with the group The Funky
Bunch, "Good Vibrations" (featuring vocal excitement by Loleatta Holloway), Marky Mark has shown a genuine understanding of hiphop style
and politics. By giving Holloway respect (providing her the visual presence Martha Wash was denied by Black Box and C + C Music Factory),

Marky Mark transcended the obvious need for street smarts and hooked up with hiphop's earlier, dance-music influence.

Since it is impossible for any white rapper to achieve originality (the axiom "Too Black, Too Strong" becomes "Too White, Too Late") attempts at combining identification with imitation (such as 3rd Bass's "Steppin' to the A.M.") wind up disingenuous. When 3rd Bass automatically assimilates street slang and fly rhythm, it is automatically suspect. But on "Good Vibrations," Holloway's sizzling, piercing growl, which reduces all listeners to stupefaction, made Marky Mark's "difference" a pertinent fact. He seemed justifiably awed yet game—a white rap boy up against the gale force of sensual Black art. Speaking between Holloway's chorus, Marky Mark played out a good-natured cartoon of the racial-sexual envy that makes whites blush.

Call it a secret shame, perhaps, because this race-sex thing is rarely gauged properly by the mainstream without shifting the balance of cultural authority. Marky Mark's youth and callowness, relative to Holloway's age and power, is almost a mythical demonstration of white desire and Black fecundity. The multiethnic, largely Black Funky Bunch (a six-person crew that includes two women) helps maintain Marky Mark's cultural context. That's usually the first thing denied by white crossover acts and counterculture theorists like the Beats and Norman ("The White Negro") Mailer.

This cultural egotism is the main thing Mark learned to avoid from the example of his older brother Donnie Wahlberg of the insufferably derivative New Kids on the Block—a group that could succeed in pop but never in rap. Donnie Wahlberg produced Marky Mark's debut album *Music for the People* (Interscope) and co-wrote most of the tracks. This funk-heavy album fulfills the hiphop ambition Wahlberg showed on "Games," the 1990 rap single from the last New Kids album. The other *Music for the People* tracks stay within proven Black pop formulas. (In 1994 the group acronymized its name to NKOTB and released a lame imitation of Snoop Doggy Dogg's sexism called "Dirty Dawg.") For instance, the second and third singles, "Wildside" and "I Need Money" were essentially cover versions of records already marked with strong ethnic referents.

Like many younger siblings, Mark dives into the depth of his older brother's commitment to Black pop, but the surprise on *Music for the People* is the breadth of the Wahlbergs' pop savvy: from the intense house of "Good Vibrations" to the sex rap "Make Me Say Ooh!," which uses only the revving-up bits of Marvin Gaye's "Let's Get It On." Marky Mark's whispered rap bites L.L. Cool J's loveman pose, yet he gets over, because how many white kids would know the right Gaye parts to use? This show of instinct seems impressively genuine in a third-generation pop addict. It doesn't discredit Marky Mark, but it clarifies the passion for Black pop that one hears in his records.

White communion with Black style is nothing new, but Marky Mark perfects it—politically, if no other way. This happens as a benefit of Marky Mark's naiveté, something that a producer as smart as Hank Shocklee can't quite manipulate. Shocklee's white rapper projects, Young Black Teenagers and Kid Panic and the Adventures of Dean Dean, are too "Black," too slick. The amazingly inventive productions for these groups (Young Black Teenagers was a test run for the soundscapes Shocklee perfected with Son of Bazerk) strained the white rappers' plausibility. A similar anxiety effects the musical inventions of writer-producer Sam Sever (3rd Bass and his own duo Downtown Science), which can't be called innovative without choking on the word. Clunkier funk, like Marky Mark's or The Beastie Boys', would have been a more credible mode for these white rappers.

Shocklee gave his acts more sophistication than the public could recognize—or even wanted to. Such semi-adept white rap provokes a tricky debate about cultural authenticity. Rap performance and linguistics connote particular social, ethnic experience. The use of this idiom is not a right to be earned but a given. For the middle-class, suburban Black kids who assume street manner and philosophy, it implies a particular knowledge and empathy that is assiduously maintained by social circumstances, if not genetics.

For the moment, rap's codes are inimitable; that's why TV and radio commercials can parody rap without diluting its potency. White rappers who try so hard for Black style confuse the music's communication. Gerardo, J.T., even Falco may know the form but not the essence. And though their tone may get close, their intent is unclear. The issue is not whether there is good music or acceptable rapping on *Radioactive, The Cactus Album, Young Black Teenagers, Licensed to Ill* or *Music for the People* (there is) but whether these records can give comparable pleasure and enlightenment.

It's difficult to actually *hear* some of this music, because the impetus for it is unknown, its purpose uncommunicated by the halting meter and the white voice (as Marky Mark identified) trying to pass as nothing unusual. Hiphop is such a rich culture that its audience can thrive without paying attention to white rappers. But instead of dismissing this white subgenre, it's best to understand that the audience is not indifferent. It's just that its needs (which will determine the shape of hiphop to come) preclude any records or artists who are shams.

Hiphop has so many styles that it can't be accused of racial exclusivity, but its ethnic specificity is crucial. Rap's seemingly casual expression actually developed as the careful, forceful, personal articulation of social groups without access to America's dominant language and media. Even records as disparate as Young M.C.'s "Bust a Move" and Naughty by Nature's "O.P.P." are informed by this expressive urgency. Both evince an African-American yearning to claim, protest, enunciate. The significance of speaking—as an expression of identity and a form of power—gives hiphop endless fascination.

In Ed O.G. and Da Bulldog's "Speak Upon It," the Boston-based group perform the necessary function of interpreting history and recording it for the artists' sanity and the audience's awareness. "Speak Upon It" retells the Charles Stuart scandal in which a white Boston man killed his pregnant wife for an insurance settlement. Stuart's claim that a Black man murdered his wife provoked a police riot by the Boston municipality in which an innocent Black man, William Bennett, was arrested and charged with the killing. Ed O.G.'s account of this social disgrace is as serious as Scripture; his purpose is to make sense of an unjust world if only by keeping this horrible tale fresh. It is instant folklore made eternal by the rapper's intensity and a blues-righteous backing track.

"Speak Upon It" is a classic example of what makes hiphop special; it contains a mythmaking, muck-raking imperative about racial and social affronts that white showbizzers cannot be expected to have, an anger they dare not show. Unexpectedly, Marky Mark's "Wildside" makes the grade. Of course, "Wildside" can't match the deeply pleasurable nuances of Ed O.G. and Da Bulldogs (their "Gotta Have It" and "Bugaboo" show the rich, humorous foundation for their ethnic identity), yet it is a remarkable display of empathy and a strong polemic.

On "Wildside," Marky Mark narrates several real-life tragedies, but the Stuart case is the song's center. Hearing its details relayed is proof of Marky Mark's social consciousness. His voice isn't mature enough to sound bitter, but his sense of outrage gives this Boston Irish kid an undeniable emotional link to Ed O.G. and Da Bulldogs. Marky Mark's hiphop consciousness in "Wildside" is another form of homage, this time to the political status of African Americans that even whites are coming to share. The video begins matter of factly with a burning American flag— the kind of inflammatory image Marky Mark was able to get past MTV censors after 2 Black 2 Strong & the MMG's *Burn, Baby Burn* video was stopped.

Marky Mark's racially enlightened social protest is also an advance for white pop, as demonstrated by "Wildside's" bassline from Lou Reed's "Walk on the Wild Side." Bad boy Marky purposefully follows Reed's lawless example, but he stops short of Reed's bohemian white-negro tradition. "Wildside" covers Reed studiously but leaves out his chorus intro "And the colored girls say . . . ." This is intentional and smart for its implicit Afrocentric acknowledgment. There's no exoticism in Marky Mark's crossover; he maintains his own identity without circumscribing an Other. (This healthy approach to pop means he'll never have to cover Reed's masochistic-racist "I Wanna Be Black.")

"Wildside" speaks on a level of social identification that hiphop represents better than any other contemporary art form. (The video for Marky Mark's antigreed screed "I Need Money" boldly spotlights the era's villains, starting with George Bush, Charles Keating, and Michael Milken and ending with Ronald Reagan.) Marky Mark touches realities that more adept white rappers, like Jesse Jaymes or Kid Panic, avoid. His empathy allows him to express the tension felt by the new, vocally empowered white working class. Songs like "Wildside" and "I Need Money" provide cross-racial, emotional solidarity; it's hiphop with a purpose, not just radio fodder. Marky Mark isn't simply in it to win it.

Young Black Teenagers' best track "Daddy Kalled Me Niga 'Cause I Likeded to Rhyme," only added to the racial static it attempted to calm. There may be no resolution to the cultural tension provoked by the class and race divisions of rock 'n' roll and hiphop, but the integration happens best when it happens unostentatiously, as in De La Soul's sampling of Wayne Fontana and the Mind Benders on "My Brother's a Basehead" or Marky Mark's "Peace."

Marky Mark relishes that hiphop salutation for more than fun. He poses its ameliorating notion against the "racial tension" and "fussin' and cussin'" he knows he will provoke in some whites and Blacks. His hiphop gregariousness extends to the white b-boy image he cultivates: backwards cap, exposed muscle, peekaboo briefs and low-riding jeans.

Since whites can't cut it vocally in hiphop, where the texture of African-American speech is as musical an element as the samples used, the visual image is all important. Marky Mark knows that the white assumption of this image is the reason he and Vanilla Ice and Gerardo exist and prosper—they're the nonBlack mediators of hiphop aesthetics. But he avoids this racist trap by dint of his boyish, cartoon eroticism. No match for the sexual images of L.L. Cool J, King Sun, Chuck D, Big Daddy Kane, or Treach, Marky Mark instead simulates their swagger and energy in a way that's as amusing as it is flattering.

Marky Mark delineates how new styles of white fashion result from cultural transference; his hiphop-era innocence presents something new: working-class confidence that proudly maintains the source of witty behavorial innovations without trading it in for middle-class snobbery (his good-sense *Interview* magazine statements on class).

If Public Enemy represents Blackness as (among its many meanings) a metaphorical condition recognizable to any unempowered person, Marky Mark underscores that proposition. He says "peace" in imitation of hiphop attitude, but it's also fellowship, his communion with home-boys as social and ideological neighbors. Marky Mark takes such honest pleasure in hiphop phrases that when his voice goes surfer-boy flat saying "wooord!," he still demonstrates the process by which slang moves through culture from Blacks to whites and between generations. Marky Mark himself becomes the site of racial/cultural exchange.

Marky Mark's style may be transparent (the underwear bit suggests that he knows white sexual fear and racial naiveté are inseparable from his success), but his effort is forthright. Marky Mark's manner and delivery capitulate to Black style in ways that Vanilla Ice and Tairrie B. don't. It's flattery with intelligence, and on "So What Chu Sayin'?" he defines the entire racial/aesthetic complex of white rappers:

> See, some do hiphop and forget how it started
> They claim their white complexion
> Ain't the reason why their records charted
> Please!
> Man, it's so easy to see
> When a white dude raps
> The public calls it a novelty
> Even me, although I take it seriously
> Some dislike me because of my r-a-c-e
> But I won't quit and I won't stop
> 'Cuz I do hiphop just because I love hiphop
> I never claim to be vanilla
> I'm Irish American
> And never did I claim to be African American . . .
> With respect to the Old School
> That created this art form
> It comes from the heart
> Not from critical acclaim
> 'Cuz that's just the same as the political game.

If hiphop can inspire a white American kid to such cogent cultural analysis that shows respect for others and sees politics even in rock criticism, it surely will outlast all its detractors. Marky Mark makes the prospect of All-American rap a little less frightening.

At the moment Marky Mark disgraced his rap credbility by selling it out to a racist Calvin Klein ad, he released his best record. "You Gotta

Believe" (again produced by brother Donnie) confirms Marky's naive rap faith, but it doesn't take off until female vocalist Darcelle Wilson wails encouragement and Marky delivers his most urgent, rhythmic rap. It makes a good farewell disc, insisting on Marky's good intentions in the face of the media's backlash expose of his juvenile-court rapsheet for ethnic and gay bashing. It's a pitiful end for what should have been a happy American story, but this disc shows it's still a classic story.

Marky's growth out of white Boston's racist, insular environment into being a front man for an integrated rap group and a gay icon is the bildungsroman that American fiction celebrated before hiphop. Now, with new nonwhite examples of Horatio Alger (superficial) success, Marky seems to be doing penance for nothing more than reminding the larger society of its hypocrisies—the race baiting and gay bashing that white males indulge in as a rite of passage and big business's noxious exploitation of sexuality. Now the insincerity includes appropriating Marky's rap bona fides (and showbiz gimmickry) and attempting to convert it into images of white erotic supremacy. A Black rapper's sexuality would upset the balance of trade, even though the nasty look of a white thug rapper like Everlast is equally threatening. Marky conveys the innocent dumbness of probably most white rap aficionados. His very innocuousness has been turned against him. And still he insists, for the best reasons you can imagine, "You gotta believe!"

*The City Sun*
February 12, 1991

# LIES AS TRUTH

M ORRISSEY SAID IT BEST: "In our lifetime, those who kill/The news world hands them stardom."

The complete corruption of contemporary movie culture has been brought to light by *Bugsy*. It's a factitious biography of the gangster and killer Benjamin Siegel, focusing on his involvement in Hollywood in the 1940s and his "invention" of Las Vegas (a story told better in the Moe Green scenes of *The Godfather*). Siegel's interest in leisure activity as the end point of his social ambition provides screenwriter James Toback with a fake postmodern irony. This ass-backward view suggests that Siegel's individual drive separated him from the venality and shallowness of these mainstream institutions and made him, somehow, an existential hero—rebellious man pursuing a great vision, and at tragic, personal cost.

This is a simple, obscene lie, but Toback has gotten away with it (to judge from the film's critical acclaim and ten Academy Award nominations) by imitating his fantasy of Siegel's quest. *Bugsy* is the ultimate telling of the spoiled genius/Jewish gangster tales Toback has been making on his own (usually with Warren Beatty as a behind-the-scenes, uncredited producer) in such films as *Fingers, Love and Money*, and *The Pick Up Artist*. Those were extremely idiosyncratic movies, full of ethnic compulsion, strained technique, and effortless naughtiness. (Toback lacked the finesse to be gauche, yet he could be disarmingly gross as in *Fingers'* poolside seduction speech about erotic textures.)

Toback's films had a rude honesty that might have seemed original if Norman Mailer hadn't already polished off raunchy intellectualism, but it was enough to keep Toback on the fringes of the film industry. With *Bugsy* Toback gives in, selling short the ethnic subtext of the films he personally directed, and goes mainstream. The one filmmaker interested in the sexual and ethnic peculiarities of social behavior—who believed in the psychological and cultural details that distinguish individuals—here capitulates to trite gangster mythology.

Siegel's assimilationist drive is deemphasized as an attempt at glamour. Toback shows his move out West, his elocution exercises, and his haberdashery as behavioral tics, certainly, but without indicating any cause or meaning besides acquisitiveness or the desire for refinement. The film implies that Siegel, who responded violently to the nickname "Bugsy," merely was trying to improve himself by dressing up his image. Toback does public-relations work for gangsterism.

Another way of putting this is that *Bugsy* is part of the Hollywood tradition that carelessly sensationalizes social fact. The backstage view of Hollywood and Vegas empires gets close to the mechanics of American pathologies, showing how Siegel's personal neuroses join the construct of social power and egotism already in place. But the view, in the end, is morally simplistic and escapist. When Siegel meets the ruthless showgirl Virginia Hill on a Hollywood sound stage, Toback and director Barry Levinson turn their encounter into a shadow play, focusing on a silhouette of their pert profiles. The tactic reveals nothing, but it reinforces a compulsion toward ignorance and delusion: those silhouettes represent how egotists see themselves and how Hollywood encourages us to view human complexity.

Siegel and Hill's banter (they team up to cheat the mob) recalls the flirtations in *Body Heat* (clichés spiked with obscenity), and the unremarkable story of Siegel's underworld dealings link up with countless gangster-movie conventions. Levinson shoots all this dryly, almost desultorily; his pace fuses dullness with ineptitude. It's probably an attempt at giving viewers think time to distance themselves from what one reviewer called the "swanky fun." But that's an aesthetic delusion. *Bugsy's* "irony" *is* socially irresponsible—and irrelevant. After the *Godfather* films, it is unconscionable to make a gangster film this divorced from social context. Coppola's artistic and moral triumph was to show the full horror of the Corleones' lives while making direct emotional contact with the audience. Instead, Toback and Levinson do what's cheap and easy in movies.

*Bugsy* retreats from the great truth of Coppola's art, which might explain why reviewers find it so "entertaining"—it's a guilt-free movie, a Reagan-era excrescence. It is not fundamentally different from last summer's cheapo *Mobsters,* in which Bugsy Siegel, Meyer Lansky, and Lucky Luciano were shown as Little Rascals who, in addition to killing people, happened to be visionary entrepreneurs. *Bugsy* also takes this insane view in an epigraph that praises Siegel's Las Vegas as a capitalist marvel.

Valorizing racketeers suits 1980s Wall Street sensibility; *Mobsters* and *Bugsy* defy any criticism of their depraved protagonists. And Warren Beatty, who produced and starred in *Bonnie & Clyde* twenty-four years ago, should know better. That movie was accused of glamorizing criminals even though it submitted them to an unprecedentedly shocking, horrific death. Actually, its edge came from representing 1960s disaffection and antisocial impulses in figures that appeased the counterculture. *Bugsy*'s link is with the powerful and indifferent; it inspires weak nostalgia rather than political reflection.

Beatty, who once had an exemplary, progressive movie career, has made a more drastic capitulation than Toback. This ultimate expression of Beatty's ego is a complete turnaround toward the deceptions his earlier films revised. *Bugsy* doesn't keep pace with the smart genre revisions of DePalma's *Scarface* and *The Untouchables*, films that expressed a new awareness about crime and gangster myths. This awareness would emphasize an ethnic and social sense as issues important to the current cultural era, but *Bugsy*, like *Dick Tracy*, can be seen as white pop's last gasp. Its most fascinating subtext is the filmmakers'—and Siegel's—ethnic denial.

Toback's denial is an intellectual's version of Siegel's (and Beatty's) street cunning. It allows them all to get over in a society that is built on ethnic rivalry, class resentment, and the various methods concocted to exploit those biases (e.g., Hollywood, Las Vegas). Beatty's part in *Bugsy* is the film's biggest lie. He gives an energetic, unconvincing performance in a role he is all wrong for, apart from the disingenuousness he imparts to the notion of a Jewish gangster being just like any other. Beatty may be street-smart, but that doesn't give him street credibility; his charming, hesitant manner isn't feral; it lacks ferocity. His noisy outbursts and his offhand dismay (in a terrible, sentimental scene where Siegel mishandles his daughter's birthday party and a mob confab) are charades. Beatty's now taut, waxen glamour is hollow; it doesn't evoke the ethnicity needed to make sense of Siegel or even the emotional force that William Hurt used to transform the ethnicity of the Jewish protagonist he played in *The Doctor*.

As a Hollywood icon, Beatty may well suit Siegel's (and Toback's) own personal fantasy, but Beatty is incapable of portraying that ethnic contradiction—and Toback seems afraid to write it. (Gregory Peck's performance in *Gentleman's Agreement* may be the only time Hollywood's come close.) This kind of denial is understood as the secret meaning of Hollywood. (That's why *The Wall Street Journal*'s reviewer could say, "*Bugsy* seems so convincing because Mr. Beatty plays him very much like the Mr. Beatty we all think we know.") But Toback and Beatty and Levinson go along with the secret rather than expose it.

*Bugsy* ought to be about the conditions that turn assimilation and ambition into psychosis or that trigger social derangement. These points were made by Alain Resnais's use of Jean-Paul Belmondo's iconographic presence in the antiromantic biography of the French criminal *Stavisky*. . . . The title's ellipsis shows that Resnais wasn't dealing in fake irony. His film was a meditation on delusion, politics, and ethnicity, its art deco look patterned after *Trouble in Paradise*. Yet, Resnais understood psychological projection. When the secretly Jewish Stavisky, owner of the Empire Theater, asked an actress, "Why do you make such a point of telling the whole world you're Jewish?," he got a startling answer that revealed the paranoid atmosphere in France at that time—the circumstances that inspired him and that eventually conspired against him.

Such truth is only a fraction of what Toback omits from *Bugsy*, but it's part of the age-old Hollywood corruption that disguises ethnic reality for wholly inappropriate and misleading fantasy. Siegel's greed and his relationship with the misogynistically presented Hill (Annette Bening) are meant to be understood as an innocent American romance right down to its *Casablanca*-style airport scene. Fools will cheer.

*Bugsy* isn't the first movie to suggest that a gangster was a doomed romantic, but to insist on this point in the full knowledge of Hollywood prevarication—minus social context—is insipid.

*The City Sun*
February 26, 1992

# DAUGHTERS BITES THE DUST

AFROCENTRICITY IS a terrible thing to waste, especially if it is the only means some contemporary artists have for connecting with an audience. Julie Dash's *Daughters of the Dust* proves that Afrocentricity by itself is not culture but can—as they used to say down South—kill it dead.

There's something like naive arrogance in this movie about African American matriarchy. Set in 1902 in the Sea Islands near South Carolina—the Gullah region where the Black inhabitants sustain vestiges of African language and mysticism—the film attempts to reclaim history through didactic recreation. It's about the Peazant family (reads like peasant, pronounced like pissant), whose women are preparing to make the transition from indigenous island life to mainland assimilation. The story is overcast with a sense of loss. Dash, who wrote the film as well as directed it, is certain that the family's move will cost them more than they ever can gain, so she weighs the family dilemma against "progress." But what Dash seems in favor of preserving is vague, sentimental, confusing, and banal.

There are lots of eager actresses on view in *Daughters of the Dust* but not a single freshly observed character. They're all types—not from a declarative, conventional realm of dramatic exposition but from such allegorical forms as dance and poetry and political-spiritual parables. Cora Lee Day presides as Nana, the seer; Barbara-O is Yellow Mary, who seeks reconciliation with her heritage (I think); Kaycee Moore as Haagar is anxious for a new life in a new territory; Alva Rogers as Eula, the granddaughter, is burdened by historical knowledge and future uncertainty. The leading male figure is Adisa Anderson as Eli, whose manhood in the company of these women depends on his ability to maintain his African spiritual faith.

None of these characters interacts on any clear, consistent basis. The film is a series of gnomic encounters and pseudopoetic recitations, paced by shots of the performers, in middle-class garb, lolling in trees, strolling along beaches, or rowing in boats. Each fuzzily conceived scene is meant to convey an existential idyll: Here are Black folks displaced from "home," yet in a better place than their urban descendants at the other end of the century ever can know.

This assumption is terribly subjective on Dash's part; she ignores what's Afrocentric in Black urban industrialized cultures. Contemporary urban despair (which has encouraged many Black folks in Northern cities to relocate South) here is translated as ideological nostalgia. Dash is like an Afrocentric travel agent who offers a limited number of vacation options.

Dash's sense of the lifestyle that was most edifying for Black people is twisted up with her desire to document and preserve Gullah culture (the credits call the film "a Geechee Girl production"). This agenda is part of what prevents her from making a sensible, clear presentation of her subject. Her Afrocentric arrogance demands that ignorant nineties audiences strain to follow reenacted rituals and patois that are familiar only to a few.

As a screenwriter, Dash shows no evidence of following a Gullah literary or theatrical form that communicates itself through emotional force. The barely intelligible dialogue is shouted, mumbled, or intoned in mixed-up rhythms, according to each performer's personal preference (and skill or lack of). Every scene is a puzzle; it reminded me of a junior high field trip to see a French classical theater troupe perform *Phèdre*. But even in French, *Phèdre* made sense if only because the actors gestured effectively.

At the heart of *Daughters'* failed attempt at cinematic lyricism lies Dash's utter ineptitude at staging and blocking scenes. (Her subsequent PBS film of Urban Bush Women's *Praise House* showed remarkable improvement in this area, but that also could be due to the work's previous conception.) The performers here related to each other as awkwardly as amateurs in a school pageant, and the folly reached a peak when Alva Rogers did her frenetic mad prophetess scene. (The excellent Kaycee Moore, so memorable in *Bless Their Little Hearts*, is given little to do but yell and roll her eyes.) And which actress is Yellow Mary, anyway?

Just when you're most discombobulated by this movie, there will be a moment of stunning obtuseness like that Rogers number or some narration by "the unborn child" such as "I am holy and I am whore. I am barren and my daughters are many." Greg Tate, a close friend of Dash's, writing in the *Village Voice*, called this "an unprecedented achievement in terms of world cinema and African aesthetics." I have never met Dash, and I call it slow, precious crap.

And what, to American movie audiences, is African aesthetics! Ousmane Sembene and Idrissa Ouedraogo make emotionally lucid films with awesome, pristine skill. They don't hide temerity behind a schoolmaster's vanity about improving the sensibilities of deprived viewers. If Gullah culture means so much to Dash, if Afrocentricity is important to her, she's got to get across to an audience what a knowledge of history means and convey a sense of how history actually felt as it happened. Those are the things that movies as different as Spielberg's *The Color Purple*, Jan Torell's *The New Land*, and Martin Ritt's *Sounder* did superbly.

If my tone sounds a bit uncharitable, it's because for years now a lot of hope has been invested in Dash's project. But this isn't simple disappointment; it's despair—anger—at the sorry spectacle of serious, intelligent film people like Dash and her cinematographer, Arthur Jafa, making pretentious Art that is both remote from viewers' sensibilities and drably executed. *Daughters* is full of verbal and visual dissociations and symbolic imagery that never gather force simply because the ideas behind these tropes have not been transformed in a way that delights or intrigues the senses. You can pass time counting the slow-motion promenades or the impenetrable shots of a half-sunken statue.

Yet, as this mess piles up, it builds an underlying sense that its obscurity is a virtue—African aesthetics that you'd better get used to. (Wonder what Fela would say after waking up from this movie?)

At a *Daughters* screening, a trio of brothers in parkas and caps downed chips and soda and then began to talk among themselves. After asking them to quiet down, I realized their misbehavior was a sign of defeat—they were bored and so was I.

No matter how often Black folks have been disgraced at the movies (Lionel Martin's *Burn, Hollywood, Burn* video for Public Enemy), there remains a healthy threshold for entertainment. This doesn't mean trash like *Father of the Bride* is the answer any more than *Daughters of the Dust*. Simply put, the fascination of a face, a recognizable conflict, an arresting image are the basic things a filmmaker has to provide. *Daughters of the Dust* is more committed to a cultural elite's Afrocentric polemics than in the pleasures that excite one's imagination.

Interminable shots of women in long white dresses playing with a tattered parasol evoke nothing but a dreadful Black bourgeois fantasy of refined cinema. There's more life—more Afrocentricity—in the last X-Clan album cover, on which a pink Cadillac journeys into the blue-black ionosphere seeking heroic ghosts. The great image had wit—the missing element in Julie Dash's seriousness.

*The City Sun*
January 22, 1992

# BACK TO THE FUTURE FOR FAITH

A RRESTED DEVELOPMENT'S "Tennessee" is, currently, the single of 1992 because of its multisided view of wonder. This neo-blues written by Speech (Todd Thomas), the group's twenty-four-year-old leader, wonders about the future, in the present, through a musical style from the past, and it is, of course, wonderful to hear.

Each line about disillusionment followed by one about striving has the beauty of church testimony: a personal witnessing that one assents to with pleasure and certainty. This is the rare hiphop record with a convincing spiritual underpinning: Speech is on a search for a home (Tennessee as a state of mind), but it's the kind of search Geto Boys can't even conceive. And when Speech leads a new verse in this testimony saying, "Now I see the importance of history," he shows a realistic awareness that shames PM Dawn's loony tunes.

Hiphop sorely needs some spirituality, and after the innocuous beatitudes of *Of the Heart, Of the Soul, and Of the Cross*, it's a relief to find a hiphop spiritual quest that honors hard-knocks Black experience and eschews hippie daydreaming. For that reason, Speech's passion may hit more profoundly as r&b than as (white) pop. The subtle references to A Tribe Called Quest and Sly Stone are more authentic and invigorating than left-field-but-still-wack samples of Spandau Ballet.

Like all pop revolutions, hiphop is about making new culture out of old culture—making music your own—and that's what "Tennessee" does spectacularly. It's clear that Speech heard and understood Prince's obscure reference to Tennessee in "Alphabet St." as a cultural marker signifying a dream place of historical, musical, and libidinal importance. Thus is Tennessee a triply endowed ideal.

Behind Speech's dulcet, wise-child lead, a female oracle chants, "Home, home, take me to another place." Arrested Development have the charming intention of shifting hiphop's interest away from such venal, craven centers as New York or Los Angeles. They point the way through music: a primarily vocal, Southern-inflected rapping style with strong but casual blues riffs asserting the human touch the way record-scratching used to. And then there's the amazing, modern bluesman lyrics:

> *Walk the roads my forefathers walked*
> *Climb the trees my forefathers hung from.*

At last! Billie Holiday's "Strange Fruit" gets a response that's empowering rather than pathetic. And it took the recent revolution of rap music's exhausting young Blacks' political and religious disenchantment to do it.

Speech embraces religion not like a young fogey conservative; he talks to his God in terms as smart and modern as those New Order used in "Touched by the Hand of God." "I know you're supposed to be my steering wheel/Not just my spare tire" are the words of a contemporary reawakening, followed by words of uneasy devotion: "You was there to quench my thirst/But I am still thirsty."

"Tennessee" contains evidence of an important realization based on felt experience rather than New Millenium convenience. Arrested Development have a healthy response to the degeneration of Black society. Speech's personal sense of loss (death looming in the family and community) inspires his search for what once united a people. ("Fishin' 4 Religion" makes a distinction between "church" as institution and fellowship.) Speech doesn't merely proselytize for a church; he's rapping for the sustenance—the hope—that people used to find in spiritual communion, the very thing Black politics alone has been unable to supply.

Arrested Development's debut album, *3 Years, 5 Months and 2 Days in the Life of . . .* (Chrysalis), is as cumbersomely titled as PM Dawn's but it has simpler, more persuasive stylistic shifts from blues talking ("Tennessee"), playground shouts ("Mama's Always on Stage"), funk jams ("Fishin' 4 Religion," "U"), love songs ("Natural") to urban-folk character sketch ("Mr. Wendel") and group-chant parables ("Give a Man a Fish"). This young band of three guys and two women from Atlanta, are smart enough to know that their best groove is ideological, and they keep the homilies flowing on discreet rhythms with occasional intense grooves.

It's the friendliness of their sound that lets pronouncements such as "Can't be a revolution without women/Can't be a revolution without children" play even though Speech seldom shares the lead with women or children. The album is good enough to overcome such naive lapses (and the group is good enough to still deserve a better name).

Speech, who previously wrote colloquial editorials for a Southern Black newspaper run by family members, is careful to avoid the doctrinaire attitudes of most Afrocentric religiosity; he preaches agape with politics. The ebullience is most apparent on "Children Play with Earth," a back-to-basics ditty that isn't all stargazing ecology; it's also a fundamentalist's parable. ("The dirt that made you/Get acquainted with the earth/ The earth that eventually will take you/And the world that hopefully will again awake you.")

None of Arrested Development's allegories and style spinning is as brilliant as that of hiphop's greatest philosophical autodidacts De La Soul, but Arrested Development have the one thing De La Soul doesn't have: innocence. Speech raps about death and "my people keep messin' up," but his innocence shows in the spiritual solutions he proposes in tracks like "Raining Revolution." He has a childlike faith that De La Soul have not yet settled for in their secular fervor. (Regeneration and renewal may seem more likely prospects in the South.)

That means there's room in hiphop for Speech and Arrested Development to do something new, something original. The album's best cuts, "Tennessee" and "Fishin' 4 Religion," are tough, dreamy achievements that will force hiphop to reconcile history, politics, and belief, and grow up. That is, develop further.

Maybe the group should call itself "A.D." to indicate the rebirth of down-home moral sense and its musical profession of hope after so much death.

*The City Sun*
April 22, 1992

# FAB 5 FREDDY COMMERCIALIZES THE REVOLUTION

URING THE RECENT Los Angeles holocaust, in which desperate people hoped for a revolution, Fab 5 Freddy put it worst: "It's goin' on, y'all. It's goin' on!"

Actually, all that was going on was another Saturday episode of *Yo! MTV Raps*; Fab 5 Freddy used as background the L.A. turmoil and a protest rally at Columbia University to help rapper YoYo promote her new album. Reality became grist for hiphop's ever-grinding wheels of commerce. It was only last year that Fab 5 Freddy joined George Bush's war machine, urging *Yo! MTV Raps* viewers to support the troops in Desert Storm.

This brownnosing instinct for trends has made Fab 5 Freddy famous enough (that is, acceptable to the mainstream) to receive a ten-page profile in *The New Yorker*. Yes, *The New Yorker,* which has never given Spike Lee a favorable review, helped Fab 5 Freddy promote himself as a culture maven in the Andy Warhol mode. *What up!*

It was that June 1991 article that previewed Fab 5 Freddy's pop exploits this time as a hiphop lexicographer; his own dictionary has just been published, *Fresh Fly Flavor: Words & Phrases of the Hip-hop Generation* (Longmeadow Press). Coming on the heels of Nelson George's "Buppies, B-Boys, Baps and Bohos: The Complete History of Post-Soul Culture" in *The Village Voice,* Fab 5 Freddy's book makes the authoritarian aims of buppies unmistakable.

These pathetic documents reveal something sadder than the gall of Fab 5 Freddy and Nelson George; each publication represents a terrible development in which African Americans crassly exploit their culture under the guise of expertise. Fab 5 Freddy and Nelson George are not artists but purveyors — b-boy con men, not b-boy intellectuals. With their eyes on business, they produce marketable reductions of Black experience. Their TV shows and books simplify the nuances of Black thinking and living. Black Americans gain little insight from this, but white America—the purveyors' ideal audience—can purchase fake entry into contemporary exotica.

This crazy opportunism—"crazy" as in "insane" and (per Fab 5 Freddy) "abundance"—occurs at a historic moment when young Black artists demonstrate vigorous imagination to a society poised to accept their talents. Fab 5 Freddy first seized this chance in the early-eighties downtown New York art scene as a graffiti hack. But the integrity and political impulses implied in Afrocentric consciousness are easily subverted by the mainstream's accommodation.

As fake impresarios, Fab 5 Freddy and Nelson George put a self-serving price on something that should be invaluable, and soon it becomes horribly inauthentic and its originality betrayed—as happened with graffiti.

Disaster is inevitable given the mainstream's willingness to use Black culture and conscript a few reliably unchallenging hosts: MTV embraces rap for its commerciality, not its essential value; *The Village Voice* would never reduce twenty-six years of white Western history to fifteen-odd pages-plus-pictures, yet an insidious pop racism says Black culture deserves nothing better.

If "The Complete History of Post-Soul Culture" was no more than a clipping service for Madison Avenue executives who are eager to cash in on a subculture's energy, *Fresh Fly Flavor* can serve a similar function for ad-slogan writers. And James Bernard—a junior-league Nelson George—provides Fab 5 Freddy with an approving introduction from the white-sanctioned vantage point of *The Source* magazine:

**Fab 5 Freddy helps to facilitate understanding like an ambassador and gives us a valuable reference point, like Webster.**

***Fresh Fly Flavor* will help you catch up and keep up.**

Obviously, the only people who need a phrase book such as this are visitors. It's doubtful that Black American history has ever spawned so many translators and interpreters. Freddy's book and George's article appear on the cultural scene like signposts turned upside down. You don't need them to find home, and only outsiders will be misled. Yet, as examples of literature or journalism, these two *things* lack originality and spirit. They're upside-down accidentally—not in defiance of the encroaching pirates and parasites, but in cahoots with the exploitation. Morally upside-down.

*Fresh Fly Flavor* contains nearly 500 photographs of Freddy (born Fred Brathwaite), but there is little effort to make serious sense of hiphop slang as a legitimate example of mutable language. It's no equivalent to either Raymond Williams's *Keywords* or Zora Neale Hurston's *Mules and Men* or even an EPMD album. It's all cheaply simple (or simply cheap).

An entire page is given to define *hype*: "1. To overly build up and exaggerate. 2. Also means something is really good." The phrase *I'm with that* is defined: "I agree."

*New jack swing* conveniently is defined with a plug for the movie *New Jack City*: "Also, I must shamelessly add that yours truly was the associate producer," Freddy writes. He even does some logrolling for another businessman when the term *living large* is used in a sample sentence: "Russell Simmons, the owner of Def Jam Records, RUSH Productions, and several other companies, is definitely *living large*."

A hilarious example of Freddy's capricious scholarship comes with the *mackin'* definition that cites the song "Yankee Doodle" as the source instead of Caribbean or Creole derivation of the French term *mec*. This nursery rhyme preference is a telling clue to Freddy's disrespect and infantilization of Black linguistics.

His trivializing is most apparent in the *dope* entry. Freddy credits Old School rapper Busy Bee but gives a lame explanation. "Its common usage also reminds us that a key ingredient in ultra urban, contemporary counter-youth-culture is to flirt with what's wrong, take the negative vibe and power, and turn it all the way around to make it serve a new purpose, yet with the shock value still intact." That's what you tell the authorities— the same jive Henry Louis Gates pulled when defending 2 Live Crew.

Freddy's wack explanation has no regard for the beauty of speech and the mystery of cultural connotation. An expression like *dope* or *bad* contains the experience of menace and shock; it suggests a stimulation that changes one's perception while at the same time flouting received morality. Freddy's entry is from the outside looking in—the typical way hiphop gets dissed by its spokespersons.

Fab 5 Freddy isn't merely craven, though; he seeks to emulate Warhol out of a native cynicism about the business of culture. But lacking Warhol's sense of high irony, Freddy mostly seems complicit with the business rather than provocative. His instincts must have been itching while L.A. burned; he seemed to be longing for the kind of catastrophe that might have given *Yo! MTV Raps* an even bigger audience share. That a music show host could so blithely plug for revolution—after touting jingoistic militarism—is just plain unprincipled. That's as low-down and ironic as hiphop can be.

Hiphop is certainly a cultural movement, but most of all, it's an opportunity for people like Brathwaite and George. Instead of using this predominantly verbal form to express a genuine understanding of personal experience, they opt to sell superficial aspects of it. The sorry truth is, Black culture makes room for this in the breadth of its experience and human license: There's a sympathetic and fond tolerance of the itch to succeed, to make money and live comfortably. But instead of clarifying that humanity and need, Brathwaite and George contribute to the white comprehension and control of it. Their latest works amount to crib notes for Trivial Pursuit.

*The City Sun*
May 13, 1992

# APOSTASY: ANTI-HYPE IN FOUR STEPS

☐   *1*

"**C**ICELY TYSON came and cried." No, that's not another of the *Village Voice*'s salacious intimate confessions; it's a quote from one of the *Voice*'s relentless editorial promotions of *Daughters of the Dust*. Tyson's response to Julie Dash's film was used in a way that made it seem a combination erotic and sentimental experience. The *Voice*'s monitoring of this film's freak success clarifies its relation to the trendiest political biases. That makes *Daughters* the Black woman's equivalent to *Thelma and Louise*. The movie is more interesting for what it means to people than for what it is as a work of art.

But let's distinguish that affective meaning from actual meaning. The current stage of American film culture (specifically, as created by African Americans) mixes together the ambition of artists and the desire of audiences. Any movie will do because it need only be an object for both parties' projection, and the perfect film for such an era is one banal enough to follow well-known ideas about positivity and progressivism.

*Daughters of the Dust* has become a hit by appealing to the frustrations of women who feel left out of the African-American art competition. This serious, hardworking group is concentrated in New York in enough numbers to make Dash's feature-length debut a bigger local hit than it is ever likely to be anywhere else in the country. Once again, New York has a disproportionate influence on the national cultural temper.

This is good to the extent that it might shed light on the efforts of other African-American women who are putting up a mighty struggle to express themselves in film or video (Mary Neema Barnette, Pamm

Thomas, Paula Walker). Yet, this too-easily pleased audience is, I'm afraid, unworthy of any filmmaker's best efforts. By demonstrating their presence and enthusiasm, this feminist audience may encourage some filmmakers to stretch, or simply to produce, with the confidence of knowing there are people who want to see what they do. But the sad part of the *Daughters* phenomenon is that things look bad for any filmmakers who aren't willing to massage this eager group's prejudices or who don't have friends in high media places.

It's a little frightening to imagine the kinds of movies *Daughters* actually might inspire: conceptually diffuse, structurally vague polemics that lack immediacy and astonishment. Sure, there are various ways to make cinema, but the best way to keep the art form interesting is by making it vital and revelatory.

Suspiciously, no one who praises *Daughters of the Dust* can relate specific insights or information—not even a moment when the whole pastoral impresses itself on one's consciousness as a strongly perceived experience (such as the knifing scene or masked-ball scene in *Chameleon Street*). The *Daughters* reports are all about effusive praise and weeping. These mushy responses are sad and infuriating. When will Black people stop being pathetically grateful for the tiny beneficences tossed their way? When will they demand more from a movie than characters who are never clearly introduced and a plot that is almost impossible to follow or recite?

Frankly, it's not possible to buy the claims made for *Daughters* as high art, simply because: When has the genuine pop audience ever cared for high art in the form of elliptic, allegorical movies! *Daughters* wouldn't make it on Times Square, in Flatbush, or on Fordham Road, and there's no reason it should.

It may seem like apostasy to kick *Daughters of the Dust* again, but it is because a recent re-viewing of *Chameleon Street* confirmed what a really great, effective movie can do. I refuse to settle for less.

□  2

Two days before John Singleton became the first Black person nominated for an Academy Award as Best Director, I pointed out to a friend the minimal display of craft in Singleton's *Remember the Time* video. Instead of showing the stages of the stickman's trick, Singleton cut to a slave girl watching the stick's ascension. That cut amounts to basic cinematic skill; it extends the meaning of an action by implying its continuance and adds a point of view to the audience's own. Singleton's work in *Boyz N the Hood* is, at best, similarly skilled and functional and—at times—expressive.

Still, the Oscar nomination for *Boyz* seems to certify Singleton's conventionality (and mediocrity) more than it proves his talent. Like Barry Levinson's, Sydney Pollack's, and Paul Mazursky's rush to sign up Steven Soderbergh after the opening of *sex, lies, and videotape,* the Oscar nomination only shows how the Hollywood community recognizes Singleton as one of its own. His simplistic, stereotypical evocation of the Black urban experience works in familiar commercial movie terms.

One can be happy for Singleton's individual acceptance and success—but not for long. It happens in contradistinction to the neglect mainstream film culture habitually has shown to superior work by such neglected Black artists as Spencer Williams, Bill Gunn, William Greaves, Charles Burnett, and Wendell B. Harris.

Singleton's Oscar nomination only distracts one from the distressing reality that makes the *Boyz N the Hood* phenomenon pall: that the movie's success does not reflect an audience's unadulterated response to film content but its successful manipulation by the mainstream Hollywood system—complete with the perversion of social consciousness that comes from accepting the predictable story line's too-neat settling of modern American tragedy. *Boyz N the Hood* represents the hideous triumph of venal sentimentality.

Singleton will earn praise when he rises above the cheap blandishment of this Oscar nomination. At twenty-three, he is the youngest Best Director nominee in history and he has the chance to overcome it. But he also has the risk of succumbing to its implicit delusion that a clichéd approach to the human condition is a sufficient means of communication.

□ 3

These bitter thoughts were prompted by the happy occasion of seeing *Chameleon Street*'s first return engagement in New York at the American Museum of the Moving Image (AMMI), on February 22 [1992], sell out the house and turn away patrons. This should encourage movie lovers to ask other exhibitors to program this important, remarkable movie.

*Chameleon Street*'s first commercial release last year was sufficient to put Harris in the running for the National Society Film Critics voting for Best Film, Best Director, Best Actor, and Best Screenplay—all well-deserved citations backed by perceptive critics who'd seen the film in Los Angeles, Chicago, and New York. *Chameleon Street* should have enjoyed the celebration that attended *Boyz* and *Daughters,* but it was scuttled, locally, by *Village Voice* feminist politricks and, nationally, by the lack of mainstream pressure (i.e., hype).

But the film has true merit: Harris's weird, daring, provocative investigation of the modern American psyche makes *Daughters* and *Boyz* look like the trivial gestures of children. *Chameleon Street* makes adult demands on viewers by withholding judgment and easy categorization of its vain, brilliant, psychologically messed-up character. Harris is an artist in the profound sense of Dostoevsky and Ellison; he doesn't take the easy Dash-Singleton route of making his protagonist *likable*. He puts William Douglas Street's professional life in the context of his personal life; the man society can't tie down is shown in the trap of family and marriage — a second set of bourgeois restrictions.

Harris depicts, with humor, the exploits of a man whose social circumstances are tragic — that immediately makes it more complex than typical movie fare. It doesn't fit conventional notions about independent films and certainly is not the typical, self-righteous screed that Black filmmakers are expected to produce.

□    *4*

Harris, a talented Juilliard graduate who didn't get the breaks of his fellow alumni Robin Williams, Patti LuPone, or Kevin Kline, assimilated a lot of Western culture and cosmopolitan sophistication before finding himself stuck in Michigan working for his family's industrial films business. His identification with Street's slipperiness and daring resulted, no doubt, from his own straining, frustrated ambition and wit. And evidence of Harris's tension — his vivid, nearly solipsistic intelligence — is what's on the screen. It goes deeper than some pose of "African aesthetics."

*Chameleon Street* isn't straight out of a ghetto about homeboyz hanging in the hood or juicy daughters whose business is strictly dust. In fact, *Chameleon Street* is about the psychological complexity that most American movies (especially those about race) cover up. Harris hooks into the deep, scary ambivalence most people who dream about "Black cinema" (or more precisely, who dream of breaking into Hollywood) don't even dare think about: the meaning of individuality, the nature of social relationships that have everything to do with one's intimate (yes, sexual and psychological) history. The issue of identity that Woody Allen disguised with a joke in *Zelig* is taken quite seriously, even though Harris's film is also a comedy.

The links of private and public behavior that catches Street's ego in social quicksand (such as the restaurant confrontation with a bigot or the disastrous foreign-exchange student ruse) are so bold, their content may seem embarrassing or shocking. The hysterectomy scene and the knife game are both hilariously morbid. These moments go beyond the kind of tribal protectiveness that Black pop artists usually assume. Harris bravely pushes past the reassuring acknowledgment of racism, hurt, entitlement, defiance, and "pride" that African Americans know as a group and that they take sustenance in confirming with one another and opposing against a hostile world. Harris depicts Street as if he were not part of a group but as a human being responsible for his own actions.

This is a thoroughly disorienting, completely unexpected approach for a movie about a Black person (anyone) who is not a certified winner or loser. Harris's artistry is as tough and original as Robert Altman's, Orson Welles's, Charles Burnett's, or Bill Gunn's in that it isn't immediately clear what one ought to think of his protagonist. This isn't a ready-made polemic like such hogwash as *Thelma and Louise* or *Silence of the Lambs;* this is the complex poetry of a conflicted individual, which pop audiences are never ready for. Each viewer has to figure out Street for himself or herself.

The process may take a while in a cultural climate debased by commercialism and cronyism; Harris stands lonely like the French film eccentrics he homages (Godard and Cocteau). He shows the individuality it takes to make movies that matter, to do justice to experience that is personally felt and honestly considered.

*Chameleon Street* is a seriously talented person's attempt to find a means of expression he can call his own. And that, in the popular arts, is a heroic endeavor. It risks being unpopular, risks not being distributed, and risks being misunderstood. Harris defies the niceties about Black cinema that Donald Bogle mouths in his cheerleading notes for the AMMI "Black New Wave" series.

The not-niceness of *Chameleon Street* centers on Street's terrible misogyny. Blind viewings of the film make some people criticize this; they miss how Harris exposes the central male problem at the base of Street's dilemma. (They also miss Street's equation "Nat Turner = Justice" and his reading of *The Clash of Races*. The film is a subtle consideration of the machismo that cripples Black liberation efforts.)

Yet even these responses are better than sisters weeping in the aisles; *Chameleon Street*'s power provokes hard questions about sexism. But do we only worry about propriety when a movie is bold enough to make us really think?

*The City Sun*
March 4, 1992

# METALLICA TALES

"I T BOILS DOWN to what new stories you can tell," Chuck D said on the subject of white rock (Springsteen, in particular). But sometimes the old stories can be meaningful and told with power. In "Wherever I May Roam," Metallica performs the neat trick of submerging American politics beneath metal mythology. Manifest destiny is expressed as a cry of freedom and, in a final coup that critic Robert Palmer traced back to blues legend Robert Johnson, the political urge is wailed from beyond the grave:

> *Carved on my stone:*
> *"My body lies but still I roam."*

"Wherever I May Roam" is fueled by an idea of entitlement and privileged instinct; restlessness and dissatisfaction become the basis for a creed. It's played exultantly (by a band that knows how to use guitar chords to stirring effect) but is weighted with dread—perfect for a song of desperation. The mood here, as on the band's 1991 eponymous album, is that all-American defiance-in-the-face-of-overwhelming-disillusionment. There's an implicit fear of territorial limits that Metallica refuses to acknowledge—an authentic neo-con delusion perpetuated by restating conventional platitudes: "Call me what you will / But I'll take my time anywhere / Free to speak my mind anywhere / And I'll redefine anywhere."

With its raging, grandiose sound, Metallica makes this determination primal and irresistible. It's the same hardheaded American will heard in Springsteen's "Badlands" but, fourteen years later, done with melodic fits and starts—hints of something less than innocent. In Metallica's nihilistic lullaby, "Enter Sandman," escape was related to isolation and ignorance: "Exit: Light / Enter: Night / Take my hand / We're off to Never Never Land." That's how a generation of white American youth claims its inheritance—with anxious self-revealing honesty.

The album hits greatness in these songs that admit ambivalence. There's a mixture of pity and pride like that found in the most tortured, passionate rap. Both musics are rooted in the sins of American social tradition. Their common story is precisely the tension the artists feel. It's primarily in Metallica's music but also in James Hetfield's punk-Ahab vocals; the way he growls, "Yeah, yeah" at the end of "Wherever I May Roam," to convince himself of his sovereignty.

An equally significant tale is revealed in Kirk Hammett's closing guitar lines that imitate an exotic, Middle Eastern figure. Yes, this is the anthem Desert Storm deserved: a scary, withering siren. On the album it is followed by "Don't Tread on Me," which confirms the ideology of the New World Order by opening with a quote from *West Side Story*'s "America" but distorting it in the same way Jimi Hendrix played "The Star-Spangled Banner."

The old story Metallica tells also clearly defines the American political heritage that is usually left unexamined. And it's not what is carved on the Statue of Liberty; it's the message inside presidential rhetoric. On the album Hetfield sings, "I'm your hate when you want love / I'm your life and I no longer care." That song is titled "Sad but True."

*The City Sun*
June 17, 1992

# THE HAMMER &
# THE POP SICKLE

PRESIDENTIAL WANNABE Bill Clinton would make a bad DJ. His willingness to judge and condemn Sister Souljah without full knowledge of her political agenda or her aesthetic program was not only rash but typically rap-phobic. It recalls the same disrespect constantly shown to Public Enemy—essentially a white's exercise of his presumed superiority. Clinton's disdain for how Sister Souljah might be regarded by some (Black) voters resembles the narrow view of white journalists who pass moral and political judgment on rappers in the guise of music criticism.

These white pronouncements exhibit how profoundly disturbing Black expression can be to people in power or those seeking power of their own. That's what's at stake in rap—the chance for Black folks to speak for themselves and gain power through speech. The facile argument that political rappers are hypocrites for taking (and making) white corporate money ignores the fact that the freedom to speak, the thrill of self-expression, is worth more than money and outlasts political fashion. That's why whites secure this privilege for themselves. Sister Souljah's album *360 Degrees of Power* (Epic) counts as a jam primarily because she seizes an opportunity that's usually forfeited by Black artists who have nothing to say, who only want to make money.

Some rap artists take the phrase "freedom of speech" for more than a platitude; it's mythic, full of promises not yet met in day-to-day living. It carries the potential for social achievement and self-fulfillment. Ironically, rappers base this potential in the workings of a capitalist industry that would seem to be the root of their troubles. They make a very American show of democratic faith that then gets dashed when the system displays its prejudices by such restraints as warning labels and media attention that is either withheld or hostile.

It may be the privileges enjoyed by white journalists/politicians that keep them from understanding the extraordinary importance *expression* has for Black artists (it's tantamount to that of the open road for whites), but these critics of rap compound their insensitivity by attacking rappers' arguments rather than the quality, style−or art−of their expression. This is a method of controlling public discourse and limiting potentially subversive speech. It continues the tradition of dismissing Blacks' intellectual capacity, denying their aesthetics, and accusing them of social misconduct.

This is a repressive tendency in the popular arts, and Green Gartside saw it coming in his 1982 Scritti Politti song "Asylums in Jerusalem." As a cultural apostate−a Structuralist outsider−Gartside understood the paradox of finding sanctuary in pop music and the offense one risked by using that form to enunciate individual, transgressive, or radical views. His self-consciousness only brought him closer to the Black pop experience as he sang about Black paradigms and his own desire: "Let him hip, hop, hippity-hop, now hurry . . . with his hammer and his pop sickle, they'll put him a hospital for good."

The utter charm of that tongue-in-cheek warning doesn't detract from its seriousness. It's proved true every time a rapper is "institutionalized," or put through the wringer of public censure because the status quo gets irritated. Empowered journalists and politicians vilify rappers the way journalists and politicians once demonized communists. Gartside's cute pun perfectly captures the way pop music can go from being a sweet confection to a powerful, threatening weapon of counterdiscourse. His suggestion that pop can subvert capitalism is as disquieting to people who object to social change as it is inspiring to many rap artists. Like Gartside, hiphoppers are self-conscious about the subversive potential that long has been a spiritual secret in Black pop. This enables rappers to accuse, renounce, and defy with such remarkable energy and an unflagging sense of justification.

Many pop critics and politicians just don't get it. Clinton's foolish response to Sister Souljah's wild rhetoric seems a weak replay of last fall's Ice Cube controversy. That, too, was an exercise on behalf of the socially preferred (and empowered) done in the guise of moral authority. Ice Cube's attackers ranged from the usual rock cretins in the press to such demagogues as Curtis Sliwa's subfascist campaign to get all Ice Cube videos banned on MTV.

It was difficult to defend the normally obnoxious Ice Cube, whose latest album, *Death Certificate* (Priority) was full of his usual half-baked spite in such woof ticket songs as "The Wrong Nigga to Fuck Wit" and "Man's Best Friend (is a gat)." But while most of the album shows him guilty of poor thought and meanness, his critics trumped up charges of anti-Jewish and anti-Korean bigotry. Specifically, Ice Cube was condemned for two cuts on a twenty-track album. Essentially, his personal politics were deemed less important than the offense critics chose to single out—and by singling it out, they ignored the context of Ice Cube's anger. More important, they (deliberately?) failed to recognize the measure of his intellectual progress in the album.

*Death Certificate* has a banal concept: The first half, called "The Death Side," is full of nihilistic songs, and the second half, called "The Life Side," contains songs about rebirth and reconstruction. But the movement from dark to light actually occurs only on the three penultimate tracks—"Color Blind," "Doing Dumb Shit" and "Us"—that display a crude but genuine social consciousness and a complex analysis of Black self-destruction. Critics relegated this serious part of the album to insignificance. (Not even Henry Louis Gates dared a *New York Times* op-ed piece on the cultural authenticity of Ice Cube's lyrical gibes.) The meaning of the critics' diatribe was clear: Urban ideology and Black self-expression are unimportant next to the esteem of preferred ethnic groups and privileged classes. Critics refused to acknowledge the passion in the self-accusations of "Us." It may even be that they couldn't *hear* the colloquial beauty of Ice Cube's introduction on "Steady Mobbin' ":

> *You got to know that "Steady Mobbin' "*
> *Is not just the name of this jam*
> *But a way of life*
> *Bound together by motherfuckers known*
> *To break 'em off somethin'*
> *Give it to me!*

Ice Cube's warm, familiar voice leads off a viciously sexist tune, but the sound and the message are inseparable, and so, each is complicated. A human being is rapping on "Steady Mobbin'," and his cadences root both his most clever and most vile expressions in a credible experience, a probable mindset. Dismissing this record is a form of escape—and cowardice. The truth in "Steady Mobbin' " is what makes the near transformation of "Us" possible; the former recognizes human failing; the latter achieves an understanding. Aspects of both are what's significant about Ice Cube's tone of voice, and it's that tone that must be appreciated in order for him to be fully understood. Ice Cube is able to reach a point of larger humanity only because he is comfortable in his speech and has come to formulate and analyze his experience in honest, sincere terms.

The terms of most of the best, challenging music are, like it or not, impolite. Popular art gives a platform to artists as well as hacks, the intelligent, and the foolish—and combinations of the bunch (as does party politics). Rap is special because, as usual, it expands the meaning of the term *party politics* mainly by emphasizing the *art* word in the middle. Trouble begins when critics and politicians don't understand how politics become central to the experience and expression of these artists. The bourgeois notion of art as refined diversion forgets the wonderful, direct expression found in folk culture. Artists like Public Enemy don't just revel in linguistics; they glory in rhetoric because they have a passion to communicate the personal and social concerns that others would deny.

White critics used to the functionality of folk-music protest and long-suffering blues often don't appreciate rap's transformation of issues into passions. It's easier for them to accept Black sexuality in music as natural expression without realizing that the increased politicization of Black American life also has inspired a natural musical expression of political ideas. This is as much a fact of late-twentieth-century capitalism as a McDonald's in Moscow. But this inevitable talk-back music is necessary and good.

It's complicated, too. Scritti Politti's "Asylums in Jerusalem" is also about stress and cultural neurosis—the Western social conditions that inspire a more self-conscious, agitprop art. Contemporary political artists have to reconceive ideas of entertainment as part of the way they understand their own lives. That's why Public Enemy could make its great albums without the traditional love song; there's no lack of love or faith but a radical rethinking of how love and faith can be applied and expressed in the modern racist world.

This truth replaces the romanticism of rock nostalgists who like to think that sixties chart hits like "Dancin' in the Street" and "Respect" were recorded as civil-rights themes. But that era had its own openly political artists, like Curtis Mayfield and Sly Stone—prototypes for the contemporary artists who combine musical fervor with ideological commitment. (Strange that the movies would mythologize a sixties musical genre appreciated for its lack of politics by substituting a contemporary group of white "soul" singers called The Commitments. It was an obvious attempt to ignore the political sense of pop that's so outstanding in a modern white Irish soul group like Dexys Midnight Runners.)

The post-sixties era has seen politics reanimate pop—especially in the past fifteen years—so that dialectical arguments can be used as song lyrics and even style issues like facial reconstruction and hairdos become prime cultural issues. Politics shouldn't be left to politicians. Pop has taken on politics for good.

*The City Sun*
June 24, 1992

# BLACK TO HIS ROOTS

Y ES, ANOTHER ARTICLE on RuPaul but not just to spite small-minded readers. It's because the new RuPaul video, *Back to My Roots*, is a great, wonderful, important thing. "Everybody ain't able," LaWanda Page says at the beginning. What that down-home adage means in RuPaul's nineties ambisexual concept is a leap of faith across the borders of gender, race, and whatever political constructs happen in between.

The *Back to My Roots* video launches RuPaul's full-length album *Supermodel of the World* (Tommy Boy) in grand, hilarious, heartwarming style. As directed by Randy Barbato, it is one of the few pop videos to revel in Black physiognomy and the various notions of glamour that Black folks create—whether Afrocentric or Hollywood-derived, a drag queen like RuPaul has access to all of them. RuPaul sets the video in his mother, Ernestine Charles's, beauty salon on Auburn Avenue in Atlanta, as a personal and cultural homage—he goes to the source of personal reinvention, the actual factory of self-made Black men and women.

Just as the song plays with ethnocentricity by turning the title phrase from "Back to My Roots" to "Black to My Roots," the video makes clear that he is not so banal or humorless as to reduce his life imperative to a dry political slogan. RuPaul demonstrates, more effectively than some street-corner haranguers and their musicmaking peers, that Blackness contains multitudes of reasons and styles—fried, dyed, and laid to the side! That's slang taken to polemic-poetic heights.

Along with shout-outs to his homies (Miss Earlene, Burnetta, Little Baby Boy, Korneisha), RuPaul calls up various hairdos and Barbato throws hot colors, key lights, even a Nintendo grid, on each one: Corn Rows, Jheri Curls, Afro Puffs, Hair Weave, Braids, Extensions, Asymmetrical Shrew. Every style is modeled by RuPaul, but in a blond wig and corresponding apparel—a ploy that can only throw cultural nationalists into a politically correct tizzy more confounding than the expected homophobic panic. For the chorus sequences, where dozens of Black folks show off different 'dos in their own hair, to their own liking, RuPaul makes pluralism and unity seem fun—but only after illustrating the Black cultural forms in which people take pluralism and unity for granted.

Going further than either Digable Planets' "Nappy hair is life" statement or the Naughty by Nature video closeup of Treach doing his own braids (*Everything's Gonna Be Alright*), *Back to My Roots* zeroes in on a Black universal: "Unh uh! I'm tender-headed!" That youth-and-ethnic-specific phrase deserves to be preserved in art (like the lice scene in *The Long Day Closes* and the hair-combing scene in *The Color Purple*). And in RuPaul's art, it signifies the mental pains, the *work* of self-presentation and self-invention.

There's no one way of being Black he shows. And whichever you choose is beautiful and powerful if you believe in it. The techniques of reinvention parallel the techniques of survival that all oppressed groups — Blacks especially — have had to develop. Frank Browning puts it well in his book *The Culture of Desire* (Crown): "Employing wit and the critical parody of camp [unravels] the hidden forgeries of their own inherited cultures and then self-consciously constructs new cultural forgeries that they know are destined to dissolve."

RuPaul's makeover in drag demonstrates the chameleon qualities of resilience, adaptability, and defiance that Black people learn intuitively. That's what's meant by *Everybody Ain't Able*.

Roots are implanted in the soul by the memory of early experience, by the practice of rituals and styles as humble as someone knocking, burning, untangling the kinks on your scalp. You can see RuPaul's art as being all about untangling kinks. The *Superstar of the World* album won't make the world forget Sylvester, but it does justice to that triumphant Black drag-disco legacy, adding RuPaul's witty politics. (Again, "House of Love" should become a popular anthem.)

It's doubtful if any drag act has confronted the mainstream as irrepressibly as RuPaul. His video postures as a gospel powerhouse, a banji girl, or *Miss* Ross don't offend. They're full of happiness. Even TV stiffs like Arsenio Hall and Donnie Simpson have found their wariness melting away before RuPaul's grinning onslaught. This brother's image isn't so much female as joyful and free. His smile and sincerity are too strong to even accept condescension. RuPaul's singing and showing off shout a great big YES to life. Good folks in the world can only assent to it.

*The City Sun*
June 30, 1992

# SWEAT AND L.L.

A T THE END of the millennium, it's the most persistent and sincere cry to be heard across the land—whether in Naughty by Nature's "Everything's Gonna Be Alright" or this exquisite duet "Why Me, Baby?".

The pairing is perfect: the rapper who never gets down on his knees and the singer who lives there. They add up to the ideal love man, blending egotistical charm with deep, selfless need. This song is even better than the Tresvant/Jam-Lewis "Sensitivity," simply because these performers' vocals seem truer to their feelings; they're able to show as well as tell. It's in the contrast of their utter emotionalism that all this begging can sound as meaningful as an existential question.

"It seems like ninety-nine years have gone by since the last time I talked to you," L.L. says, beginning his flashback story of humiliation and hurt. He can't help sounding coy, but with Sweat in the background pleading, "My baby, my baby," the two undercut each other's pretensions.

Listen to the way L.L.'s told-ya-so rap teases: "You were the center of my world." It may sound like giving in, but there's pride and possessiveness in that admission. It needs Sweat, taking the heart of that phrase—the "center of my world"—and spinning it, to make the sentiment wound.

"Why Me, Baby?" is a stirring combination of what men experience and what they desire. Although each vocalist speaks on both issues, between them they reveal where truth and fantasy differ. The pathetic tale of seeing an ex at the movies provides an apt setting for introspection. L.L. sees her sitting there "with the next man"—a description that situates himself as just one in a line whose turn already has gone. He then recalls other moments of exclusion: "Caught you on the phone a couple of times but it was always your cousin, stepbrother, just a friend." Each relation that he *isn't* is mentioned with increasing dejection. L.L. is capable of various sad expressions, yet his superb dramatics are enhanced by Sweat's melodious runs. The mood Sweat creates gives L.L.'s reminiscences an unfathomable, haunting quality. You can't tell when exactly his depression has carried him away.

Sweat is such a good singer that his deadpan tone is never so dry as a moan; the lubricious edge to his sound means that more than his heart is pumping—his belief in love is firm, ya know it. That's no surprise from the singer-author of 1990s "Make You Sweat," a raunchy seduction song but with a sublime intro and a James-Joyce-gone-gospel climax: "Yes. *Yes.* Yes. Yes. Yes-yes-yes-yes!"

With a faith in love that's still devout, Sweat doesn't make glib statements like any ol' dog in the pound. He has a gift for ennobling the basic urge. An earlier song, "I Knew That You Were Cheatin'," peaked with a long repetition of "No, no, no, no," each rep dissolving disbelief. Sweat portrays his vulnerability as a fall from grace. And somehow, he confronts it without misogynistic blame. *That's* romantic.

L.L. is fully equal to Sweat's emotional ingenuity. His presence helps certify Sweat's breakthrough: "Why Me, Baby?" sets a new standard in romantic pop, building upon "I Need Love's" innovation in 1987. A sensual vocalist like Sweat can express what he feels, but it takes a verbal wiz like L.L. to articulate as cogently as "If my heart had eyes it would cry." Thank God for CDs, 'cause if this record was on vinyl it would melt.

The version of "Why Me, Baby?" on Sweat's album *Keep It Comin'* is good, but the CD single remixes by Marly Marl are astonishing. The song gets turned into a sexy, dreamy ballad and then, with embellished lyrics, a hiphop about-face. Sad as ever, L.L. and Sweat seem to come out of their solitude and recognize each other as homeys with the same kind of love trouble.

They even trade memories like veterans of the love wars.

> *Keith: Was it good?*
> *L.L.: Yeah.*
> *Keith: Was she right?*
> *L.L.: Yeah.*
> *Keith: Every night, did she hold you tight?*
> *L.L.: Yeah!*
> *Keith: Nice and tight. Did she bite?*
> *L.L.: Umm-hmm!*

The "Hip Hop Mix" offers dialogue and gallantry; the faces men show to one another without exposing their hearts. In a sexist world, where Eddie Murphy's *Boomerang* is considered fun, this is the most commercial (obvious) version of "Why Me, Baby?" Yet it's not all that commercial when it's positioned on the CD as a revelatory contrast, exposing the many sides Adam presents to Eve.

Of course, Sweat and L.L. expose more and laugh harder than *Boomerang;* they've got the confidence that comes with artistry and heart.

*The City Sun*
July 29, 1992

# DECONSTRUCTION OR SYMPATHY

*Of what cannot be seen, of what is hidden, there is no possible symbolic use*
—JACQUES LACAN ON DIFFERENCE

ALLING HIS fiction feature debut *Swoon,* Tom Kalin announces his openly gay interest in exploring the homosexual image on screen—and controlling it. His point: Movie images can be so full of libidinal, cultural, and political meaning that their richness can make you faint with ecstasy. But a more fitting title might have been *Deconstruction or Sympathy,* because *Swoon* marks a new generation's theory-based choice to dismantle oppressive history and narrative instead of the previous tactic of fond subversion, like the laughing/weeping responses to Vincente Minnelli's *Tea and Sympathy,* one of the inane fifties Hollywood films about sexual difference.

This is a crucial thesis for gay people, whose identity and dreams are expressed in mainstream culture furtively, if at all. Every socially oppressed person has a complex relation to pop culture that includes finding political significance in its details or investing it with special—often camp—affection. ("The knife edge between joy and pain," according to one film scholar.)

Kalin's subject choice of twenties "thrill killers" Leopold and Loeb complicates a swooning response. He's interested in the way a primal, private passion for film synchs with the external world—specifically, how a modern, conscious viewer adjusts historical offense. Leopold-Loeb become Kalin's test case of sexual repression because their sexual habits were perceived at the time as the cause for pathological behavior (the line used in their defense by august counsel Clarence Darrow). Kalin also indicts the cultural misrepresentation of homosexuality in Hollywood's own Leopold-Loeb legends, such as Alfred Hitchcock's *Rope* (1948) and Richard Fleischer's *Compulsion* (1958), by reenacting several scenes from those films.

It is Kalin's project to demand a more sensitive, morally responsible viewing while at the same time outing movie homoeroticism and cultural homophobia. He implies that Hollywood repression destroys the possibility of gay empowerment. As a reaction, the film occasionally turns into a thoughtless defense of Leopold-Loeb as if they were ACT-UP's equivalent to the Scottsboro Boys or Sacco and Vanzetti—making Kalin's politics seem imprecise, to say the least. But the best and strongest idea in *Swoon*'s concept is its gay analogy: the linkage of homosexuality and cinematic pleasure.

To do this, Kalin has to violate the credibility and accuracy of his tale. *Swoon* retells the Leopold-Loeb story through assorted narrative tropes: biopic drama, documentary footage, a card game in drag, nondiegetic performances of Von Masoch's *Venus in Furs*. These dislodge the history of the murder case as a central cinematic event and replace fact with imaginative—often anachronistic—fiction. For the most alert modern filmgoers, Kalin's approach is, by now, familiar from the radical historical narratives Derek Jarman produced in *Caravaggio, War Requiem,* and *Edward II.* There's no pretense of authenticity; these filmmakers share the creative excitement of forcefully bringing modern consciousness to bear upon the classical experience of movie watching.

In *Swoon,* the sight of a mobile phone (like the presence of a typewriter in *Caravaggio*) asserts that the film is a work of its time, but also that the period story has an essential, contemporary relevance. Kalin doesn't hide his ideology behind an objective point of view, nor does he acquiesce to received notions of "deviant" behavior or to social consciousness. All such implicit pretenses of the Hollywood costume drama—and previous Leopold-Loeb films—become a joke in *Swoon.* The filmmaker's use of multiracial bit players and such devices as a phrenological diagram sequence satirizes 1920s psychiatric quackery and the film's conservative Chicago setting (while making in-jokes about 1990s New York avant-garde filmmaking).

This movie deliberately has no past tense, which means that the presentation and reshuffling of incidents in Leopold-Loeb's act of murder, the trial, and the years of their prison terms form a continual present. It constantly begs one's critical regard of movie artifice. This sensibility refutes the biases of an unenlightened past and of its dominant (subtly repressive) politics. In their place Kalin substitutes his own preferences: a consciously pictorial, rather than "realistic," visual style (Ellen Kuras's photography makes *Swoon* the lushest-looking black-and-white movie

since Isaac Julien's *Looking for Langston*); and up-to-date erotic codes—
Tom Schlachet's (Loeb's) flexing biceps are displayed in a sleeveless
checkered shirt that puts a touch of Christopher Street in the Scott
Fitzgerald ambience.

These devices are intellectually arousing on one level but suspicious
on another; the film's erotic candor isn't the same as fine understanding.
Kalin proceeds on the questionable whim that by claiming—and validating—Leopold-Loeb's sexuality he can redeem them. But to snatch
L&L's gayness whole from the jaws of bigoted history is a dangerous
sentimentalization. Can a valorizing sexual politics be based on the
behavior of those who cancel out their humanity? After all, the issue here
should be murder, not fucking. Kalin gives L&L more than the tolerance
the world withheld; he romanticizes their innocence. It's seen in both the
butch Loeb's pathetic tendency to pass for straight and Craig Chester's
performance as Leopold in the prison sequences, delicately shading in the
fragile emotions of a man confounded by his own obsessions and by his
lover's and the world's indifference to him.

*Swoon* goes from complexity to confusion, suggesting that sexuality
and Jewish ethnicity accounted for L&L's incarceration and subsequent
defamation. Kalin turns his intelligent act of revision into silly special
pleading. His script (an unfortunate collaboration with *Village Voice*
writer Hilton Als) goes unnecessarily vague on the intertwining of
sexuality and ethnicity. L&L's personal use of the word "pussy" (taken
from court records) only hints at their private identities—a teasing reference to the curious role playing of these teenage Jewish intellectuals who
adopted Nietzsche's superman theories (as a masculine fascism) but with
no intimation of an ethnic or cultural paradox at work. Their lack of
Jewish consciousness contrasts with their sexual deviousness. This aspect
of *Swoon* may represent the filmmakers' own fantasy of gayness as a
release from ethnic and social constraints—a Nietzschean delusion that
the Leopold-Loeb case should serve to disprove.

Coming from Apparatus Productions, the New York independent
film group with a postmodern bent, *Swoon*'s depiction of a chapter
in American gay oppression ought to be below-the-belt effective as
well as academically highbrow. And though *Swoon* seems intended
to offer liberated truth and exalted sexuality, it is weakened by the
assumption that classical Hollywood's suppression of sexual and ethnic
politics left gayness unaddressed. Kalin's struggle against a hidden gay
history and a normative Hollywood treatment of queerness is, unfortunately, based on his own facile misperception. This fault—which can be
felt in *Swoon*'s broken rhythms and halting attempts at sinuous montage—

stems from new, dogmatic gay politics more than an openhearted gay sensibility.

Todd Haynes, director of Apparatus's *Superstar: The Karen Carpenter Story* and *Poison,* described that sensibility in an interview with *L.A. Weekly's* John Powers: "Films like some of Hitchcock's or Sirks's have these weird, perverse, complex perspectives that can be far more gay than most movies about gay themes—because they're coming from an outsider's perspective and change *how* you see things." For Kalin, whose film background is documentary, issues of redress override any sensual cinematic effect Haynes referred to. Determined to excoriate any spurious depictions of gayness, he forgot something about the film's fundamental erotic attraction—which explains why *Swoon* never lives up to its title.

Kalin got that title from the notion of enigmatic, unexamined pleasure set down in Jacques Lacan's heavily perused 1975 essay that cited Bernini's statue of St. Theresa as a representation of female difference. The commonly suppressed (secret, sexual) ecstasy of women as defined and constructed by men inspired Kalin's effort to revise the deprecating, censorious depiction of homosexuality by mainstream (implicitly, heterosexual white) media. *Swoon* was made primarily as a falling-away from *Rope* and *Compulsion.*

It's one thing—a good thing—to challenge Hollywood ideology for its still insufficiently recognized racism and homophobia. But it's just another fabrication to treat a pair of outlaws as rebel heroes. When British pop star Morrissey sang about the sixties gangsters The Krays, he turned an erotic obsession into a critical reading of an entire society. Kalin's view of Leopold-Loeb lacks such moral sense, and it confounds the process of oppressed-group mythmaking by falsifying L&L's social meaning. *Swoon* is, in fact, a new false myth whose only virtue is the eradication of the dominant point of view. Kalin finds the deficiencies of past gay images uninstructive, but he is blind to the moral lessons that come from the discipline of acknowledging difference everywhere, even in naive films.

Lacan understood how patriarchy reified its sexism through subjugated images of women, but previous generations of artists (gay and straight) also understood the beauty of subverting such a rigid ideology. They dealt with what could not be seen by using inference and vivid symbolism. Vito Russo missed these achievements in his book *The Celluloid Closet,* and when Kalin slights them in *Swoon* he misses out on one of the great misunderstood pleasures of the movie past.

*Swoon* presents the currently fashionable impatience with inauthentic or demeaning gay representation that should—one day—forge a more honest, direct gay representation. For now, we have a culture gap. At one time a pure, lively cultural exegesis happened automatically when audiences responded to closeted Hollywood films. Before Lacan enunciated it, movies like *Compulsion, Psycho, Rope, Miss Lonelyhearts, The Member of the Wedding, A Place in the Sun, Rebel Without a Cause,* and *The Wild One* offered a coded appreciation of gay behavior and sensibility. Most of these, in turn, inspired poster iconography that was the pop equivalent to Bernini's St. Theresa. Hung on bedroom walls, mailed on postcards, these images—Brando in leather on a motorcycle, Clift in a prison cell—received special acceptance by fans. The states of concupiscence, neurasthenia, tenderness they evoke are powerful tokens of nontraditional masculine behavior and male peacocking. Openly significant, these images predate Lacan's "The mystery of the woman can be seen, in all its evidence for the man, for him." To transpose this theory—to understand it in gay terms—is a process of empowerment through delight; a "male" point of view is deemphasized when men themselves become objects of contemplation. These fifties icons gave release from Hays Code repression. Ideas, expressions, looks were communicated that expressed gay desire, sensitivity, tension. Audiences who picked up on these elements practiced an intellection that had to thrive outside the academy (which even today insists on analyzing movies through heterosexual paradigms).

This pop sophistication is exactly the brain work, the heart need, that structuralism is about. One of Richard Dyer's essays in *Heavenly Bodies: Film Stars and Society* (the 1986 follow-up to his pioneering 1979 book *Stars*) describes the intensity of gay male identification with movie star Judy Garland: "Garland works in an emotional register of great intensity which seems to bespeak equally suffering and survival, vulnerability and strength, theatricality and authenticity." A similar relationship is developed with the images certain fifties movie actors presented through their more flexible, idiosyncratic, androgynous performances—Anthony Perkins's trembling, Farley Granger's meekness, Montgomery Clift's delicacy, Brando's open sensuality, James Dean's ambivalence, Julie Harris's and Brandon DeWilde's pansexuality. The attraction of their styles lay in what Dyer saw as evidence "of the way that social-sexual identity has been understood and felt in a certain period of time."

These were the years Tennessee Williams's plays were filmed with impeccable casts, yet were traduced—castrated—through censorship. Even the gay content of Robert Anderson's *Tea and Sympathy* was turned into an embarrassed, snickering self-righteousness. Hollywood seemed unable to grow along with the advancing psychosexual visions of artists in other disciplines. A gay undercurrent is all that keeps many of these films fascinating today as illustrations of an alternative consciousness struggling out despite artistic repression.

And yet some actors, performances, characters really did come through, and spoke to gay audiences. In *Compulsion* and *Psycho* (1960) there is the obvious, perplexed exhibition of masculine difference, locating it in the disturbed behavior of killers fictionalized from real life—mainstream projections of social taboo equated with moral terror. While this is unarguably homophobic, one's political objection changes in the face of Dean Stockwell's Judd (the Leopold counterpart in *Compulsion*) and Tony Perkins's Norman Bates—still two of the finest gay characterizations in American cinema and among the most eloquent portraits anywhere of the sad young man. Yes, it's a limited gay archetype, but it also draws a definitive emotional crisis.

These are marvelous, *romantic* performances, done within the limits of mainstream convention but bravely pushing past them through nuance and detail that are delicate, sensitive—and, shockingly, unacclaimed because they seemed unconnected to the normalizing tactics of the vaunted Method. But much like the Method, these performances used sex as glamour (Stephen Heath's phrase). One responded kinesthetically to the actors' display of subterranean emotions, fascinated by the revelation of a different sexual being and a different sensitivity.

The sustained artifice and truth of great acting like Stockwell's and Perkins's is superior to the academic extrapolation of *Swoon*. Their performances give a rich understanding of the diversity of human behavior, the tensions that arise from strict social pressure, and the agony of self-fulfillment. This subtext, so elemental to the Freudian drama that flourished after the Second World War and made a mark on fifties Hollywood, formed a link between individuality and gay experience. (What Dyer calls "to turn out not-ordinary, after being saturated with the values of ordinariness.") These movies dramatized the dilemma gay people know from confronting social conventions.

If the unconscious idea behind *Compulsion* and *Psycho* was to demonize homosexuality, it is remarkable how much sympathy Stockwell and Perkins were able to draw. They create an understanding of their characters as people, and hence an understanding of gayness where none existed before and especially remarkable in a context where gayness is shamefully hushed. The ardent devotion of Stockwell's Judd Steiner to Bradford Dillman's Artie Straus hits notes of passion and melancholy that even an eighties out film like *Another Country* could only make explicit but not *felt*. In *Psycho*, Perkins limns the confusions of repressed sexuality. His performance is cagier, more humane, more radical than the jokey responses panicky critics and audiences prefer to have toward Norman Bates's identity crisis. It is, actually, a crisis of inhibition—the ultimate closet scenario. Perkins turns it into a prestructuralist satire when he nervously stammers the world "falsity," making that critique of the mainstream's stereotypical depictions of masculine difference into a mangled utterance. (At first it sounds like a difficult, tortured pronunciation of "fallacy"; more ironically, it sounds like a nervous "phallus.")

Norman's struggle to reconcile aspects of his personality with his assigned social role fits a grotesque idea of queerness—no less so than in the psychobabble explanation at the film's end. But much of *Psycho*'s greatness lies in the contrast of Norman's mental stress to Marion Crane's; she is the film's first psycho, the "normal" person who goes "a little bit crazy sometimes." The scene of their yearning misconnection is one of Hitchcock's most poignant. In a film largely about the repression of sex and social roles, the gay and female protagonists are cases of oppressed self-destructives. It can be clearly understood that their crimes are not caused by sexuality, and that such prejudiced reductions (as happened with Leopold-Loeb) are laughably insufficient explanations of the mystery of human character.

No doubt Hitchcock arrived at this pinnacle through the previous quasi-gay characters in *Strangers on a Train, Shadow of a Doubt,* and *Rope,* characters that were dry runs for Norman's complexity. *Rope,* particularly, evinces an early naiveté that made oblique reference to the nature of the relationship between the John Dall–Farley Granger characters. It's this dreadful innuendo of "discretion" that Kalin is up against as it has embarrassingly returned to today's movies, particularly in *The Silence of the Lambs.* The gay groups that objected to *Silence* based their protests on a jejune reading. Sure, "Buffalo Bill" (Ted Levine as Jame Gumb) is a rampaging serial killer, but he exists in a circumspect context that allows director Jonathan Demme to defend him against antigay allegations. In truth, the film's other main characters—Clarice Starling (Jodie Foster) and Hannibal Lecter (Anthony Hopkins)—have the kind of singularity and difference (hypersensitivity as special sexuality) that suggests they, too, are gay. Demme's three protagonists demonstrate a range of gay archetypes, but so subtly encoded (more so than in fifties films) that their *difference* makes no difference. And here is where protestors—and Kalin—can legitimately balk: the characters' lack of sexual affect makes them unresonant. Their gayness remains unempowered, hidden.

Take a fresh look at *Compulsion* thirty-four years after, even at a TV print that compresses the CinemaScope images into telescoped pop-art fragments. Leopold-Loeb's criminality takes on a charged-up expressionism—a startling representation of their Jazz Age, supermen neuroses. It begins with a postcoital (getaway) scene as intense and hyped up as any in *Bonnie and Clyde;* Fleischer's exploitation style asserts its own aesthetic distance as rigorous as the formal disruptions in *Swoon*. The secreted meanings suggest a widescreen *Caligari*—a vision angled and distorted by the euphemisms of its time—but inside it all is the beating heart of Stockwell's Judd: angry, intelligent, passionate. That Stockwell would dare the finest performance of his career as a gay man (in one scene revealed as the owner of a teddy bear with subtle, beyond-camp seriousness) prefigures the same avant-garde impudence he showed as the pop-art freak lip-synching "In Dreams" in David Lynch's *Blue Velvet*. Stockwell achieved the rejection of social role and sexual stereotype that the cooled-down acting in *Swoon* merely outlines (Kalin makes Leopold-Loeb's top/bottom distinctions seem schematic rather than personal). Stockwell's acting triumph supersedes *Swoon*'s narrative convolutions simply by the demonstrated fact of individual personality that slips both the confines of narrative convention and the dictates of a radical politics. Stockwell, like Perkins, lets one *see* gay emotion separate from a pathological case study. An early audience of gays and straights could correctly appreciate this as a sophisticated achievement.

It occasioned pleasure in seeing (*la jouissance de voir*) rooted in the exhibition of unorthodox male eroticism and sensitivity; Perkins's fragility, Stockwell's desire. Kalin withdraws from these film experiences, refusing an important interpretive reflex of film consciousness. But the structuralist antics of *Swoon* leave it unclear how much pleasure—or swooning—can be had when gayness is analyzed more than it is made understandable. Kalin's approach may have outsmarted itself.

*Film Comment*
July 1992

# A SOULJAH'S STORY

W HEN CHUCK D drafted the community activist Lisa Williamson to be the female voice in Public Enemy, he attempted to
avoid the usually hopeless process of educating and politiciz-
ing a pop performer. By starting with one who was already politically savvy, he stood a good chance of transforming the hiphop female
stereotype: The image of an around-the-way girl would only be deepened by a girl who knew her way around popular rhetoric and social
history.

From the moment Williamson made her debut as Sister Souljah (a
sister who was the essence of all things and approved by an Afrocentric
deity), her temper and strident voice (Richard Torres called her "the Dr.
Ruth of hiphop") didn't quite fit the Public Enemy profile. Her first
recording, "Buck Whylin'," went a step past agitprop and closer to sheer
agitation ("WE ARE AT WAR!"). She didn't break the MC Lyte-Queen
Latifah-Roxanne Shanté mold; she simply didn't fit anyone's idea of a
good time.

A Black Boadicea, she expressed female righteousness as a warrior,
not a nurturer. No-nonsense by nature, Sister Souljah would push the
perimeters of hiphop away from partying and transcendence by emphasizing instead the political basis of all American and Black experience.
She since has proved, with the release of her album *360 Degrees of Power*
(Epic) and the furor made over it by Bill Clinton and the media, Chuck D's
instincts to be too good. Hiphop does indeed allow for the musical
expression of political ideas, but that development can only disturb a
cultural system committed to frivolity.

Critics who claim *360 Degrees of Power* lacks the necessary dope
beats and phat rhythms for hiphop approval have not really listened to
it; they're actually expressing their displeasure at the effrontery of a
woman who won't dance/sing/rap solely to the rhythm of sensual escape.
Her producer, Eric "Vietnam" Sadler, sticks to the Public Enemy mandate
that pop music can be political. Sadler and Souljah's music to protest
by is bebop Brechtian; they emphasize the drum's message as well as its

sound and that—in the increasingly commercialized hiphop nation—is a radical faith.

All this makes Sister Souljah the first female hiphop artist who can be taken seriously. Despite Latifah's bodacious smile, the form has not yet produced its Billie Holiday, Diana Ross, or Aretha Franklin, but Souljah is comparably authentic. Her virtues are extramusical; she can express the urgency of her feelings. She can't always wait for the music; she only tries to as a pretext. Her essential ambition is to justify Afrocentric intellection and loquacity as updated venerable practices.

Her opening speech fits a wonderful legacy:

> *Most people won't accept my activism and this album until after I'm dead and the blood's all over the ground. Maybe in a year, or two or five. Then all the money-making blood suckers will come out with hats, coats, buttons and posters and maybe even movies. And people will lie and say "Yeah, I was down with her! She was bad! Yeah, she was fine! She gave those white people hell, ya know!" Well the truth is this album is from my heart to my people based on my experiences with America. Furthermore, this album is from one* lonely *but powerful Black soldier.*

That declaration is followed by the piano fills, choral wailing, and congregational moaning of a church service. It's a blatant pop-gospel crossover, but unlike most, this isn't designed to make you feel good but to further the potential of Black oral tradition. Lonely but powerful, Souljah evokes the historical figure that has gotten the least play from Afrocentricity's ascent: Black women missionaries, Sojourner, the martyr of Baldwin's *The Amen Corner.* Even the new breed of skeezer-journalists eager to pump up the most scabrous trends have denied this figure, left it a blurry myth.

Souljah is the only female rapper to *consider* a poor righteous teacher ethic, who is willing to accept sacrifice as a condition for telling it like it is. The Black missionary who eschews fashion (whether kente cloth or a thumping rump) scares people through her arrogance and righteousness. My guess is that this alienates rap womanists less than Souljah's defiant lack of glamour. But what they miss, what they fail to acknowledge, is the missionary's zealous concentration. It's what gives her the power to tell it like it is. And the pleasure—the art—of *360 Degrees of Power* is Souljah's blunt, tireless ability to call a spade a spade ("African Scaredy Katz in a One Exit Maze"), to tell the truth and shame the devil ("My God Is a Powerful God").

It never should be forgotten that the great thrill of hiphop is its imaginative reclaim of the beat and the voice. These ubiquitous skills are often used in show business to betray Black people, but political rap curates those qualities by giving them a self-empowering focus.

Most critics and politicians don't realize that to argue Souljah on such points as "Two wrongs don't make a right, but it damn sure makes it even!" ("The Hate That Hate Produced") is to miss what makes her attractive, compelling, entertaining and, at times, artistic. Her astringent pronouncements clear the air of fluff and drivel.

The plain truth is that there is a lot of truth in *360 Degrees of Power*. What appalls conservatives sounds liberating to others. Her litany of complaints targets a general ignorance that comes from the suppression of political and racial discussion. It's a wittier level of discourse than Shahrazad Ali's scapegoating.

> *African people, too scared to call*
> *themselves African*
> *And too dumb to know the difference if they did.*

This isn't simple name calling; she uses the colloquial sense of dumb, meaning the deliberate, capitalist act of protecting old ways of thinking and behaving.

Souljah's oration is not especially lyrical, but she is hilariously precise. Criticizing Black people who "will fall for any damn thing / Will boogie into the 21st Century / Without a plan, without a clue / Still divided," she seems as observant and shrewd as a grandmother. Most of the tracks here qualify as satirical folk wisdom—you call it a rant only to deny its sense and authenticity.

The best track is "Killing Me Softly; Deadly Code of Silence," a duet with Ice Cube that features his best vocal performance yet: "In '92 Ice Cube come a little bit Blacker / Buck, buck, buck down the cracker / See ya driving in your Cadillaca through South Central / And I just might jack ya." He parries Souljah's didacticism with sheer rhythm. Their teamwork proves hiphop to be a limitless musical and political form. Their styles blend well and so do their perspectives.

Cube warns: " 'Cause you teach freedom of speech / As long as Black men don't say Howard Beach or Bensonhurst / Tawana and Latasha / We ain't forgot ya / Don't say Jew or Korean / You're acting like a bad human being." He sums up the political racism that is denied in most political-candidate rhetoric and music-critic diatribes. The emphasis on speaking, Black political utterance, cuts to the heart of hiphop as an art form and as a controversial social act. *360 Degrees of Power* defends the form and attacks its attackers from many angles on each of Souljah's thirteen tracks. Her passion is as legitimate as Latifah's "How do I love thee? Let me count the ways"; it's just that Souljah continues "The Wrath of My Madness" after Latifah dropped it.

On "Killing Me Softly," Souljah goes off, listing America's violent historical atrocities until her voice cracks in a crescendo of anger and pain: "AND AMERICA IS RESPONSIBLE FOR ALL FORMS OF VIOLENT DESTRUCTION OF AFRICAN PEOPLE THROUGHOUT THE ENTIRE WORLD / WHY AMERICA, IN FACT, IS EVEN VIOLENT IN AMERICA." She knows it's overstatement, but you know it's true. Calling Souljah a crank ignores the issue.

"Killing Me Softly" is an ideological romance, with Souljah pledging devotion to Cube's own caustic manner: "Some think he's right, and some think he's wrong / But Sister Souljah, I like him / 'Cause I like 'em strong!" It's bad that she later tells him, "Don't change," because he plainly needs to grow, but she recognizes his essence as a system-bucking speaker, and that at least is something to admire.

Hiphop may never produce an album more self-consciously audacious than this. One track overlaps Souljah screaming, "George Bush is a terrorist! He creates terror in the minds, hearts and neighborhoods of Black people!" against a white-bread female voice complaining, "Oh, no, it's her again. Why won't she stop yelling!" It's a funny, healthy trope that gets expanded on "Brainteasers and Doubtbusters," in which the tape is left running and we hear recording studio engineers ridiculing Souljah's stridency. It's worthy of De La Soul but it draws a harshly realistic picture of the music-industry paradox – the unspoken joke among Blacks and whites who must make money and politics off of each other.

There's no denying the impasse is great, but what angry hiphoppers have on their side is the refreshing vigor of sizing up the situation even though people who sit at the social controls don't want them to. Implicit throughout the album is a blood frankness. Souljah says a lot of things that many think Black people are too naive to notice and too frightened to say. She satirizes politeness and ridicules mendacity.

"Brainteasers and Doubtbusters" ends with a description of how white power effects Black people that can only be called a revelry, an uncomplicated defense of Black linguistics. The pleasure of saying this is in Souljah's voice even when she gasps with her last breath, "Fuck all of you, that's right I said all of you!"

Johnny Rotten knew there were occasions when you can say no more than that, and Souljah's sentiment held – before and after the Democratic

National Convention—as truth and as uncompromised entertainment. Her consistent point is that Black speech is a defiant art form. She has made a classic album to prove it, and won't need to make another.

*The City Sun*
August 19, 1992

# ICE-T GOES BUCK WILD

CE-T, CAPITALISM'S FRIEND, promises that his next recording will be "even worse" than "Cop Killer," the song that enraged law-enforcement groups across the country. Does that mean he'll finally come up with "new and improved," "100-percent-pure" anger?

Last month, when Ice-T bowed down to political pressure and conveniently asked his record company, Warner Bros., to delete "Cop Killer" from further pressings of the *Body Count* album, he made the decade's sorriest demonstration of confused pop ideology. Trading ethics for economics, Ice-T took the juice out of his usually hard-core defiance. He exhibited, instead, a naive complicity with the powers that be.

Aggrieved but not astute, Ice-T has become a puny martyr—a role that now seems a clarification of all the others he has played. Whether as a pimp, drug pusher, or cop killer, Ice-T has made many good records in the tough, wary, angry, and witty voice of the oppressed. He could make antisocial belligerence sound justified by detailing the personal and political insults that provoke it.

With all of this, Ice-T mastered the commodification of anger. The most remarkable aspect of *Body Count* is his transubstantiation of Black temper and perspective into the heavy-metal idiom. His loud, careening band of Black metalheads is good enough, and Ice-T does his rants with such appropriate gracelessness that the album's high points— "KKK Bitch," "There Goes the Neighborhood," "Evil Dick," "Momma's Gonna Die Tonight"—are hilarious camp.

This move was artistically insignificant (especially compared to the sophisticated genre hopping Public Enemy does in each half of "I Don't Wanna Be Called Yo Niga" or what Morrissey does on *Your Arsenal*). But it was commercially shrewd.

Ice-T's metal rap consolidated his reputation with the largely white audience he was presented to in last year's "Lollapalooza" tour. But if political hiphop is predicated on higher terms of social consciousness and civil disobedience than the petulant fantasies of white metal, then the zippy, delirious humor of *Body Count* effectively smashed those terms: It makes the legitimate protests of society's victims into a harmless joke anyone can enjoy. That, ironically, may be precisely what brought Ice-T and "Cop Killer" to Simi Valley consciousness and, thus, ruin.

It could be argued that Ice-T's crossover indeed made him the mainstream's boy; his ironic character studies became their arsenal for combating freedom of speech. And instead of remaining intransigent and subversive — by staying hard, angry, and defiant — Ice-T voluntarily set the precedent for nineties clampdown by censoring his own record.

He may have trashed First Amendment principles by withdrawing "Cop Killer," but Ice-T did not — really — betray himself. His "sacrifice" could ingratiate only him with the corporate executives at Time-Warner; he took the fall for them — a precipitous fall from grace. Now one can clearly see that, for many hiphop artists who perform the canny trick of moral suasion in their politicized music, there is no principle that is held more strongly than business.

There was a hint of Ice-T's capitalist devotion at this year's New Music Seminar, at which he appeared on the rap artists' panel and advocated a vigilante beatdown on bootleg-tape peddlers. He showed no comradely understanding of grass-roots hustling by streetcorner brothers and no mercy for financially strapped consumers who are faced with greedily marked-up prices.

Apparently, Ice-T would impose capitalist arrogance only upon the unempowered; he didn't take advantage of Time-Warner's omnipotence by laughing in the face of those miffed police groups who proposed a boycott of all Time-Warner companies. Here was an opportunity for the most daring subversion of all — challenging America to do without the press, cable TV, and even *Batman Returns!* — but Ice-T has made the marketplace safe for the status quo.

If there was inside pressure from his record company, Ice-T could have saved himself from disgrace by admitting it. Chuck D did as much in 1989, and Sister Souljah has not pulled any of her singles. Instead, Ice-T stayed true to a pimp's small-time vision, showing a typical record-industry hack's intimidation.

In the history of Black empowerment, this amounts to a personal shame and public scandal. The hiphop artists who champion the rights of Black people to speak their minds and challenge authority need to understand that even a business deal is a political act but it does not limit the conditions of moral behavior. If hiphop artists are not willing to go all the way with the ideas they profess—if they aren't willing to sacrifice a few royalties—then they will be doomed to repeat Ice-T's cowardice.

Is that a harsh term for Ice-T? Here's a harsh fact: In Detroit, this month, parents of students at Malcolm X Academy, a public elementary school, convened to discuss whether they would relocate the school from a predominantly white neighborhood. The academy had been defaced with spray-painted swastikas and picketed by tattooed, hostile white residents threatening violence should any of the five- to eleven-year-old students attend the school.

On August 13, the parents announced their commitment to the school, vowing that their children *will* attend and *will* be protected, however necessary. They displayed the sense of history—and principle—that Ice-T, counting his money, lacks. The Malcolm X Academy parents demonstrated a love that is deeper, more mysterious, than anything described by rappers' facile politics.

Ice-T's aptitude for selling anger is null and void. He simply doesn't say what he means or mean what he says. When an artist chumps out this way, he's even too pathetic to be a laughingstock.

*The City Sun*
August 26, 1992

# BOOM IN HIS HEAD!

T HE BEAUTY OF plain talk and the efficacy of profane language make "Rodney K" a major event in contemporary social discourse. It's also a funny, exciting record—just about the only thing worth one's attention at this cacophonous moment in African-American intellectual history. "Rodney K" is the flip side to "Clean Up Man," the first single by Willie D (William Dennis ) since he left the Houston rap group Geto Boys, and it has the same raucous, down-home appeal of such notorious Geto Boys' songs as "Mind of a Lunatic" and "Mind's Playing Tricks on Me," but without any of the piety.

Willie D's vulgar record counters the most acclaimed voice of polite Black diplomacy—specifically, Rodney King's public statement in the middle of last spring's Los Angeles uprising, "Can we all get along?" Dazed, pitiful, and uncertain, King made a maudlin display of Black futility. And Willie D slams him for it. The most shocking thing about this record is that even if you question Willie D's rage, you can't help but understand it. ("Rodney K" begins with a woman's voice crying, "We're tired of it!")

At the 1992 Democratic Convention there were other equally pathetic displays, as Jesse Jackson, Barbara Jordan, Aretha Franklin, and Jennifer Holiday provided the entertainment without remotely affecting the policy platform of the white folks in charge. The question is no longer "Who speaks for the Negro?" but "Whom is the Negro speaking to?"

All those proper voices seemed lost, whereas Willie D's charged-up impudence finds a home—finds unassailable logic—in the dropped consonants, dialect tones, and cussed bons mots of Black vernacular. But "Rodney K" celebrates more than a voice; it revels in the expression, the psychological sense of place, that defines the common Black American condition. And with this burden, carried lightly on the tongue, Willie D commands the serious attention and the ethnic legitimacy that desperately is being sought by another set of African-American spokespeople, the niggerati—from Cornel West to Henry Louis Gates Jr.—now having a crisis of conscience in the pages of the nation's white press.

In the five years since rap has become the superior art form of contemporary culture, there hasn't been a single academic theory that mattered as much. No Black scholar has written an essay, edited an anthology, or contributed an op-ed piece as cogent, inspired, artistic, meaningful, or pleasurable as "Bring the Noise," "The Booming System," "Say No Go," "Nighttrain," or "Rodney K." The public knows this automatically, and the Black intelligentsia knows it with chagrin. That's part of the reason Black scholarly attacks focus on rap music and its attendant politics. Eggheads envy the b-boys for their direct link to the people and so try to match hiphop popularity through the white (mainstream) media.

One reason it's so wonderful to see the voice go up against the word in "Rodney K" is that it pulverizes the education president's worry about illiteracy. Rap audiences get better poetry and more intricate philosophy than anything inscribed on those dead trees titled *The Content of Our Character* or *The Signifying Monkey*. The hiphop generation is a generation of writers, in the literal sense, plus avid listeners (i.e., readers, in the best sense) who understand and appreciate the ideas communicated.

The art of "Rodney K" is based in the confidence that Willie D and his audience/generation have in the thought and language that see them through a hostile world. The intelligence they develop for themselves has been learned—felt—and not borrowed from textbooks, seminaries, or literary quarterlies. Angrily enunciated "Rodney K" evinces a radical intelligence that may be dismissed superficially as "ignorant." But Willie D's Southern wit makes a detailed rebuke of those accommodating, polite wastes of breath.

By the time Willie D tosses out his fifth f-word on the ("Fuck that nigger!") chorus, you can be sure Shelby Steele, Gates, and West won't let themselves hear past his crudeness. And this thought adds to the record's joy. Willie D dismisses them in his ridicule of rhythmless, tired Blacks chanting "The Negro National Anthem." On his sixth f-word, Willie D turns "Rodney K" into a magnificent broadside:

> *Fuck all that singin'*
> *I'mo be too busy swingin'*
> *That's the problem with Black folks*
> *Always want to bust a note.*

That's the finest rap trope since Public Enemy's *Apocalypse 91*. It transmutes sexual instinct into habitual passivity to show what's wrong with conventional methods of Black protest. Willie D don't wanna

> *. . . hold hands and form rallies*

*And down niggers who fight back in Cali*
*I'm down with the niggers who's maxin'*
*Fuck all that goddamn protestin'.*

It's the traditional means of resistance that Willie D rejects as insufficient. He earns the right to this by his professional association with the Rap-A-Lot record label, based in Houston, where Geto Boys repaired after their big-label deal with Geffen Records (through Def American Records) fell apart in 1990 following "Mind of a Lunatic."

Being on the fringes of rap's mainstream ensures the possibility of genuine hard-core records. The Geto Boys' bust-up has resulted in an unusual flowering of talent in Scarface's Dostoyevskian album, *Mr. Scarface Is Back*, and Bushwick Bill's surreal confessional, "Ever So Clear." The artistic daring in these post–Geto Boys' recordings measures the independence artists feel when they don't have to play the major-label rules (such as Public Enemy bleeping its own tracks). The security of a rebellious audience means they're not beholden to any elite group and so don't have to kowtow like the head of Harvard's African-American Studies department or professors seeking tenure at a mainstream university.

These creative and political conditions are more important than any evanescent "street credibility." Willie D and his credited producers—Crazy C, Bido, Roland, and Goldfinger—keep the beats jumping as a show of creative freedom throughout the album *I'm Goin' Out Like a Soldier*. The rushing rhythms on "Rodney K" often are rooted to melodic piano flourishes—a combination that recalls the inspired, chaotic Bomb Squad sound of *Fear of a Black Planet*, another radical touchstone.

Willie D may be farther "out there" than Chuck D, but he's also, obviously, more inside. "Rodney K" is as uncompromised as it is heartfelt. Willie D explicates the complex emotions that King's televised address provoked. That sad portrait of humility and forgiveness got broken down each time TV news directors chose to rebroadcast it. What looked like a simple human moment was revealed, through repetition, to be ideological propaganda.

The anguish in King's voice evoked a Christian charity that seemed anachronistic and—even worse—incongruous. King addressed nothing that most oppressed Americans feel in the 1990s, only the shame that might be felt by a white (Christian?) dominant class. Willie D's outrage comes out of the realization that King's appeal to white American power was deliberately misdirected toward the powerless. Willie D responds to such bizarre twists in contemporary racial discourse by damning the corrupt, foolish behavior of Black folks who appoint themselves spokesmen before assessing the situation. He berates the slave tendency for injuring oneself to please whites. At one point, he unfortunately borrows Ice Cube's homophobia, but he's best on his own:

> *Rodney King, goddamn sellout*
> *On TV crying for a cop*
> *The same motherfucker*
> *Who beat the hell out ya*
> *Now I wish they woulda shot ya.*

Martyrdom in the sixties made more sense than the attrition of nineties injustice. A social system that does not inspire faith only, logically, can inspire rage, so "Rodney K" is pitched somewhere between the absurdism of Kafka's *The Trial* (Joseph K) and the political passion of *The Autobiography of Malcolm X*. Therein lies the continuing horror story of the Black experience as a daily nightmare that one can only curse but not change. Willie D's language portrays it exactly:

> *Fuck that motherfuckin' sellout ho*
> *They need to beat his ass some mo*
> *Fool talkin' 'bout "Stop the violence"*
> *When niggers can't even shit in silence.*

For Willie D and most Black Americans, silence is an unknown quantity—like peace, freedom, safety from harassment. The song's hectic pace pushes past any relaxation or ease; the whole record is a rocking boat, a vehicle conveying the nation's instability.

This is the most sense anyone has made of the L.A. disturbance. Willie D related the compounded grievances ("Didn't nobody set a fire for Willie D / When them laws beat the fuck out of me"); he describes civil disobedience as a historical pattern ("That's why the niggers stay out of check / Cuz that's the only thing rednecks respect"); and he has words for politicians ("We don't want your welfare checks / Niggers need a real job to buy a Rolex / And until we get it / We gonna' keep throwin' them things / Fuck Rodney King").

Rodney King becomes an ultimate figure of scorn, because he allowed himself to be used (further) as a figure of white control. Despite Willie D's livid tone (the quick righteousness in his voice), "Rodney K" contains great pity for that abused man, and that's why it is a great record. You first may have to understand the full scope of the Simi Valley tragedy to taste the pity in Willie D's rant, but it's also in the song's gravely developed ideas—the daring, serious leap from King to other unsuspecting Black puppets.

*I still got a lot of grudges*
*It's high time that we take out some judges*
*And congressmen and senators who cheat us*
*And all of you so-called Black leaders.*

Willie D is aware of the delusions suffered by high-profile Blacks who presume to lecture on Black civility, and he's artist enough to portray that voice, too. The CD single version's final coup is a meeting with "that ho-assed" King, who, in a wheedling Stepin Fetchit voice, brags, "Ah, man, they paid my rent up for a month, man, and everything. They gave me a year supply of Right-on Curl. They take care of me." That voice is the definite sound of sellout. The three gunshots that follow it fulfill the promise of Willie D's opening—"Boom! In his head. Boom! Boom! In his back. Just like that." It's a killing in effigy.

"Rodney K's" violent rhetoric is far less harmful than the real-life assassinations conducted by the cadre of Black intellectuals jumping on the Black anti-Semitism bandwagon. These attempts to silence Black discourse according to the terms and preferences of a white media elite are as vile as if Rodney King had fired the gun that killed LaTasha Harlins.

Black vigilantes like Henry Louis Gates Jr., do not hold intellectual freedom precious. Gates lacks the camaraderie of rappers who list scores of shout-outs in the liner notes of their albums. He doesn't recognize how difficult and rare it is for an African American to find and broadcast a voice of his own.

This chastising tendency is, itself, elitist, as demonstrated by people whose small degree of prominence fosters a sense of moral superiority. It's a feeling Rodney King also might have felt as he slicked back his hair and put on new duds for the TV cameras that previously had shown him beaten. That both the pampered and abused can behave as overseers supervising out-of-check Blacks shows the utter confusion that keeps Blacks from thinking independently. Willie D says it tight:

*This shit is deeper than Vietnam*
*There ain't no room for the Uncle Tom*

Again, it is necessary to assert the seriousness of the American racial holocaust before the mainstream (Oliver Stone) idea that there is only one major modern American catastrophe. This may be a Black point of view, but it admits a rooted social identity. That's what the crusading Black academics envy next to rappers' cultural leverage. In a *Village Voice* discussion between Cornel West and Patricia J. Williams, both bemoaned their lack of consequence among Black Americans without connecting it to the remoteness they feel by working in white academic sinecures and refusing to write for Black-oriented publications. (In a hilarious feat of self-justification, Gates, in the *Voice*, described *Tikkun*, one of West's writing berths, as "not primarily an African-American forum.")

Black academics, reluctant to give up the prestige of white acceptance and approval, still want to use their own curriculum vitae as the definition of Black history and morality to which every Black should aspire. And Willie D has words for them, too:

> *Brown-nosin' cuz you was chosen*
> *By the whites*
> *To make niggers act right.*

Those select lines may describe no so-called Black leader better than National Book Award winner Shelby Steele. Caught in an uncharacteristic nonplussed moment, Steele wailed on his *Transitions* magazine interviewer Julianne Malveaux: "I am a 'Black nigger' from the South Side of Chicago. I'm not a cool guy and I don't just take that shit. I understand that I have to live my life, certain goals and ambitions that I have . . . and if you get in my way I'll try to wipe you out. If you get in my way because I'm Black, I'll try to wipe you out, I'll try to hurt you."

Only a challenge to a Black academic's intellectual authority could make bourgeois Steele talk like a stereotypical rapper. Where's the AK-47? In the essays that accuse Blacks of loving their victim status, and those *New York Times* editorials that call Blacks the enemy of Jews.

These Uncle Tom positions (and privileges) can be maintained only by making other Blacks look bad. No doubt Henry Louis Gates Jr. benefits professionally from posing himself against Leonard Jeffries. But it's cowardly that Gates does so without ever engaging his "opponent" in an intellectual discussion. (Gates's personal rap song also must be, "If you get in my way I'll try to wipe you out.")

In the end, all this backbiting and cultural assassination isn't enlightened at all. It suggests the age-old antagonism of uppity house niggers fighting the field niggers, and the truth of this struggle comes out in petty rivalry over white favors. Steele to Malveaux: "Damn right! Get into the mainstream. Goddamn right! If you're not in the mainstream you're dead. Jews are in the mainstream. They have a culture and a community. . . . If you get out of the mainstream where are you gonna go?"

Perhaps to Houston, where the best modern art is being made this year.

Plainly, Black academics lusting for prestige, power, and money turn their backs on the very idea of a nonbourgeois Black society as legitimate culture or community. And this is why hiphop's faith in language shows a faith in the people who speak it. Willie D speaks it, not like a professor: he speaks it to make it sing.

In the most startling and moving lines of "Rodney K," Willie D rises above anger and transcends the usual hard-core rap commitment to money:

> *You can't lead the Black struggle*
> *And be friends with the enemy, Motherfucker!*
> *While you tryin' to keep your fuckin' job*
> *Black folks gettin' robbed*
> *But when it's time for the revolution*
> *I'mo click-click-click*
> *Fuck this rap shit!*
> *Cuz money ain't shit but grief*
> *If you ain't got no peace.*

Willie D's vulgar, countrified rap is absolutely visionary. It takes in contemporary sorrow, and hopes for a future of change. Offering to junk his profession is more than the academic cultural assassins ever have dared to say. And Willie D's warning "money ain't shit but grief" shows a greater wisdom than the eggheads know. Gates's suspicious morality is too closely tied to social advancement; Willie D shows that you don't have to leave the ghetto to have integrity.

*The City Sun*
October 21, 1992

# THE AWFUL TRUTH
# SNAGS POP

*How I love the complicated things of life.*
—FROM "SUCH A LITTLE THING" AS AD-LIBBED BY MORRISSEY IN CONCERT

ORRISSEY'S LAST New York appearance at the Paramount, September 18, ended with the British pop star singing before a two-story poster of an extremely dissolute Elvis Presley. This backdrop was revealed as Morrissey launched into "The National Front Disco." Surely, the pairing of a rock deity with a song about British fascism was intentional, but no New York paper reviewing the concert made mention of it.

Elvis irony, a familiar tool in Morrissey's constant subversion of rock-'n'-roll orthodoxy (Elvis was the sleeve star of The Smith's single "Shoplifters of the World Unite"), displays an ambiguous view, celebrating rock tradition and satirizing it. No such complexity was apparent in the recent *Village Voice* music item tying Bill Clinton and Albert Gore to Elvisiana, a habit of white contextualization not far from National Front dogma and one of the continuing nightmares of pop discourse.

Morrissey queers all that in "The National Front Disco," a great, troubling song that connects fascist politics to the mainstream rock culture that denies it, even—especially—in blurbs that attempt to tout Democratic presidential candidates.

"The National Front Disco" dares to do what Morrissey sang about on 1990's *Kill Uncle* album: "Telling you all that you never wanted to know / Showing you what you didn't want shown."

Asked about the sentiments of British racists that go uncondemned on his latest album *Your Arsenal*, Morrissey answered, "I understand the level of [their] patriotism, the level of frustration and the level of jubilance. I understand the overall character. I understand their aggression and I understand why it must be released. You might be surprised by that. But I just understand the character. I just do."

It's the "just do" in Morrissey's explanation that won't do. A complete understanding of the phenomenon of racism as evidenced in English social habit and such rituals as football games and pop concerts (two of the most evocative settings on *Your Arsenal*) would have to recognize its relation to the history of nationalist aggression and warped psychology and its peculiarity as a postcolonial fact. Morrissey's "just do" seems to accept foul social custom as the unchangeable nature of things. But *Your Arsenal* isn't so simple that this observation is served up plain or contentedly. With his usual daring and intransigence and wit, Morrissey confronts the unpleasant aspects of every social contract.

The pop star wily enough to contribute "You're the One for Me, Fatty" to the narrow-minded catalogue of romantic platitudes insists on providing "some hope and some despair" as a balanced, realistic expression. It's surprising Morrissey has never written a song called "Nothing Is Easy," yet his blithe pronouncement of everyday tragedies makes life's dis-ease a palpable thing, an aesthetic force.

"The National Front Disco" is an improbably intricate balancing act where several points of view on fascist fashion come to terms but not a conclusion. Whatever politics Morrissey personally holds get subsumed in the dialectic and the emotion of the lines like "Where is our boy? Oh, we've lost our boy" and "England for the English"—all sung wistfully over a rousing, jumpy rock track.

Morrissey is examining a complicated cultural thrill that recently has been located in the seventies skinhead movement (the subject of his concert's first large poster) but that probably goes way back into the history of cultural chauvinism. He's remonstrating against the depoliticization of pop culture by emphasizing its typical (not nice) political use.

American white rock critics especially don't want to know about fascist potential in rock-'n'-roll culture, just as their eighties antipathy toward The Smiths showed their hostility for nonheterosexual expressions of desire. (They prefer the antiBlack ravings of Lou Reed and Axl Rose.) Morrissey's campy political art is too confrontational; it spoils the ordinary boys' fun. The iconic use of Elvis Presley and the rockabilly underpinning of *Your Arsenal* (plus Morrissey's and his band's retro appearance) insists on complicating the fun of pop culture.

Certainly there's no easy line drawn between what Morrissey loves and loathes—just that damned "understanding." He takes rock out of innocuous irrelevance and gives one's enjoyment a heavy price. The whiteness of this music isn't simply a fair enough compliment to the hard-won ethnocentricity of hiphop; instead, it indicates a self-consciously isolated idiom.

The *Glamorous Glue* video deals with this anomaly as Morrissey and the band perform a sound check. The only listener in the club is an old Black man; his sage face is edited into shots of the guitarist Alain Whyte's amazing visceral slide guitar fingering—a blues-rock connection that is identified, then updated when the old man puts a dollar down on the table and walks out of the club carrying a fiddle under his arm. That moment of racial/cultural alienation recalls the "Fuck you" Sandra Bernhard suffers from a Black listener at the end of her movie *Without You, I'm Nothing*. That, too, could be a Morrissey song title, and the candid discontent in *Your Arsenal* says almost exactly that.

*Your Arsenal* is only as good as the truth it contains. It's in the nervous rush one feels from "The National Front Disco," its headlong guitars and mixed emotions. The absence of naiveté feels like enlightenment and it is. By using "Disco" to follow "We'll Let You Know," Morrissey admits his love of England then connects that love to its vicious, hateful extreme. ("You don't need to look so pleased," he sings.) This is the only sophisticated move in pop's political discourse outside of rap. Perhaps it takes a blatant acknowledgment of racism to expose its shape to others. It's not too strange a tactic for the artist who wrote "Late Night, Maudlin Street."

Morrissey sets the tone for this culture examination on "Glamorous Glue," where he sings election-year trauma: "We won't vote conservative / Because we never have / Everyone lies / Nobody minds."

An artist who won't lie to himself is the only kind worth a damn. Morrissey's integrity has always been tied to his self-mockery and fearless defiance. On "We'll Let You Know," *Your Arsenal's* aural montage of football hooliganism, the sound of a chanting crowd is called to musical order by a sharp, rowdy whistle. That piercing noise is then linked to the subtle shrillness of a recorder as heard in Elizabethan-set plays and movies. It traces a tradition of English thuggery as Morrissey sings, "We may be cold or we may even be the most depressing people you've ever known. We are the last truly British people you will ever know."

In concert he places palm to forehead during these words to forestall rebellious cheers and to exaggerate his distress.

These dramatic-pathetic gestures leave room for ridicule more than fright. And a joke has always been Morrissey's code for a mistake, an error, a painfully human transgression. Most people feel no compelling desire to understand fascists and racists and so won't face the huge challenge of *Your Arsenal*. But there will only be delusion—no hope for progress—until they do.

*The City Sun*
November 11, 1992

# POP STAR POLITICS

ECAUSE SPIKE LEE has white people on the brain, his new film is about the shock wave Malcolm X created in American society, not a biography of the martyred Black Muslim spokesman. At three hours plus, it's a movie with a theme but not a subject.

*Malcolm X* avoids character study and sticks to a chronological review of the man's life. This merely replicates the cycle in which Malcolm X's anger and awareness went unheeded until later generations of deprived, abused, curious, and desperate young Blacks needed his messages. It's like the Bay Area rapper Paris's pop reiterations of Black Panther principles. But Lee doesn't use artistic details and sensitivity to show the political and spiritual conditions Malcolm X experienced (which are still relevant). Instead, Lee uses this story and its meaning shallowly. He addresses the mainstream's skepticism about his own seriousness by reiterating the slain speaker's dedication and risk. This primer on Malcolm X fails to illuminate those everyday intricacies of political consciousness that made *Do The Right Thing* so vivid.

Lee's demand that only a Black filmmaker could tell this story proves fallacious before the enigma of Malcolm X's character. An artist's best bet is to show how much any character is like ourselves, and surely Lee understands the fierce anger that Malcolm X articulated about Black American suffering under white domination. But the hypocrisies of his own anger (such as his impulse to make statements that irritate white folks) reduce Malcolm X's political, philosophical study and preaching — his *edge* — to spitefulness.

This kind of morally justified arrogance can be profound (check out *Lawrence of Arabia*), but Lee is unprepared to deal with it in Malcolm X or himself. Lee's superficiality is dramatized when Denzel Washington as Malcolm X shuts out his wife, Betty Shabazz (Angela Bassett). That closed door symbolizes the intransigence — and egotism — that Lee prizes as strength.

All Lee knows is that Malcolm X lived and died; as a capitalist purveyor of pop politics and Black fashion, Lee doesn't know what Malcolm's conflict of principles meant. Case in point: Lee's whole bogus front two weeks ago about preferring to be interviewed by Black reporters was just more publicity for *Malcolm X*. His essential purpose was to stave off the resentment building up in the Black media about largely white mainstream media being given immediate, privileged access to the *Malcolm X* production and screenings. Lee's challenge to the racial biases of the mainstream media was hypocritical; he simply could have taken his promotion straight to the Black press. (An early diversionary tactic was to contact a local publicity firm to slowly handle the Black media while Lee and Warner Bros. proceeded with their white media campaign.)

The fealty Lee demands of the Black media (he told a convention of Black newspaper publishers that *Malcolm X* should be their cause, too) matches his intimidation of the white media. But while going from the ranks of independent filmmaking to Hollywood production deals, Lee's greatest gift has been for making white people pay attention to him, and this is the primary impulse behind *Malcolm X*.

Lee treats Malcolm X as a pop star whose achievement was fame rather than enlightenment. The struggle Malcolm made to find knowledge and dignity, to believe in himself, to love people—that is, to be Black—is made to look easy, like a series of steps one takes toward making an Oscar acceptance speech. There isn't a single incident in Malcolm X's life that Lee gives the texture of a moral crisis. Washington's spoken narration often tells the conflict that Lee can't dramatize—such as Malcolm's devotion to the Honorable Elijah Muhammad (slyly portrayed by Al Freeman Jr.). It's the same simplistic presentation as the early scenes of young Malcolm's eagerness to conk his hair. Washington makes even this display of being naive too obvious; he cheapens the jivy passion of zoot suits and processed hair, leaving out the cocksure attitude that goes with *knowing* you're hip.

Lee misses how this certainty, this intellectual pride, was a constant of Malcolm's character; he makes an ingenuous assumption that a person is defined by hair, dress, and style of politics. The root of this is Lee's own faddish beliefs. Instead of a politicized bio-pic, he's made an Afro-pic—a fashion accessory. He's unable to distinguish even the first good scene in the movie—Malcolm's jail term and tutelage by a Muslim inmate, Baines (Albert Hall). The dictionary study that gives Malcolm the intellectual key for deconstructing white ideology is an obvious but stale revelation. It's less imaginative than the two sisters' linguistic lessons in *The Color Purple* and less trenchant than the prison learning sequence of *South Central*. No doubt the *South Central* scene owes a spiritual debt to Alex Haley's *The Autobiography of Malcolm X*, but it's in the right spirit. The education works as the characters' deliverance from pain and ignorance, not merely as a rite of passage. Where Carl Lumbly's Ali gave a piece of his soul to a young brother, Hall's Baines merely pontificates to Malcolm. Throughout the film, Malcolm's familiar speeches seem rote, strangely devoid of personal cost or conscious strategy. They ring inviolable and self-important, like the Jim Morrison songs in *The Doors*.

Oliver Stone's influence is unmistakable here. Lee borrows the hagiography of *The Doors* and the signifying structure of *JFK*. Perhaps Malcolm X means as much to Lee as Jim Morrison and John F. Kennedy do to Stone ( a "shining Black prince" put up against a messianic egotist and a white knight), but Stone also was dealing with the fundamental ways in which history, legend, fandom and heroism are manufactured. In *JFK*, Stone's obsessive manipulation of film stock and visual media gave his pursuit of truth a passionate mania. Lee does it only to show off—and sloppily (8 mm CIA footage of Malcolm in Mecca includes a shot of the CIA men themselves). The use of artifice that made *Do the Right Thing* so amazingly timely doesn't fit Lee's essentially realistic approach to historical truth. He treats the past as a stunt, depicting it in the rush-and-freeze-frame manner of Scorsese's *GoodFellas*.

These Stone-and-Scorsese styles might have been combined in some daring, postmodern way to scrutinize the roots of Black nationalism, revealing a history of both valor and corruption, but Lee's ambition is not so sophisticated. Emptying out a rented bag of tricks to keep *Malcolm X* interesting, Lee shows the most insipid, embarrassing misapplication of technique since Woody Allen's *Husbands and Wives*.

Lee's effort to make *Malcolm X* an important movie is a "dick thing" (his is five minutes longer than Oliver Stone's). The very methodology of a $35 million pageant goes against *Malcolm X*'s political significance, so viewers need not feel unnecessarily charitable toward this mediocre film. Yes, it flows better than *Mo' Better Blues* and *Jungle Fever*, but this refined production, its cost and bigness, do not matter—it's just a drop in the ocean of cinema.

However, the way it distorts the spectacle of African-American history is discomforting. Lee's recreation of Harlem's heyday lacks the immediacy of the old New York in Scorsese's *GoodFellas* and *Raging Bull*. This quaintness may satisfy Lee's desire to confer Hollywood-type glamour on Black American history, but what's the purpose of prettifying what Hollywood never lied about, only ignored? Lee cannot achieve a credible street aura. He has a jive-time sensibility that may strike a cord with those who enjoy the cartoonish scene of Malcolm and his running buddy, Shorty, (played by Lee), bopping down the streets in their fancy threads, but this is dishonest nostalgia and inexact culture. The bebop suaveness needs a grim urban contrast to explain its appeal. Delroy Lindo—the great actor from *Joe Turner's Come and Gone*—

provides a sense of rough, troubling experience as West Indian Archie, the numbers runner who teaches Malcolm to hustle, but he's the only fully conceived character.

Malcolm looks twerpy next to West Indian Archie, and even his harshest moment—a bigot-baiting humiliation of his white mistress—seems jejune; it expresses petulance rather than a world view. Shorty's temperament doesn't so much contrast Malcolm's as provide a distracting example of obsolete coloredness. Lee likes to play these wack characters, but except for Mookie, he never enriches his protagonist with that ambiguity. He holds the tall Denzel figures of Black manhood in rigid awe. Split between jive and rectitude, Lee tries to mix pizzazz with harsh politics. The result here is the miserable jitterbug production numbers. They are an inept director's preening—as foolish-looking as the yellow hat with the Robin Hood feather that Lee wears in the opening scene to announce, "THIS IS MY MOVIE!"

Such arrogance, smartly displayed, would be okay if Lee used it to disturb the audience's relationship to the deceptive attractiveness of pop fashion, but he wants to impress more than enlighten. This Hollywood polish cannot be taken seriously as political filmmaking—especially now with the Jean-Luc Godard retrospective at the Museum of Modern Art illustrating the relationship between commitment and formal rigor and between radical ideology and visual beauty.

Cinematographer Ernest Dickerson has not changed or sharpened his pretty style; his golden view of past misery turns racism into fable. This confusion is part of the film's dangerously conventional structure; when the Nation of Islam finally turns against Malcolm—actions leading up to his assassination—the anticipated betrayal is so old-fashioned, it's clichéd. (And worse than a Christ complex, Baines's line "The ministers think Malcolm is getting too much press" suggests a Spike Lee complex.)

Lee's best film work this year was his Prince music video *Money Don't Matter 2 Night*, in which he complicated Prince's lyricism with an agitprop assemblage of news footage and turgid family melodrama—at one point he daringly matched the line about an Uncle Tom to a shot of Gen. Colin Powell (in *Malcolm X*, Lee makes the same word-image match with a shot of Dr. Martin Luther King Jr.). *Money* sustains an immediate clamp-down on the Black family. *Malcolm X* lacks the same conceptual cohesion.

An extended newsreel montage that Malcolm supposedly views on television is simply trite, and the Rodney King beating footage that opens the film is merely facile. (Already rap's Willie D has outstripped Lee's political discourse with the magnificent agitprop song "Rodney K.")

When Lee dissolves from the King beating to a burning American flag to an iconic X, it is not just an overload; it's incoherent. His immediate sense of outrage makes him present the King beating as America's ultimate race crime when there are too many other candidates—in fact, there's a whole history of inspiring, enraging sorrows. But Lee begins with the kind of trendy misunderstanding one would expect from a facetious network newscaster. It proves how the entire concept of *Malcolm X* is keyed to the marketable moment and not to a deep-seated African-American need.

*The City Sun*
November 11, 1992

# MALCOLM X'D AGAIN

HEN *TIME* MAGAZINE calls a film biography of *Malcolm X* "tepid" and *New York* magazine calls it "solid," only one thing can be said for sure: The figure of the slain Black politician has been thoroughly domesticated. This may be part of a natural cultural process at work despite daily promulgated racism—yesterday's headache becomes today's pillow just as yesterday's tragedy becomes today's big-budget Hollywood extravaganza. The shocking thing is that the agent of this process is Spike Lee, a so-called outspokesperson (Albert Murray's term) who pretends to shake up America's white-dominated culture industry while trying to attain all its benefits, from money to influence.

*Sellout* is too common a word for an outrage of this shame and magnitude. The full horror of Spike Lee's *Malcolm X* didn't occur to me while watching the film, with its various, silly look-at-me tropes (a widescreen moonscape; a purely fanciful trip to South Africa to film an endorsement from Nelson Mandela). Since the film has little aesthetic significance, its real meaning and effect can be seen in surrounding media treatments—the numerous talk shows in which Lee and his star, Denzel Washington, reiterate Malcolm X rhetoric while selling their Hollywood product.

This deception happens within the confusion of Black careerism. First, there's the Catch-22 of being important (rich and famous) enough to make people listen to you but saying only marketable things so that you can become rich and famous (important). In the hiphop era, this is most easily accomplished by making art (product) of previously sanctified things—ethics and ethnicity. Genuine artists who have only their lives to trade on constitute a larger part of African-American pop culture than any other ethnic group. The history that bears this out is also a history full of compromises—stemming from both collusion and betrayal. However, the only thing that justifies these desperate acts and these practical facts is the amount of honesty in the art—the raw truth and plain essence that usually get Black artists ghettoized as being difficult, controversial, without crossover appeal.

It's exciting when a Black artist becomes mainstream and can keep up the level of difficulty (like Prince), but unless that happens, there will be trouble. Black artists whose work gets too far away from their personal thoughts and habits risk devaluing the very experience that inspired them. This was probably difficult for Spike Lee to ascertain during his constant battle to affront the white mainstream, but it happened quickly and it was simple. Here's how:

By transforming his impatience with American racism into an easily packaged emblem—the X cap—Lee automatically voided the meaning of the sign. X for exploitation, X marking the spot of buried treasure, X meaning anything but the sorrow of a people without identity. Lee managed to reverse the original intention of the sign by converting it into merchandise. After turning the X into a style that can be effortlessly purchased, and imitated, he shortchanged its value even while it seemed to become profitable.

Acquiring X necessitated no learning, no experience, no private affection or enmity other than recognizing a current fad. In response, a sarcastic white youth was recently seen wearing a cap with the insignia Y.

The culture is filled with so much misrepresentation and dishonesty that, sometimes, it seemed the mere utterance of a fact or a defiant point of view would be sufficient to clear the air and set things right. But now it's plain that no matter how many sound bites broadcast Malcolm X's most challenging thoughts, they unfortunately enter the air as air, not lightning. This doesn't negate the possibility that somebody might hear the words and start to think, yet the context of their new, Time-Warner sponsorship suggests that far more people will hear Malcolm X's words as merely discomforting and will tell themselves, Don't worry: It's just a movie.

Malcolm is killed a second time, in fact, by the misdirected enthusiasm of a Black entrepreneur who thought he could continue Malcolm X's mission by dealing with Hollywood on its own terms. Lee's own ideas are not comprehensive enough to accomplish this assault successfully. The two schisms that defined Malcolm X's career—ignorance /consciousness, religion/worldliness—are not dealt with. Lee, too, wears a cap rather than feeling Malcolm X's spirit.

That explains why, in the film, Washington comes off petty—lukewarm rather than hot, angry, calculating, intimidating, brilliant, ornery, or, in a word, undeniable. Lee has blanded out Malcolm X's character to make him worthy of a big-budget movie that could recoup its cost by attracting (but not offending) millions of viewers. The *Time* magazine critic who called *Malcolm X* "tepid" is the same one who called *Do the Right Thing* "irresponsible"; this demonstrates the no-win conditions of a contest in the mainstream. Lee should have realized that the only thing he had to lose was the deepest, most personal meaning that Malcolm X has for him (if any). Whatever viewers he lost with a too-harsh portrayal would be worth losing (as the *Time* critic proves, Lee never had them on his side anyway).

*Malcolm X* is compromised by Lee's contradictory hipness. He wants to be accepted by Hollywood while chipping at the ideology for which it stands. It can't be done. Better filmmakers than Spike Lee have failed at it, but unlike such heroic examples as Eric von Stroheim, Orson Welles, and Brian DePalma, Lee has his ego tangled up with Black political imperatives. He's willing to exploit the political ideas that came out of years of suffering and many struggling, hopeful generations for his own aggrandizement.

Despite the political awareness Malcolm X preached, Lee makes no single statement or incident dramatically potent – or personal. This implies that Malcolm X's axioms are mere slogans to Lee. He doesn't proceed by Malcolm X's ideas; he hides behind them using a convenient sense of righteousness to fuel his career assertions and distract from his compromises. The most "imaginative" filmmmaking stunts in *Malcolm X* portray, instead, Lee's competition with other filmmakers. Of course, he comes up short, but Lee never looks tinier (or more small-minded) than in the flashback scene of a Klu Klux Klan attack on Malcolm and his family. To seal the moment of racist aggression and Black humiliation, Lee shows the KKK troupe riding off toward a huge illuminated moon dominating the nighttime horizon.

It's an insensible effect, a hollow visual epiphany that coheres with nothing else in the movie. Certainly, to portray the KKK as Halloween goblins goes against the historical facts that *Malcolm X* reinterpreted as examples of real-life, political evil. Instead, this costly visual effect fights one of Lee's own spiteful battles. The moonshot is a perverse quote of Steven Spielberg's *E.T.* that Spike Lee connects to D.W. Griffith and the KKK as a stupid show of his contempt for *The Color Purple*. This kind of iconoclastic gesture requires more than nerve to be successful; it isn't the same throw-down to pop tradition that Public Enemy made, slighting Elvis Presley in "Fight the Power," mainly because Lee doesn't have the artistic ammunition to make Spielberg look trite the way PE made Elvis look pale. In the end, Lee wants to steal the amazement that was central to *E.T.*'s exploration of childhood awe. Does Lee's moonshot mean Malcolm was in awe of the KKK or that Spike is in awe of white filmmakers whose success he envies? The confusion is sheer lunacy.

On this level, *Malcolm X* is a piddling rewrite of movie history. Lee plays a pitiful game of misinterpreting Hollywood's white liberal past as if it were all lies. This narrowness contradicts his stated respect for Malcolm X's evolution from hate to love. In the film's bizarre finale, Nelson Mandela appears speaking to a classroom of Black South African children whom Lee has introduced in a series of close-ups testifying, "I AM MALCOLM X!" This is a rip from the superb 1970 Hal Ashby–Bill Gunn film, *The Landlord*, in which a white liberal visited a proto-Afrocentric academy and, in a series of close-ups, various cherubs stood up to declare, "I AM BLACK AND I AM BEAUTIFUL!"

Spike's version acutely says much less, but it accurately portrays the commercialization of Black consciousness to today's youth. It's an arrested development from self-regard to style (or perhaps from a period of revolutionary awareness to a Halloween-style assumed identity). This is a consequence of Malcolm X's being discovered first by rappers reclaiming Black history in personal disc expressions and their political-artistic renaissance being imitated—co-opted—by Lee, a less serious pop artist.

Lee neglects what rappers have been good at: There's no continuity between Malcolm X and the legacy of Black intellectuals (and no reference to Frederick Douglass or Marcus Garvey). Lee's pop star Malcolm emerges from prison a full-blown thinker-speaker as incapable of personal politics as Lee himself.

This Malcolm X without rough edges is the last thing Amiri Baraka and his group of naysayers expected when they challenged Lee's ability to tell Malcolm X's story, but it's part of the neutralizing they feared. Already those dissenting voices have been lost, crushed beneath the powerful weight of Hollywood hype.

Once again, capitalism is the force that subdues Black individuality. All this current (temporary) interest in Malcolm X rises from Hollywood-generated publicity. Many Black folks are willing to go along with the hype, not for the sake of Malcolm's politics but for the mainstream legitimization. This is the same kind of pride that always trips up Black show business, whether it's Ice-T siding with corporate interests or Spike Lee deciding he should have the same privilege of spending time and money on a film folly as Oliver Stone and Richard Attenborough.

Lee's essential con job was to refurbish Malcolm X, but Malcolm X was not Martin Luther King Jr. It is misleading—but typically Hollywood—to pretend that Malcolm X matters because of his late ecumenicism. The film would seem to confirm the wide acceptance of Malcolm X and his message, but this acceptance is on a false premise. Spike himself doesn't risk controversy; the proof of his politics-into-safe-entertainment is in his choice of Arrested Development to provide the movie's theme song instead of the more appropriate rapper Sister Souljah. You've got to wonder how many of the stars who turned out for Lee's premiere would be as supportive of a contemporary rebellious Black political pop star like Sister Souljah. Plainly, all this *Malcolm X* hoopla is not a celebration of ideas but of Hollywood commerce.

The only way to redeem this scandalous sellout would be to radicalize moviegoing and movie watching. (Imagine the blistering, charismatic, brilliant Malcolm X that *Chameleon Street* auteur Wendell B. Harris might have created.) With no formal innovations or controversial content, Lee's film has made Malcolm X safe for box offices everywhere. This mediocre film is a setback to all the artistic advances of the hiphop era. Let the mourning begin.

*The City Sun*
December 2, 1992

# HISTORY GETS KICKED BY FANTASY

*/ /* |'M HISTORY! No, I'm mythology! I don't care what I am; I'm free!"
shouts the Genie (Robin Williams in a peripatetic vocal performance) of the animated film *Aladdin*. The Genie's emancipation at
the very end of this *Arabian Nights* adaptation takes the wildest spin ever
seen in a big-budget movie of *The Thousand and One Nights*. Americanized to a very modern and popular degree, this story of an Arabian
street kid who falls in love with a princess and is helped by a genie in a
bottle emphasizes the same values—self-awareness and sexual equality
for women—that were also neatly packaged in two previous Disney
cartoon features, *The Little Mermaid* and *Beauty and the Beast*.

Those were popular updates of superficial themes that the Disney
animators mostly treated as mush. By comparison, *Aladdin* is a fairly
tensile, political cartoon; the schmaltz and pseudo-Broadway music score
are minimized in favor of verbal humor (supplied by the voices of
comedians Robin Williams and Gilbert Gottfried) and visual slapstick (in
the style of the antic Warner Bros. cartoon classics).

A new theme breaks through in *Aladdin*'s comical (rather than merely
magical) transformations and miracles. The anachronistic references to
TV game shows and modern slang in the ancient Persian setting is a
volatile experiment. It mixes history and legend with an awareness of
their contemporary, political interpretation and usage.

The poignant (not simply exuberant) idea in the Genie's exclamation
comes from more than his long-awaited participation in democracy or
humanity. The Genie, who metamorphoses as ostentatiously as the animators' pens will allow, represents the license taken by modern culture-
producers to make of history anything they want.

It's a very different message than earlier generations got from *The
Thief of Bagdad* or *The Golden Voyage of Sinbad*, which exhibited a
romantic, Western view of what Edward Said identified as Orientalism.

Adults are more likely to appreciate the comic references in *Aladdin,* but these comfortable modernist anachronisms are still, somehow, distressingly misleading. A new, brash version of post-Orientalism is announced from the opening narration: "It begins on a dark night with a dark man with a dark purpose."

Fascination with the mysterious Other is part of the project's origin, the *Aladdin* press kit notes:

> The story of "Aladdin and the Enchanted Lamp," quite possibly the best known story ever written, has come to be regarded as part of *The Thousand and One Nights,* or *Arabian Nights,* a collection of fewer than 200 folk tales, derived from the Indian, Persian and Arab cultures with origins dating back to 850 A.D. In actuality, it appeared for the first time between 1704 and 1717 in a 12-volume translation by Antoine Galland, a gifted French story teller and professor of Arabic who not only translated the tales but adapted them to suit the tastes of his French readers. Galland also invented plots and drew material together to form some of his own tales. The story of Aladdin is said to have been told to him by a Syrian friend and scholar. The tale of Aladdin was further popularized by British author Richard Burton.

*Aladdin* continues this Western practice, borrowing mythology without borrowing the culture. The first characters shown are identified as "my pungent friend," "big-nosed, camel-loving"—all said humorously but in a way that denies the lesson Spielberg finally learned in *Indiana Jones and The Last Crusade* about the sanctity and sovereign independence of non-Western cultures. The good Princess and Aladdin are drawn with slightly tanned skins and irregular features (large eyes, rounded noses), but this isn't more than a first, tentative step toward multicultural fantasy.

The most suspicious set piece is the magic carpet ride song, "A Whole New World," where Aladdin, the Princess, and the perky magic carpet free themselves from Middle Eastern turmoil and take a nocturnal tour of the globe—defying ethnocentricity—that ends even farther east, in the more Oriental China. "A Whole New World" is actually about cultural imperialism—the global village concept reduced to a romantic marketing strategy. The cynical tone is set by the use of recycled Broadway music when rap, world beat, or a Persian trance score might have provided a new consciousness. The sequence remains Western even to the point of falsifying history: the truth about the nose job performed on the Sphinx is shown as an innocent blunder instead of the actual racist vandalism ordered by Napoleon. Who says this is good entertainment for the family?

The cartoon illustration on the record sleeve for Digital Underground's single "No Nose Job" had far more wit and honesty.

Hollywood's way of confusing history, mythology, and reckless creative freedom has been the predominant theme of this year's movies, from Merchant Ivory's depoliticized version of *Howard's End* to Francis Coppola's extravagant but pointless *Bram Stoker's Dracula*. Even Jean-Jacques Annaud's soft-porn version of Marguerite Duras's *The Lover* ridicules itself as an honest view of this culture and race mixing in the past. The actress who plays out the metaphor of Europe's careless exploitation of Indochina incurs an unexpected level of antipathy when her lack of talent reveals the filmmaker's primary interest to be pornographic rather than political. The bimbo actress becomes more hateful than imperialism itself.

In *Malcolm X*, Spike Lee demonstrates the way even Afrocentric Hollywoodites go in for glossy historical pampering. And the season's two biggest epics, *The Last of the Mohicans* and *1492: Conquest of Paradise*, both show the extent to which white people go easy on themselves.

These are not truly revisionist histories. They're historical pageants that enact the same old Eurocentric hoopla and self-celebration, but with a shrug of the shoulders thrown in to show the filmmakers' political consciousness. In *1492*, Ridley Scott has Frank Langella lament the dismantling of a Spanish mosque, saying, "I have a feeling we're destroying a beautiful culture," then moving on as Scott moves on to photograph the splendors of Queen Isabella's court and the picturesque destruction of indigenous Americans by Gérard Depardieu's fake-noble Columbus.

It isn't a matter of filmmakers not having politics. (Certainly *1492* star Sigourney Weaver's statement to England's *New Musical Express,* "You can't blame the Spanish for [Native American] genocide," proves otherwise). Entertainment movies like these scenic epics about the European claims on the North American continent merely disguise the political aims and intentions of the people who make them.

These movies are fables, but they have a purpose—only one of which is to daydream; the other is to instruct. The implicit lesson is that the eighteenth-century settling of the Northeast American territory and the sixteenth-century exploration of the non-European world were only regrettably destructive and exploitive—it is a nightmare only for anyone who doesn't benefit from it today.

White pseudohistorians like Scott and *Mohicans* director Michael Mann treat the European expansionist past like a trust fund. Mann, in fact, ignores all the modern reinterpretations of the James Fenimore Cooper Leatherstocking tales (the racial-sexual subtext scholar

Leslie Fiedler explicated) in favor of conventionally trashy Hollywood adventure-romance. Daniel Day-Lewis's miscasting as Hawkeye recalls the ludicrous oddities of Al Pacino in *Revolution* (Day-Lewis's pale spindly legs and changeable accent are not those of an early American explorer).

Mann's most modernist trope is the cliff-jumping scene, so recontextualized that it unfortunately recalls a scene in D. W. Griffith's *The Birth of a Nation* where a white virgin fleeing from Blacks jumps through "the opal gates of death." If the neoracist implications were not apparent to Mann while making the film, he should see his movie with a real nonwhite, urban audience, whose catcalls do not sympathize with Mann's subjectevily racist vision of American tragedy. As Chingachgook, Indian activist Russell Means cuts an authoritative figure (a sop to *Dances with Wolves*), but there's no advancement in a movie about the "settling" of America where the only genocidal impulse is spoken by an overzealous Indian who hates whites. *Mohicans* is so far from history, it can only be considered fantasy.

Both Scott's and Mann's films, with their deceptive visual and sentimental splendors, amount to reparations for whites.

*The City Sun*
December 9, 1992

# ERASURE, *POP!*

A FTER ERASURE's touring show "A Phantasmagorical Entertainment," this greatest-hits collection is one of the most necessary and wonderful releases. It not only commemorates a superbly produced pop show—the most delightful cultural evening of the year—but it helps certify Erasure's near decade of excellent but underrated work.

When synth-composer Vince Clarke broke with Alison Moyet, his female partner in Yaz ("Situation," "Move On'" "State Farm"), he searched for a new vocalist-lyricist partner, experimenting with a few Brit-pop veterans until meeting newcomer Andy Bell. Their first album together produced the teen-swoon anthem "Oh, L'amour," with Bell turning Moyet's own husky singing style into an androgynous enigma.

It was on the second album, *The Circus* (1977), that Erasure lived up to its name—wiping away synth-sex ambiguity and creating a passionate, political, openly gay album of pop that worked on many levels.

"Hideaway" poignantly and emphatically urged coming out. "It Doesn't Have to Be Like That" pondered hate between groups ("A heart on the inside's the same as any other / Are we divided? / Why do we have to suffer?), then enlarged the song's moral-social field with an mbaqanga chorus that moved concern from homophobia to apartheid. "Sexuality" and "Sometimes" were both sexually and emotionally explicit ("It's not the way you leave your clothes sprawled across the bedroom / It's not the way my emptiness fills with your desire").

From there, one of the great overlooked albums of the eighties, Erasure advanced to create the hit machines *The Innocents* and *Wild!*, where they explored both love pangs and romantic fervor while expanding the synth turf to include club stomps, cabaret ballads, and a splendid variety of camp gems.

"A Phantasmagorical Entertainment" found visual equivalents for all these styles, including a combination Agnes DeMille ballet and spaghetti-fringe western that mixed Ennio Morricone existential prairie blues with high-energy disco. Bell, in high heels, showed off his ebullient stage presence while a muscled cowboy cavorted with Clarke sashaying

334 □          THE RESISTANCE

in zaftig Mae West drag. The pantomime was narrated by Bell singing "Who Needs Love Like That?"

For all the glitz, the point was simple: not antihetero but a spoof of the sexual models that people mistake for love and fulfillment. The Erasure stage show, catalogue, and *Pop!* itself are all about the poignant longings that keep art and popular music going.

It may be a special province of the most searching gay culture; the line of articulation that runs through this well-selected compendium shows what makes Erasure's specialty special. The Smiths had a greater, more devastating wit, Pet Shop Boys are more pristinely sophisticated, but Erasure commands an effervescent lack of subtlety. If the Smiths make you smile and the Pets make you wink, Erasure make you grin (that, perhaps explains the group's large faithful following of Japanese teenage girls).

Erasure's last release, the cover EP *Abbaesque,* was pop scholarship that revealed the source of their unusual musical philosophy (Erasure's hoppity single "Star!" is a good-hearted, worthy rewrite of the upbeat Abba formula: "You gotta look real hard / Is it in your heart? Yeah, it's in there somewhere"), and though *Abbaesque* is a drab disc, the stage performance of that same took flight. *Pop!* includes Erasure's hiphop version of "Take a Chance on Me," which is enough to prove the sturdiness of the Abba canon and the strength of pop emotions that at first look trivial. When "Star!" poses the question "Did you ever have a lover leave you for another? / Take your love and kisses for granted?" Erasure also are questioning pop aesthetics—equalizing the value of sorrow and love and kisses, an uncannily piquant proposition.

The deceptive strength of gay pop defines both Erasure's career and the track that anchors this collection, "Stop!" This 1987 single has a harsh, driving beat and brassier harmonics than one is used to in synth-dance-pop. At first an antihomophobia protest march, the song has an enthusiasm that also addresses shy love. But then, most remarkably, it becomes a pledge of faith in the age of AIDS:

> *We'll be together again*
> *I've been waiting for a long time*
> *We'll be together*
> *And nobody ain't never*
> *Gonna disconnect us*
> *Or ever separate us*

Here is Andy Bell's most impassioned moment on record, his uniquely exultant-melancholy tone infusing heartbreak with a triumphant-sounding defiance: "Stop! / Stand there where you are / Before you go too far / Before you make a fool out of love."

Erasure's smart fun never forgets the torment that love costs in a cold society. Tracks like "Love to Hate You" and "Am I Right?" are as complex as romantic pop can be; whipped up into a pounding dance-frenzy, this stuff gains philosophical weight.

Clarke and Bell rationalize pop therapy on "Drama!," a love dissection that spares no one, chooser or chosen:

> *Your shame is never ending*
> *Just one psychological drama after another*
> *We are guilty*
> *And how we ever entered into this life God only knows*
> *The infinite complexities of love*
> *We're not to sacrifice the art of love*
> *God only knows the ultimate necessity of love*

No one else is making more blithely profound records.

*The City Sun*
December 16, 1992

# REMEMBRANCE OF SONGS PAST

*I can't look at it hard enough.*

—OUR TOWN

SENTIMENT ISN'T a shameful word, and if Terence Davies's new movie *The Long Day Closes* gets the wide audience it deserves, it might effectively reclaim that precious element from its abusers (such execrable films as *Ghost, The Prince of Tides, Rain Man, Driving Miss Daisy, This Boy's Life*). Rather than patronize audiences by making them feel good about what they already know, Davies reveals what viewers are not conscious of about their own memories and—most radically—about popular art.

Both *The Long Day Closes* and Davies's 1989 *Distant Voices, Still Lives*—each film a chronology of his white English-working-class family—are rich in sentiment, but being rigorously formal exercises combining the melodrama, the musical, social critique, and avant-garde experiment, they most intelligently should be considered masterworks of the postmodern era, Davies's sentiment about his own biography occasions a conscious use and exploration of the pop art experience. The movies and songs he grew up with make a Top Ten of sense memories and then are recycled into the art he currently creates. For Davies, this process is a natural—integral—part of modern living, proven and justified by these complex family histories. Though not representative of a political-cultural movement like the French New Wave, Davies's idiosyncratic movies amount to a one-man wave. By re-creating his family's pleasures and days with a profound fidelity to the sentiments that are linked to class, religion, and sexuality, he simultaneously alters the common perception of how cultural legacy becomes a private one.

This happens on both the quotidian level, where art intersects everyday life as part of social ritual and cultural practice (the pub gatherings and holiday chorales in *DVSL*), and on the psychological level, where a song occupies a person's subconscious and is instinctively expressed in an emotional response (Angela Walsh's unforgettable rendition in *DVSL* of "I Want to Be Around to Pick Up the Pieces" sung in defiance of her husband's brutality). In order to illustrate this insight, Davies reconceives his fondest film genre, the musical, the way Proust reconceived the novel as a mode of autobiography. Davies reinvents the musical after relating to its forms and sounds. As Proust wrote, "What is this palpitating in the depths of [his] being must be the image, the visual memory which, being linked to that taste, has tried to follow it in [his] conscious." Although a child of the fifties, Davies demonstrates a very contemporary license: he doesn't need a narrative excuse to enjoy the emotional release of song. His creative freedom comes out of the pop era, when music seemed to float through the ether, experienced via the radio or the whim of any individual with a tune in his soul.

Departing from the operatic-Broadway-MGM tradition this way allows Davies to employ sentiment and the secret, suppressed feelings of his characters without being coy. He elevates the musical from a subgenre of fantasy into poetic realism, thus avoiding the debased representation of emotion known as camp. This break with convention is also a breakthrough into a great postmodern understanding of the way political and social ideas are contained in and perpetuated by culture. Such sophistication is usually associated with gay sensibility as an inverted specialty: the result of artists submitting to generic formulas within the institution of the musical. But Davies, who ironically professes no interest in rock 'n' roll (*The Long Day Closes* ends just before the moment of rock 'n' roll's explosion), nevertheless benefits from pop music's subversive, oppressed group impulses.

It may be that only a movie buff will note the way Davies liberates Doris Day's "At Sundown" from the narrative entrapment of *Love Me or Leave Me,* or appreciate his hiphop-era sampling of the most trenchant narration from *The Magnificent Ambersons* as part of his own soundtrack. But these tropes are more aligned with pop music's radicalism than with the Hollywood-Broadway tradition Davies says he admires. The sentiment he wants to express is too strong to wind up generating an *Aladdin* or a *Cats;* Davies's idiosyncrasy is closer to another contemporary Englishman, the pop singer Morrissey, whose 1986 song "Rubber Ring" epitomizes Davies's relationship to pop.

*The passing of time leaves empty lives*
*waiting to be filled*
*I'm here with the cause*
*I'm holding the torch*
*In the corner of your room*
*Can you hear me?*
*And when you're laughing and dancing*
*and finally living*
*Hear my voice in your head*
*And think of me kindly*

It's sung from the postmodern point of view of *a pop record* just as *The Long Day Closes* begins with the sound clip "It's not like you're introducing a film" (from *The Happiest Days of Your Life*) in order to tease the "voice"—the point of view—of the medium. Godard would approve; so would the New Wave's mix-genre modernism (Pauline Kael: "Loving the movies that formed [their] tastes, [they] used this nostalgia for old movies as an active element in [their] own movies") to be taken to the next stage, and Davies does. Songs and movies contribute to the feelings that define one's personality, so Davies refers to this pop material reverently, wondrously, and unironically as pure emotional phenomena—even though it also exists as the markers of a particular social period.

While the New Wave adapted movie lore to the present (Godard's Bogie-into-Belmondo, Falconetti-into-Karina simply transferred mythologies), it was literally a modern movement (*Jules and Jim* treated the World War I era as here and now) and spent little time accounting for the particular experience of nostalgia. Davies's connection to the pop art past is the sort of thing often condemned as a timid or alienated person's substitute for living a normal life in the present. But Davies's entire autobiographical project—starting with his first films, the black-and-white trilogy (*Children, Madonna and Child, Death and Transfiguration*)—searches out the roots of sensibility in the past, in the various socializing experiences of school, religion, and art

The formative nature of pop is Davies's most profound subject, as it is for the New Wave acolyte André Téchiné, whose 1976 film *French Provincial* (*Souvenirs d'en France*) was a landmark reclamation of modernism for one's personal history. The way Téchiné related seven decades of a pop-loving family's life, each decade in the style of a different genre, demonstrated art's special significance, using culture as both evocative memoir and psychological key. (In his later films Téchiné maintains a pop-lore subtext to provide an amplification and grounding of his ambiguous characters' life stories.)

Téchiné and Davies's aesthetics, emphasizing styles of film- and musicmaking as historical codes, were also sociological responses to modernism. Given the transformation and avoidance of camp in their serious use of pop elements, it's fair to say that their methods represent a changed gay political perspective. Davies's wrestling with gay identity (the specifically Catholic guilt struggle of the trilogy) rejects the formerly subjugated gay social position; nothing is hidden in his identification with pop. Instead of the tension between dominant culture and subordinate groups that social critic Dick Hebdige said "can be found reflected in the surfaces of subculture," Davies and Téchiné boldly open up songs and movies to express a fuller, unembarrassed range of human experience. *The Long Day Closes* is the first great movie about an explicitly gay child, and that particular detail only deepens the film's universality. Davies's personal stories (like the ones Téchiné tells in *Scene of the Crime, Les Innocents,* and *J'embrasse pas*) are about a community's nonconformists. By showing characters nourished on innocuous, sentimental songs and movies these movies expand on the uses of pop's enchantment.

"Love is now the stardust of yesterday, the music of the years gone by," Nat "King" Cole sings in *The Long Day Closes* as Michael Coulter's camera first searches the rain-drenched, dark, empty tenements of Liverpool. Cole's recording lives even though the people who first responded to it have aged, died, or gone away and their homes decayed. The past is not sentimentalized, but the emotions begun in it linger, structuring Davies's vision. The 1940s, Second World War setting for *Distant Voices, Still Lives* and the 1950s, postwar era of *The Long Day Closes* are observed with scrupulous visual detail: brick council houses, flared dresses, interiors with never enough electric light. Davies stays true to the idea of kitchen-sink realism but without the facile class conflicts of those sixties British films that were more about aspiration than political criticism.

*DVSL*'s concentration on the intimate familial conflicts—the tyranny of patriarchy as inflicted by the laborer father and suffered by Davies's mother and siblings—is more political than a story of social striving precisely because it is so personal. This, too, is a strategy of the postmodern era, reflecting the age's psychoanalytical study of art and custom. Hebdige notes:

> Social relations and processes become appropriated by individuals only through the forms in which they are represented to those individuals. These forms are . . . by no means transparent. They are shrouded in "common sense" which simultaneously validates and mystifies them. It is precisely these "perceived-accepted-suffered cultural objects" which semiotics sets out to "interrogate" and decipher.

This explains the process Davies indulges with such emotional amplitude through his presentation of the beauty of song and the thrill of
carnivals and movies contrasted with working-class anomie. Scenes of
classroom daydreaming about ships or a leisurely walk with Mother, both
scored with heartrending folk songs, are the best semiotics because the
study of signs happens while luxuriating in their complex beauty. Some
reviewers were unable to recognize Davies's extraordinarily subtle revelations in *DVSL* of the common bond in pop's expression of ideology and
the subversion of pop sentiment. They missed how those musi⌐al numbers
in crowded living rooms with live, often *a capella* singing (a legacy from
Altman's *Nashville*) made it possible for characters to sing a song as the
statement of their sad, humorous, *coping* reaction to domestic or social
circumstance.

Preserving his singular reaction to pop, Davies has grown beyond the
art that formed him. His musicals are not replications of a harmonized
world, such as Kelly-Donen and Minnelli depicted in Davies's youth, but
a new kind of musical about the most basic kinds of conflict: ghettoized
individuals finding the lyrics and the music necessary to express their
salvation. Davies's period recreations have a verisimilitude unlike the
patriotism of, say, the Noel Coward–David Lean *This Happy Breed*
(1945), and much closer to *Ambersons* (of course) and even *Long Day's
Journey into Night*. In *The Long Day Closes*, the scene of Mother (Ma-
jorie Yates) singing, "If I Had My Life to Live Over" is a reprise of the
earlier "Me and My Shadow" scene showing the generational endurance
of misery. In this mix of musical sentiment with an unflinching, drab
atmosphere, Davies achieves what social historian Raymond Williams
once called "A particular way of life which expresses meanings and
values not only in art and learning, but also in institutions and ordinary
behavior. This analysis of culture . . . is the clarification of the meanings
and values implicit in a particular way of life, a particular culture. . . ."

A startling example comes in *The Long Day Closes* when the older
Davies siblings have their revelry interrupted by a Black man asking
directions; their hostility to the visitor critiques, through pinpointed
racism, the insularity of the culture in which they thrive. It's Davies's
much more complex way of looking back in anger.

This paradox has a powerful fascination for Davies. Reaching back
into his own childhood for *The Long Day Closes* (*Distant Voices* was a
*prenatal* vision), he finds its essence preserved in pop artifacts as vividly
as in his own memory. The swell of emotion evoked by a fifties pop string
section, the calm of Nat Cole's tenor, are touchstones, still potent evidence that certain lives were led and passions felt. Davies's use of these
exquisite sounds—including the numinous 20th Century-Fox fanfare by

Alfred Newman—restores a sensibility. These elements are manipulated in a way that captures pop art's spontaneity. As Greg Solman suggested, the title *The Long Day Closes* implies the conclusion to a passing phase, but Davies's recall relays the process of change with a rich ambiguity and makes it momentous.

"I can't look at it hard enough" is what the heroine of Thornton Wilder's *Our Town* cried when visiting her past. Her nostalgia describes the intensity of Davies's method: he paces images slowly, down to Ozu- or Bresson-like contemplation, in order to hold on to memory. (One audacious moment out of many in *TLDC* features a Michael-Snow-style meditation on the light and time changes apparent on a bedroom carpet.) The difference between *DVSL* and *TLDC* can be described as memories Davies can't get rid of, memories he won't let go. The degree of obsessiveness in each film is unusual—especially in that freak of commerce, the English-language art film—but it keeps Davies from making a blithe or uninteresting memorial. His torpor has emotional weight and, despite the longueurs, it conveys the central dynamics of his family-life experience as vividly as Dreyer's *Master of the House*. The past, for Davies, is as mystifying and irreducible as contemporary experience.

*The Long Day Closes* is the happy side of his family's chronicle. The memories that are not ecstatic (like the visit of the Black outsider) are the memories of Davies coming to consciousness. Teen actor Leigh McCormack as Bud gives the young Davies some of Jean-Pierre Léaud's *400 Blows* alertness. Bud's frequent glances toward the camera index his quiet, pampered intelligence collecting these memories and internalizing personal critique. The film is too self-conscious to fake a kid's discovery of the world; instead, it is about the more subtle activities of his *learning* how the world and fantasy, sense and sentiment, interact.

Davies's central epiphany comes when Bud attends a geology lecture on erosion. Taken from an actual school text, Arthur Holm's *Principles of Physical Geology,* the instructor's oration is pure poetry. "Life force cooperates in the work of corrosion. It is the cumulative effect of several processes. Wind erosion . . . Rain erosion . . . Glacial erosion . . . Water erosion." With a sonorous, theatrical emphasis on "erosion," and the word printed in large block letters on the chalkboard, Davies slyly suggests Bud's eroding childhood and innocence. (The idea is carried foward in a moment of hellish loneliness in the coal cellar). "Erosion" is also a poetic symbol for Davies's obsession in this film: eros and the act of, state of, result of.

*The Long Day Closes* offers images of love pulled up out of the dark of memory and made precious because of their seeming rescue. (When

Davies constructs a psychological composite for Bud's loneliness, the aural pairing of George Minafer with Miss Havisham is so uncanny it seems stolen from one's own pop biography.) Through distance and wisdom, Davies's average life seems charmed; and through stylized spareness it also seems unexaggerated: Bud and his sister Helen (Ayse Owens) perform "A Couple of Swells" using the living room doorframe as a proscenium. It harks back to Minnelli's lush *Meet Me in St. Louis,* but the modesty of the siblings' pleasure is both vulgar and transcendent. Occasionally a bickering neighborhood couple, Curly and Edna (Jimmy Wilde and Tina Malone), bring their own prepossessing version of glamour based on showbiz into the Davies home. These diverse sequences happen in a random thematic stream-of-consciousness order that is justified by the intensity of Davies's vision. Sensuality is followed by piety anticipated by melancholy—a procession of memories as piquant as an aroused mood.

Davies proves himself one of the few British directors capable of psychically powerful imagery. The film's final scene—a majestic nighttime cloudscape—is a marvel comparable to the light show in *2001,* yet it has a more moving simplicity. The cosmic view it alludes to is, aesthetically, the logical conclusion for a movie with such a carefully wrought perspective on private joy and personal trauma. The film's greatest moments confirm Davies's lack of self-indulgence: the single shot of a family Christmas recalls a still-life, but one vibrant with Davies's gratitude for his loved ones' vivacity and togetherness. As a way of distilling the poignancy of loss, it's also the brightest image in the film.

And then there's the virtuoso "Tammy" sequence in which the movie rises from Bud's solitude and considers a larger, social view. Davies lap-dissolves overhead shots of Bud playing by himself, then the audience at a cinema, next a congregation at Mass, followed by regimented rows of school children—all cadenced to the sound of Debbie Reynolds singing "Tammy:" The audacity of matching seriousness to kitsch is breathtaking. It shows how the sweetness of pop culture makes loneliness and grim routine bearable. With each of the song's chord changes, Davies's imagery deepens into unsentimentalized political fact. There's a dual consciousness here: Davies's understanding of the hard life of work and conformity, and his hope in pop culture that gives voice to impossible longings for individuality and escape.

Caught up in appreciation of pop's surfaces, the depth of our feelings, we may find that the sentiments we share with family and friends elude us. This—Davies's truth—is the truth we can't look at hard enough.

*Film Comment*
May 1993

# AMATEUR MEANS LOVE

P UT MOVIES in the hands of people with a story to tell rather than those who simply want to make money and you're likely to get something infinitely interesting. That's the most you can say for Ruby L. Oliver's *Love Your Mama,* but it's a lot more than can be said for *CB4.*

Oliver's semi-autobiographical story is about a Black Chicago family in which the mother prays, struggles, and suffers, the father drinks and cheats, the teenage son steals, and the teenage daughter gets pregnant. That last fate was Oliver's own, but her recounting isn't self-obsessed (although she casts a lovely, credible nonactress, Carol E. Hall, in the part). Oliver's experience has developed her perceptions—the family itself seems fertile for disaster, yet Oliver concentrates on the personal philosophies that see them out of the depths of poverty and the pathological crime, addiction, and self-destruction that go with it. The film is Oliver's attempt at making relevant cinema, and that, today, is a radical concept.

In the extremely commercial hiphop era, many Black filmmakers seem drawn to the art because of the fame that comes with it, the conventional Hollywood allure. The goal is not self-expression but success. Oliver has the two distinctly separated. Before making *Love Your Mama,* the previous twenty-seven years of her life were spent establishing a chain of child-care centers, overcoming obstacles in her life and community without selling her ideals, her principles, or her dreams short or cheap.

Certainly, to have made a film based on her own struggle is a form of self-promotion, but Oliver's healthy exercise of her ego has a rare honesty and sincerity. When she sings the film's theme song over the end credits in a high-pitched, idiosyncratic soprano, she drives home her inspiration and motivation:

> *Look at me, I'm alive*
> *My dreams are alive*

*My hopes are alive*
*I'm alive, I'm alive, I'm alive*

The movies could use a little of this personal graffiti, and *Love Your Mama* offers the pleasure of recognizable human (Black) life.

It's in the details, from the Southern colloquialism of a clinic report about "the claps" to the mother's repeated admonishment to her unruly offspring, "I'll kill you before the white folks do." *Love Your Mama* comes from a once-familiar experience of African-American coping.

Oliver demonstrates her survival, but the film celebrates the instilled mother wit that got her through.

The movie has a homemade earnestness, a *positive* amateur quality. You're reminded that the word "amateur" originally described a practice done for love, not money. The strongest images Oliver creates as a writer-director are of the mother pinching a child's chin (mama strength) and a telepathic crosscut between a tragedy and the mother's intuition that goes back to D. W. Griffith. These modest directorial choices are real, they have all the sophistication that matters. (When Oliver hypes up a theft with exciting music, it only shows her susceptibility to Hollywood corruption.)

The benefit of this type of homemade cinema is that it keeps cinema — the culture of big pop images — down-to-earth, not off into the unprincipled faddishness of commercialism. *Love Your Mama*'s mother wit and family sense are the very things Ernest Dickerson and Gerard Brown failed to bring to *Juice,* even though that movie started out with some interesting family setups and domestic atmosphere. And there is nothing in *Boyz N The Hood* that matches the reverberating homily in Oliver's scene of a son trying to hide a crime from a parent. "You're lying to me!" the mother (Audrey Morgan) asserts. "And if you'll lie, you'll steal!" she adds, adducing the essence of the matter.

If for no other reason, *Love Your Mama* is significant for preserving that particular homey logic. It's related to the morality that is missing not only on the streets but from most of the new movies from Black Hollywood.

*Just Another Girl on the IRT* recalls *Love Your Mama* only in the scene where the protagonist gets bad counseling at her high school. Oliver overplayed her messagey hand by not indicting the principal who threatens a student with no graduation simply for pot smoking. That extreme penalty belongs to another time, whereas the point in Leslie Harris's debut film is to emphasize the effrontery of a student, Chantel (Ariyan Johnson), who won't take a principal's threat. Chantel's response is to curse. The word "fuck" comes out of her mouth like $CO_2$, and this impudence—although it gets her nowhere—is the most the movie has going for it.

The pleasure that Chantel takes in speaking puts *Just Another Girl* on a different level from most movies about troubled teens. Harris concentrates on the esprit of mouthing off in a way that is apt for the era (the fifties-set British film *Wish You Were Here* captured some of this). Plainly, it also has much to do with Harris's attempt to claim for girls some of the discursive space that Black males automatically command in the hiphop era. *Just Another Girl* features a music track of shrewdly chosen songs to fill out the world through which a young girl has to maneuver, including one of the great Son of Bazerk tracks, "Are You Wit Me," and—an unofficial main theme—Nikki D's "Daddy's Little Girl."

Harris celebrates female brashness, and Johnson gets every verbal nuance down; she makes each cracked, high-pitched, or elongated phrase fun to listen to. "All I'm doing is expressing my opinion," she says in a way that dares people to contradict. She expresses attitude the way most people smile. But Harris doesn't seem to understand that Chantel's loud, defiant chatter is a form of emotional armor that an artist ought to pierce. Chantel creates a distracting suspense in every scene: Will her profane fly-girl's narration become a confidence shared with the audience, or will she bluff us, too?

The movie falls off and seems dumb when it sticks on Chantel's level while she stumbles into the same, age-old, teen-pregnancy trap as Ruby Oliver's surrogate. It starts to seem like an afterschool special rather than an authentic expression like "Daddy's Little Girl" itself.

Perhaps Chantel shouldn't be made to seem like just another girl on the IRT; perhaps something is inherently condescending in the significance Harris places on the generality of Black female behavior. The marketplace may stipulate an outsider's point of view (stereotype), but Harris could validate her efforts only by making her character as specific, perhaps as individualistic, as possible—even unique. Knowing about such differences is all that separates a personal or respectful point of view from a patronizing one.

The closest Harris gets is a scene where Chantel and a homegirl take the money a boyfriend gave Chantel for an abortion and go on a shopping spree. The girls use money and consumption to stave off responsibility. This mall-culture insight makes Chantel just another contemporary American kid—at least in her desires and immaturity. And though it's refreshing to see this behavior "from the 'hood," it still isn't special enough. Chantel winds up seeming a concept suited to the commercial fashion, and Harris seems less "alive" as a filmmaker than Ruby Oliver. This nice-try debut is superficial; saying that also should indicate that, unlike *Love Your Mama,* it just doesn't seem to come from under the writer-director's skin.

Robert Rodriguez's *El Mariachi* is another debut from the 'hood—an action film shot in Mexico for only $7,000. It's personal in a different way, reflecting director-writer Rodriguez's sensibility rather than his personal experience. Yet, like Oliver and Harris, Rodriguez shows what's important to him: apprehending the mainstream moviemaking apparatus.

*El Mariachi* has gotten Rodriguez where Oliver and Harris only can dream of going: He has a two-year production deal with Columbia Pictures as a reward for successfully turning his preoccupations with Latin culture into efficient commercial formula.

This isn't an obvious horror story, because *El Mariachi* is the work of a deft film student, an amateur only in the sense of having a limited budget. If Rodriguez has anything more to express than the zest of action and the elegance of formal skill, it will become clearer only with later work (as Spielberg's artistry became apparent only after his several made-for-TV movies).

Filmmakers of color can justify themselves by displaying the insight of a new vision or a technique that is undeniable. Oliver, Harris, and Rodriguez have demonstrated varied approaches that make popular culture, *in vivo,* exciting even when the movies themselves are less than astonishing. Although Rodriguez seems less serious than Oliver and Harris, his accomplishment is equally hopeful simply because he is capable of taking big-screen focus away from white middle-class clichés. His quick editing and relentless pacing recall Costa-Gavras, but if there is a political content in *El Mariachi* that is comparable to *Z* or *The Sleeping Car Murders,* it is buried so deep in the subtext, it is barely perceptible.

Rodriguez's story of a traveling musician (Carlos Gallardo) mistaken for an escaped convict and hunted down by the convict's rival—a gringo—combines cultural naiveté with a nearly overwhelming sophistication. It's the problem of expressing oneself distilled into *El Mariachi*'s significantly simple narrative and its contrasting complicated form. How the mariachi musician saves his life is, in part, a joke on Hollywood genre reminiscent of the changes spaghetti westerns played on white American historical mythology—the triumph is through ethnic change, of course. *El Mariachi* has made Hollywood listen to the marginals. (Rodriguez's production company is called Los Hooligans, Harris's company is named Truth 24 Frames Per Second, after Godard.) But how Rodriguez pulls off this artistic-commercial coup—and whether or not he will in the future—will be key to the struggle for a film culture among people for whom having something to say is more important than saying nothing for profit.

# THE HUGHES BROTHERS GET CAUGHT IN THE CRAP

*M*ENACE *II SOCIETY* opens with retaliation. Two young Black males in a Los Angeles Korean market act ill—drinking, cussing—then kill and rob the store owners. It's big-screen payback for the LaTasha Harlins murder that most of America forgot about, but the way *Menace* directors Albert and Allen Hughes exact this revenge is as phony as anything in *Falling Down*. The Hughes Brothers' scene perverts recent social history to make a troubling, faddish point, but its naive retribution is not nearly so clever as the Korean joke in *Boomerang* that got the Hudlin Brothers in trouble.

The Hughes Brothers have made an insipid piece of protest art, a movie about Black-on-Black violence that is so self-infatuated, so loc'ed on the slick, new forms of Black urban angst that it quickly implodes. Only the impulse to glamorize the ghetto in MTV color fields, fancy camera moves, and shortcut sociobabble (an insulting speech about survival by Charles "Roc" Dutton) seem authentic; whereas the Hughes Brothers' examples of damned youth are phony from beginning to end. Rapper Too Short appears handling a shotgun and asking, "Ready to put a hole in a motherfucker?" It's the kind of fake hardness designed to be accepted by white rock critics who like to see young Blacks go wild.

*Menace II Society* is chockablock with clichés, which may explain why it impresses white and Black middle-class reviewers. This is the version of African-American life that is easy to condescend to. It not only fits all the stereotypes about the ghetto—especially the ones sold to the public by the media's coverage of last year's L.A. explosion—but the film's team of twenty-year-old twin directors and their twenty-three-year-old screenwriter Tyger Williams revel in these clichés. It's the only truth they know or feel comfortable with. Like too many rappers, the Hughes Brothers accept the meager representation of Blacks received from denigrating media images as not merely better than nothing but worth something if only for shock value itself. When twin brothers make a movie whose lead character is named Caine, it's too obviously pathetic to be pathological. It's a sign of a generation desperate to assert its own significance and taking the handiest label that also appeases their feelings of rejection by validating circumstantial/delusional outlawry. (The only good aspect of this is the absolutely justified pleasure the Hughes Brothers take in presenting Black teen faces; these actors may lack credibility, but they all look good.)

We have just entered the hiphop exploitation era in which this mark of Cain also happens to be fashionable and commercial. So the Hughes Brothers are unprepared to oppose the trend by extracting from this milieu a single close or intimate relationship—the scenes of Caine (Tyren Turner) with his girlfriend Ronnie (Jada Pinkett) are alternately banal and preachy; scenes of Caine with his grandparents are ludicrous, like *Repo Man*'s domestic scenes played without satire (although Arnold Johnson's appearance as the grandfather is laughable for reasons that elude the Hughes Brothers; they may not know that Johnson with his cartoon-croak is more or less immortalized as the conman-raceman title character in the 1969 Robert Downey film *Putney Swope*); and the scenes of Caine with his homies are just fronting with all male-ego defenses up.

Deep into the hiphop exploitation era, these deficiencies exist as a form of shorthand; the Hughes Brothers are clearly communicating with each other in pop culture codes that don't mean much beyond their clichéd surface. Caine refers to his best friend Old Dog (Larenz Tate) as "America's nightmare: young, Black, and didn't give a fuck." It is, predictably, a teen-romance description, the kind young men may share to make themselves feel alive and dangerous. But it also pushes buttons for the establishment—middle-class whites and Blacks—who are used to fearing that nightmare stereotype or patronizing it as a product of social decay. At any rate it keeps *Menace II Society* on the fake level. For fools it will pass as gritty realism.

At their young age, the Hughes Brothers seem incapable of discerning truth from spurious pop lore—and many in the pop audience make the same mistake by indulging hiphop excess as a reflection of these perilous times. The Hughes Brothers use a music-video-age stylishness that has become the era's currency—a truth of a kind—instead of concentrating on aspects of character or psychological nuances. Caine, a moral orphan, describes his doomed parents as "Daddy sold dope, my mother was a heroin addict." This lower-depths narration is laughable; some distancing—like, say, the ironic narration of *Barry Lyndon*—is needed here to put ghetto sentimentality in perspective. But the Hughes Brothers (using a from-the-crypt voiceover style) settle for less by accepting the distortions of Black pop. (This is actually a regression from hiphop's most remarkable narratives, which are usually too vividly engaged with modern living to use that old *Sunset Boulevard* style. A first-person narrative song like Cypress Hill's "How I Could Just Kill a Man" is a more acute and chilling examination of "normal" psychosis than *Menace II Society*).

The evidence is in that Korean grocer opening and the flashback that immediately follows it—first to the 1965 Watts Riots, an uninformed beginning for establishing the inculcated social frustration of L.A. Blacks; next, to a multicolored view of a murderous adult card game (featuring Samuel L. Jackson in a fright wig as Caine's father). This is childish fantasy in every sense. At least *Boyz N the Hood* and *South Central* moved forward through time to convey a progression of its characters' personal histories without copping either of the Hughes Brothers' old movies or corrupt society excuses. The Hughes Brothers simply are in love with hiphop stereotypes without questioning them, and it's this completely uncritical acceptance of pop garbage (and the moral trap it disguises) that does them in.

"Do you care whether you live or die?" Caine is asked by his grandfather, and his first response, "I don't know," rings hollow to the sense of purpose that even jobless, loveless, uneducated ghetto kids possess. The Hughes Brothers have a suspicious sense of morality—they appeal to the middle-class ideas of escape and uplift. This message is assigned to the girlfriend, both uppity and friendly, played obnoxiously by Jada Pinkett. But she isn't ever convincing as the woman who once loved Caine's role model, the in-jail O.G. Pernell (*South Central*'s Glenn Plummer in the film's only good performance); she's simply the Hughes Brothers' sop to authority, the high-yellow voice of reason.

The ultimate copout to pop crap is the way the Hughes Brothers combine overamplified ultraviolence with sentimentality: when the inevitable tragic drive-by finally happens, these boys don't have the fidelity to truth, or the artistic guts, to stun the audience. By sparing Pinkett's sickeningly cute child, the Hughes Brothers show their distance from genuine tragedy. If they mean to convey the terror and loss in Black America today, then they, no less than gangbangers, have to sacrifice the child. The "street knowledge" in this film is just a game, and the Hughes Brothers' score is 0.

The Hughes Brothers are renown for two movie statements: "*Boyz N the Hood* was just an *Afterschool Special* with cussing" and "*Straight Out of Brooklyn* was just a tragic episode of *Good Times*."

These bon mots have traveled through the Hollywood grapevine, credited to other people, but now the Hughes's own movie *Menace II Society*, is their latest statement of television aesthetics (MTV flash and superficiality) intersecting the pretensions of socially conscious Black Hollywood.

No better than the John Singleton-Matty Rich movies, *Menace*, in many ways, is worse. It panders to the most sensational aspects of urban Black mythology with a couch-potato assumption that that's all there is to it, and the recent *Village Voice* film supplement touting *Menace* showed that same idiocy to be the operating principle of mainstream pop critics who glom onto Black controversy. None of those stupid pieces scrutinized the Hughes Brothers' inconsistent characters or facile technical display. Various invocations of DePalma and Scorsese proved how little those reviewers knew about movies, and their inability to discern *Menace*'s glamorous loathing of *those kids* showed that they knew nothing about Black street life.

Nelson George's profile of the Hughes Brothers was another fence-straddling promotional job that never got around to the front-page head-line's promised study of ghetto movie formulas. George, a Black pop hustler, performed an Arsenio Hall, welcoming the Hughes Brothers in-to the big money game—menace to menace—without ever addressing what it means for Black professionals to take advantage of the business opportunities afforded by the exploitation of African-American social trauma. Like *Menace*, George's *CB4* trivializes Black life for economic-entertainment value. Both the Hughes Brothers' drama and George's satire accept the stereotypes of gangsta rap as the full expression of Black American experience. For such lucky, naive beginners and venal cynics, their own careerism is the only positivity necessary.

An early version of *Menace* contained a reference by Jada Pinkett to her new job "doing some filing, typing, getting coffee. It pays 31." In the final release version, her salary was revised to "24." The difference is significant only because it shows how little the Hugheses know about the labor market, but their incredulous detail passes as truth among middle-class journalists. None of them objected to Pinkett, white Hollywood's ideal of a virtuous Black woman used to idealize African-American morality.

Praising *Menace* requires an ignorance about the politics and moral-ity of movie technique. Each of the reviewers, veterans of rock-'n'-rap controversy, responded to *Menace*'s cartoon violence like gray-haired matrons at a cockfight. (Jean-Luc Godard definitively answered complaints about movie gore, saying, "It isn't blood, it's red.") But they didn't realize that without an understanding of who any of the characters were—the understanding one got from *Chameleon Street*, *South Central*, *Tougher Than Leather*, *Do the Right Thing*, *Cape Fear*, *My Own Private Idaho*, *To Sleep with Anger*—the Hugheses' violence was affectless.

The *Voice* writers fell for the inanities of MTV shorthand, a convenient artifice that distances them, saves them from the full artistic experience of recognizing themselves in any of the film's characters. (That's beyond the Hugheses anyway.) The whole comedy of white and mainstream hiphop criticism is located in this fondness for patronizing Black anger—praising when it tickles, condemning when it offends. *Menace* presented a Rorschach test, exposing the prejudices of the hiphop cognoscenti; the Hughes Brothers stereotypes help fulfill Harry Allen's fantasy of Black retribution, Manohla Dargis's pretentious erudition, Playthell Benjamin's generational envy, Ann Power's feminist paranoia, Robert Christgau's impervious disdain. All these attitudes get fed into the general misunderstanding of Black art and politics. And that's a greater menace than the Hughes Brothers' juvenile nihilism.

*The City Sun*
May 28, 1992

# AIN'T NUTHIN' BUT A GENOCIDE THING

THE VIDEO *Ain't Nuthin' but a G Thang* ends with the credit "Directed by Dr. Dre." If the L.A. rap artist Andre Young actually did direct the video, then he has made one of the most accomplished debuts in film history. It's a rhythmed narrative that follows the song's story, fleshing it out with such authentic-seeming ghetto-life details as a cluttered front yard, a near-chaotic late-morning domestic interior, a fridge stocked with 40s, and a party sequence of Black folks rocking—leisurely, happily. Their groove—a lifestyle of music-driven distraction—is not disturbed by Dr. Dre and his boys' vicious boasts or by the siddity, long-haired female who walks through; she gives attitude to all the homeboys until two of them douse her with spritzes of malt liquor. The jets of brew are a sexualized image of how men can get off acting out their hostility. Certainly this kind of behavior belongs to the notorious Dr. Dre, even if the pacing and compositions are the work of some uncredited editor and camera person.

Dr. Dre presents himself as a visual auteur (his images are more evocative and memorable than anything in the current, ridiculous *Menace II Society*), just as his album *The Chronic* (Interscope) is the work of a musical auteur. He stands as one of the finest creators of hiphop cultural ambiance, musical curators and coordinators of various rap performers' voices that there is in pop today. *The Chronic*'s street-hard aesthetic and "gangsta-cruel" ethic provide a beautifully consistent tone (perhaps only the more politically sophisticated *It Takes a Nation of Millions* rivals its coherence). And if Dr. Dre is the man to credit, he's also the man to blame.

Look at him in his own video. His wide, knowing face shows a comfortable smugness—he has the confidence of a leader that befits a record producer or gang tough. The rappers who surround him—Snoop Doggy Dogg (the album's most featured rapper and flamboyant star) and

The D.O.C.—are immediately charismatic and have more dramatic voices than Dr. Dre. But Dr. Dre, just short of sullen, shows an uncanny authority; even when he smiles to make a brotherly (G thang) connection, he still looks mean. It's a big, imposing face: obdurate, ambiguous—not pinched and etiolated like, say, Dinesh DeSouza (a face you'd like to hit), but a field of puzzling temperament, full of potential calm or violence. Dr. Dre's video image is crucial to understanding *The Chronic* because it helps put a human face on evil.

Dr. Dre isn't shy about showing the inhumanity that, on record, can be enjoyed as an artistic abstraction. His ease with this life can be seen in his face as it can be heard in his production, which is derived mainly from George Clinton's Parliaments—the same party-people ethos that informed Son of Bazerk's "Lifestyles of the Blacks in the Brick." But Dr. Dre's musical vocabulary, though sufficient, is limited to the entrenched musical tastes of gangbangers. This is telling; he's stuck in the same deep-but-narrow rut as the ghetto damned who can't imagine other ways of grooving or a better way to live.

One of the most resonant lines that Dr. Dre orchestrates on *The Chronic* is of a guest artist rapping. "I can't be faded / I'm a nigga from the motherfuckin' street." It recalls, "You are about to witness the strength of street knowledge," the line John Singleton borrowed to begin *Boyz N the Hood* (a far less compelling movie than the video Dr. Dre has directed). Originally it was the opening line of *Straight Outta Compton*, the album that introduced Dr. Dre and his former bros Ice Cube, Easy E, and M.C. Ren to an unsuspecting world as N.W.A. *The Chronic* extends the cartoon "reality" of *Straight Outta Compton* into a vivid, ear-pleasing representation of ghetto/gangsta sentiments. Dr. Dre has a secure command of atavistic Black beats (basically P-Funk but rarely used with such subtlety) and atavistic machismo ("Never hesistate to put a nigga on his back," goes the chorus).

If the vocals were stripped off *The Chronic*, it wouldn't simply be full of dope beats as *Straight Outta Compton* is praised; it would be a masterpiece of emotional suggestion, groove, and musical finesse. But *The Chronic* falls short (thankfully) because of the raps that are a vital part of Dr. Dre's concept. The nihilistic words that he and Snoop Doggy Dogg parry so nicely ("It's like this, it's like that, it's like this and uh") complete his vision as much as the images seen in the *G Thang* video—and that vision won't do.

Although *The Chronic* offers the same fuck-it-all urban fantasy as *Straight Outta Compton*, this worldview is no longer dismissible as childish; its offense is serious and real. Dr. Dre's improved musicality – calmly loading tracks with spoken dramas, sound-effects comedy, and slow-drag atmospheric instrumentals—has no equivalent in his sociological perspective. *The Chronic*'s world of heartless competition among Blacks is speciously amoral the way *Straight Outta Compton* was speciously political—both albums reveal an artistic stance in love with demoralization when demoralization pays.

Of course, before it ever paid, it pleased. There's a lot of pain in this album, but it is well disguised as fun. This is not the joy of music. The very beat-consciousness and street sense that L.L. Cool J speaks of as "The beat is so funkified and nasty to the bone / People be dancin' alone" (from "A Little Somethin' ") are missing here. There's a depth in L.L.'s observation; it's love—of music and of a people who communicate through music, sometimes subconscsiously.

But I think Dr. Dre is expressing just his own nasty pleasure, his complex sadism. (In his directorial debut, he has the gall to present an analogy to the real-life female battary he was sued for perpetrating as if it were nothing more than a frolic. This is an artist who gladly would romanticize his people's destruction.) L.L. and Son of Bazerk have Black manners psyched out in ways Dr. Dre doesn't get close to, and that makes him a less valuable artist.

Let's face it, Dr. Dre has a genius for the musical sound, the cultural rhythm of Black hopelessness. Yet artists are not objective or impersonal conduits; his creativity is his personal pressure valve. But his observations-and-replication of street life shows no reflex. Dr. Dre's art expresses his jaundiced view, the corruption he accepts without question. That makes *The Chronic* a half-truth, half-lie and eventually worthless, as is the "wisdom" the Geto Boys' Bushwick Bill is invited to relay: "There's three types of people in this world: Those who don't know what happened, those who wondered what happened and people like us from the streets that *make* things happen."

The "happening" is all forms of Black urban death, and *The Chronic*'s casual, curious, almost happy view of genocide is bound together, weak-mindedly, with the social forces and deceptive cultural pleasures that keep the death system coing. Greatly amusing tracks such as "G Thang" and "F--- Wit Dre Day" and "Lil Ghetto Boy" are like dishonest, immoral movies that mix up an audience's desire with an audience's "romantic" self-image and then ultimately placates their frustration—disarming them spiritually by giving them a groove to get lost in. *The Chronic* has been high on the album charts since its release last winter. Millions of people are rocking to its decadent death call without ever stopping to notice or think why.

The album's best track, "The Roach," is a funny, debased pop confessional where *Cannabis sativa* is celebrated as an opiate of the people; with the radio DJ/post-P-Funk voice strongly implying that pop music serves the same function. It's the only track, mixing "bomb bullet" metaphors with sexual urge, then hunger, then dissatisfaction, that represents the way contemporary Black minds willingly, happily have gotten fucked up. "That's why they call this shit the chronic!" Dr. Dre's vocalist says, stoned and lost, unaware of his own suicide.

This feel-good ignorance is the shame of (mercilessly commercialized) pop culture and a particular scandal when produced by a Black artist at this stage of widespread social desolation. For all *The Chronic*'s tough talk and vulgar revelries presented as "pure," "primitive" Black American reality, it actually abuses the license that should be seen as hiphop's great advance over previous pop-music trends—the freedom (and pleasure) to reintroduce audiences to the most precious, significant parts of themselves that usually go unappreciated.

This criticism should not be mistaken for the kind of censorship the Rev. Calvin Butts currently is advocating. Troubling "art" cannot be eradicated or rehabilited before the conditions that produce it are resolved. But still, one can ask, is Dr. Dre worth a damn? The answer is a provisional yes. Hiphop shows that musical genius is plentiful in America today, so we don't *need* Dr. Dre, whose "The Roach" is the only perception on this album that the world never had before. Yet, on "The Roach" he gets past pretending that addiction has no pleasure or is an evil easy to say no to and offers this insight clearly, beautifully.

*The Chronic,* a near masterwork, wasn't done merely for nasty delectation—as Dr. Dre told Arsenio Hall, his mom is down with the profanity on the album because she gets paid from it. Since Dr. Dre already has played the dozens on himself, one only needs to point out that for all his street wit, *The Chronic* doesn't match the wisest, most profound political pop moment pre–Public Enemy: "You can please yourself but somebody's gonna get it."

*The City Sun*
June 2, 1993

# WHEN THE MENSCH COMES OUT

A T THE BEGINNING of her career Barbra Streisand, an icon of middle-class showbiz if ever there was one, actually sang rock 'n' roll. In spirit. The 1963 *The Second Barbra Streisand Album* is the proof; Streisand's instinct for covers matched her peer Aretha Franklin's. Even without a beat she turned conventional sentiment upside down, changing the refrain of "When the Sun Comes Out" from "suddenly the sunlight came" to "suddenly the cyclone came / I'll never be the same."

"When the Sun Comes Out" and "Anyplace I Hang My Hat Is Home" were sung violently—in the days before "Star Search" this impolite emoting meant something. She went at these songs as if to destroy them—or at least their middle-class, respectable, hierarchical culture—in order to make this art form her own. As a young artist in an "adult" arena, she scaled the edifice of showbiz (carving her own imprimatur) with nothing like respect for the form, just reveling in music and emotion and the chance to be different.

But Streisand didn't always keep the promise of those audacious revisions. The progress of her career, and her maturity, meant that she would relent, singing pop ballads "classically" or else rocking awkwardly in the seventies. Streisand had embodied an original, personal sensibility, going against the showbiz current like a talented—but proud and assured—outsider. Ego often got in the way when she acted the diva on film and record, but a forthright inspiration (singing "Lover Man" in 1965 like a radical romantic refugee) reminded the world that show tunes weren't a discipline but a form of pop art rising from the gut, shaped by nerve and buoyed by humor—an anarchic, rock 'n' roll approach.

This was politics, and they resurfaced last winter when Streisand previewed "Children Will Listen" before the Clinton inaugural audience. "What are the ways that parents abandon their children? When they say, 'It's all your fault?' 'You're a sissy?' 'I hate you'?" Those questions signaled her current political aggression, a personal and career development certified by *Back to Broadway* (Columbia), Streisand's new album of standards. Repeating the formula of her 1990 *The Broadway Album*, she's inspired by something more substantive—an understanding of her position as a pop figure and also as a private citizen of a society in crisis.

"Children Will Listen," a Stephen Sondheim composition from *Into the Woods*, is a perfect vehicle for Streisand's dual consciousness. It allows her to address her loyal following while also confronting the world that wrote her off as a rich, irrelevant institution. That inaugural introduction connected social concerns with personal ones, all conveyed through a popular-song form that isn't merely entertaining but instructive. The only integrity we expect from artists these days is aesthetic, but Sondheim's song fuses her commitment into a passionate, enlightened warning against the private, domestic politics that inevitably become public policy, social oppression. The song, which equates parental directive with law, demystifies authority by holding it accountable to the listeners' (and the singer's) emotional life. Streisand sang as a parent, but also as a person opposing the neglect of authority.

The specific intent of Streisand's political address didn't turn her live performance into agitprop—her Boycott Colorado initiative is just one of the meanings to be read into it—but a clue to the source of her subtle (special) pleading is right in the song's title: "Children," the drag queen sobriquet for young followers, places Streisand's performance in the vernacular it was no doubt destined for. She acted on her pop star privilege to simultaneously address a mainstream and subcult audience. Her apparent comfort with this multivalent discourse fulfilled a constant—if not always on-track—artistic ambition.

Apart from that voice, which won Streisand widespread admirers (and is now a richer, if less sterling, instrument) her public stature is based on representing the feelings of subcultures—Jews, women, gays—and investing their interests with passion. Lately she claims that status with bold discretion. On *Back to Broadway* Streisand performs as a showbiz relic on two songs from *Sunset Boulevard,* but the album's heft is in the role of the "children" symbolizing the disenfranchised, disaffected group needing to resolve the tensions and causes of their social distress. Streisand ennobles that plea with a singer's zeal. Going back to Broadway represents an abstract, symbolic journey into her empowering past.

This is a real return to Streisand's "roots." The icy slickness of *The Broadway Album* (a *New York Times* album-of-the-year pick after all) seemed simply a career strategy. But *Back to Broadway* revisits the Show Tune with genuine motivation and political impulse. That's what you hear in the studio version of "Children Will Listen"—a cleaner, less raw recitation than at the inaugural but powerful still. The artist gets behind the song, pushing it not as notes, but as feeling. Singing, "Careful the spell you cast / Sometimes the spell may last past what you can see / And turn against you," Streisand sounds as modern as Tracy Chapman targeting the circle of urban violence on "Bang, Bang, Bang." Emphasizing how children will "see-ee-ee" and "ler-ur-urn," Streisand unfurls the melisma that made her a white-girl phenomenon thirty years ago. A harder take on the word "listen" produces volatile syllables that recall her once-innovative approach to show tunes. Just as the point of the song seems to have renewed her passion, she regains her artistry.

Streisand's true roots are not in bowing to the Broadway institution but in messing with it, revealing its often disguised sources in the impudence and creativity of subcult, ethnic performance. In the sixties the delight of "Sam, You Made the Pants Too Long" and "Second Hand Rose" was that Streisand performed them as more than mere novelty numbers. Nightclub audiences may have heard them that way—perhaps the way Clinton hears "Children Will Listen"—but the core of those songs impressed an ethnic, Jewish pop heritage that few artists had the confidence *or* talent *or* wit to make part of a modern pop repertoire.

Why not remake/remodel Broadway heritage to say something relevant? *Back to Broadway* has two other political tracks. A duet with Johnny Mathis on a medley of "I Have A Love/One Hand, One Heart" has an unmistakable Black-Jewish resonance that redeems the sappiness of yet another *West Side Story* cover. (It connects subliminally with the "Children Will Listen" lyric "Nothing's all Black but then nothing's all white.") Trading lines with Mathis, Streisand adopts Black phrasing, intoning "Ahhh, have a love" that is more complicated than Crown Heights, and their harmonizing on the line "Even death won't part us" becomes even more profound.

Her playful "Luck Be a Lady" invokes feminism, with Streisand adding "Stick with me sister" hood. She makes the objectifying tale an empowerment ditty—kitsch but refreshing. That's more than Streisand does with the Andrew Lloyd Webber numbers. "With One Look" and "As If We Never Said Goodbye" sound like any Streisand track from her middling *Songbird* (1979) to *Yentl* (1983) period. When she wakes up midway through "Some Enchanted Evening" and "I've Never Been in Love Before" or makes easy hash of Michael Crawford on their "Music of the Night" duet by giving astonishing tenderness to the minor chords, she's doing nothing more than any good pro would do.

But a pop star's political renaissance is a rare thing, and this album is the evidence of a person stirring to life inside the star. The lyrics to "Move On" make a romantic statement of the need to get a grip, but it's the remarkable performance of "Children Will Listen" that takes hold of the imagination. It offers warning, wisdom, and advice with a veteran awareness that the melodies and verses a singer sponsors are not just material but part of a serious, social act. This subtly radical move is consistent with the irony of Streisand's showbiz-defying Jewishness. If Sony Music's execs want to prove themselves more courageous than Washington, they'll bypass "Speak Low" as the album's obvious, innocuous single and push "Children Will Listen," where Streisand speaks loudly.

*The Village Voice*
July 12, 1993

# JANET
# AND MADONNA
# USE THE LEXICON OF
# FUNK

A RECENT BELL HOOKS quote holds that "We [Black people] have no public discourse on sexuality." And last winter's publication of *Erotique Noir/Black Erotica* (Doubleday) would seem to sustain that "intellectual" bias by its air of discovering hidden delights. *Erotique Noir/ Black Erotica,* a tome of sex-oriented belles lettres compiled and annotated by a trio of Black scholars—Miriam DeCosta-Willis, Reginald Martin, and Roseann P. Bell—makes the mistake of being too literary. There's not a single song lyric in the whole book, although the greatest tradition of African-American writing—especially erotica—is the sex song.

Madonna knows this; Black erotica is the impulse behind *Erotica* (Maverick/Sire), her best album or, as Richard Torres says, her *first* album. And Janet Jackson knows it, too. Jackson's new album, *janet.* (Virgin Records), comes out of the entire taken-for-granted tradition of Black public discourse on sexuality—the pop record. The album title itself is a wacko pun acknowledging Janet's pop ubiquity—in lowercase letters—and her "period." It's done for clarification. After all, Bobby Brown's "That's the Way Love Is" jumps—even Merle Haggard had a song called "That's the Way Love Goes"—but Janet Jackson's song of the same title comes with an altogether different, subtle rhythm and languid mood. The tune is hardly there, but its very being is dialectical, eloquent, and suggestive.

Madonna's custom of borrowing from Black or Latin pop styles, then recasting them for mainstream (white) consumption and understanding is the subtext of *Erotica,* an exploration of sexual mythology that borrows subculture like a cup of sugar. It's not only a fount of inspiration but the guiding style of Madonna's personal and musical expression. Madonna performs her own scholarship by alluding to the pop past and reworking previous statements on sexual expression and identity.

Consider the videos for the album tracks, each one a revised version of earlier sexual cultural modes. *Erotica* was a compressed history of stag films; *Bad Girl,* a remake of the 1977 disco-era alarm *Looking for Mr. Goodbar; Fever,* a nineties updating of Peggy Lee's 1950s classic confession of lust; *Rain,* a video-era examination of that post–World War II aphrodisiac staple, Orientalism. And in the great *Deeper and Deeper,* Madonna combines historicism with her pop-art consciousness.

Devoted to seventies pop culture, *Deeper and Deeper* returns to the era of mainstreamed decadence, typified through disco and the Andy Warhol publicity zenith. The time period is specifically chosen for the moment artistic, sexual, and racial subcultures came above ground, claiming their right to be but also expounding many of the anxieties and complexes that supposedly tied up previous generations and have returned to haunt the AIDS era. Hoping to learn from their liberated – and doomed – examples, Madonna addresses the contemporary riskiness of sexual identity through the more adept, freer, richer modes of seventies, pop, specifically Black pop.

*Deeper and Deeper* is loaded with iconography that evokes the seventies sexual Götterdämmerung, but with more angst and alienation than admiration. Madonna, in her white Afro, mingles with the denizens of the demimonde, most memorably a Black man in a pimp suit who laughs, openmouthed, showing big, rapacious teeth. She's endangered, perhaps, but she looks worn, close to jaded but far from innocent. Rubbing against unbridled Black sexuality has coarsened her whiteness and innocence. Experience comes with worry; that's the tension that animates the song "Deeper and Deeper" (perhaps her best – or equal to "Into the Groove"), which turns the mystery of falling in love into the mystery of adult sexual experience, the bottomless drift into uncontrolled lifestyles.

The *Erotica* album, an important collaboration with dance maestro Shep Pettibone, is also Madonna's most explicit; her taunting and aggressive language isn't simply the latest taboo, but it's the mode she interprets as essential to the eroticism and the frankness of Black disco – anything else would return her to Donna Summer euphemism and camp, so Madonna has to update it to nineties brashness. Thus, tracks like "Did You Do It?" and the irresistible "Thief of Hearts" (a couple of steps behind RuPaul) take advantage of contemporary bold expression.

Discussions of oral sex and vicious name calling are part titillating, part liberated, but thoroughly risqué. The chances Madonna takes on *Erotica* reveal a white redefinition of self through templates of personality and behavior set down by people of color and their art. Madonna takes outsider art inside herself. Her personal affection and risk distinguish *Erotica* from the pandering, Sir Richard Burton example of white exploitation, yet their actions are very similar. The private, white discourse with Black sexuality is also a public discourse that automatically imbricates Black discourse.

This Madonna paradigm was mythologized twenty-five years ago in the Julie Andrews movie *Star!,* a musical biography of the stage actress Gertrude Lawrence. At the film's climax, Lawrence has trouble performing the "Poor Jenny" number from the Gershwin Broadway show *Lady in the Dark* until she is taken uptown to the Cotton Club and observes the chorus line's jazzy, sensual style, which she appropriates without acknowledgment but to her own roaring success. The film's narrator acclaims Lawrence's weakly imitative jazz performance "a theatrical miracle." The miracle is how white media shamelessly constructs its aesthetics and politics after the abuse and exploitation of other cultures. It's a pattern—a legacy—and Black artists usually stay oblivious to it while also keeping ahead of it. Madonna's *Erotica* proves what *Erotique Noir* doesn't: that Black folks lead the public discourse on sexuality even when they don't initiate it.

"Does she get funky?" a conscious Caribbean woman asked about PJ Harvey. Then the Janet Jackson album arrived with the answer "yes." Because Jackson does get funky, she doesn't have to deal, as Harvey does, with the obsessions and anxieties of unarticulated sexuality and frustrated sensuality. Jackson coos her typical entreaties rather than singing—or pondering—them according to the white art-rock approach.

"Go deeper, baby. Baby, don't stop," "I feel so good I want to cry" are expressions of sensual urging; Jackson submits to the kind of romantic fulfillment that is ever taught, exemplified, idealized by pop. Obviously a young woman takes on these thoughts through growing up listening to pop and then connecting those musical examples to her hormonal development, then to her experience.

Producer-songwriters Jimmy Jam and Terry Lewis's idea throughout *janet.* —their third collaboration with Jackson—is to define the singer's sensuality within the context, the tradition of Black pop's femininity. The foundation for this is more pop than adult—the Supremes.

Using samples from "Love Child" (on "If") and "Someday We'll Be Together" (on "You Want This") supplies the album's youthful thematic undercurrent. This record is about the first bloom of physical ecstasy, of feminine discovery. Jam-Lewis don't borrow song structure (in fact, the Supremes' sample riff doesn't really work on "If"; it just seems an imitation of the shuffling noises on "Rhythm Nation"), but the samples are tokens, references to a youth they (and the pop world) remember as innocence. There's a slight disjuncture in the use of the Supremes, though. Diana Ross's piquant voice had a special sound, whereas Janet Jackson's wispy vocal hardly seems up to the task. It's sometimes buried on "If" and seems most inadequate in the later tracks, mostly ballads. (The CD bonus cut, "Oops," is a straight-up Supremes rip, but Janet's singing and Black-American-princess coyness palls; it's an embarrassment next to Sarah Cracknell's purely joyous girlgroup vocalizing on Saint Etienne's "You're in a Bad Way.')

The album's Lil Louis knockoff ("Throb") is the type of musical construction that depends on real singers or voices with strong personality. Instead, Jackson and Jam-Lewis provide cute approximations of what's needed (similar, yet inferior, to Madonna's own Lil Louis biting). But even this is a form of communication, Janet taking part in a public discourse on sexuality by answering back to her showbiz role models. "This Time" does the same by combining Stevie Wonder chord clusters with Kathleen Battle, who provides uncannily human (sensual) atmospherics; it's the album's most successful track. "This Time" takes pleasant listening very far past the mere makeout/background-music utility of the ballads into a widely understood pleasure that includes an awakening of romantic sentiments. It gives an aesthetic equivalent of gratification. The track's array of female voices is more politic than a siren song; it takes delight in the pure sound of female utterance. That's the reasoning behind Chuck D's rap on "New Agenda," a salute to Black women that gives Janet her closest yet proximity to rap polemics. It's a political acknowledgment of certain sexual-social facts (though "Revolutionary Generation" is better). Janet's voice is set off against Chuck's as an individual sexual presence. This isn't verbal articulation, but it makes a strong point—a sentient connection as well as public discourse. That's the way Black pop goes.

*The City Sun*
July 7, 1993

# TINA TURNER CELEBRATES RACISM WITH SEXISM

Tina Turner highlighted her recent Radio City Music Hall opening night concert with a version of "Proud Mary" that, from the first tick-tock guitar notes, summoned the ghost of Ike Turner. The celebratory, sold-out audience didn't mind—Tina doesn't attract a thinking crowd. She has become a specious pop martyr, beloved by white gays and Black women for survival after victimhood. But the Radio City concert was a bizarre ceremony as hollow as the practiced screeches Tina lets out while scurrying across the stage.

Turner's stage show isn't about music (her band of mediocrities only come to life when posing as white men for her to sidle up to); isn't about emotion (the formulaic British pop that is her repertoire is inane); and isn't about artistry (Tina sang well but routinely, ballads and rockers were simply given her typical brazen once-over). This tour commemorates Tina's further deification via Hollywood in the current popular bio-pic *What's Love Got to Do with It?* But none of this signifies a triumph of human spirit over sexism; it is, instead, a triumph of sexism over racism.

Perhaps the most egregious moment out of many was Tina's perfor-mance of "Private Dancer," the awful Mark Knopfler composition that titled her 1984 comeback album. Throughout her lame recitation, white men were springing out of their seats to applaud. Here's what got them up:

A maudlin, pseudo-confession by a woman of the world who agrees to being pimped on her own terms. "I'm your private dancer / A dancer for money / Do what you want me to do / Any old music will do," Tina croaked. She wasn't being ironic—it's her credo. Her white male fans' adoring response doesn't soothe her past suffering from an abusive hus-band with unconditional acceptance. Their following is on condition of

Tina's new subjugation—a former abused wife now an exploited whore. She's gone from one pimp to a million pimps. "Private Dancer" lays all this out, but Tina's Reagan-era ascension poised her career-minded self-exploitation to be considered a cultural norm, morally superior.

Seen live, the spectacle of a fiftyish Black woman strutting the stage with her short skirts hiked up to expose her nether juncture and being applauded for it by a crowd filled with white men was uncomfortably close to the action in the *Private Dancer* music video. In the metaphorical clip, Tina plays a "dancehall hostess" bored between johns/clients. Richard Torres has interpreted "Private Dancer" as a pathetic updating of the *Sweet Charity* dance hall hostess number "Hey, Big Spender," but Tina's self-serving pathos strikes me as a Baby Boomer's version of the classic "Ten Cents a Dance" without the devastating melodramatic crescendo. Instead, the *Private Dancer* video climaxes with Tina lying on the dance floor while white men pelt her body with roses (a double allusion to a bawdy Bette Midler *Rolling Stone* cover). But those roses don't symbolize love—they represent the excrescence of white men's most base estimation of Tina Turner's worth, and she revels in the metaphorical scum. The Radio City concert brought out the major Tina contradictions—the kind of political, ethical points glossed over by the movie—such as her now compliant performances for mainstream (white) audiences of the kind of gut-bucket antics she claimed Ike *forced* her to do. If Tina's really through with Ike, why is she still performing "Proud Mary"? The song makes no sense in her current, predominantly white touring group—no one growls Ike's basso profundo, and the two white-girl substitutes for the Ikettes prance insipidly and don't muster the call-and-response fervor ("Go ahead, now!") that charges the song. The Ike arrangement itself is weakly imitated but not so badly that it doesn't expose how banal *all* the other material is. (Her "nice and rough" intro has become a Laurie Anderson spoof.)

A camp anomaly, Tina enters and exits the stage with tacky, wacky kitsch, using a forklift stairway or a crane that allows her to hover over her celebrants. There should be a sense of triumph when a Black woman commands legions this way, but Tina doesn't sing a lyric or hit a note that feels honest or inspired or that justifies a gay or female audience's faith. Opening with the garbagey "Steamy Windows (zero visibility)" doesn't inspire the kind of personal response Madonna gets from "Deeper and Deeper's" earnest "My love is alive and I'm never gonna hide it again!" Instead, Tina's a heartless trouper, simply working the crowd because it pays.

Tina creates no sluttier image than her middle-aged effort at dancing: She scoots about with one fabulous leg lifted like a urinating canine, or else she crouches and grunts. This kind of dancing certainly is raunchy, as Angela Briggins has suggested, but it's also despicably "clean;" Tina bends and spreads her legs for "family entertainment." Nothing worse than a corn cob is likely to plop out.

Is it fair to say that at the moment of her widest pop-culture renown, Tina is a disgrace to women? As the lady sang "I'm your private dancer / A dancer for money / Any old music will do."

*The City Sun*
July 21, 1993

# RUFFNECK AND BRASSNECK

MC LYTE GOES THROUGH a voice change on "Ruffneck" (First Priority Records) that's as fascinating as a boy's who is going through puberty: full of the same conspicuous, silly, embarrassing, charming immature signs of "maturity." Her well-known hard delivery keeps its baritone oration, but it assumes an extra toughness to match the latest notion of accepted sex roles.

It's a great performance. MC Lyte snaps out the sharp ragamuffin syllables with thrilling, jumpy speed. She paces her words less for sense than for the emotion that speech rhythm connotes. "He's a ruffneck so dats ah-ite!," she says, approving of a young man's demeanor. Lyte's got more than Brooklynese down, yet something ain't right.

First, she's adopting a more commercial, deliberately hard-core sound that proves pathetically desperate and unsuccessful on the album *Ain't No Other* (except for "Ruffneck" and the title track). Second, "Ruffneck" shows "O.P.P.'s" influence on rappers who previously sought to enlighten or to celebrate street innocence. MC Lyte's new bad girl act competes with other female rappers on terms that may not really be her own (morally schizo, she's at least several personalities away from "I Cram to Understand U Sam"). You can tell it's done for money when the chorus goes, "I need it in the morning so I gotta have a ruffneck." She's after the popularity of TLC, who certified a new image for hiphop females—those spunky sisters got over the way Lyte and previous female hiphoppers never did.

The imitative "Ruffneck" is Lyte's most rocking track ever, but it's something of a miscalculation. TLC and "O.P.P." made their impact through melody, not just hardness. To take on "O.P.P.'s" callous attitude toward sex and TLC's "Ain't 2 Proud 2 Beg" shamelessness, without the complicating, soothing musicality, only further traduces the love hunger those songs described.

Lyte descends to the sexual idealization of Apache's "Gangsta Bitch":

> *I need a dude with an attitude*
> *All he needs is fingers with his food*
> *Evil grin with a mouth full of gold teeth*
> *Startin' beefs is how he spells relief*
> *Actin' like he don't care*
> *But all I gotta do is beep his 911*
> *And he'll be there*
> *Right by my side with with his ruffneck tactics*
> *Ruffneck attitude, the ruffneck bastard.*

The way Lyte's voice squeezes out the adjectival naughtiness, straining to be as tough as the words she's speaking, you can hear joy—or at least a vocalist's momentary belief in the song's sentiments. Plainly Lyte responds to "Gangsta Bitch" as a challenge to real-life options. But it's unclear if she means to parody Apache's inherent comic distortion of female traits. Neither Apache nor Lyte bothers to explore the kinds of strength that Black boys and girls have to learn—they just jump to celebrating the hard street postures: "Showing little respeck / Now that's a ruffneck!"

Apache's inspired obscenities leaned naturally toward satire (and the subtle suggestion that he wanted a "bro" as much as a "bitch"), but even when Lyte's rap is most playful, she can't help but raise doubt about the "masculine" traits she extols:

> *Boxer shorts*
> *Everything is fittin' large*
> *But he don't have to be large to be in charge*
> *Pumpin' in and out and out and in*
> *And here we go*
> *He knows exactly how I want my flow*
> *And that's slow.*

The word "exactly" is ingeniously stressed in Lyte's rat-a-tat phrasing; it supplies a rhythmic and verbal contingency that qualifies the blunt praise of appetite and instinct. And this difference is both mature and, I think, feminine. Can a woman who says, "He ain't gotta be large to be in charge" really want a ruffneck? Lyte's record encapsulates the development of romantic expectations. But her tiny contradictions come from trying to keep up with pop's dubious sex-role streotypes. While puberty views behavior in extreme terms, it is experience and knowledge that make gangsta bitches, ruffnecks, sex machines, and juicy fruits seem ridiculous or insufficient to how men and women play out their affections.

Simplisitic sex pop like "Ruffneck" may have charm, but it can lead to the kind of trouble David Gedge sings about in The Wedding Present's great 1990 song "Brassneck." Like MC Lyte, Gedge's unusual voice portrays a personal history of sexual development. He has a deep, choking growl that's far from mellifluous—the kind of voice I used to fake when answering the telephone before puberty—but he sounds sincerely anguished. Instead of witty lines describing barbaric traits, Gedge demonstrates male soft spots—tenderness if not exactly refinement. Gedge reveals the masculinity that aches, a *sensitive* rough voice. He may sound like a brute, but he sings the brutality of love relationships that are not thoughtful, careful, or helpful enough. The harshly melodic guitar band with its incessant drum kick spur Gedge's emotional dips and peaks:

> *The first time you came over*
> *Remember saying you'd stay for good?*
> *No, I didn't think you would*
> *Well we couldn't have been closer*
> *But it was different then*
> *That's all in the past*
> *There, I've said it now, at last.*

The title "Brassneck" refers to the insensitivity of a romantic ideal; Gedge responds the way everyone has to a particular roughneck or gangsta bitch—with reflection and lament:

> *Now I sent you that letter*
> *To ask you if the end was worth the means*
> *Was there really no in between?*
> *Well I still don't feel better*
> *I just wonder if it could be like before*
> *And I think you just made me sure*
> *But then that's too good for you*
> *I might have been a bit rude*
> *Or wrote it in a bad mood.*

Gedge's question, "Was there really no in between?," makes his own contingency issue. He's less certain than MC Lyte about how satisfactory are extreme sexual roles. Knowing the fickleness of human nature, Gedge rejects the simple romantic ideas usually found in pop: "I just decided I don't trust you anymore," he says, reaching a stage heavier than Lyte.

"Brassneck" is moving where "Ruffneck" is only exciting; Gedge is better at questioning the precedent of role playing. He recognizes the differences made by experience, how lovers actually rough up each other — "I think I know what it means / It means I've got to grow up / It means you want to throw up" — and how this friction leaves people at odds with each other. He's in romantic hell.

Asking for sympathy, originality and trust from a love object, Gedge's letter points out the aloofness that is based in sexual strategizing rather than intimacy. By showing the emotional variety within masculinity, Gedge personifies the hope that men *can* have feelings.

The process of recognizing those feelings can be painful but not futile, and that's the most helpful example pop can provide to listeners whether during puberty or its twin condition, adult romantic stress. Our culture is already so overloaded with encouragements of male insensitivity that, without thought, the lack of heart becomes fetishized (as MC Lyte has done). "Brassneck" uncovers chauvinism, "Ruffneck" enshrines it. Pop artists need to inspire listeners to find the in-between. Ruffnecks and brassnecks need to be broken.

*The City Sun*
June 30, 1993

# REINTRODUCING CARL FRANKLIN

N THE EXTRAORDINARY second half of Carl Franklin's HBO mini-series *Laurel Avenue*, several of the Minneapolis characters go to church on Sunday. They have individual responses to this sermon:

> You know youth is a gift of God, too. But it's not a gift that's supposd to last forever. Memories should last, but not the childhood. Not biologically, or mentally. We have got to grow to maturity, to responsibility, to leadership. But we live in a land where maturity and the responsibilities of adulthood are not stressed. No. Umm Uhmm. We bow to youth, childishness, frivolity. Why be gray, dependable when you can dye your hair? Abandon your responsibilities. Buy more toys, play more games.

Certainly there's a message here, but it's not *the* message of the film; it's what the film demonstrates in the way it dramatizes the efforts of an entire family to mature, be responsible, get along, stay alive. *Laurel Avenue* exists in direct opposition to the childishness and frivolity of *Menace II Society* and the upcoming *Poetic Justice* while being more exciting and sexier than either of those hiphop melodramas. Director Franklin and screenwriter Michael Henry Brown, who gets a solo credit for Part Two's script, approach contemporary Black American life with the sobriety of adulthood without the usual dullness that appellation typically implies.

*Laurel Avenue*, produced by *Roc* star Charles Dutton, is as good a piece of art as has been made in this country in the past twenty years, and this achievement is almost shockingly unexpected. A TV movie (even on cable) about African Americans threatens to meet the bourgeois demands of obvious social criticism or moral uplift, and the first half supplies all of that (as did the sententious *Frank's Place*), though with a measured, observational ease that suggests theatrical cinema rather than emphatic TV. This could be the result of compromise (the first half's story is credited to Brown *plus* Paul Aaron).

But then *Laurel Avenue* bursts the bounds of the medium, becoming more contemplative—and like that cool, levelheaded sermon—more stylistically daring. In Part Two, the Arnett family starts to act like a family, rather than a body politic, split up into neat representatives of urban problems. The actual number of family members increases as their personal concerns get elaborated and more detailed. The truth of the world seems to be bursting from inside each handsome, emotionally animated face. Their lives don't seem determined by plot; Brown and Franklin seem simply to be following each person's mystery rather than their dilemma.

There's the stable but easily fooled father (Mel Winkler); the mother who plays piano in church but can't warm to her children (Mary Alice); the fraternal twin sisters (Juanita Jennings and Rhonda Stubbins-White), whose actions repel the love they feel for each other; a brother (Monte Russell) looking for a safe hustle; a schoolteaching brother (Scott Lawrence) who gets his middle-class righteousness challenged; a younger daughter (Malinda Williams) surrounded by troublesome suitors; a nephew (Vonte Sweet) torn between street camaraderie and the awesome burden of kinship. None of these characters dominates the narrative, and Franklin and Brown even add sidelong glances at the crises of outsiders— a white high school athlete with a gripe, a Black one afraid of success, a homeless woman. *Laurel Avenue*'s plots keep widening and deepening like Altman's *Nashville* (the movie of movies), and its this intense and unpredictable momentum that makes it so extraordinary.

From *Green Pastures* to *The Jeffersons*, from *Beulah* to *Menace II Society*, Hollywood's tradition of Black portraiture has been conventional, which means stereotypical. Franklin and Brown take startling narrative leaps, showing artistic courage and faith in their subject. In a regular *Village Voice* reduction, *Laurel Avenue* was called memorable only for it's cunnilingus scene, but that's not the only one of the film's innovations.

Franklin's frankness about a Black couple's sexuality blasts stereotypes (and racist critical condescension like the *Voice*'s) in the same way that it confounds a viewer's tendency to be judgmental about film characters. Mary Alice's variation on her matriarch roles is as superbly acted as ever (*To Sleep with Anger, Sparkle, I'll Fly Away, Fences*), but Mrs. Arnett's punctiliousness and her passionate sense of failure reveal the human depth that Hattie McDaniel, Ethel Waters, Claudia

McNeil, and Esther Rolle were never allowed to show. Dan Martin's career- and family-conflicted husband is a new-to-movies variation on the Black stud. Martin's bedroom duties may be a TV milestone, but they also give his characer the kind of dimension that few actors since Brando in *Last Tango in Paris* have enjoyed. Martin's intimate scene with his wife (Gay Thomas) is less about sex than about the facets of character that make human beings phenomenal: Martin comes across distinctive, generous not conservative, modern not traditional, and over all *complicated*.

Both Stubbins-White and Jennings as the polarized twins—a junkie and a cop—flesh out their roles past urban schematics and create palpable humans with unexpected susceptibilities. Through them, Franklin and Brown Afro-Americanize Jean Renoir's adage "Everyone has their reasons." The richness and ambiguity of those reasons put *Laurel Avenue* above typical pop drama and capture the flow of life. This movie doesn't make points. In the family party scene, the church scene, and a silent moment of father-and-daughter watching late-night TV together to pacify sleeplessness and anxiety, it *points out* behaviors and meanings usually left unexamined.

The chief surprise here is Franklin's direction. I was unconvinced by his debut, last year's overrated *One False Move*. The script was trite—extremely predictable—and the acting was uneven: excellent (Bill Paxton) to terrible (Cynda Williams). Plus the first sequence of Black people slaughtering each other just seemed sensationalistic—nothing that followed matched or supported that horrific opening. But the key to Franklin's talent was in the horror; the Black folks being slaughtered presented recognizable faces to the camera; they related to each other in uncanny flickers of vulnerability and familiarity. And that's the way the teenagers curse in *Laurel Avenue*—not with profane bravado, as in *Menace II Society*, but using words as armor against insecurity and a disguise of the ignorance they all are ashamed of.

Franklin's art makes the actors' connections look and sound undeniable. (That's part of the reason the killings in *One False Move* felt offensive, the degree of pain overwhelmed the movie's insight.) It's not a strictly realistic technique, like British director Mike Leigh's, but a stylized essence that comes from a mature, responsible artist's regard for the lives he depicts. Hollywood's hiphop directors don't have this knack, but it's common to the finest Hollywood melodramas, like *From Here to Eternity* and *The Last Picture Show*, and the deepest independent art films, like *Killer of Sheep* and *My Own Private Idaho*.

I'm using cinema comparisons because it's just the bad luck of racist Hollywood that relegates *Laurel Avenue* to cable TV rather than movie theaters. A struggling playwright scoffed at *Menace II Society*, citing the dread conditions for nonwhite artists in Hollywood. "Try being a Black filmmaker trying to make a movie in Hollywood about anything but hiphop gangsters and you'll find out what *hard* is." Carl Franklin has maneuvered in the system to make a beautiful work of movie art *for television*. *Laurel Avenue* is not a toy, not a game—it's good enough to inspire the hope that a new future starts here.

*The City Sun*
July 21, 1993

# SIMI VALLEY AESTHETICS

I F PEOPLE LEARN how to watch movies from watching good ones, then the past decade of corporate formula, inflated pulp, and critically acclaimed drivel must result in a visual illiteracy of frightening proportions—something even more alarming than the statistic of *Indecent Proposal*'s grossing an embarrassing $100 million.

Consider, just to start at a suitably ludicrous level, the Sharon Stone defense. Stone saturated the media last spring, feigning shock about the beaver shot in *Basic Instinct*. She got away with her victimized-starlet role (her best acting yet) because no one—critics or paying customers—seems to know how to look at movies anymore. Director Paul Verhoeven and cinematographer Jan De Bont did not steal a sneak shot of Stone's pubic hair. Any alert viewer saw that the shot was a close up insert requiring a special lighting and focusing setup that could only have been done with her knowledge and compliance. But Stone's outrage makes a good self-protective fantasy.

As does the Simi Valley jury's calamitous reinterpretation of the Rodney King tape as a police training film. We're talking about a verdict that left fifty-one people dead, $775 million dollars in property damage, and Southern California's white middle class permanently paranoid and strapped for the next throwdown. That's a score to make the heroes of *Die Hard, Terminator 2,* and *Rambo* envious. A fatuous connection? No, merely the kind least favored by film pundits: the classic art-politics link. That jury of American citizens enunciated a conjoined approach to society and image watching that exposes ideas dominant in our cultural habits and our national sense of self. Simi Valley aesthetics—in which the indecencies of social prejudice, legalized sadism, and narrative illogic can be found in a single sorrowful image of an unarmed Black man being hit fifty-seven times in eighty-one seconds by a gang of whites—are the bequest of an unjust social system and a culture of absolutely debased visual media.

Photojournalism has recorded many atrocities since Matthew Brady's time, and in the past few years home videocams have probably captured just as many. But George Holliday's videotape of the assault on Rodney King, chosen for this year's Whitney Biennial exhibition, is one of the primal images of the contemporary world. Like the little boy holding up his hands at the Nazi concentration camp, the Vietnamese youth having his brains blown out, the JFK motorcade, the napalmed Vietnamese girl, and the Kent State coed screaming with her arms outstretched, the Holliday video crystallizes an era. But unlike the others it's a ghostly image of nighttime, underworld, almost subconscious doings by a post-sixties army of the night, acting out the mean frustrations of the Reagan-Bush revolution where law runs amok, making examples—victims—out of the defenseless. Holliday caught a cowardly, anarchic show of might within the guise of law enforcement. His video overwhelms movies and TV series as the decade's single most indelible, conscience-haunting spectacle. Though real, not a product of "artists," and though video, not film, the Rodney King video redefines visual aesthetics.

So far Walter Hill's videological *Trespass* has been the only Holly-wood movie to consciously manipulate post–Rodney King spectatorship. (Spike Lee's use of the footage in *Malcolm X* was merely agitprop, documentary.) Hill alternated film and video imagery in a postmodern allegory about race war, deliberately invoking the audience's awareness of race and politics as objectified by visual media. But the lack of other references doesn't mean that the King video has been ignored. It has, in fact, been pervasive. It's in the country's bloodstream, changing the pulse—the connotative rhythm—of everything we watch. (It palpitates, subliminally, in Martin Scorsese's *Cape Fear* when authority figure Nick Nolte arranges a gang attack on Robert De Niro and watches the assault from a—now familiar—distanced vantage point.)

The Holliday tape in all its gruesome actuality—spontaneous life turned into a mechanized phantom-image in which technical distortion teases one's sense of disbelief—makes you blink and refocus as few fiction films have done lately. The facts on view slowly realize a racist-fascist dream. Sociology and psychological dread were combined, exposed, and then, in the sunlight of a Simi Valley courtroom, given twenty-four thumbs up—way up.

It seems right to assign film critics a share of blame for Simi Valley aesthetics; the press's absurd laudatory response to phony, violent trash like *Menace II Society* shows a warped social sense that bad movies encourage and critics, through their ignorance, affirm. Examples abound, especially when movies depict the nation's racial trauma. The historical misrepresentations of *Mississippi Burning* were often praised without apology (celebrated on the covers of *Time* and, yes, *Film Comment*); a year later, some of the same reviewers condemned *Do the Right Thing* as inflammatory. Even film reviewers who ignored theatrical engagements of Henry Hampton's astonishing civil rights documentary *Eyes on the Prize* rushed to promote Ken Burns's factitious revisionism in PBS's *The Civil War*. The deliberate, patronizing fantasy of *Driving Miss Daisy* fulfills the racist fantasy of conservatism, and critics applaud choosing nostalgia and resisting the contemporary reality of increased ethnic and class separatism.

If critics don't resist the moral and factual imbalance of movie fiction, society's tendency to reify its fears and prejudices goes unchecked; lies become part of the national mythology. It's almost as if *The Birth of a Nation* were constantly being remade (see Michael Mann's *The Last of the Mohicans*), but with far less craft.

This wave of clumsy, politically specious filmmaking occurs naturally in a period of social retrenchment. As much as anything in Soviet Russia, recent American movies have been under the influence of an unconscious politically determined cultural program. Facetious complaints about MTV misplace the blame in an increased superficiality in filmmaking, empty flash and dazzle. But it's worse. The Reagan-Bush revolution in media control was coterminous with Hollywood's enfranchisement of television's most craven culture-for-commerce practices through the handiwork of British advertising hacks: the visionary Ridley Scott, the opportunistic Alan Parker, and most devious of all, the exploitative Adrian Lyne. All three, utterly unscrupulous, base their films in the indulgence of the most fashionable, regressive social moods. The shortcuts of advertising technique that Hollywood adopted during the eighties have helped to obliterate the syntax that makes movies expressive and readable. A typical Adrian Lyne scene, such as the traffic-directing sequence in *Flashdance,* structures images not for their narrative logic but for visual pacification. The image content is actually negated—without significance it merely reflects back the audience's inertia, holding them in place until the next dialogue segment. A Reagan-Bush-Quayle speech similarly utilized political cant, asserting the status quo while appealing to the public's reticence and disinclination to think. Reagan-Bush used objects of secular worship and appropriated patriotic symbolism, tactics similar to the non-sequitur montages of the Brit-Hollywood school. (Lyne turned Demi Moore's bed romp with dollar bills into a fetish in *Indecent Proposal*—whereas the scene's stylistic predecessor, ZaSu Pitts's mouthing a coin in Stroheim's *Greed,* was *about* the fetishization of money.) By distracting attention with innocuous but pleasing imagery, eighties-nineties films avoid provocation and active or critical thought during viewing.

Simi Valley aesthetics are the end result of this anti-Eisensteinian approach to film. Instead of constructing thought in the manner of Soviet montage, modern movies obstruct it. Audiences robotically watch movies until told what to take in or think by the next dialogue—or by the Los Angeles Police defense attorneys who attempted to subvert the Rodney King tape. It's like *The Nation*'s review of *Jurassic Park* observing, "There's nothing for the forebrain to do." But the reviewer was blaming Spielberg's Eisensteinian sci-fi spectacular for the modern moviegoer's refusal to think while enjoying, or analyze while watching. People no longer know what they're looking at at the movies—sometimes critics least of all. As modern movies plunder endless cinematic gimmicks, critics, at the same time, ignore the significance of form and theory. This genuine postmodern irony showed its conservative roots, its susceptibility to Simi Valley aesthetics, this summer when critics praised the fake reflexivity of *Last Action Hero* over Spielberg's intellectualizing and DePalma's surrealist tricks in the previous summer's *Raising Cain*. Postmodern fictions questioning film-watching convention disturb, while Arnold Schwarzenegger–John McTiernan destroy all avenues of comprehension in their nihilistic celebration of meaninglessness.

*Last Action Hero* was guilty of serious sociological insult by ducking responsibility for urban violence and codes of machismo that young males ingest from Schwarzenegger cinema. The choice of a guileless white protagonist (Austin O'Brien) refutes the reality (and imaginative needs) of the nonwhite and third-world fans who are targeted by the violent machinations of Schwarzenegger, Stallone, Willis, Seagal, et al.—the Terminator as the cinematic equivalent of malt liquor. *Last Action Hero*'s ode to calamity is not avant pop but contemptuous of its audience. Schwarzenegger's vanity leaves him many levels of morality away from John Singleton's recent, hope-restoring statement, "I know my audience is the Steven Seagal audience, but I want to give them the kind of movie they can think about when they leave the theater."

Critics' reluctance, or inability, to examine form and audiences' tendency to misperceive cinema first came together in a significant eighties folly presaging the disaster of Simi Valley: In Woody Allen's *The Purple Rose of Cairo* (1985) the meanings of images were no longer fixed and cinema was trashed. In fact, by promoting Allen as a major artist of the period, critics exhibited a retreat from the experimentation with form and the politicization of the arts that distinguished the post-Vietnam/Watergate-era golden age of the American Movie Renaissance.

*Purple Rose,* a pseudonaturalistic Depression-set fairy tale, embraced film-buff nostalgia by constructing a fundamentally nonpolitical approach to culture and its significance. The New Jersey hausfrau Cecilia's (Mia Farrow) escape to the movies was the absolute reverse of the *pop* meanings Arthur Penn used the movies to evoke in *Bonnie and Clyde.* Typical of the nontheoretical Allen, movies are depicted condescendingly as an innocent pleasure whose implications could never be more than trivial. Allen does not expose the era's blinkered ideology. When the film-within-the-film's actors walk off the screen or comment upon their cinematic entrapment, wisecracks by the onscreen audience members, who are stupefied or bemused by the spectacle of moviehouse anarchy, are in a similarly passive vein. Allen's conceit may seem complex, but it is consistently, determinedly shallow. What is intended to be a jarring, humorous contrast between life onscreen and off succeeds only in the short dialogue between a prostitute (Dianne Wiest) and a screen idol (Jeff Daniels). Allen for the most part blends his fantasy of Depression-era chic with his nonintellectual fantasy of thirties Hollywood as a golden age of narrative folly. An usher's cry, "I'll get the manager," suggests the political nature of the audience's ignorance: they have no awareness of where images or story come from; a reflexive reliance on the manager suggests their compliant, unquestioning response to authority.

The critical acclaim for *Purple Rose* proved that people know nothing—or have forgot all—about how movies work. Meanwhile, the film's unrealistic view of work (and unemployment) exposes the detrimental aspect of Allen's romanticism. All action in *Purple Rose* is devoid of ideology; that's the general, escapist view of art that the Reagan-Bush cultural revolution reinstituted. *Purple Rose*'s implication about "entertainment" for the good of the oppressed sanctioned eighties viewers to disengage from the previous decade's sophisticated approach to film watching. (*Zelig,* in 1983, was more extreme and so, for its first half, funnier.) Allen's crazy comedy doesn't go the distance of alienation and bedazzlement like DePalma's *Raising Cain,* which invites audiences to question the form of the film they're watching or the nature of the society depicted. Allen aims instead for laffs and boffo piety, a giddy idiocy as embodied in his sentimentalized heroine.

But as Cecilia sits mesmerized by the screen, she (and the audience that not only identified with her but shared her pathos) submits to the most oppressive, bourgeois deception. Though modeled after the heroine of Fellini's *The White Sheik,* who idolized a photo-novel comic strip (a fact critics conveniently missed), Cecilia actually embodies the zombified audience of the TV era. In fact, *Purple Rose*'s illogical concept is based in Allen's instinctive but poorly thought-out reaction to television. Films don't emanate from the screen but are projected from the back of the theater (to wax poetic, from the audience's collective wish to the screen that reflects back collective dreams). The way Allen shows the first cracks in his film-within-a-film concept, complete with audience response, the effect is not of a metacinematic experience but of a TV sitcom with a laugh track.

Allen is unable to distinguish film experience from TV experience because he lacks the theoretical curiosity and formal seriousness to challenge anyone's assumptions about how media means. *Purple Rose* shows no intelligence about diegetic or nondiegetic pleasures. Like a Simi Valley defense attorney, Allen relies on a layman's status-quo interpretation of images, no matter how absurd. Keith Gardner correctly suggests that this counterrevolution carries out a further debasing of classic cinematic inquiries and experiments, specifically those in Buster Keaton's *Sherlock Jr.* In silent films the manipulation of technique and audience perception was fundamental to the art form's growth (the same methodology was repeated by the French New Wave and teased in the moviehouse scene of Godard's *Les Carabiniers*). Keaton played subversively with the relation between audience and screen: to challenge innocent presumption about screen emanation, about genre, about cinematic form and the relation of visual media to reality.

*Sherlock Jr.* investigates intellectual projection; *Purple Rose* celebrates viewer indolence. Godard updated the projection-vs.-passivity theme in *Sauve qui peut/La Vie* – particularly the slow-motion sequences that broke down events into iconographic frames. The point was not simply to question the image but to behold its microscopic detail as evidence of a larger, awesome recorded truth that turns cinema/video into a palimpsest superior to fantasy or prejudiced supposition. The Simi Valley jury's response to the slowed-down version of the Holliday tape happened without such an inquiring, conceptualizing basis. They saw a different scenario because that's what they preferred to see. ("Rodney King was not being abused, Rodney King was directing the action," one juror said on *The Phil Donahue Show*, demonstrating as much knowledge of direction as the stars of *Sneak Previews*.) But this autistic insistence happened also because contemporary audiences are ill equipped to think about movies in the abstract. They're ready to believe any half-baked fiction they've been told to accept.

Such passive spectatorship may be the direct result of television, and it has infected film culture so drastically that even a big-screen sitcom, *Broadcast News* (1987), was hailed by critics as a sophisticated, behind-the-scenes look at the personalities responsible for electronic information gathering and dissemination. *Broadcast News* presented another embarrassingly simple distortion, yet critics and audiences let themselves be tripped up by a blatantly dishonest piece of montage crucial to the story's moral lesson. Tom (William Hurt) violates the movies' oldest canard, the integrity of journalists—a contemporary joke if ever there was one—by faking compassion for an interview subject: he cries on camera, once the interview has been completed, so that his tears can be shown off in a crosscut from the subject to himself. Writer-director James L. Brooks pretends that this standard TV interview technique is a breach of telejournalism ethics. To make the point, he has Jane's discovery of the ploy—she's the "smart" neurotic feminist news producer (Holly Hunter) in love with Tom—serve the dramatic purpose of alienating her from the star newscaster. But who could believe that savvy Jane would be hoaxed by this—as Brooks hopes the audience will. Her implausible innocence matches Brooks's pretense; it's a double demonstration of the era's obtuseness and corruption. Yet critics went along, and through this mistake—a fault of filmmaking incompetence and lack of ethical rigor—*Broadcast News* encouraged a cynical rather than critical distance in viewers. But it's an especially dishonest, eighties cynicism, carefully designed to protect and abso!ve the powerful folks who work in media.

The *Broadcast News* hoax is based on denying the theoretical principle called suture—the editing together of discrete material to form a cohesive meaning. By not applying this, a filmmaker can only anesthetize a viewer's basic mental alertness—the Simi Valley jury's ignorance about the connecting logic of even individual, split-second frames shows the terrible replacement of basic literacy, intelligence, and imagination with dupability. That's the shame hidden inside *Broadcast News*. Attention to such details of filmmaking—which some critics think gets in the way of fun or readable criticism—is not necessarily esoteric. It once was part of the joy to be had in movies and their reflexive practices, whether by Griffith, Welles, Eisenstein, Hitchcock, DePalma, or Spielberg. Their technique thrills audiences while simultaneously instructing them on the intricacy of visual expression. It is not designed to settle interpretation or deny viewers' authority, as does the TV news routine of fake interviewer-interviewee communication.

*Broadcast News* made a hash of modern sophistication by trivializing TV form and obvious subject-object connections. Instead of scrutinizing Tom's narcissism, the film condemns him as it supports, romanticizes Jane's self-righteousness. Meanwhile, Brooks neglects the true journalistic issue of bogus, slanted news coverage—specifically, the traditional, white-majority control of news broadcasting. The mythology and stupidity surrounding news media was also evident in the smart-ass appreciations of the Belgian film *Man Bites Dog,* a cinema verité boondoggle that never clarified who was behind the camera taking delight in the actions of a European serial killer—a perfect postmodern conundrum to bewilder critics unsure of what they're doing or watching. The arty pretenses of *Man Bites Dog* are also a form of political projection where fact, reality, and truth are omitted by elitist whim. If this art-politics link seems too ideological, or disproportionate to the emotional investment that filmmakers and filmgoers and film reviewers bring to cinema, that's just the very unease that has been inculcated in the popular audience for at least eighty years by an industry that sold dreams as a front for collaborating with many social injustices.

The refusal to identify with news subjects or with politics in *Broadcast News* and *Man Bites Dog* parallels the Simi Valley jury's neglect to imaginatively perform suture between the separate, slowed-down images of the Holliday tape. Modern audiences have been distracted from the necessary, exciting film-watching process of suture that visualizes the relation between conscious and unconscious, imaginary and symbolic ideas. That process, the British Film Institute's Pam Cook writes, seeks to understand "our narcissistic relationship to the rest of the world in which others are seen as ourselves." The jury's inability to make imaginative connection with the beating of Rodney King favors white egocentricity. They, like Hollywood with its penchant for cop-authority-figures as protagonists, are stuck in a racist, narcissistic rut.

A frightening truth becomes apparent: the unexamined artifices of mass media can preclude any certainty about events. The callow, gullible spectator is then helpless against any challenge to the evidence of the senses. That's how a jury, twenty-two years after *Z*, ten years after *Sauve qui peut*, two months after a Los Angeles judge misread the surveillance-camera footage of LaTasha Harlins's killing, could approve a specious analysis-interpretation of the Holliday tape. ("We got the jurors to look at the case not from the eye of the camera but from the eyes of the officers" bragged Laurence Powell's attorney, Michael Stone.) Even slowed down to infinitesimal increments and microchronic blurs, the fact of Rodney King's abuse is incontrovertible. Truth does not change by changing the speed of visual presentation, but modern audiences are kept from understanding the facts of what they see because unconscientious critics and immoral filmmaking promote the primacy of subjective fantasizing. This isn't the same as being desensitized to violence (the initial Schwarzenegger effect) – it's being desensitized in, not responsible for, one's own perception. And it happens through a political allegiance to authority above all else. Even the truth before one's eyes.

"You think a videotape can't be tampered with!" a digital graphics expert (Tia Carrere) says to Wesley Snipes in *Rising Sun* before going on to demonstrate the latest electronic gimmicks of image doctoring. *Rising Sun* director Philip Kaufman is not above using post–Rodney King rhetoric while borrowing techniques from *Blade Runner* and yet steering clear of any moral/political implications in his story. (Kaufman seems far less socially aware than are Reginald and Warrington Hudlin, who cleverly inserted a LaTasha Harlins reference into the wittiest dialogue of the New York–set comedy *Boomerang,* connecting their movie to life offscreen.) In his slick, neo-Hollywood manner, Kaufman demonstrates how the lessons of Simi Valley and the makegood second verdict easily are subsumed by an industry intent on keeping audiences docile. The film's electronic cutting-and-pasting sequences are worlds away from the exercise and uncovering of visual technology that made Antonioni's *Blow-Up* and its noble descendants—Coppola's *The Conversation* and DePalma's *Blow Out*—such epochal and richly expressive inquiries into the nature of human perception. Kaufman's movie about transcultural perception is as blind as its variously xenophobic or condescending, egocentric characters.

There is a subtle politics in the act of image making of which all image watchers need to be aware. *Rising Sun*'s crime thriller fantasy is irrelevant to the need of the contemporary audience to realize how the interpretation of spectacle is not simply subject to manipulated imagery but requires an ability to understand the context of events. Such manipulations are nothing more than ethical cosmetics used to dress up the corpse of America's ego by a filmmaker reluctant to give away the funereal practices of modern, disingenuous Hollywood. Kaufman's *Rising Sun* reflects the dormant politics of an American prodigal who had escaped the nation's most recent perplexing crises by making two ersatz European movies (*The Unbearable Lightness of Being* and *Henry and June*) that could only satisfy a determinedly unpolitical mind dead-set against films that distract from the illusions of romance and sex.

The same hardened subjectivity was apparent in the acclaimed Steven Soderbergh's *sex, lies & videotape,* a naive comedy of manners derived from the VCR revolution and the attendant misunderstanding of what constitutes a close encounter of any kind. Soderbergh contemplated James Spader's "celibate" asceticism as the condition of a spiritually vacant, postmodern age, but the premise was naive. Spader's amateur stroke videos were the discharge of many actual, if impersonal, *relationships.* He exploited women and abused them; his emotional penetration was nothing less than obscene. Soderbergh misunderstood Spader's complicity with his strip-and-tell subjects and failed to examine the politics of flesh-and-blood sex versus sex in the age of mechanical reproduction. In 1989, numerous critics preferred this inexact, mildly pornographic fantasy to *Do the Right Thing,* dodging political art—and the complexity of modern spectacle—and thereby anticipating Simi Valley aesthetics.

Movies like *Basic Instinct, Indecent Proposal, Purple Rose of Cairo, Broadcast News, Man Bites Dog, sex, lies & videotape, Last Action Hero, Rising Sun, Mississippi Burning,* and *Driving Miss Daisy* are selfish, purposeless acts perpetrated by the kind of people art critic John Ruskin condemned in 1887 for "retarding the arts, tarnishing the virtues and confusing the manners of your country." The tragedy of Simi Valley comes of the corrupt machinations of a culture committed only to slackening the tastes and civic aspirations of a populace by flattering its solipsism, beguiling it, deceiving it under the ruse of "entertainment." It's perfect that Simi Valley is home to the Ronald Reagan Presidential Library: a monument to the Hollywood stench that rose to poison our political air.

If the moviegoing public is to avoid a doomed future of Simi Valley idiocy, then film critic juries, like courthouse juries (that means everybody), will need to learn the craft they're judging and sharpen their ethics and aesthetics.

*Film Comment*
September 1993

# REVOLUTION TO REVELATION

THE HIGH IRONY of Pet Shop Boys' single "Go West" is also an artistic strategy of *deep* feeling. It adds an astonishing climax to *Very* (EMl), their new album of love songs and political songs informed by gay sensibility.

"Go West," a disco anthem, balances nostalgia with contemporary awareness, glee with sardonicism. This adaptation of a seventies Village People song follows the VP formula of a stentorian male-chorus putting exaggerated testosterone heft behind a list of simple entreaties: "TO-GETHER!" "I LOVE YOU!" "THIS IS OUR DESTINY!" But Neil Tennant's fey, *almost* dispassionate, lead vocals catalyze the track. The two types of male voices blend to take the song out of the realm of comedy; it's a demonstration of the cultural strides pop music has made since the disco seventies, when the Village People brandished homosexuality as a series of stereotypes, satirizing, in the very sound of hypermasculinity, the limits of the gay and straight sexual ideal. Pet Shop Boys add to that complicated spoofing their own serious mock seriousness. It's a beautifully open consideration by artists who are usually chided for not being out. Despite its cool tempo the cover is rather brazen, and the audacity of PSB's automatic revisionism makes it all the more thrilling. Tennant's calm voice contains the realization that the Village People "joke" is, in fact, a natural truth with which we have come to live—and die.

The merging of dance music styles and eras in "Go West" is deepened by the sociological fact of what those styles mean: a representation of early gay-lib esprit and nineties AIDS-era yearning. PSB's "Go West" isn't a lament for lost innocence; its emotional power lies in the observation of past innocence and an insistence on hope. Tennant, partner Chris Lowe, and producer Stephen Hague turn seventies folly into modern faith—an act of progressive gay humanism that smashes the petulant decadence of a good, second-rate group like Suede. On *Very,* PSB write and perform their wisest and most trenchant tales of modern romanticism. Essentially, if subtly, gay-themed songs like "Young Offender," "The Theatre," and "One in a Million" and the acutely poignant "Dreaming of the Queen" strike universally human (that is, pop) responses. The tense hesitation and lush swooning of "To Speak Is a Sin" improve on PSB's 1990 "Nervous" and finally answer the despair of The Smiths' "How Soon Is Now?" with an equally magnificent levelheadedness. The sense and sensibility in the songs on *Very* can provide the argument against the ignorance of homophobia (the songs are about things everyone experiences), but that effect is propelled by the undeniably musical pleasure of each track.

The ecstasy of "Go West" comes from the VP chorus that now sounds like a martialed initiative (as in Erasure's "Stop") – proud voices on parade:

> *TOGETHER! We will fly so high*
> *TOGETHER! Tell our friends goodbye*
> *TOGETHER! We will start life now*
> *TOGETHER! This is what we'll do*
> *GO WEST!*

But the seventies-style chorus also suggests a lost battalion, and the idea of PSB marching on for innumerable fallen soldiers *who sang so strongly that their voices would always echo* makes the song's cheerfulness bittersweet and devastating.

When the chorus hits its final crescendo, PSB leaps forward to a technobeat coda – a flat-out epiphany. The move is from revolution to revelation (1990s "My October Symphony"). It's dance music relieved of earthly fetters and social constraint. The men's voices become quieter, faint, almost cosmic. Without campiness the phrase "go west" is a memento mori and the track becomes a requiem.

In the *Go West* video, director Howard Greenhalgh uses the notion of requiem to reveal another level of meaning. Tennant and Lowe are shown leading an army of gym-fit, white-attired men up a stairway to some nebulous heaven, the final destination after marching through Moscow's Red Square. Various symbols of Communist patriotism are contrasted with the image of a ruby-red soul-sister idealization of the Statue of Liberty. (The Black female presence in disco is, of course, pure sexual politics.)

Greenhalgh specialized in futuristic, sci-fi imagery for Snap's video *Rhythm Is a Dancer*; for *Go West* he uses a similar mix of live action and computer animation not to represent the abstract concept of rhythm this time but the West as a political abstraction. Greenhalgh's spiraling towers, scarlet monuments, celestial staircase, geometric birds, and heaven-bound troops are fantasies that pose the fall of Western capitalism. Through these aural and visual symbols, the AIDS era becomes the means for PSB to chronicle simultaneous political and spiritual tumult.

*Go West,* a highly ironic video, comments on contemporary political faith. It turns the muscular shapes and vaulting angles of socialist realist art into a homoerotic cartoon. What's camp in this vision—what's scoffing, otherworldly, absurd—in fact carries the force of political criticism. Westward-leaning enthusiasms and foolish optimism ("We will find a place where there's so much space!" "Baby you and me / This is our destiny") are skewed by the neofascist implications of the video's ghostly shock troops.

The video's political symbols are less romantic than the song's sexual ideology, and so it is skeptical rather than elegiac. But the basis of these dual readings is part of PSB's pop sophistication—from the bird chirps out of the classic Soviet film *The Cranes Are Flying* to the subversive use of camp. *Go West* manages to be both exultant and cautionary, an artwork of uncommon richness.

*The City Sun*
October 27, 1993

# IN THE BEDROOMS OF AMERICA

"WET PUSSY. I know all about that," a character says sorrowfully, facetiously, hopefully in Robert Altman's *Short Cuts*—a brazenly heterosexual-centered film. That statement focuses the social disorder that begins in the homes—and expressly in the bedrooms—of America.

It's hard to think of any other movie that presents such a panoramic view of American life yet concentrates on the intimate deceptions and dependencies of individuals. It's the kind of feat one expects of Altman, but even his past large-themed movies—*Nashville* (1975), *A Wedding* (1978)—were different from *Short Cuts'* ever-shifting and rebalancing of moods and tones.

Altman bases his interweaving of twenty-two characters on the writings of Raymond Carver, and though the overall tone of the film recalls Carver's dry melancholia, this is less significant than the abundance of Altmanesque humor and irony. Not only is that "wet pussy" line consistent with the film's sexual motifs—love, water, birthdays, drinking, urination, bathing, posing, smelling, fish are everywhere—but the vulgarity and candor are part of the film's lively, very American style and artistry. Altman and his cast of funny/sad actors seem free to personalize and delineate the stress in our culture. This is a gallery of idiosyncratic, naturalistic performances.

The actors' autonomy structures *Short Cuts* like a museum exhibition—every performer is a work of art depicting the film's predominant themes. Altman alternates each one so that their actions (a nude with a basketball floating in a Hockney-like swimming pool) and their dialogue ("Your father was a prick. That's the long and the short of it!") play off one another. You note the similarities and differences, and as the film moves forward, the connections enlarge the meaning and amplify the moods on display. One of the most violent scenes is, ironically, the quietest in the movie: An estranged husband (Peter Gallagher), desperate to get back with his now-uninterested wife (Frances McDormand), sneaks into her house and vandalizes it methodically and maniacally. Gallagher's psychological tumult is conveyed inconspicuously, but his derangement and emotional isolation are the common thread of the movie. Sex isn't the only explanation for his agony, yet it locates human distress in a universal soft spot.

*Short Cuts'* heterosexual emphasis is unusual and deep enough to stand in for a worldwide malaise, though this aspect of the film is probably its most personal. After *That Cold Day in the Park* (1969), *3 Women* (1977), and *Come Back to the 5 & Dime Jimmy Dean, Jimmy Dean* (1982), this movie represents Altman's most successful exploration of female psychological mystery – mainly by having a naturalistic, sociological framework. Instead of treating women as mystical entities, Altman dramatizes the mysteries of sex as a dilemma that has an impact on the way the world works. It is fundamental to the country's well-being. Altman gets at intimate secrets here; he doesn't pretend solutions. It's in the predominance of sexual imagery – the candid nudity featured during a husband-wife argument (Matthew Modine and Julianne Moore); a post-coital douching scene that conveys threatening marital detachment (Anne Archer and Fred Ward); the different kinds of innuendo that go on between a wife questioning a husband about his fidelity (Madeleine Stowe and Tim Robbins); and another wife (Jennifer Jason Leigh) doing in-house phone work for a sex-call line while her husband (Chris Penn) suffers shock and jealousy.

Many of the scenes in *Short Cuts* play with ideas in a fashion distinct to Altman where images, actions have the weight and resonance of symbol or metaphor but actually fit into the film as just another element of mundane life. It's an extraordinary strategy, part of what enables Altman to create great, imaginative art without using conventional plotty storytelling devices. This three-hour, four-minute film moves swiftly but – most impressively – smoothly. Altman provides a masterly, Olympian view of the many different lives under consideration here.

The film is full of elegant, astonishing-yet-simple transitions from one character, situation, location to another. This often is accomplished with a cut between scenes focusing on a repeated object, word, or activity that links the scenes – but then varies the sense of its first use – or else by the leisurely, gliding movements of Walt Lloyd's camera that combine the images in a scene, providing a subtle, narrative arrangement of the action without limiting its meanings.

One example of this prodigious technique occurs when a waitress (Lily Tomlin) driving home from work accidentally hits a boy on his way to school. Tomlin attempts to help while the boy gathers his books and walks home, refusing to talk with a stranger. At the end of this frustrating exchange, Altman pans right to a school-crossing traffic sign with the silhouette logo of an adult helping a child. The contrast of people with iconography is heartbreaking—Altman poses the ideas around which our society is constructed with the reality of the way people really do live. It's theory vs. truth, a powerful, innovative use of image content, central to the way Altman gets underneath the mythological delusions of drama and human relations. He cuts the crap—the comforting lies—of movie romanticism.

In *Short Cuts*, Altman complicates the way movies are ordinarily watched and understood in order that viewers understand the way other people's lives fit with or fall away from their own.

It is through an examination of the emotional relationships people share that *Short Cuts* becomes a fascinating, unassailable social vision. It's the proverbial personal-is-political concept portraying the way personal frustrations affect how people interact outside their homes.

The sexual entanglements of the couples in *Short Cuts* reveal the different politics that people have. These soured relationships take off from Carver's short stories, but Altman cuts into Carver's prose not to do him justice but to do him a favor. This film offers a richer vision than anything in Carver's literature, not just through the advantages of cinema's sensual, kinetic effects (the stunning opening sequence of a helicopter fleet, fitted out in green and pink lights, flying in formation through the nighttime sky, spraying pesticide on the Southern California territory), but through the democratic fairness and plangency of contrasting social strata and psychological type, as well.

Each couple may be noncommunicative and frustrated but—like Tolstoy's concept of families—they are so in special ways, in distinct circumstances. The contrasts bring out not only individuality but also a larger understanding of the social temperature when numerous personal crises converge. This happens in several group sequences: at a nightclub, a hospital, a diner, a terrace barbecue. In the latter, male-female, person-to-person tensions are locked inside veiled recriminations: A key exchange happens when a wife, made up as a clown, tricks her husband, saying, "It's me. I can change, but I always come back." This scene (backed by the song "I Don't Know You" on the soundtrack) crystallizes the differences that bewilder people. It updates the private revelations of Albee's *Who's Afraid of Virginia Woolf,* along with Mike Leigh's *Abigail's Party.* Altman repeats the situation, affirms its truth, when a horror film makeup artist (Robert Downey Jr.) uses his wife (Lili Taylor) as a grotesque model while taunting her about her past domestic abuse.

It's a bizarre treatment of emotional terror and dependency worthy of DePalma.

All this makes *Short Cuts* a great film about the unintentional failures that Americans inflict upon one another. On one level it's a singularly disturbing vision, yet, it's also an exhilarating feat of human perception. Without being specifically "political," *Short Cuts* provides an understanding of what has seemed to go so wrong in the culture. These characters' lack of a spiritual center conveys the shifting, quaking terrain of contemporary living. *Short Cuts* differs most from *Nashville* by the cultural displacement of religion and music—the unifying forces that signify a society's stability. No one goes to church, but the music here is primarily an appropriation, a white version of jazz (sung by Annie Ross tartly playing a singer who is alienated from Lori Singer as her classical musician daughter). Profoundly, jazz is used here the way it is used most commonly, as a background noise. Altman's adaptation of Carver deals predominantly with whites, but Altman's inclusion of Black people on *Short Cuts'* sidelines—a jazz mutation—enlarges the film's sociological view. They are another part of the whole disturbing social mix. It happens mainly in the nightclub scene ("Underneath Art Blakey," the maitre d' says to arriving guests), where Darnell Williams as a testy ex-con intimidates an alcoholic Tom Waits, and later propositions Jennifer Jason Leigh. The characters' inability to see into each other, past stereotypes, is a devastating dramatization of American cultural distancing. The use of jazz becomes, incidentally, a sign of cultural aberration.

*Short Cuts* is a great, unsettling vision. Some reviewers have complained that Altman's filmmaking is different from Carver's written intention, but this anticinema, literary bias is completely ignorant of the special qualities that make movies a valid and unique art form equal and often superior to literature, and there are few examples finer than *Short Cuts*. By not constricting the meanings of the many stories and images on screen—by giving the multiplicity of life infinite significance—Altman has made a movie that reduces most others to insignificance.

*The City Sun*
November 3, 1993

# THE WRONG NOTES

J ANE CAMPION's version of feminism sentimentalizes women's predica-
ments and attempts to make fools of us all. *The Piano*—her third,
again overrated, feature film—has the maudlin hysteria of a romance
novel, except that New Zealander Campion adds on the kind of weighty
sexual politics she thinks are new but were fashionable in the Western pop
literature of twenty years ago.

Holly Hunter plays Ada, a mute nineteenth-century British woman
assigned to wed Stewart, a New Zealand landowner (Sam Neill). She
travels Down Under with her prepubescent daughter and a grand piano in
tow. That's metaphor luggage—female innocence and sexuality. In the
New World wilds, Hunter gets a sense of her disenfranchisement. Resisting her husband's sexual advances, she stalls, waiting for him to have her
piano hauled from the beach by Maori native/servants. But her husband's
lack of interest sets up the illicit sex-and-liberation plot device: A nearby
Maori foreman, Baines (Harvey Keitel), buys the piano from the husband
(despite Hunter's protests of ownership), then uses it as an instrument of
sexual blackmail. He'll allow Ada to come to his house and play the piano
in exchange for sex.

Campion's idea of feminine assertiveness comes in the couple's secret
bartering; Keitel proposes sex for each of the piano's eighty-eight keys;
Hunter counterproposes sex for every one of the black keys. This isn't
mere effrontery; there's a contemptuous racial subtext in those color-
coded keys that Campion never explores. *The Piano* is filled with facile
details and images of daunting nature, threatening environments, primitive society, and furtive sexuality. But this obviousness is winning Campion acclaim instead of the derision she deserves.

*The Piano* sets back feminist thinking through Campion's simple-
minded romanticism. Her lachrymose critique of patriarchy adds nothing
to our understanding of how patriarchal intimidation is part of a larger
system of oppression. Yet, Campion's white-feminist subjectivity has
been championed far beyond more adventurous feminist explorations
such as *Daughters of the Dust,* even *The Color Purple.* This movie's

hothouse, insulated politics distorts the feminist ideas that were originally meant to radicalize people's awareness of the stifling social traditions that also effect men and nonwhite people.

Campion's phoniness begins with that cumbersome titular symbol.
Hunter's piano isn't a playful, impudent device like the singer Melanie's
"brand-new pair of roller skates"; it is a product of European cultural
development—an item as politically determined as the selfish sexuality
Hunter freights across the globe. A shallow artist, Campion is unaware of the
symbol's full implications. She's too impressed with the idea of a woman's
personal possession and the glory it confers upon her—a very oppressive
European tendency. There's a word for this: colonialism. But Campion
doesn't devote a single image or line of dialogue to exposing colonialist
treachery. The subjugation of the Maori is just the way things are—Hunter
shows no sympathy, or even interest, in the plight of other oppressed people.

In a bizarre twist of feminist logic, Campion connects Hunter's
liberation to the actions of a Maori man who is, implicitly, saved from
savagery and illiteracy not by his native culture but by his exposure to
Western music and white female sex organs.

(Sometimes Campion gets so carried away in her tendentiousness that
she forgets a plot point: The climax turns on a note Hunter scribbles and
has delivered to Keitel, who is still unable to read!)

*The Piano* takes advantage of the debased feminist politics of the
current era. Scenes of Hunter's sexual awakening are titillating in nearly
pornographic ways—the Hunter-Keitel trysts evoke Victorian images of
rape/subjugation, while a conjugal scene between Hunter and Neill leans
toward the propagandistically prurient. (She explores Neill's anus, teasing the stereotypical site of male vulnerability—an unlikely point of
female interest and a far less interesting scene than the one in *A Night in
the Life of Jimmy Reardon*, of Meredith Salenger's nervous curiosity
about River Phoenix's penis.)

For Campion to present, in 1993, a mythical feminist heroine with a
politically loaded sex organ is laughable enough, but to complicate the
protagonist's burden by also making her (selectively) mute is downright
ludicrous. The whole purpose of seventies pop-feminist art was to give
needed voice to the anguish and ideas of oppressed women. In 1972 Joni
Mitchell sang:

> *You've got to try*
> *If you're feeling contempt*
> *Well then you tell it*
> *If you're tired of the silent night*
> *Jesus! Then you yell it*

*Condemned to wires and hammers*
*Strike every chord that you feel*
*That broken trees*
*And elephant ivories*
*Conceal.*

At the same time Laura Lee advised, "Stand up and fight for your love rights!" (And she didn't mean only orgasm.)

Campion is unable to strike every emotional chord, and she must never have read or seen *The World According to Garp*, which one would have thought satirized the idea of mute feminist martyrdom to a fare-thee-well with the crazed, militant Ellen Jamesians.

Yet Campion isn't even consistent with her own conceit—her mute heroine is given the advantage of *narrating* her story to us. Campion isn't skilled enough to convey passion or ideology through expressive images. With cinematographer Stuart Dryburgh, Campion gives every image a hollow romantic luster as if the sea storms and dark twisty woods of New Zealand were analogous to the soul of Hunter's squat, pinched-face victim. Hunter's casting evokes her frequent use by playwright Beth Henley, who specializes in grotesque female masochists. Like Henley's, Campion's tactics are contradictory and her dramatic style clichéd.

Anyone who remembers Ingmar Bergman's explorations of female psyche (*Through a Glass Darkly, Persona, The Silence, Face to Face*), or who saw the intelligent, sensual explorations of feminism and colonialism in Claire Denis's *Chocolat* or Jan Troell's *Zandy's Bride,* should doubt all claims about Campion's masterly technique. It's essentially praise for her position as a white, mainstream would-be stylist and is refuted by the denouement, where Hunter and piano, leaving New Zealand by sea, both fall overboard. Inadvertently, the scene is edited like a *Monty Python* skit even though the metaphorical idea of Hunter loosening her umbilical connection to the piano and rising to her own rescue comes out of Canadian novelist Margaret Atwood's *Surfacing* (c. 1972). Campion doesn't even trust the nobility of tragedy; she's playing a pseudoempowerment game of making self-absorbed white feminists feel good about themselves. This is evidenced by the film's happy ending, with Hunter learning to speak and openly making out with her Maori lover on the porch of her all-white house. The scene is not just berserk wish fulfillment but it celebrates the very economic, political, class, and ethnic structures of privilege that many white feminists take for granted. Jane Campion wants to fret about oppression and enjoy it, too.

*The City Sun*
November 17, 1993

# THE TAMI SHOW

"**N**o one has seen Reality perform," Tami Akbar says, describing her hiphop girl group, Reality, but also summing up MTV's "The Real World", a continuing episodic series that in 1992 documented a household of New York youth, this year a household in Venice Beach, California, and is scheduled to host a third group in San Francisco next year. It's a peculiar institution.

> *I'm a slave, I'm a slave, I'm a slave to your lovin'.*
> *I can't resist the flavor of your kissin' and your huggin'.*

That's the rap Tami uses as part of her Reality act—she's seen practicing it, recording it, and finally presenting it onstage before an audience of friends and family. This prisoner of the stage showboats throughout the twenty-two episodes, stealing the series from the five other roommates that MTV execs have grouped her with for six weeks.

The original "Real World" gimmick is based on the 1973 public television series "An American Family"—a continuing series that peeked in on a white middle-class American home. Shot on film rather than video, "An American Family" offered documentary drama revealing the parents' marital breakdown, a son's admitted homosexuality. As if countering the sitcom mythological view of American domestic life, "An American Family" depended on the shock of real life and unscripted behavior, but it was a smug TV coup. Cinema verité technique was used without admitting the degree of intervention by the video crew (a conceit Albert Brooks satirized in his 1979 movie *Real Life*), and this, essentially, is the legacy MTV follows. "The Real World" is less a counterpoint—to, say, "Happy Days" or "Beverly Hills 90210"—than it is an up-to-the-minute commercialized alternative to the drama of American adolescence. What Hollywood movies like *The Breakfast Club* formulized during the eighties, ironically missing—avoiding—the developing hip-hop, metal, punk, and grunge cultures, MTV now appropriates as part of its basic function as a conduit for youth consumer culture. "The Real World" was "created" and produced by Mary-Ellis Bunim—a producer of the soap operas "Santa Barbara," "As the World Turns," "Search for Tomorrow," and "Loving"—and Jon Murray, whose background is in syndicated television sales. By selecting a deliberate "cross section" of young adults, these MTV execs gathered their own test group of exploitable attitudes. The "Real World" families—dormitory cliques without supervision—represent the type of audience MTV wants to attract and the types of consumers they want to mold.

## □ *NOTHIN' GOIN' ON BUT THE RENT*

Tami Akbar doesn't simply want to be a rapper—she means to be seen. Like Eric Nies, alumnus from the first "Real World" and now host on MTV's "The Grind", Tami is less an all-American youth than an all-American huckster. The only skills she demonstrates are those of an actress, flashing anger, joy, or deviousness with unconscious abandon. Her eyes are on a specific type of stardom: VJ heaven. And sure enough, midway through the series Tami appeared co-hosting a day of MTV programming, along with one of her Venice Beach roomies, an alcoholic Irish immigrant named Dominic. Later, during the series run, Tami introduced a morning of MTV videos while sharing a bed with another white male co-host.

Like every Black VJ on MTV, Tami occupied a strange position: *objet noire*. But on "The Real World" she also represented the mainstream's preferred version of Black person, a shameless, accommodating exhibitionist.

None of the other Venice Beach roomies was as interesting as Tami, partly because television has accustomed (if not inured) us to white domestic and social habit. Tami isn't exactly a homegirl, but she can turn on the Black act as easy as snapping on earrings and she's down with the latest forms of flirtation and temerity. For all the phoniness of "The Real World" and its haute bourgeois concept of reality, Tami brought the series endless fascination. She is the genuine, horrifying item: a Reagan-Bush baby, a petulant go-getter in her twenties. As a product of her times and as a sign of the times, Tami took this cunning, calculated broadcast—and its opportunity for her selfish, small-minded display—as a chance to turn the life of a young careerist into the single most amazing Black female character in contemporary pop culture.

## □ *THE BOY WITH THE THORN IN HIS SIDE*

Tami was instrumental in one of the most outrageous malfeasances in television history: the ousting of one of the "Real World" participants through kangaroo-court extortion. The victim was David Edwards, a young Black man struggling to be a comedian.

The trouble began during some housewide horseplay: "The Real World" roomies were joking around in Tami's bedroom; to everyone's amusement, David playfully pulled Tami out of her bed and into the corridor as Tami scrambled into the bathroom laughing. Seconds later, Tami bounds into the hallway: livid, cursing, threatening. She taunts David to fight—"We'll go head up in this muthafucka!"—while the white roomies stand back shocked, frightened.

The first respondent is Beth S., a white roomie from the Midwest, who in earlier episodes had been encouraging David to have a romance with Tami. In her perfervid imagination, Beth tells Tami that the horseplay incident was an attempted rape. The accusation spreads throughout the household, linking up with the roomies' unconscious fear, disrespect, suspicion of David, the lone Black male. Their confusion and ignorance are epitomized by Irene, the Chicano roomie who works as a deputy police officer (she had been shown working as a bailiff in a courtroom, her face rigid with hostility rather than strength). Irene joins the campaign against David, correcting one of the white male roomies' contention that David might be innocent by asserting, "You don't know what was in his head."

Irene's Daryl Gates attitude to demonize Black males was a pathetic example of how racism extends even to people of color. It contrasts Tami's refusal to try to clear up the matter; both women of color simply want David out. "I don't feel safe with him in the house," she admits to the assembled roomies, later adding, "I can't tell you how hard it was for me to keep from killing him."

Tami's ruthlessness (in an earlier episode the white male roomies referred to her as "Tami Norman Bates") makes her intimidating and unignorable. Egotism powered her confrontation with David. She enacted a showdown to impress the flabbergasted roomies—and the larger audience of white viewers across the country.

## □ *THE HOUSE THAT JACK BUILT*

"The Real World" toys with the reality of socializing, of racial and sexual intermingling by constructing unnatural occasions, and by putting these kids beyond their own achievable class, economic groups, abodes—and waiting for some civilization to occur.

Yet in the style of bourgeois hypocrisy that MTV practices, true reality is covered up. (The one thing Tami says you can agree with is, "No one has seen Reality perform.") There's no nudity, profanity is bleeped, and brand names on T-shirts and caps are blurred. Plus the producers, directors, and editors of the scenes (who do a yeomanly job of sifting through hundreds of hours of material) conspicuously stay out of whatever altercations or disputes occur. MTV acts like insensitive gods looking down on the insufficiencies of the rock culture it is selling and celebrating.

It would take moral courage, honesty, to break through "The Real World's" format to provide an understanding of the pop life today's young adults experience. But scrutiny is not the series' aim—just selective voyeurism. MTV controls the meanings of the real-life happenings.

Both Tami and David, California-living softies (soft of mind and heart), are so different from the two Black subjects of "The Real World's" New York group—rapper Heather B and writer Kevin Powell—that it's plain MTV definitely wanted opposite types to Heather and Kevin, politically conscious East Coast agitators who were unafraid to acknowledge their roommates' racist behavior. Tami and David don't complicate the scenarios with any kind of hiphop politics. Both are in show business for the same reasons they are on "The Real World"—to get over. Their ignorance makes even the worst traits of Heather (belligerence) and Kevin (hiding behind the inanities of *Fly Boy in the Buttermilk*) more interesting than the vapid, West Coast hedonistic greed that Tami and David exemplify.

## □ *SHE WATCH CHANNEL ZERO*

The David episode would have turned out quite differently from the young comic being booted from the beach house with a politically savvy Black male in the role. David seemed unaware that the whole setup was just the functioning of MTV/Time Warner racist and capitalist opportunism. Instead, David gets suckered by his own jokey, mock integrity—self-destructive political strategies learned from the Eddie Murphy race humor he emulates. David abetted his own victimization.

The household's free-floating fear of Black males went unchallenged by David's passivity, his weak pranks and quips (although the moment he enraged Irene, standing up to her bigotry by calling her a midget, was priceless).

When it was time to replace David with a new roommate, MTV pretended to let the group choose, as if the entire sad, anarchic episode were an example of democracy in action. Obviously, the chance of entertaining another Black male roomie was out of the question; the group's new choice (Glen, a white slacker and rockhead) proved the stereotyping and fearfulness underlying both editions of "The Real World." David had signed on to be a media guinea pig and took part in a larger insult, suggesting the incompatibility of the young Black male as a naturally antisocial creature.

Tami, on the other hand, contributed to the notion of Black female co-optation. Her venality confirms the worst view possible of Black women as vain, hateful, selfish, greedy "bii-yaaches" in Dr. Dre's pronunciation—the pronunciation MTV took to heart in its regular programming this year and fully sponsored.

## □ *NUTHIN' BUT A G THANG*

It starts with Tami arriving at an airport with a brother towing her luggage: Plainly, she's a user. Later, on a road trip to California, she takes offense at the use of the word "trash" by a white country roommate named John. On the TV series "Studs," Tami cheats with one of the male contestants by making secret dates to prepare the answers they'll use with fake spontaneity to win a dream trip to Jamaica.

"When we win, I'll spend my $600 on me and he'll spend his $600 on me," Tami says. But when they eventually lose (Providence be praised), Tami cuts the guy down. "I'm sorry we didn't win," he tells her, and she responds, "I'm sorry we're not going to Jamaica." She refuses to date him anymore, sucking her teeth when he asks if she'll call him. "If you're waiting for me to call, you'll be waiting a long time."

The abortion episode offers Tami's most sympathetic moment. Her mother—only fifteen years Tami's senior—appears, wondering how Tami, who works at an AIDS center, "with condoms all over the place," could allow this slipup. The camera follows Tami from the moment she announces her pregnancy to her appointment at the abortion clinic. This intrusion on her privacy is audacious (it's the only episode to carry a parental advisory), but it's part of Tami's ongoing star turn. Rather than conduct private business offcamera like Aaron—the blond, Orange County Republican-surfer roomie—Tami again pitches herself into the spotlight. It recalls the episode where Tami decides she's gaining too much weight and has her jaw wired shut—anything to get attention.

Tami presents a negative image at MTV's behest fully cooperating with the demonizing of Black youth. Selfish, she quits her job at the AIDS clinic, at first giving one day's notice; insidious, she agitates an argument among the group when they take a sponsored trip to Cozumel, Mexico; homophobic, she defends her insecurity when a new roommate, Beth A., comes out as a lesbian. "Am I a bigot?" Tami asks her other roomies, who only stare back, too depressed and ashamed to answer her.

Throughout "The Real World," the image of Black youth as presented by Tami (and David) offers a frightening demonstration of how the media can manipulate perceptions about behavior. The entire dormitory premise, in which the social experiment of living with others becomes a metaphor for growing up in rock and hiphop America, is built on the flimsy premise that everything here is spontaneous and honest—in opposition to the Heisenberg principle.

This dorm of shallow, pampered kids, whether from wealthy California backgrounds or the streets (Tami relates a period when she and her mother were homeless) gives a frightening picture of Americans' inability to be fair, to be anything other than self-involved.

The David calamity, with its surreal parallels to the Anita Hill-Clarence Thomas fiasco, suggests that for all MTV's shrewd, behind-the-scenes meddling, and all the roommates' narcissism, this really is the real world. People are like this—cowardice and selfishness are real—and these are just junior examples of our nation's now and future corruption.

*The City Sun*
December 15, 1993

# TOWARD A
# THEORY OF
# SPIELBERG HISTORY

□　*1.*

"Witnessing," a term repeated in the most doctrinaire reviews of *Schindler's List,* actually happens only once in the movie. Steven Spielberg "witnesses" the tribute he has arranged in which survivors of the World War II Holocaust file past the gravesite of Oskar Schindler. It is a perfectly situated affirmation of the gratitude and humanity that a group of people express toward a man who saved their lives. The profound optimism – the goodness – of human experience has always been the subject of Spielberg's greatest art: *Close Encounters of the Third Kind* (1977), *The Color Purple* (1985), *E.T.* (1982) – each an ebullient fantasy. But there's no awareness of this sensibility in the widespread hurrahs for his latest drama.

Typically far from the mark is David Denby's praise of Spielberg's "anger" – imputing a petty vengefulness to the motives of the most benevolent filmmaker of all time. The tendency to turn Spielberg into Moshe Dayan (a Scheherezade into a sabra) suggests other frightening reasons for the movie's praise. With *Schindler's List* critics have reduced Spielberg's art to a hegemonic tool for promoting mainstream historical interests – an implicit policy as pervasive as the refusal of white critics to see the meaning in a Black story like *The Color Purple. That* film is Spielberg's most audacious feat of "witnessing" – a poetic act of revelation rather than partisan reportage. But the critical line on *Schindler's List* misrepresents Spielberg's artistry.

As a piece of witnessing, *Schindler's List* is almost as disingenuous as the Oscar-baiting statements Spielberg has made about growing up, expressing his Jewishness, and so on. He gives in to contemporary social and historical mawkishness by pretending a special significance here. It's the typical middle-brow equation of solemnity with seriousness. Spielberg's skills see him through, but *Schindler's List* is weakest as history, strongest at evoking the emotionality of the events depicted. Of all the techniques he employs — fast cutting, chromatic shifts, emotive lighting — the most specious is the pretense toward documentary realism. It's a desperate, unoriginal tactic for a fabulist-stylist who became a legendary filmmaker by always surprising the audience, freighting a dinosaur theme park with ethical comment, putting irony into a kid's fascination with Mustang fighter planes.

Similarly, *Schindler's List* is a dream of the Holocaust. But its newsreel trope is too literal-minded; in the age of "Hard Copy", audiences' need for an authenticating format can devolve into an ahistorical thirst for atrocity as spectacle. To look past the poetry in Spielberg's Holocaust is to see less in it. When Spielberg and cinematographer Janusz Kaminsky chose to shoot in black and white, they conformed to a somewhat fallacious theory that this particular historical event could not be adequately rendered in color. Spielberg's claim "I have no color reference for that period" forgets William Fraker's zesty recreations in *1941* and Allen Daviau's luminous *Empire of the Sun* images in favor of newsreel "reality." Kaminsky's b&w — a superlatively achieved combination of documentary style, natural light, and dramatic stylization — actually serves a banal, reverential function. (Only the shifts to color for scenes of religious ritual, shots of the little girl in the red coat, and the final scene in Israel attest to Spielberg's postmodern interest in activating viewers' consciousness, and his still-estimable creativity.)

If the film falters, if the director is anywhere untrue to his gifts, it's in the pretense to b&w realism. This confuses his private, inventive use of mythology with an absolute historical reality. Recreating the shock of genocide and discrimination, Spielberg adds nothing to the understanding about how pogroms happened within European political history. This may seem sufficient to those who simply want the fact of the Holocaust confirmed, but it is, *imaginatively,* a small accomplishment.


□   2.


Never forget that Steven Spielberg proved himself a serious artist long before he took 35mm b&w cameras to Poland for *Schindler's List*.

*Indiana Jones and the Last Crusade* (1989) addressed history intelligently, elegantly: revisionism and fun in one. Crossing the globe with newfound respect for previously dominated cultures (Indy's Western belief in museum curatorship is opposed with his father's faith), Spielberg opened up his viewfinder to wonder. He gave serious attention to the World War II era and the fascist thrall of Nazism in personal, original ways. Although critics have been reluctant to admit that the farcical tone of the Indiana Jones trilogy and *1941* (1979) were worthy of their admiration, those movies went to the heart of the pop imagination.

Spielberg accomplished a postwar, postmodern miracle in those films—criticizing the political gestalt of the virtuous, prosperous West with the pop ethos of Hollywood fantasy, the tradition of which he is the truest heir. *Schindler's List* may fulfill an obligation Spielberg felt as a Jewish American—and tributes from industry Jews such as Billy Wilder suggest he has kept a faith with the Jewish founders of the industry. But that's a false, biased assumption. *1941*'s devotion to the pre–World War II sense of pop culture as wild, racist, naive—unmandated except by the principles of capitalism and pleasure (i.e., Americanism; i.e. Hollywood)—shows Spielberg shrewdly deflating cultural sovereignty at every turn; indeed, he opens the film with an impious spoof of *Jaws* (1975).

*1941* astutely turned homey, U.S. imperialism (and the world's subordination to it) into a satirical jamboree—a first, important step toward changing popular attitudes about Hollywood prerogative. Spielberg made the change memorably in *The Last Crusade*'s inspired incident wherein Adolf Hitler autographs Indy's father's personal diary. It unexpectedly summed up the psychic, historical weight that the fascist legacy exerted on the pop imagination. (An indestructible Nazi insignia is a significant "Never Again" motif throughout the trilogy.) Such clever business didn't necessarily identify Spielberg as Jewish, or as a history scholar, but it evidenced the wit, the political preoccupation, and the sensibility of an auteur.

□   3.

Spielberg is the rare Hollywood plenipotentiate not to settle for the status quo practices of the industry—until now. That means *Schindler's List,* rather than being his greatest work, is actually, in some poignant, infuriating way, his most compromised. Surely an artist who works unfettered—and magnificently—in the Hollywood system, who can portray an industrialist's saintliness (and dedicate that sacrifice to the late

Warner Bros. president Steve Ross), is aesthetically at home in genres that define the emotional life in hugely popular, sentimental terms.

In fact the terms by which *The Last Crusade* can be recognized as a great work of humane and artistic contemplation were explicated thirty years ago by Andrew Sarris's manifesto "Toward a Theory of Film History" in *The American Cinema*. Sarris's important distinction between expressive art and sociological entertainment is the kind of critical clarity that advocates of *Schindler's List* have almost completely muddled. Reviews of that film, whether pro or con, aggravate the current disaster of debased popular taste. As Sarris prophetically suggested, *Schindler's List* is being foisted upon us tendentiously. It's this decade's *Gandhi*.

It isn't only Spielberg's artistry that these *Schindler's List* reviews demean through he's-finally-grown-up cliché or he's-still-trivial myopia. *Schindler's List* itself has been misread, misunderstood, "appreciated" (which is to say, trivialized) for the wrong qualities. It's as if obviousness were an artistic advance. *The Nation* provided the best twist: "Spielberg has in fact converted his incapacity into the virtue of restraint." Can the man who directed the most splendid, heartfelt Hollywood entertainments of the past twenty years accept that praise, that dismissal of his life's work, as reasonable? Do critics who think Spielberg incapable of passion and intelligence genuinely credit *Schindler's List*'s historicity?

Answers may lie in that widely disapproved climax when Nazi businessman Oskar Schindler (Liam Neeson) has delivered 1,100 Jewish political prisoners to safety after protecting them under the ambivalent wing of capitalist patriarchy. He confounds the Nazi regime's extermination plan by insisting that his workers are essential to its wartime productivity. The ploy is expounded throughout the film in a number of deceptions and a series of last-minute rescues, culminating, once the Allies reach Poland, with Schindler releasing his workers. In response, the grateful Jews with mostly middle-class skills who have toiled as laminators, machinists, and foundry workers forge a ring for Schindler out of their gold teeth fillings and he accepts it with a tearful speech. Though the contrite language is plain, it's a Shakespearean cry of humility. It's also the most purely Spielbergian moment in the film.

Not to dismiss several memorable scenes that imaginatively convey surprise, shock, pathos, but Schindler's expression of gratitude transcends the familiar catalogue of misery. It's a concretely plausible show of decency. Until then, Neeson's performance is rather opaque. Schindler's transformation is only revealed in this speech: materialist Schindler—a vain, devious man—holds to a bourgeois sense of reason, but his apology and self-accusation redeem it. Critics who reject this scene as overly sentimental fail to understand how it works *morally*—like the climaxes of all Spielberg's films. It is a spiritual moment. Spielberg avoids the insulting concept of a great man's noblesse oblige; Schindler's humbling becomes a sign of grace bestowed upon his beneficiaries and the audience of moviegoers who observe its reenactment.

For two decades now, Spielberg has explored the emotional, thus spiritual essence of movie spectacle. Audiences have often been right there with him, recognizing and appreciating moments of grace. The box-office success of *The Color Purple* proved the public's readiness for advanced Hollywood fiction, and Spielberg's radical deployment of generic tropes. Critics' aesthetic awareness should have been excited by this sign of the director fulfilling a fragmented public's hunger for unifying emotional revelation; making a successful Hollywood movie about a Black lesbian confirmed Spielberg's auteurist consistency as a crowd pleaser par excellence.

Think back: A grown man's trepidation intercut with the slapstick tragedy of a drive-in Road Runner cartoon—*The Sugarland Express* (1974); a panicked mother distilling her frustration through artful renditions of mountains—*Close Encounters;* a Japanese sailor weeping at the (mistaken) thought he has demolished Hollywood—*1941;* elderly sisters regaining paradise and innocence by playing patty-cake—*The Color Purple;* a lonesome boy's sensory remembrance of his father's aftershave lotion—*E.T.;* a woman's bicycle race to proclaim the fragility of her love without waiting for the (unseen) response in kind—*Always* (1990); and a group of adult orphans finding themselves in the moment they pay tribute to a woman who cared for them—*Hook* (1991). These scenes are among the many trenchant episodes in Spielberg's cinema that critics have rejected as fanciful. Lacking sensitive, imaginative eyes, they can't recognize Spielberg's poetic distillation of human experience, his respect for emotion as the evidence of spirituality. The plots that get dismissed as utopian optimism are sincere expressions of a generous sensibility that constantly redefines human experience in pop terms.

The Holocaust-movie concept of *Schindler's List* gets in the way of Spielberg's visionary expression; it keeps some from seeing Schindler's speech as remarkable. Despite epiphanic scenes directed with Spielberg's impeccable narrative rhythm (a boy's quick life-saving game with luggage left in a street), his experiential mystery (the unkillable factory worker), and multilayered visual splendor (the snowy-ashy nighttime arrival at Auschwitz), they fit into a construct that is, frankly, less compelling than Spielberg's usual working through fiction to claim the essence of a moment or expand its meanings.

☐ *4.*

No scene in *Schindler's List* is as great as the letters sequence of *The Color Purple,* which explored narrativity in popular dramatic, rather than academic, terms. Working in montage, Spielberg combined the story's Southern U.S. setting with images of Africa that illustrate a series of letters sent to Celie (Whoopi Goldberg) by her sister, Nettie (Akosa Busia), from whom she has long been separated. One startling cut from Celie in Georgia, looking behind her, to a shot of an elephant coming through the trees in Africa, conveys her engrossed, transported interest. The parallel construction is similar to the letter sequence of John Ford's *The Searchers* in the way the story moves forward in two directions at once, but it's more culturally and politically enlightened. *The Color Purple* serves a timely social function by metaphorically connecting Celie, an uprooted descendant of slaves, with a newly revealed heritage — a fresh and by no means common Hollywood endeavor. The letters sequence, a genuine act of deconstruction, was itself an auteur's demonstration of rare heroism. It showed how the dissemination of history — witnessing — involves practices of imaginative rendering as well as historical recall: a leap of faith as extraordinary as Oskar Schindler's.

This great sequence provides the movie with a modern, multicultural purpose; the action in the African scenes implies the historic intrusion of Western industry and Christianity. Crosscutting between African musicians and an American chain gang of Black prisoners chanting a work song sums up one of the American holocausts. Spielberg's transitions epitomize the social displacement and cultural continuity of diaspora. It may not be his personal story or that of white and Jewish film critics, but it is emotionally and historically comprehensive.

Advancing from the political conservativism of *The Searchers,* Spielberg explores the communication of ideas and history that is central to the modern awareness of ethnic representation and the uses of pop culture. His methods are so ecstatically vivid that critics mistook this for condescension. It was anything but. In *The Color Purple* Spielberg attempted a first — applying Hollywood's entire fictional apparatus to create a romance about African Americans, all the while adhering to the pop-feminist politics that marked Alice Walker's novel as a modern work. *The Color Purple* is the most successful example of the eighties interest in cultural signs and signifiers of African-American and Hollywood history that there is in mainstream American cinema, and it is the quintessential example of Spielberg's sophistication. (The sight of Celie hiding a letter from Africa behind a hymnal and reading it alone in church expresses the need for Black disengagement from Western influence.) He expanded on it in *The Last Crusade*'s self-reflexive, accordionlike compression of the Indiana Jones series' play with history, anthropology, and colonialist lore (not for nothing do the recurrent religious rituals in *Schindler's List* involve play with light).

A degree of this postmodernism may inform *Schindler's List,* including the impulse to change American movies' anti-German conventions. But it has been further submerged by hegemonic reviews that turn the director's vision of the Holocaust back into a more conventional, vague view of history. This is why the pseudo-documentary style—so much less inspired than the pop didactics of *The Color Purple* is suspicious. The black and white austerity claims an objective truth, whereas the Technicolor, symphonic *The Color Purple* daring to present Black Southern life as something other than Walker Evans docutragedy—challenged audience preconceptions. At the top of his game, Spielberg counteracts conventional social mythology through a revivifying of genre; the docudrama pretext of *Schindler's List* loses that narrative anchor.

Acclaim for *Schindler's List* presumes that only now does Spielberg show an interest in history; it still denies his interest in revisionism. In truth, reviewers are congratulating Spielberg for making a historical movie that, unlike *The Color Purple* and *The Last Crusade,* does not disturb their view of the past or upset their perspective on pop culture. The film's few detractors resent (as they resented *The Color Purple*) his powerful spiritual-political suasion.

□   5.

For those who know Spielberg's work, *Schindler's List* seems less expressive than *Close Encounters, E.T., The Color Purple, The Last Crusade, 1941,* and *Empire of the Sun* (1987), because its story is circumscribed, not by the factual requirements of history or Thomas Keneally's book but by the culture industry that has accumulated around the subject of this century's European Holocaust. The surreal, visionary *Empire of the Sun* and the hellzapoppin *1941* seemed more personal reimaginings of the Second World War partly because their child's-eye view is Spielberg's unique purchase on human experience.

Unfortunately, much of *Schindler's List* fits prescribed Holocaust lore, the kind of thinking Pauline Kael once ridiculed in the phrase "Nazi junkies." A pornography of suffering—and revenge—that sneaks into movies on this subject can be read between the lines of the film's rapturous notices. (Spielberg told the New York Film Critics Circle their reviews "were not like reviews, they were like personal essays.") Even the waterfall of acclaim for Ralph Fiennes's charismatic performance as Commandant Amon Goeth smacks of Nazi-junkie masochism. Dreamy-eyed Fiennes could be one of the stars of the porn film *Mein Cock,* but his acting is not more skilled than Ben Kingsley's nuanced portrait of bookkeeper-listmaker Itzhak Stern.

Like *E.T.,* the other film on which Spielberg eschewed storyboard-ing, *Schindler's List* pares down the director's visual dynamics. Though this pleased his detractors, he ought to remember that their objection to his *style* is basically a distaste for what makes movies exciting. One moment in the film has a legitimate cinematic thrill: the sequence when mothers are separated from their children epitomizes Spielberg's genius for connecting emotional purposes to compositional vectors. As with the *Orphans of the Storm* separation of the sisters in *The Color Purple*, this scene recalls Griffith's command of primal emotions and narrative vigor. The Spielberg twist (and plus) comes with the very Hollywood principle of "proportion." A single mother separated from a child is usual. (It was acted definitively by Madge Sinclair and Leslie Uggams in *Roots* and has since been used as a bogus, dull cliché in *Sophie's Choice*.) But two hundred mothers running after their abducted children belongs to a most powerful artistic vision. It's a moment in which Spielberg has suc-cessfully reimagined the terror of the Holocaust in an original way. In that scene, the literal rush of emotion kills you without the nicety of taste and "truth." It is passion made essential, kinetic, made into cinema.

Call that scene a magnanimous gesture. Its primacy is the kind of thing most Hollywood directors can't do or do badly, and so turn Holly-wood filmmaking odious. Spielberg is often cursed by a critical estab-lishment that can't see the difference between his élan and a hack's blatancy. Those mother-child emotions needn't be trivialized or dis-dained—Spielberg employs them honestly (familial emotions are not simply manipulated but well *understood*), and his sense of Hollywood inflation contains a sensible assessment of the Holocaust experience. He restores dignity to the undignifying effect of a pogrom wherein individuals are *reduced* to faceless numbers, routed en masse. Spielberg's insistence on primal emotions in this scene ranks with Gillo Pontecorvo's at the climax of *The Battle of Algiers;* the masses become undeniably human despite the effort to dehumanize them.

Complaints such as Leon Wieseltier's in *The New Republic* and Frank Rich's op-ed in *The New York Times* that *Schindler's List* celebrates the 1,100 Jews Schindler saved without a thought for the 6 million killed is fatuous mathematics and narrow-minded ethics. They miss the funda-mental fact that the movie interprets the mass experience of Jewish oppression. It's not a story of individual suffering, and Spielberg would be as fraudulent as Nazi junkie Agnieszka Holland *(Europa, Europa)* if he pretended to describe that torment singularly. He relays the Holocaust as it comes to him: as a people's tragedy. The little girl in the red coat who triggers Schindler's compassion is a perfect Spielberg symbol for humanity, but he reenacts "personal" Jewish history without specific differentiation. Schindler and Goeth stand apart as stylized, slightly awestruck visions of the German Other—angel and devil portrayed as ambivalent human extremes. But the Jews are ennobled when called upon, in the end, to display nobility as opposed to piously asserting it.

Not even Spielberg's personal holocaust interpretation has satisfied those "Never Again" drumbeaters who want a movie that parcels out sanctimony and guilt. That's the other side of the hegemony Spielberg dangerously plays into when he affects "seriousness" and "realism." Such naive Holocaust politics beg to be misconstrued; *Schindler's List* might have been an even stronger movie if it clarified itself as a *version* of history rather than a document of the real thing. All those film critics' awards showered on the film but not on the man who made it directly show a higher regard for the subject than for the artistry.

But *Schindler's List* is best experienced as something other than a Holocaust history. Steven Zaillian's script is not nearly as politically sophisticated as the John Milius–Larry Gross outline of genocide and racism in Walter Hill's *Geronimo*. Zaillian's lucid charting of events—from ghetto mandate to prison transport to Schindler's factory ruse—is substituted for any analysis of class or the dialectic of policy vs. experience that brings a political history to life. Spielberg rivals *The Garden of the Finzi Continis* in early scenes that show middle-class Jews shocked into awareness of their third-class status, but the complexity of ethnic oppression is never focused except to be simplified as mundane evil, cut off from social/political design.

Certainly the way Spielberg emphasizes emotion and morality is about as fine as Hollywood has ever managed on this subject. But it has led to some gross, polemical exaggerations. David Denby's claim that "rage brings out [Spielberg's] intelligence" projects the critics' own responses onto the film's political reticence; *Schindler's List* has nothing like Kurosawa's informed, masterfully tempered anger in *Rhapsody in August*—a view of World War II critics chose to ignore. Even *Swing Kids* was politically savvier: director Thomas Carter used the Third Reich era as an analogy to contemporary cultural racism. *Swing Kids* brought home to the era of hiphop censorship the dilemma of fascism—politics as people commonly perceive and practice it—in terms *Schindler's List* achieves only once: when Nazi troops storm a Jewish apartment building, ransacking homes while one soldier sits at a piano and delights his comrades with his playing. "Bach? Is it Bach?" "No, Mozart!" Spielberg slyly mocks the Germanic tradition in that instant—a demonstration of the political uses of art, flirting with post–World War II skepticism without resorting to mere castigation. That brief, brilliant moment touches on the tension between culture and nationalism that is a guiding principle of Spielberg's creative intelligence.

□  6.

*Schindler's List* falls into the not-always-artful but often sanctified tradition of Holocaust movies even though Spielberg enhances that tradition by finding a story that is hopeful rather than accusatory and despairing. He returns the "favor" Spike Lee paid in *Malcolm X*—when the Ku Klux Klan ride off into a bright, full *E.T.* moon—by emulating Lee's modern-day documentary coda. And as usual, Speilberg does the unexpected. The memorial sequence of Schindler Jews and their offspring laying stones on Schindler's grave carries the moral conviction Lee hoped to get from Nelson Mandela's appearance at the end of *Malcolm X.* Lee's polemicism failed because he never showed a simple connection between the living Mandela and the dead Malcolm X. *Schindler's List*, however, is very much about the connection between a member of the Nazi party and the European Jews. Victims and victimizers all discovered a spiritual commonality. The European Holocaust was but one of history's atrocities, and Hollywood's dealt with it before. The real-life evidence of gratitude, of love given and returned, testified to in the coda, is something new and overwhelming. Spielberg's intuitive dramatization of boundless ecumenical faith, hope, and charity extends, as always, to the way he updates Hollywood genres to meet the most contemporary emotional needs.

Now that Spielberg has played his trump card, it will be interesting to see if critics respect him when he goes back to the subjects he knows best.

*Film Comment*
March 1994

# DAP AND A SLAP FOR ICE CUBE'S MIXED MESSAGES

W HEN *THE NEW YORK TIMES'* token Black critic chose Tupac Shakur's *Strictly for My N.I.G.G.A.Z.* as album of the year, the choice seemed so obviously wrong that it must have been done to make a point—to prove the critic's independence or maybe just to irk the *Times'* honchos. But the gesture canceled itself out since America's media elite have pegged Tupac as a nut—harmless except to himself or (better yet) to his people.

A much smarter—and fiercer—album-of-the-year maneuver would have been *Lethal Injection* (Priority Records), by Ice Cube, an artist who still strikes fear and animosity in white media makers. Ice Cube stands for untamable Black social resistance. He provokes such contention among powers-that-be in journalism and the music industry that that *Times* critic could have salvaged token status by turning from minion to mole.

Straight up: *Lethal Injection* isn't nearly as good an album as Ice Cube's previous *The Predator,* but it interestingly holds to his agitator principles. (The track "Enemy" is pretty damn fine—a veritable hit in a fair market.) It proves that even in white corporate America, a kind of Pyrrhic victory is still possible for those open to the idea of challenge without sellout. Cube demonstrated as much on *The Predator's* "Dirty Mack":

> *There goes a* Billboard *—pull it*
> *And see if I'm still No. 1 with a bullet*
> *What the fuck do I see?*
> *It looks like The Predator*
> *Is gettin' dissed by the editor*

*Look: The vanilla wafer caper*
*Is to lynch a nigga on paper*
*But I'm much too Black for the goddamn cracker*
*Huh! Dirty macker*

Slinging his rhymes amid cheery, squawking soprano sax and rip-pling organ fills, Cube achieves an incontestable kind of beauty. This is a jazz and rap fusion used as revenge. Cube arms himself with hiphop, taking the age-old, symbolic boasts into the realm of political debate. Frankly, he's never made a better track than this, and the verbal ingenuity and musical pizzazz of "Dirty Mack" underscores the triumph Cube describes. While presumed reggae enthusiast and *Billboard* editor Timo-thy White launched an unprecedented editorial campaign against Cube for allegedly racist remarks, the L.A. rapper was still *selling,* still *charting.* The white media's objections didn't matter in the face of popular accep-tance, and Cube got juiced from it: He rhymes "cracker/macker" by giving both words a sly, resonant drawl. You hear strong, jazzy confi-dence in Cube's voice, and he got that from Chuck D's example.

*The Predator* is Cube's Public Enemy album; the East Coast influence that started with the production of *Amerikkka's Most Wanted* is fulfilled here. From the exuberant musical burst of "When Will They Shoot?," Ice Cube uses sound audaciously, strategically, like Public Enemy. No West Coast rapper has made an album as raucous as *The Predator,* as hard, or as politically intense. That PE formula is part of what the industry-driven Dr. Dre onslaught was meant to counteract. The success of apolitical Death Row music was designed to weaken the impact of hiphop, also proved by recent Cube attacks that complain he's fallen off musically.

That's nonsense: "Wicked" has a startling, trembly thump, and "When Will They Shoot?" quakes like "Nighttrain" or "Welcome to the Terrordome." It's a song about paranoia in the hiphop era but it also, in L.L. Cool J style, tells its tale through the metaphoric summing up of current hiphop culture. You could reconstruct all of early 1990s hiphop from this track alone, with the shout-outs Cube uses and the combo of East Coast agit-jazz and West Coast lyrical flow.

Tracks like this and the oft-celebrated "It Was a Good Day" and the unparalleled assessment of the L.A. uprising, "We Had to Tear— —Up," make *The Predator* a thrilling album to return to. Although it was dissed almost universally by the press upon its release (reviewers followed *Billboard's* lead), *The Predator* is actually a massive achievement. In apology to Cube's hard-pressed followers, my appreciation of *The Preda-tor* was a matter of returning to it. Much of Cube's mixed messages of mission-and-meanness is off-putting, and the concept of embracing *an-*

*other* version of "hardness" made me overlook his political underpinning that—throughout 1993—became an increasingly important distinction from Dr. Dre. But the similarities are there, too. In the largely wonderful "Check Yo Self," Cube's homophobic snap (and the video he directed that depicted swishing with the admittedly inspired line, "You used to be a Don Juan/Now you're just 'Toine") strain one's tolerance for his otherwise admirable aesthetic challenge to (white) power.

But Cube is the ultimate example of hiphop paradox; not 100 percent defensible, he's yet got a core of valiant Black political consciousness—something Dr. Dre and most commercial rappers absolutely lack.

*The Predator* responds to the Rodney King beating and the first Simi Valley verdict with raging humor and witty anger—similar to the way PE's "Terrordome" answered the Yusuf Hawkins murder. On "Who Got the Camera?," Cube personifies the Rodney King experience in terms of hiphop celebrity; he's learned his PE lessons well and even rivals *Fear of a Black Planet* on the self-produced aural collage "I'm Scared," which intercuts recorded white incomprehension with Black insistence. After all this, *The Predator* ends with "Say Hi to the Bad Guy," a song that explains his persona without apology.

At his most juvenile, Cube called himself "The Wrong Nigga to Fuck With," but *Lethal Injection* proves that the press backlash was one of the best things to happen to him. It caused him to reflect, thereby making one of hiphop's most interesting examples of intellectualizing and philosophizing—a sign of continuing growth. The white press would like you to ignore this; to perceive rappers simply as venal reprobates like Dr. Dre, amiable fuck-offs like Snoop Doggy Dogg, or wild-eyed malcontents as Cube once was willing to present himself. But *Lethal Injection* (taking a cue from Ice-T's *Home Invasion* white-infiltration shtick) shows Cube complicating his own rapper persona.

"To G or not to G," Cube's first line here, shows his growth process as the album's subject. He identifies with the gangsta image as a profitable social and professional strategy, but every protestation is answered by the chorus: "You got to believe in something / Why not believe in me?" It's a street shark's brag (originally used to describe the slick preacher Richard Pryor played in *Car Wash*), but a rapper like Cube hasn't got a lot of hermeneutics to rely on or proselytize. The brag reflects back on himself—he's looking for something to believe in, and his self is all he knows or trusts.

A brilliant slice-of-life tale like "Ghetto Bird" (named after the police helicopters that patrol his neighborhood as an occupying force, as in *Boyz N the Hood* and Mike Leigh's Irish rebellion film *Four Days in July*) describes the limited social vision determined for Black males. When ghetto birds command the horizon wherever you look, it may be best to look within. Cube's turn from religious agape to worldliness is the point of "Really Doe," a catalogue of his cultural engagement—details of materialism and political bitterness convey a uniquely fin de siècle sensibility. It's a beautifully rapped tune. Cube, it must be said, has the richest vocal quality of anyone in rap. Chuck D has force; L.L., facility; Snoop and Slick Rick, crazy style; but Cube has the best *sound*. Instead of Snoop's Stepin Fetchit languor, politically spirited Cube takes the rhythm of Southern dialect and matches it to urban sharpness. When he speaks, he has a brotherly *tone*, a sound you warm to—sometimes especially when he cusses. ("Word to ME! / Fuck your mother!" he contributed to Michel'le's debut album.) "Really Doe" preserves the values of Black speech one might take for granted (or discourage in a child); there's linguistic wealth in Cube's timbre and in the very phrase "really doe." The term—a distillation of "really though" or "in point of fact"—is as brilliant as the stressed pauses Michael Jackson used between "but-if" in "Black or White." By saying "really doe," Cube implies an assessment of events and announces an agreed-upon affirmation.

The way "Really Doe" works explains the nature of political hiphop; it's based in shared experience rather than diplomatic theory. It's a politics of community feeling rather than power, and in Cube's perpetually *young* voice, it's a politics that retains its sincerity, its joy, even when most angry. There isn't necessarily a program in this—it's what makes one "Down for Whatever." And whatever Cube is, he's no diplomat, but he's able to identify and evoke certain Black experiences. "What Can I Do?" tallies the crimes ascribed to Black males while questioning what other role this society offers them.

On "Lil Ass Gee," Cube (answering Dr. Dre's sentimental "Little Ghetto Boy") draws the bleak circumstances of Black male youth today. But before that is a dramatic dialogue with another male who is waiting on Christianity. Cube asks, "You ain't go do nuttin' with your life but sit here and wait for Jesus to fall out the sky?" Although his setup is impudent, this is an exchange to be taken seriously. Black media tokens like Greg Tate dismissing *Lethal Injection* in *The Village Voice* act as cultural assassins still trying to strangle Ice Cube with Louis Farrakhan's bow tie. They stupidly, intentionally, ignore evidence of the artist's naive, crude, but definite search for moral standards, for something to believe in.

Frankly, I never expected this kind of seriousness from Ice Cube, and sure enough, it doesn't come neatly packaged or fully thought-out. It is a sign of intelligence, though—not merely with a dope beat, but a heartbeat, an inchoate heartbeat. Listen to the closing track, "When I Get to

Heaven." Its failure is as poignant as most successful serious pop songs. Cube thinks his way through street knowledge, Christianity, and his infatuation with the Nation of Islam. In under four minutes, he recites volumes of Black Nationalist rhetoric:

> *Looking for survival*
> *The devil made you a slave*
> *And gave you a Bible*
> *Four hundred years of gettin' our ass kicked*
> *By so-called Christians and Catholics*
> *But I'mo watch 'em burn in the fire*
> *See, I'm a G; that's why I ain't in your choir*

It may be simplistic but it's also considered, and, most important, it's *felt*. Cube bases the song on Marvin Gaye's "Inner City Blues." (Cube's title refrain is also answered by Gaye's refrain "This ain't it.") Recent, sanctimonious pop has made Gaye's "What's Goin' On?" almost a boring cliché, but Cube chooses the stronger homage and raps the blues:

> *Cuz I see, cuz I know*
> *The church ain't nothin' but a fashion show*
> *Get the devil do a 187*
> *And they won't call me nigga*
> *When I get to heaven*

The song has a pattern of disgust; Cube's failure to turn the title into a compelling irony — into a glimmer of some kind of belief — is probably the failure a cynic expects. But it also isn't cynical enough. Cube could have used the irony of California being thought of as heaven (cf. The Eagles' "The Last Resort"). His suggestion that the Nation of Islam provides a heavenly resistance or social salvation is a weak response to the despair this song uncovers. Cube needs something stronger, and that wanting is considered, and equally important, it too is *felt*. (That Tate and the *Times* token could ignore this shows you how little they respect the spiritual lives of hiphoppers.)

*Lethal Injection*'s bleak close is a serious gesture and an abstraction. What Cube sees, what he knows, is vividly, humorously expressed on "My Skin Is My Sin," a non-album B side of the "Really Doe" single that should be the album's climax. "My Skin Is My Sin" recasts the religion issue in livelier, more concrete terms; it rocks with a rebellious thump while "When I Get to Heaven" just slumps. There's also community on this B-side track — Cube gets backup from W.C. of W.C. and the Madd

Circle—and he's hoppin' (the song is as much fun as the album's hiphop debate, "Make It Ruff, Make It Smooth"). Here, Cube says plainly what the *Times* token probably wanted Tupac to say:

> *Usin' me as a scapegoat*
> *But I don't sleep*
> *Far from a goat*
> *More like a Black Sheep*
> *And you can't stand it when I talk like that*
> *And do Black men have to walk like that?*
> *Becuz he swing low like a chariot*
> *And I got Harriet all on my dick*
> *Becuz my shoe size is much larger than a muthafuckin' 10*
> *My skin is my sin*

When he's really on, Cube flips racist ideology, turning cultural stereotype into the means of wrathful vengeance. (Sometimes he's just plain confused, as on "Cave Bitch," a reverse racist castigation of white women tied up with stupid, pseudoreligious cant.) But by now one fact is clear: Ice Cube is one of pop's best voices and—with fits and starts—he's one of rap's least static minds.

*The City Sun*
February 9, 1994

# MENACE TO SANITY?

W HEN THE NEW YORK FILM CRITICS CIRCLE met last December to vote its annual awards, critic John Simon proposed omitting the Best First Film category, a motion seconded by Judith Crist and carried by a hand-count vote. Sitting across from the *Rolling Stone* critic who had hailed the Hughes Brothers debut film *Menace II Society* as the third-best film of the year, I puzzled at his silence. Sitting next to the *Entertainment Weekly* reviewer who had praised *Menace* similarly, I also puzzled his complacence with this motion. (Happy that *Menace* was aced out of its only possible prize, I kept quiet, too.)

But what happened to the critical euphoria that had greeted *Menace*'s opening just a few months earlier? Apparently for all the critics who loved that movie's fount of Black urban stereotypes, none of them thought enough of it as a work of art to award the Hugheses along with such year-end critics' faves as Steven Spielberg, Jane Campion, Mike Leigh, James Ivory. It seemed that Black stereotypes were one thing, but Black artistry—well, no way.

This anecdote sums up the critical battle facing Black filmmakers who seem only to get attention when plying stereotypes yet still can't get respect as filmmakers. So far this year, with the release of *Sugar Hill*, *Above the Rim*, and the upcoming *The Inkwell*, Black mainstream movies remain in their infancy, they haven't yet graduated to art status—they're still part of a crude, compromised, pseudo folk art that Black folks understand as little as white critics.

"Autobiography" is the word *The New York Times* used to describe *Menace II Society* in its opening-day review. It's the wrong word, of course, but unfortunately America's newspaper of record sets the terms of the middle-class public's discourse, and that includes the way the so-called Black intelligentsia thinks and speaks. People who ought to know better followed the *Times*' lead (carried its cudgel, fulfilled its contract) by treating *Menace II Society* as if it were indeed auto biographical:

A host of Black writers convened by *The Village Voice* gave the movie cultural cachet by linking it to hiphop music. Spike Lee feted the film's directors, the Hughes Brothers, at his Brooklyn emporium at an event titled "Celebrate the Achievement." Stanley Crouch wrote a two-page exegesis in *The Washington Post* attempting to confer Hollywood lineage on the Hugheses' gangster flick. And recently Henry Louis Gates venerated the Hughes Twins' "authenticity" in a *New Yorker* article titled "Niggaz with Latitude."

All of this has been horrible to witness. The *Menace II Society* debacle is the case of a juvenile wet dream being treated as an accurate summary of contemporary Black conditions. What the *Times* and everyone else conveniently ignored was that the Hughes Brothers' flashy, extravagant vision of street violence was the usual exploitation movie's distance from truth.

The Hugheses themselves came from a comfortable middle-class background with no experience in street dealings, jail time, drug selling, or murder. Yet the white media and the Black intelligentsia were willing to stereotype them as—to use the film's phrase—"America's worst nightmare: young, Black, didn't give a fuck." And worse, this stereotyping became the terms by which contemporary Black popular art—and life—is judged: journalists' fantasies of street life become the measure of reality. This explains how neo-conservative rap-phobes such as Crouch and Gates could champion that pseudo-hiphop movie attempting to ratify its panoply of Black urban clichés.

Crouch and Gates are old hands at playing the mainstream race market; they capitalize on (white) America's guilt and loathing toward Black culture through genius grant sinecures and university tenure. Both men demonstrate insiders' knowledge (apolitical subterfuge) that allows them to recognize and secretely expound on the race profiteering that the Hughes Brothers do from the other end of the cultural spectrum. They share interest in making profit off the specifics of Black social turmoil— not social critique, but exploitation. (Gates's *New Yorker* piece was a highfalutin' bitch fest, giving the Hugheses a platform to dis Spike Lee, Matty Rich, and John Singleton—for what? The patronizing delectation of *The New Yorker*'s classist, racist readership. It also sets up the Hugheses' perfervid fantasies as the preferred vision of Black American life.) The twist comes in Gates and Crouch's anterior moralizing about Black pathologies—a calumny that *Menace II Society* simultaneously makes possible and profitable.

The problem with white American film critics is that they become shills for the industry, selling any garbage Hollywood has packaged. For Black cultural critics—and I use that term because American journalism doesn't sponsor Black film critics—the problem is becoming shills for the industries that construct demeaning, distorted prejudices about Black American life. There's the disdainful neo-con branch represented by Crouch, Gates, Playthell Benjamin, and Shelby Steele, and the celebratory cult-nat branch represented by the *Vibe* magazine, *Village Voice* stable of Black-culture writers.

Given this strange phenomenon, one may ask, "What's aesthetics got to do with it?" Because none of these writers demonstrate any appreciable knowledge of film. Crouch's *Washington Post* panegyric was a laughable jumble of inaccurate details about Hollywood history added to an absurd, film-illiterate misreading of the gangster movie genre. Crouch's inability to account for the different social conditions that created Howard Hawks's 1931 *Scarface,* Brian DePalma's 1983 *Scarface,* and 1993's *Menace II Society* is typical of the stupidity evident in much of the criticism surrounding Black films. Incompetence and ignorance prevent understanding the continuity between political and cultural eras, the racial politics that always makes any exact parallel between Hollywood's views of white gangsters and Black gangsters problematic yet is essential to understanding how a generation of postmodern Black filmmakers feed off the generic tropes they seek to imitate or turn into their own expression.

It's a case of writers who don't know anything about the art of movies having the audacity to make judgments about cinematic value and the ratio of street-to-screen truth. Aesthetic folly could be seen in the *Times'* descriptions of *Menace II Society* as "filmed in a jerky cinema verité style," and "has the jarring immediacy of a television news flash enchanced with expressionistic camera angles and color" and "blurs the line between brutal slice-of-life realism and sensationalistic gore." Despite all that, the film is praised for its social realism and political message. What's happening here—and it's also apparent in *New York* magazine's assessment of the film as "primal" and a "fuller and more wrathful understanding of the nihilism of the ghetto" and "the most striking directorial debut in the history of Black cinema" (a backhanded compliment)—is a complete dismissal of Black artists' capacity to invent. For most film critics, Black or white, Black subjects are *reduced* to their sociological correlative, judged as realism rather than art, appreciated as message rather than movie. The insult of this is bottomless, but its danger should be obvious in the way the Hughes Brothers take advantage of critics' susceptibility to stereotype and 6 O'Clock News hype. *Menace II Society* isn't a film that would change anybody's thinking about racism or the effects of poverty and deprivation in America. It appeals to status quo thinking.

And this status quo—the shitstem as usual—defines the commercial conditions that underwrite so much Black popular culture. If critics are incapable of pointing this out through aesthetic alertness or political sense, then the mess, the doom, continues. In this way the Hughes Brothers are like alternative-universe versions of the Black critics who parlay Black stereotypes into literary careers. The most egregious recent examples have been Gates's *New Yorker* pieces, but the practice has become standard: most Black critics make their bones by defending stereotypes, shoddy work, blunted thinking, sexism, greed, peevishness, and so on, as if these things were virtues of some ideal, natural Black political essence. No doubt a personal philosophical change is the only way out of this confusion, but an improved—sensible, rather than opportunistic—approach to criticism could be a start.

Writing in *Artforum*, *Daughters of the Dust* cinematographer Arthur Jafa began his paen to *Menace II Society* with a kind of baleful apology: "It is only with difficulty that I tolerate the mediocrity of most contemporary Black cinema, a trick I manage by constantly reminding myself that mediocrity is a necessary stage in the development of a mature practice." Jafa then goes on to demonstrate Job-like tolerance through the convoluted sophistry that makes him equate *Menace II Society* with Spike Lee's *She's Gotta Have It*, Charles Burnett's *Killer of Sheep*, Martin Scorsese's *Mean Streets*. Jafa's piece is excusable as cultural geography, but as an aesthetic method it is pathetically solicitous. His hunger for a Black work of film art—*any Black work of film art*—makes him tolerate the Hughes Brothers' misrepresentations to the point of embarrassment and confusion. Jafa errs with good intention; he's after an aesthetic ideal: a film that will account for the terrible state of contemporary Black American living, rage against it, and at the same time provide a cathartic, vivifying art experience. Well, we get all that in *some* hiphop music, but not yet in movies, and it's time that people stop deluding themselves about it, whether it's whites looking to justify their fear or Blacks looking to get on the film-music gravy train because Black frustration, longing, and prevarication are marketable.

If the Black intelligentsia had any power, the Hughes Brothers— makers of last summer's *Menace II Society*—would be Black culture's Spielberg and Lucas. Instead the Hughes Brothers and the Black intelligentsia are just menaces to sanity. They are colluded in the strange, essentially middle-class effort to confuse the righteousness of social indignation with the drive for success (i.e., money and influence).

*The City Sun*
March 3, 1994

# HAILE GERIMA'S FAITH

H AILE GERIMA'S *Sankofa* matters in ways that other independent films such as Tony Brown's silly *The White Girl* and Julie Dash's high-minded *Daughters of the Dust* do not. Gerima treats his potential audience – the Black moviegoing public – as an ideal audience, capable of the sophisticated process of recognizing the importance of mythology. He sets up a didactic premise of a Black Europeanized model (Oyafunmike Ogunlano) doing a fashion shoot in an African slave port, then shifts, with little ceremony, into the drama of slavery. *Sankofa*'s flashback narrative structures Gerima's very modern theme: the rediscovery of Black history.

Gerima doesn't jump all the way back to the beginning of the ordeal; the main story begins a few generations in, so that many of the slave characters in the flashback (including the model herself) speak about their sense of loss. Angry about the heritage denied them and ready to rebel against the brutal slave masters, these characters stand in for the condition of Black moviegoers (themselves twentieth-century descendants of slaves).

In this way *Sankofa* connects with the most contemporary Afro-centric attitudes. When a head slave complains to another about the agony of doing his master's bidding and is lectured on manhood; when a house slave tortures himself over imposed Christian teachings; when a matriarch declares the necessity for delicate, feminine feelings in warriors, the drama of each crisis takes on pop-art urgency not so different from the most Afrocentric hiphop.

Gerima understands the way heritage, morality, and politics have, today, become complexly tied up with pop lore. In *Sankofa* he takes part in this practice without disgracing the folk need it addresses. Recreating a hidden, tormenting history is both valiant and tricky: Gerima exploits the psychic bond made from deprivation and pride to get some of his most powerful effects: An overseer's anguish and the whipping of a pregnant woman check with their modern analogues both obviously and sub-consciously. This is, of course, the way all fiction works. (A familiar technique, it was used in Eric Meza's *Can't Truss It* music video.) But by openhandedly giving and revealing this process to the Black movie audience, Gerima may effectively lift that audience out of its naiveté, acquiescence, and intellectual slavery. It's a pop ambition that ranks with Spielberg's *The Color Purple* and Amiri Baraka's *Slaveship*.

Right now, *Sankofa* itself is part of an entrepreneurial experiment, as Gerima tests the possibility for distribution and exhibition outside the mainstream network. Like Baraka, he has radical upliftment in mind; like Spielberg he understands the profundity of pop communication. If *Sankofa* is a big enough hit (Gerima's taken it uptown, opening at Harlem Victoria cinemas, down the street from the African artifact vendors), he might inspire others to follow his risk taking. It could be the key movie by a Black independent filmmaker of the mid-nineties, making up for Tony Brown's insult, Julie Dash's elitism, and the entire hiphop world's hypo-critical neglect of Wendell B. Harris's *Chameleon Street*.

*Sankofa* may accomplish the basic work of enlightening a debased audience, but there is still a ways to go—and that's past the superficialities of Afrocentricity. The key moment in *Sankofa* is the midwifing of a baby boy (naturally, given the film's Afrocentric-patriarchal bias). The birth proclamation, "His name is Kwame, which means The Witness!," lends a religiosity to Gerima's tale. When his model-girl protagonist hears an African drummer's command, "Go back to your past, back to the source," Gerima implies that salvation will be there waiting for her. That mysti-fication rules over the *Sankofa* enterprise even (ironically) when Gerima puts a torch to Christianity.

The religion of Afrocentricity is an opiate that can only be tolerated for it's short-term effectiveness (and Gerima stretches tolerance with a two-hour-plus running time). Perhaps *Sankofa*'s premise is flimsy because it is based on a weak, romantic idea about returning to Africa. When the model girl awakes and emerges nude from her two-hour-plus shock therapy, she is greeted by a native African woman who says, "All you got to do is go back to Africa! Welcome back, embrace me!" This is simplistic even for the hiphop era of facile, skin-deep Africanists. The idea of reunion (*sankofa* is the Akan word for "return") distracts Gerima from what seemed to be his interest in history: he winds up replacing one set of myths with another, and that is not the same as enlightenment.

Gerima hammers home his points about the psychological destruc-tion Christians wrought on African Americans through the character of a half-breed slave Joe (Nick Medley), who commits the ultimate crime, killing his Black mother (Ghanaian actress Alexandra Duah) during a fit of Christian dementia. This sequence has a kinte-cloth audience flipping its turbans—and no wonder: Gerima is working out deep-seated animosity that includes a sarcastic montage of Renaissance religious paintings. Flying high on pure instinct, Gerima, the polemicist, even stages a reverse pietà: The half-breed son places his African mother's body on a Catholic altar and the sacrifice wins him back his sanity.

All this strong image making is passionate but problematic; Gerima twists the story into his own proselytizing. But it's poorly conceived. If you got rid of Christianity, racism would still be here. Unfortunately, Gerima's ideological attack (it's not probing enough to be called theological) neglects an economic analysis. That was one of the most thrilling parts of Gillo Pontecorvo's slave-trade epic *Burn!*, and Gerima pays homage to Pontecorvo when *Sankofa* alludes to a slave rebellion that (as in *Burn!*) involves the torching of sugar cane fields. Pontecorvo's leftist critique of capitalism would be consistent with Gerima's effort to compete with the Hollywood system, but he doesn't do it, perhaps because it lacks the glamour that goes with outright rebuking of European-Christian totems.

However, there's more than political glamour here; there's genuine, complicated emotion. During the vapid model girl's transition, she is stripped then branded by slavers: this brutal event is scored to a live gospel recording of the timeless "Precious Lord, Take My Hand." But this isn't a cynical irony, because Gerima lets the song linger on the sound track; its pure, raw sound underscores the first scenes of Diaspora/plantation life better than any other effect you could think of. "Precious Lord" carries a mighty legacy—it's an unparalleled account of suffering and a search for transcendence. It is not inappropriate to suggest that the only secular rival to its greatness is Public Enemy's "Can't Truss It." (Not "A Change Is Gone Come," used so mawkishly in *Malcolm X*) "Can't Truss It's" brilliant slavery/contempo narrative anticipated the structure of *Sankofa* but did the job with poetry when Chuck D says "Blood in the wood and it's mine." These words convey a haunting, material sense of history and suffering. Throughout the song Chuck D seeks moral redress, but he also expresses a moral conundrum, a loss of faith, and that's precisely the point of psychological and historical stress at which "Precious Lord" effects its transcendence. It's a Christian gospel without apology—also without shame, because it is grounded in the fact of African-American experience, in suffering that is recognized and felt as deeply as blood in the wood.

The political religiosity of *Sankofa* is a sham if it cannot admit and accept such complicated truth. The imposition of Christianity cannot be easily renounced. As even some Carribean hybrid religions suggest, there's a another side: the African adaptation of Christianity, as with Southern U.S. gospel, has been powerfully unifying and redemptive. It can be seen as an exegesis of catechism into an absolute philosophy. Modern Black audiences can be asked to apply religion rigorously, intelligently, but it's insane to ask them give it up—especially without recognizing what they've gotten from it and the emotional validation they have contributed to it.

*Sankofa* knocks at the door of the mysteries of human strength; it seems insufficient, fake—even patronizing—to assign those mysteries to Africanness. When the half-breed rages, "Prayer wasn't working. I felt responsible," Gerima turns the religious issue into an existential one. It improves on the evocation of historical tragedy in *Schindler's List* by suggesting that cruelty itself isn't frightening but that a sense of futility—a loss of faith—can be damaging.

Gerima's struggle with faith (and faith in the Black audience) is difficult. He is this month's Kwame, but to make oneself "witness" of a past you never knew is, let's face it, dreaming—an act of fantasy based on myths and trust. (The same is true of Spielberg with *Schindler's List*.) *Sankofa* is essentially a panoply of the myths Gerima has chosen to ratify his own secular Afrocentric faith. Some are clever, self-serving pop (the use of reggae star Mutabaruka as the linguistic key to the film's polyglot dialogue and rootsy character types); others are rabble-rousing crap (the many scenes of buggering rape, done to avoid the embarrassment of eye-to-eye miscegenation while also unnecessarily imputing sexual deviance).

All this makes Gerima a far-from-holy auteur: he repeats standard Hollywood corruption in the strategy of showing bare-breasted female brutalizing. Yet the rebel scenes of slaves attacking their masters are coy; the violence happens offscreen. This cheat is unworthy of a principled filmmaker. Gerima utilizes actors' faces dramatically—not one feels as remote as the entire *Daughters of the Dust* cast (although Gerima over-does the family-of-man bit at the end). But this craftsmanly knack for audience involvement carries responsibility when the dramatic thrust is toward vengeance. If Gerima wants to stir up blood lust, he has to *show it* and admit its horror. Without the ambivalence of the "Precious Lord"/branding sequence, his scenes of revolt are just trite.

The pedantic approach to history can be punishing (as *Sankofa's* model-girl demonstrates), but it shouldn't be dishonest. Telling the complicated truth is also an act of faith.

*The City Sun*
April 13, 1994

# AFFECTIONATE DERISION

*"See what happens to your life when you're born in New York!"*

—"HEARTLESS" BY LIVE SQUAD

A NIMOSITY GETS in the way of Spike Lee's nostalgia. That's not a happy assessment to make, but *Crooklyn* is a very unsatisfying film. It displays Lee's widest emotional range since *Do the Right Thing*, and generates some genuinely warm sentiments. But its view of life is idiotically simplistic.

Working from a script co-written with his siblings Joie Susannah Lee and Cinque Lee, Spike returns to the 1970s. This semi-autobiographical tale focuses on Trey (Zelda Harris), the ten-year-old girl in a Brooklyn family and her musician father, schoolteacher mother, and four raucous brothers. A casual succession of memories, *Crooklyn* is filled out with an r&b hit parade sound track, precise details of adolescent rowdiness, and vintage artifacts from hopscotch games, "Rock 'Em, Sock 'Em Robots" to a TV sitcom like "The Partridge Family" (the latter an ironic yet authentic choice).

Two stories are told: The Lee family history (here called the Carmichael family) and a chronicle of Black pop's golden age. The seventies are seen more perceptively than in *The Inkwell* as the roots of nineties pop culture and social temperament. James Brown's "Soul Power" is relevant to both eras, as is the specter of white flight. In between the affectionate moments of family togetherness and neighborhood chatter, a constant, hectic hostility erupts like music from a blaring radio (a signature Lee motif).

Chaos seems to be at the core of Lee's sensibility, and the meanness that gnaws at the tone and vision of *Crooklyn* suggests an explanation. This is a disturbed view of a family, a culture, a society. Dis-ease runs straight through it all, evident in the incessant bickering of children, the fragile emotional negotiations of an ambitious father and a frazzled mother, the ironic, distanced placations of a sentimental TV and music culture, and the anarchy of a mixed-race community where individuals struggle to pay rent and races veer toward warfare.

While *Crooklyn* seems to be Lee's least political movie, it is, actually, his most politically depressed. The title, a term of affectionate derision, comes out of a troubled consciousness. The clue is in a passing state-ment—the title phrase—that the mother (Alfre Woodard) makes in a letter about living among fools. *Crooklyn*'s drama denies the filmmaker's im-pulse toward blessed nostalgia: when the arguing and misunderstanding stop, there is death. In this sense *Crooklyn* isn't so much a look back as a meditation on New York miasma. Entrepreneur-provocateur Lee is im-mersed in the complexities of modern Black pop and the way culture and economics both tease and thwart Black social awareness. The subtext of *Crooklyn* demonstrates this phenomenon. There is no dramatic explana-tion for the disjunctures in the film—Lee's typical agitprop asides about drugs (a pair of glue-sniffing junkies) and religion (a zealous, Southern aunt). These details exist as reminders of Lee's own pet peeves and of the issues that have riven nineties Black America.

Consider that Trey's nightmare stems from a street attack and in-volves the junkies; consider that the film's most stylistically daring (and foolish) episode involves the conservative aunt, and then understand that Lee's current preteen, female protagonist is but a template for his own modern anxieties. *Crooklyn,* like Charles Schulz's *Peanuts,* uses children to represent adult temperament. The giveaway is in the obnoxiousness of the Carmichael family hellions: Lee isn't being falsely nostalgic about childhood; instead he imbues these crumcrushers with the hardened mischieviousness of nineties youth. Slapped around at home, these kids become violent in the streets—a Black urban pathology. Even Trey (whom Harris makes cute rather than lucid) lies and steals while her brothers partake in vandalism. This seventies Black family has already broken down. It's as if Lee understood his family to be unconscious harbingers of the dread future or has retroactively distorted the past to explain Black America's current malaise. Or does Lee even realize this? Unlike the beautifully nuanced affectionate derision in Ruby Oliver's *Love Your Mama, Crooklyn* offers no moral basis from which to interpret these kids.

In the Southern sequence, filmed in elongated anamorphic style, Lee ridicules Southern Christianity (Frances Foster plays Aunt Song in the same satiric mode in which she played the pious Christian in *Malcolm X*). It's as petty a caricature as the Flatbush Brothers in *Mo' Better Blues*. In *Crooklyn*, the Carmichael family's next-door neighbor is a white oddball musician (David Patrick Kelly) with an apartment full of dogs, and Lee makes comedy out of his abuse by the Carmichael kids. This, too, is petty, and it exposes Lee's inability to respect the essence of human behavior— or something worse: it may be true to the general indifference and hostility that defines New York living. You wonder what the connection is between these rotten, dishonest kids and the insensitive grownups who made a movie about them.

*Crooklyn* was a smooth enough viewing experience, but afterwards the more I thought about it, the less well I thought of it. The pleasures of seeing an era fondly recalled, including childhood memories of dinnertime, playtime, fighttime, is rare and welcome, but Lee's accuracy made me long for some understanding of what these remembrances mean. Last year, Terence Davies's *The Long Day Closes*—the most remarkable of all nostalgia films—felt personally relevant because Davies penetrated the surface of memory and pop culture. It was more about the eroticism of memory, the politics of culture and the depth of child experience. A coming-of-age movie is only worth doing if an artist conveys such an awakening to the world (*E. T.*) or a glimpse into human character (*Long Day's Journey into Night*). These are the standards Spike Lee is up against.

As the parents, Delroy Lindo and Alfre Woodard give large, emotionally varied performances, their individual wills maneuvering through the chaos. But Lee stays on the surface of the family complexities (if only he had filmed Lindo and Woodard in Bill Gunn's great family-memory play, *The Forbidden City*). Lindo and Woodard don't get a single line of dialogue that reveals personal character; *Crooklyn*'s script is shockingly unconcerned with what makes people tick and ignores the Freudian mystery of what makes parents tick. (Lindo and Woodard are two of the best actors in America, yet, sadly, their roles are less vivid than Danny Aiello's Sal in *Do the Right Thing*.)

*Crooklyn*'s best scene—a husband-wife tiff that escalates into a family brouhaha is *almost* as good as the housebreaking scene in *Shoot the Moon*. Here Lee's musical cues ("Thin Line Between Love and Hate" and "I'll Take You There") pace the rising tempers, but he can't relate this scene to anything—the strong moment just passes. It must be scary to examine one's family life (instead of dramatizing their mother's death scene, the Lee kids give her a couple of lovely, beneficent farewell scenes), but what's the point of asking audiences to look back if nothing can be learned from it?

*Crooklyn* concentrates on the detritus of pop and the viciousness of urban living sheerly as spectacle, with no interest in what art or society does to people's souls. The final musical sequencing (from "Ooh Child" to "Ain't No Sunshine" to "Mighty Love") is erudite, but ending this movie on *Soul Train*'s line dancing (after Terence Davies showed that the poignance of life can be revealed through pop) winds up trivializing the Black cultural experience. I will not settle for seeing Black life reduced to its good-timey surface. And even if *Soul Train* is the summation of human experience, *Crooklyn* doesn't show how.

*The City Sun*
May 18, 1994

# IS THERE
# A MAGIC BULLET FOR
# UNCLE TOMS?

LET'S SERVE NOTICE on two viruses known by the names Touré and James Bernard. These hiphop journalists are not important in themselves, but as servants of white media institutions, they represent a disastrous development in the discussion of Black popular culture. Touré's vindictive *Rolling Stone* magazine review of the new Public Enemy album and Bernard's similarly assaultive piece in *The Source* make it clear that the political betrayal of Black journalists has become a bigger problem, a greater threat, than the typical bugaboo about rappers' profanity.

This is the porch-nigger syndrome: Black writers sacrifice Black artists—and the integrity of African-American thought, language, music, politics—for their own benefit. The insidious thing is, they do their dirt in the guise of nurturing Black culture. It's a vile deception and a loathsome tendency (witness the stable of buffoons now appearing as token Black editorial columnists in New York mainstream newspapers).

Writers like these debilitate the social impact of Black artists' work by countermanding its ideas and encouraging its dismissal ("a hiphop moment to forget" is how *Rolling Stone*'s editors paraphrased Touré's advice). It's a wonder that young Black journalists can commit themselves to such contrary action while pretending to care about hiphop. They actually care about something else—the peculiar status that Black professionals have gained during rap's rise.

The hiphop era announced a period of deceptive acceptance for Black performers—not just rappers, actors, designers, but journalists have also received the blandishment of mainstream attention. So they become performers, too. They put on a Blacker-doper-smarter-than-thou act. Claiming the center of this three-ring media circus, they jump through "Afrocentric," "conservative," "bohemian" hoops making predictable, unoriginal goofball explanations of Black culture and then snapping at any artists who don't fit their screwed-up scheme.

In exchange for "authority" status, these writers attack any Black culture that goes against the dominant ideology. (That's Public Enemy's crime.) *And be aware: mainstream ideology now includes the "legitimizing" of hiphop.*

The institutions that sell hiphop and promote its image—from MTV to *Rolling Stone* to *The Source* and other pits in between—use this cultural base to exert political influence. It sometimes get confusing: MTV censors the political content of rap videos, then gives its "Movie Award" to *Menace II Society*. Yet it's not contradictory; MTV consistently advances the notion of nonintellectual Black art and unmitigated Black criminality and decadence. But let's get this straight: The cultural betrayal by Black journalists has become a worse problem than rappers' "immorality." Virus journalists spread this disease and unenlightenment disguised in dreads and threads as race man, b-boy, roughneck; they affect a justification of the mainstream's disdain. The result is, the mainstream legitimizes any hiphop that is predictable, unoriginal, that keeps Black folks docile, endangered, ignorant, unpolitical, trifling. So these journalists issue cultural approbations (Touré praising Snoop Doggy Dogg in *The New York Times,* Bernard celebrating thug life in *The Source*). In effect they say, "Yes, boss!"

One way of ensuring hiphop's triviality is to deny its richness, to attempt to halt its growth. The latest trick of these Uncle Tom journalists is to claim that the new Public Enemy album is out of touch. (Both writers got bitchy accusing Chuck D of being too old to be cutting edge—as if The Puppies now define cutting edge; as if "cutting edge" itself meant anything.)

Here's what these writers don't understand: Even though rap is a great form of popular art, it isn't only—merely—fashion. While Public Enemy set a temporary consciousness trend with the 1988 release of *It Takes a Nation of Millions to Hold Us Back,* the group has advanced beyond fashion to complicated substance. Public Enemy—like L.L. Cool J and De La Soul—remains a group of serious artists, even if their work no longer appeals to teenagers. Any intelligent pop critic should recognize this and allow these aritsts to develop even as they grow out of the exploitable age of pop marketing.

But Touré and Bernard hold hiphop to the flimsy, corruptible criterion of the music industry. (Clueless Touré is playing catch-up and Bernard tries to keep pace with hiphop trends.) They repeat the impatience and lack of interest of "the street"—not out of wisdom or taste but out of gullibility. Defending the most obviously calculated rap, especially gangsta rap, they pander to the kids who don't know how thoroughly their tastes and choices are controlled by a system of capitalist enterprise. This ignorance is the disease Touré and Bernard perpetuate.

Oblivious to his personal disingenuousness, Touré's own corruption was exposed in his suggestion, "The most effective way for [Chuck D] to combat the gangsta trend is not to criticize the genre but to show how commercially viable his brand of social consciousness is." Touré (dis)misses PE's point in *Muse Sick n Hour Mess Age*: Hiphop has been so thoroughly corrupted that in our mess age, commercial viability *translates* as decadence. It is a sign of moral strength and artistic integrity that PE risk commercial success, risk losing sync with a debased pop audience, by insisting on empowering lyrics and adventurous, not Top 40s, music.

There's no better example of Uncle Tomming than when *The Source*'s James Bernard snaps, "Chuck [seems unwilling] to accept the fact that his revolution is over." A Black man's impulse to resist amuses Bernard-the-lackey. Buying into the rhetoric of revolution, Bernard misunderstands the awful paradox of hiphop acceptance and Black deprivation. So by mocking Chuck D, he ridicules the tragic distance between Black peoples' dream of change and the fact of record industry control. ("Revolution" was 1988's gimmick; this year it's the method man.)

Bernard is on the capitalist's side of the bed. And no wonder, he's co-editor-in-chief at *The Source*. That magazine's leader and other co-editor, Jon Schecter, has demonstrated a peculiar anti-PE agenda ever since the Professor Griff episode. It's unpleasant to bring up the specter of Jewish revenge, but it's part of the complex white American politics that have never stopped dogging Public Enemy.

This is vendetta journalism, and it includes *The Source*'s white-boy love-hate relation to Black culture (it portrays Black outlawry as fun until it becomes as serious and dedicated as PE's dissent strategies). Aping that condescending fascination with hardness, Bernard rails at PE's conscientiousness. The boy is panicking; he'll become a backstabber if it will keep hiphop purely juvenile and inconsequential. Bernard's slyest move is to make sneering connections between PE and white rock acts (The Lollapalooza Tour). But he doesn't admit that PE records *aren't* played on alternative radio, that PE *hasn't* appeared on Lollapalooza, yet he scares *The Source*'s readership into self-hating and racist culture-phobia simply by invoking white rock. Because he isn't a deep thinker, Bernard doesn't hear blues sources in white rock or PE's distinctive reclamation of the blues. That's how thoroughly Uncle Tom journalism distorts Black culture.

It's the scornful tone, the reproachful glee of these pieces that make Touré and Bernard seem so foul, so stompable.

Bernard snipes, "Even with all of his anti-drug rhetoric, Chuck couldn't stop his man, Flavor Flav, from falling in love with the dopeman." That's ridiculous. Bernard overlooks "Gett Off My Back," one of the remarkable *Greatest Misses* tracks, where PE deals with Flav's addiction in unsentimental, groove-rich, devastating terms. Picking up white media's cudgel, Bernard tries to condemn PE for nonmusic offenses. He perpetuates the childish, hiphop attitude that heroizes rappers rather than allowing them the fallible, complicated expression of genuine artists.

But Touré's attempt at character assassination is so shaky he blames Chuck D for an offense made by Wu Tang Clan even though *Muse Sick n Hour Mess Age* isn't even in stores yet.

PE are not beyond reproach, but these Toms dis the new PE album without examining a single track and then leap to simplistic moral attacks, as if Public Enemy meant menace to society and not valiant Black expression.

The problem here is more significant than how silly reviewers rate a single album (these early bad notices prove the group is too good for fools). Touré and Bernard are caught up in a hierarchical practice designed to deride the seriousness of Black artists and keep the culture obscure.

The great thing about the hiphop era was that it occasioned the bust-out expression of Black artistry, of cultural retrieval, of art and political *appreciation*. But this is also the era of high-tech lynchings, and even pissant pop critics want in on the party. Let's reverse the string-'em-up imagery and recognize Touré and Bernard as puppets for a racist system that supports those who support it. The big question remains: Is There a Cure for Greedy Sellouts? The lure of mainstream acceptance fools these careerists. They cultivate an adversary journalism by treating Public Enemy viciously yet uncritically, thus abetting the agenda of the white media.

These folks don't really care about Black culture, but those who do will, of course, give Public Enemy a serious listen and, in turn, they'll hear that Public Enemy cares about them.

*The City Sun*
June 29, 1994

# THE STRUGGLE
# STRUGGLES

"MY FANTASIES were being played out for me in real life," says Curtis Hayes, one of the Freedom Summer participants who get to tell their story of the climax of the civil rights struggle in *Freedom on My Mind* (showing at Film Forum). This documentary examines the fantasies of real life, a significant contrast to *Forrest Gump*, which dangerously, deceptively, turns real life into fantasy.

Hayes, a large, bearded, affable Black man and Mississippi native who picked cotton as a child, now works on agrarian projects in Africa. Looking back, he says, "I had always wanted to be in a position where I could fight the white man and win." *Freedom on My Mind* shows how Hayes and many others—Black and white—got their first chance to oppose injustice. Freedom Summer in 1964 set the course for the rest of their lives.

There's such a shapely, moralistic tone to these stories—dismay, mission, depression, determination, caution, courage—that *Freedom on My Mind* sometimes suggests fable. Directors Connie Field and Marilyn Mulford put together contemporary color interviews with black-and-white footage (old and new) that make elegant transitions between present and past, history and legend. They're dealing with the artsy, liberal tradition of depicting Southern hardship (*Let Us Now Praise Famous Men*) but using a more forthright, testimonial approach that raises the level of understanding by letting individual voices construct audience perception.

This happens through the examples of Freedom Summer, where Black Southerners and Black and white outsiders (called "invaders" by segregationists) heeded a historic, romantic calling. (President Kennedy: "Those who do nothing are inviting shame as well as violence. Those who act boldly are recognizing right as well as reality.") Their actions set a paradigm for intellectual and moral development; the activists tested social custom, learned about the American political and legal system, and discovered their own faith, strengths and weaknesses.

This movie makes Freedom Summer seem the last great story American history has to offer. Bob Moses, who went from Harvard student to thoughtful activist, is prominently featured; he explains how the freedom workers' created the Mississippi Freedom Democratic Party and how its manipulation at the 1964 Democratic National Convention epitomized the hope and then the derailment of the era's moral trajectory. It ended, Moses says, in the violence of the late-sixties' street and campus rebellions and the subsequent culture of cynicism. (The latter should include the capitalistic hiphop generation who know nothing of the civil rights struggle or its principles.)

Moses's truth gets glossed over in *Forrest Gump*. Tom Hanks plays the title role of a saintly, slightly retarded, innocent white man recounting his observations of the last forty years of American history. Director Robert Zemeckis (*Back to the Future*) and screenwriter Eric Roth commendably balance incidents of human cruelty with shrewdly turned humor: The medical stupors of the fifties contrast with the rise of rock 'n' roll; sixties protests contrast with eighties self-improvement. Gump strides—runs—through it all as witness and noncommittal participant. He recalls the portentous idiot savant Chauncey Gardiner of *Being There* and the ahistorical media freak of Woody Allen's *Zelig*—pop figures created to pacify history—but he is nothing like the real-life participants in history seen in *Freedom on My Mind*.

The difference is in *Forrest Gump*'s presumption about individual naiveté and its romantic view of power as something wielded by others. Surely the prominence of these ideas perpetuates the public's ignorance, and the charm that Zemeckis works in tends to gratify mass idiocy. Hanks's beatific acting has the gracefulness missing from his other bogus zeitgeist performance in *Philadelphia*, but he, too, is in the service of a dubious political message.

Gump succeeds in life, becomes more confident, through inadvertence. The contrast of *Freedom on My Mind* shows how this distorts the self-actualizing processes of anyone who achieves real growth. Gump, who delivers his memoir while seated Beckett-like at a Savannah busstop, has a pseudo-Southern homily: "Life is like a box of chocolates; you never know what you're gonna get." But that pales next to the lessons learned by the white Northern debutantes who went South in faith, or of Dr. Endesha Ida Mae Holland, a Mississippi native who turned from prostitution to activism and relates how she was inspired by the sight of marching Black women: "They be walking with such pride. These women would walk the walk. It was so beautiful. And they titties be stickin' out a whole, long way in front of them. Mama said you could see they titties a block 'fo you see them. But they be walkin' heavy with such pride. Look like the earth would catch they feet and hold them."

In place of Holland's vivid descriptions, *Forrest Gump* offers . . . well, the miracles of Industrial Light and Magic special effects that put Gump at the center of phenomenal personal and historic moments. There's some intelligence and perception here, too, as when the film's most significant Black character, Bubba (Mykelti Williamson), has his Southern family legacy conveyed through a montage of servant scenes that set up a happy reversal later in the film. But Bubba, a fellow "innocent," is also an insulting simplification of the very sense of social obligation and human connection that happened during Freedom Summer and exemplified the best American behavior.

Field and Mulford don't neglect the difficulties of comradeship; the arrogance of white liberalism is confronted along with the resentment of the Black Southerners who, though needing whites' help bringing American law to the South, did not rely on it.

Bubba is a depressing Black image, part of the film's secretly cynical view of America as a nation of abused women (Robin Wright) and handicapped veterans (Gary Sinise), hapless misfits and mindless predators. Hanks's geniality is nothing compared with *Freedom*'s panoply of heroes, including Fannie Lou Hamer or scenes of the intelligent, sensitive young Bob Moses or the modern close-up of his brown eyes burning with a message.

When Moses details the movement's betrayal, he explains how the Democratic National Convention made room for professional people but not grassroots people. This knowledge helps explain the mixed messages of *Forrest Gump*, where professional Hollywood filmmakers take up social issues without risking their own class advantages. We're in a less heroic age, and *Forrest Gump* represents professional liberal caution of the Clinton era; this reliance on a blameless white hero is ultimately disillusioning.

*Freedom on My Mind* is an excellent film that documents a moment when many Americans actively expressed belief in power sharing. It includes their complex sense of the issues as expressed in the protest song lyrics "They say freedom is a struggle / Lord, I've been struggling so long I must be free." But *Forrest Gump* is a fantasy attempt to relieve American individuals from any sense of responsibility about history or their own lives.

Hollywood filmmakers confuse responsibility with guilt. That philosophy is what produces this sweet-natured yet horrible entertainment: *Forrest Gump* embodies Dinesh DeSouza's concept of the end of history as the end of human conscience. *Freedom on My Mind* emphasizes individuals' needs because that's where history always begins.

*The City Sun*
July 6, 1994

# A FRESH ROUTE
# TO RACISM

Boaz Yakin could conceivably have made *Fresh* just to prove Dr. Leonard Jeffries's account of Hollywood history as a white conspiracy to degrade Black people. *Fresh,* the story of a twelve-year-old crack courier in New York, is full of just about every racist cliché a white outsider could harbor or maliciously use in gossip about Black people. If (Black) moviegoers have their act together, then after seeing *Fresh* they will picket this movie to oblivion out of respect for the great civilized tradition of Black protest.

The main character, Fresh (played as a baby zombie by Sean Nelson), inhabits a world of soul-blasted killers and victims. Constructed from tabloid headlines, *Fresh* affirms conservative race fantasy, yet it's being offered with "liberal" condescension. The popular, casual acceptance of Black depravity as the unchangeable nature of contemporary American life—dubbed "ghettocentricity"—poisons Yakin's approach. This is different from the kind of shtetl consciousness that informed Martin Ritt's direction of the 1972 film *Sounder* (it was an empathic projection from his own Jewish heritage). Yakin wastes no understanding on this subject. He's of a different, harsher culture (if *Sounder* was a sympathetic post-Holocaust movie, *Fresh* is a defamatory post–Crown Heights movie). His absurd story line exposes an insidious distaste for Black life that, in fact, reverses what once was a good Jewish-liberal tradition.

*Fresh* perverts the humanist approach of movies such as *Sounder,* Satyajit Ray's *Pather Panchali*, and Vittorio DeSica's *Shoeshine* by withholding the empathy that made those movies extraordinary. The desperate lives of Black Americans that result from unemployment, government indifference and cultural disdain are not recognized by Yakin as valuable. He examines Blacks as larvae, as exotica, then arranges his drama to fit a pandering sociology. Fresh has no mother, and he lives with his aunt and eleven—yes, eleven—school-age cousins, and his father is absent (a bum who nurses his social defeat by playing chess in the park).

While Ritt, Ray, and DeSica (and Native American Steve Johnson in *South Central*) used a child protagonist as an expression of their hope for a people, Yakin's Fresh is an emblem of a destroyed people. Though Black folks have always lived under rotten conditions in this country, their belief in the future and a sense of human value created a counter-condition of hope. Yakin, a nihilist dramatist and art poseur, wants to imagine Black folks' dread destiny for them. "Yeah, you're fucked" is the message of *Fresh* as it shows a child sealing his fate through a baroque plan of vengeance that punishes the local crew of drug suppliers and thugs (especially Giancarlo Esposito doing three-dimensional slime as Estaban).

Yakin gives the boy no sense of the political forces that perpetuate Black deprivation. He trivializes the most heinous social policies and moral apathy by reducing the human rights struggle to a chesslike con game where the child Fresh deviously confounds the grownup drug lords (Blacks being such fools). This might please a political moron like KRS-One, who advises "criminal-minded" activity as a young Black person's method for beating the system, but it's a thick-headed movie device. Yakin's lousy chess metaphor uses the boy to act on conservative politicians' short-range crime fears. The ironic ending is no irony at all, since it plays out Yakin's basic premise that Blacks only—always—cheat and destroy themselves.

The clues to Yakin's disdain come early. First, in the fanciful establishing shots—an abstract, Colorform f/x of a clean American city street being blotted out by graffiti and neglect. He's making up his own playtime ghetto world rather than supplying honest social observation. Yakin seizes the peculiar hiphop era opportunity to make *his* name by joining in the Black pathology bandwagon—but art felons like Dr. Dre do it better. Yakin, applying a European art-film hubris to the subject, saps the life out of ghettocentricity. When Fresh goes home, everyone sits catatonic watching TV and Fresh himself never smiles. Every speech and camera angle shows a high-minded design to underscore the bleakness of poverty rather than the life of people who defy it (even by thriving in it—that's the irksome irony of Dr. Dre's music videos).

*Fresh* is diabolical in the way it uses racist clichés to inspire white pity and restate obloquy. In order to "save" his older sister (N'Bushe Wright), Fresh pimps her to Estaban. The slave-mentality actors are only too happy to act out Yakin's neuroses. Here is one-third of Wright's entire dialogue: "I'm just a funky ass nigger ho." As Fresh's father, Samuel L. Jackson incestuously inquires after his daughter, then offers little Fresh a beer: "It tastes like a tub of warm piss somebody farted in." In Yakin's mind, that's how earthy, profane Black folks talk.

Yakin readily caricatures adult losers, but his impulse is to dote on a troupe of really cute children—the better to condescend to you, my little darkies. The most entertaining of these is Chuckie (Luis Lantigua), the Puerto Rican kid who brags he can "bust some dope moves." Among the worst are the little girls (one wears a pinafore!), and Yakin's staging of a girl's playground killing is stupefyingly arty—the camera circles and scans the concrete leading to a trail of blood and a child's restless limb.

It's obvious that Yakin delights in filming this mayhem, using Black tragedy as his Hollywood calling card. He's an extremely crafty film-maker who one day might make an entertaining movie about something he knows. The solemn new-age score by Stewart Copeland proves the filmmakers' hateful, tony distance. Yakin implies that hiphop music is too crude for his serious message (he probably wouldn't know which songs to use anyway), and that's the bad faith that exposes *Fresh* as fraudulent.

*The New York Times* says the film can't be accused of exploitation because "it earns the right to approach this subject through the thoughtfulness of Mr. Yakin's direction." But that's exactly why it *is* exploitative. It deliberately makes sociological fodder out of the misery of others.

*Fresh* is a reminder that most white people know nothing about how Black people live or feel. And worse, it demonstrates that some whites are incapable of empathy. The most Boaz Yakin musters is pity and stereotype.

*The City Sun*
August 31, 1994

# AN IDIOT'S DELIGHT

"TAKE YOUR FOOT off the nigger!" is staged to be the funniest line in *Pulp Fiction*—it climaxes a chase between Butch (Bruce Willis), a white boxer-on-the-lam, and his Black underworld boss, Marsellus (Ving Rhames); they wind up in a sporting goods store where the proprietor pulls out a shotgun and delivers that punch line. The audience laughed both times I saw the film. But it's a laugh that sours even as one's moral disgust is distracted by what follows—an extended sequence of baroque sex-and-violence: Tied-up and abused by a pair of gun-toting deviants, Butch and Marsellus honor their macho code, then exact revenge.

That offensive line—dashing the hope of salvation with bigotry—doesn't make the world of the film's characters intrigue the audience. Casual violence (verbal and physical) occurs in *Pulp Fiction* simply as a trope, a bit of business, a purposeless piece of "fun." Writer-director Quentin Tarantino, who also wrote and directed the 1992 *Reservoir Dogs*, enjoys such disreputable aspects of pop culture; he revels in the *bad* action and *bad* manners of tough-guy characters. But Tarantino makes no distinction between low-life and genre, and this insensitivity, while flashy, funny, and attention-grabbing, borders on idiocy.

*Pulp Fiction* itself is a misleading title; it should simply be renamed *Trash*. It keeps within the shallow, thoughtless boundaries of cheap fiction (potboiler crime novels and B movies), but no ugly, mean truth gets revealed. Here's the catch: QT shows such an unenlightened, film buff's faith that he fails to redeem or improve the pulp genre in any way that matters. *Pulp Fiction* is a modernized rehash of the fast killings, stylish poses and affectations that appeal to the adolescent taste for pop.

This trash aesthetic often is carelessly valorized in the postmodern age as a preference over the staid, conventional style and pleasures of classical film and fiction. (It took the Coen brothers many years and several films before they beat this trend in the best parts of *Barton Fink* and most of last spring's *The Hudsucker Proxy*). However, QT's fallacious glorification of trash is a trickier, more dangerous method than the Coens' because he includes a smug art-consciousness—and his own knuckleheaded class, race, sex biases. QT's trash bin processes everything from Bruce Lee movies to Jean-Pierre Melville films, Jean-Luc Godard to Blaxploitation—all without discriminating an enlightened sense of what, for instance, the word "nigger" means in the contemporary world.

Beginning with the "clever" but arbitrary narrative structure QT has devised, this is a genuine, immoral po-mo artifact. Rearranging the chronology of events, QT starts with two lovers/petty robbers (Amanda Plummer and Tim Roth) in a diner; flashes back to two hitmen, Jules and Vinnie (Samuel L. Jackson and John Travolta), on their way to massacre a group of gay/yuppie welshers; interrupts that scene to flash forward to Vinnie babysitting his boss's junkie wife (Uma Thurman). A parallel shift intercuts Butch's story, the movie's emotional center; next, QT sutures in a completion of the massacre scene; then jumps back (up?) to the opening diner scene. All this fancy footwork reworks themes of male sexual anxiety and white racial fear through pastiches of action movies. It recalls the narrative games by the French New Wave in the 1960s, updated with more recent genre movie gimmicks.

But *Pulp Fiction* makes a hash of New Wave narrative innovations, which were revolutionary, in part, because they identified the modern audience's perspective. Godard's romantic heroes lamented life's failure to be like movies; pop naiveté forced them to experience an existential crisis. QT reduces life to be like exploitation films. Despite QT's narrative pizzazz and awareness of high art (his production company is called Band Apart after Godard's *Band of Outsiders* [*Band a part*]), he is ignorant of what genre means to specific (Black or white) audiences. Unlike the New Wave, QT thinks all audiences view all films the same way. Though solicitous of subversive impulses, QT then betrays them—a middle-class, middle-brow bad joke. To amend *New York* magazine's rave, Tarantino may know New Wave conventions but he doesn't understand New Wave *convictions*.

New Wave directors like Truffaut and Godard loved the concision of genre movies and so compressed narrative; they found storytelling shortcuts based on their knowledge of art and movie history and a sweet sensitivity to the pop audience's sophistication. And in *Band of Outsiders* Godard also connected pop (pulp) mythology to a sense of the political world, not simply to *more* movies. (So did Altman's *The Long Goodbye,* Benton's *The Late Show,* DePalma in *The Fury* and Leone in *Duck You Sucker.*) QT draws out his narrative and dialogue to please the movie morons who prefer talky, obvious exposition to more kinetic, sophisticated cinema. And it seems critics praise *Pulp Fiction* precisely because its story is nonpolitical—that is, backwards. *Pulp Fiction* would have been great if it included the sense of social change implicit in Blaxploitation. But instead, this is a dumb white guy's *nonreading* of Blaxploitation. Consider: QT's fancy structure denies Jules's prominence. Through "cleverness" it disguises that the real heart of the movie is Bruce Willis's glumly acted, highly conventional tale—a decidedly unhip, strictly commercial concession that sets back film culture from the corrosive satirical edge Altman advanced in *The Player*, where Willis was used as an emblem of Hollywood venality.

Jules (rousingly played by Samuel L. Jackson in familiar Blaxploitation style) is QT's cultural linchpin, but this is a specious characterization; he is underlit, thus implicitly disrespected (QT keeps his foot on Black aesthetic beauty). Given to extemporaneous harangue—no simple response will do when he can wax philosophical—Jules is QT's fantasy of the hypereloquent, violent Supernigger. In conversations with his hitman partner Vinnie (John Travolta, who affects a "Black" accent), Jules offers mysterious depths of wisdom and masculine efficiency—he's the man to Vinnie's kid. It's Nigger Jim to Huck Finn all over again.

A backward po-mo culture mistakes this as something good, which explains why some Black journalists (conservative hack Stanley Crouch writing in *The Los Angeles Times*) bend over backwards trying to excuse QT's casual cruelty as an acknowledgment of racism (similarly, liberal journalists have not objected to the film's gay massacre scene, with its hidden homophobia—another cultural ill QT flaunts but refuses to confront). QT didn't conceive the Jules-Vinnie dialogues from any observation of Black-white socializing, friendship or enmity. He has idly imagined his own exchange with a character from a seventies Blaxploitation movie. This is worsened by a later scene where Tarantino himself, playing a friend Jules turns to to hide a dead body, does a tiny soliloquy about "Dead Nigger Storage." Trigger-finger Jules/Jackson responds humbly to Tarantino's aria of white belligerence, but imagine what a clash of temperaments a seventies modernist like DePalma would have made out of such a Italian mobster-meets-Shaft moment!

Some critics, relating to QT's hipster approach, accept his slumming approbation of movies like *Black Caesar* and *Hell Up in Harlem* as a part of the mainstream's pandering postmodernism, and then, predictably, dismiss them. This is possible because QT misses the transformative essence of subculture art. White hipsters (the archaic slang applies, since QT doesn't share the social consciousness implicit in today's hiphop lingo) remain oblivious to the desperate revenge and political justification even the most debased Blaxploitation movies expressed. (All that makes those movies matter—even charm—two decades later is that inside the frivolity, some genuine anger, a sense of injustice, rumble and briefly flash on their grimy surfaces.) *Pulp Fiction* adapts Blaxploitation codes in a thoughtless way that merely reaffirms the cultural status quo Blaxploitation contrasted. QT's specious admiration of Jules is based on the traditional white hipster misunderstanding and fetishizing of Black folks' *style.*

Humanity and politics have little to do with this kind of appreciation, which is clear from the way QT gives Jules a showpiece executioner's speech:

> The path of the righteous man is beset on all sides by the inequities of the selfish and the tyranny of evil men. Blessed is he who, in the name of charity and goodwill, shepherds the weak through the valley of darkness. For he is *truly* his brother's keeper and the finder of lost children. And I will *strike* down upon thee with *great* vengeance and *furious anger* those who attempt to poison and *destroy* my brothers and you will *know* my name is the Lord when I lay my vengeance upon thee.

The use of this quote from Ezekiel 25:17 (emphases Jackson's and QT's) manages the truly postmodern feat of combining contemporary viciousness with sentimental hogwash. QT updates the stereotype of Black religious superstitions with the racist fear of Black revenge. When Jules tells the pipsqueak white robber (Tim Roth), "You're weak . . . and I'm tryin' damn hard to be the shepherd," it suggests some culturo-historical retribution. But Jules's insight is no more credible or plausible than the conversion he claims; he never avenges Black mistreatment, he just adds to it. (And accepts it from the Tarantino character.) Jules' conversion happens as a narrative trick, a joke. QT hasn't the sensibility to believe in spiritual conversion, but he isn't beyond using it for a neat fillip. So he ends *Pulp Fiction* dramatically, sardonically, with Jules's supposed moral awakening, but the amoral world of dopers, killers, and perverts belongs to Hollywood cliché, a fabricated world, a trivial thing.

*Pulp Fiction* misuses the most precious essence of pop—its evocation of emotional strife and spiritual hope (that's what critics *want* to be excited about). But QT has forgotten the great lessons of the American Film Renaissance of the seventies: to apply a myth to political reality. That has become an inspiring fact of pop art in the hiphop era. (Many hiphop artists have appropriated Blaxploitation tropes and adapted them to contemporary significance; e.g., Ice-T's compilation album *Pimps, Players and Private Eyes.*)

Yet even the old music on *Pulp Fiction*'s sound track is a sign of white hipster solipsism. Blended with familiar action, noir, kung fu, western tropes, it consolidates regressive notions of pop culture as unchallengingly familiar and harmless. The Jack Rabbit Slim nightclub scene gives a slanted summarizing of our pop heritage, featuring white fifties icons plus Thurman and Travolta doing the Twist; it denies the power of more modern styles and of Black art pleasure, which ought to figure highly in a movie subliminally about race. *Pulp Fiction* is a pop jamboree for people who dislike the cultural and political disturbances of an Alex Cox movie.

The racial, cultural mix in Cox's *Repo Man, Straight to Hell, Highway Patrolman*, and *Sid and Nancy* was part of a wonderful up-to-date worldliness. Not only a more dynamic filmmaker than Tarantino, Cox clearly understands the moral value in pop variety and the politics inherent in artistic maneuvers. Cox's punk ethos—his stories express heterogeneous versions of social behavior—are more significant than merely hip. The naive hero of *Highway Patrolman* and the American malcontents of *Repo Man* all illustrate political positions far more representative of American experience than any "cool" postures. QT's cultural vision is insipid.

*Pulp Fiction*'s mixed world of Black and white gangsters bears no relation to the real world in dress, speech, or manner, although QT is not above exploiting real-world race tension. In his "Dead Nigger Storage" scene, he implies that his own character has an interracial marriage but curiously avoids showing the Black woman's face. QT intercuts this nonportrait with another interracial couple (Black man/white woman) lounging at a swimming pool to produce a casual but meaningless frisson. In fact, that's all QT does throughout this movie.

Actually, QT traduces American pop in the contemporary style of conservative ambivalence. Think about that elite use of the word "nigger" and how vengeful Jules *allows* it from QT himself. (Even in QT's script for last year's *True Romance* there was a speech where an Italian gangster is taunted about having "nigger" blood; the invective impressed morons who think it's enough to express racism, as if it clears the air; it still affronts the conscience when used pointlessly.) I'm afraid that despite all the pop QT has ingested, he has learned nothing. When *Pulp Fiction* is praised as reviving American movies, that simply means it has reasserted mainstream conventions, and white standards of narrow, myopic social points of view. The latest movie to dress up and enshrine white cultural bigotry, it's a repository of pop idiocy—an example of Dead Hollywood Storage.

*The City Sun*
November 2, 1994

# INDEX

Breuer, Lee, 100, 101, 102
Brides of Funkenstein (musical
group), 91
Bridges, Beau, 142
Bridges, Jeff, 6, 142, 144
Briggins, Angela, 366
*Bright Lights, Big City* (film), 80
*Brighton Beach Memoirs* (film), 59,
61, 62
"Bring the Noise" (song), 82, 83, 104,
166, 310
*Broadcast News* (film), 123, 380–382,
383
*The Broadway Album*, 357
*Broadway Danny Rose* (film), 60
Bronson, Charles, 83
Brooklyn Academy of Music, 100
Brooks, Albert, 396
Brooks, James L., 381
Brooks, Mel, 61
Brooks, Richard, 170
*The Brother from Another Planet*
(film), 2, 12, 44
"Brothers Gonna Work It Out" (song),
167
Brown, Bobby, 360
Brown, Georgia, 121, 253
Brown, Gerard, 344
Brown, James, 75, 90, 243, 425
Brown, Michael Henry, 371, 372, 373
Brown, Tony, 148–150, 421, 422
"Brown Skin Girl, Stay Home and
Mind Baby" (song), 134
Browne, Roscoe Lee, 14
Browning, Frank, 290
Brownmiller, Susan, 28
"Buck Whylin'" (song), 301
"Buddy" (song), 218
"Bugaboo" (song), 260
*Bugsy* (film), 264–267
Bullard, Larry, 28
Da Bulldogs (musical group), 260
Bunim, Mary-Ellis, 396
Buñuel, Luis, 206
"Buppies, B-Boys, Baps and Bohos"
(George), 274, 275
Burchill, Julie, 25
*Burn!* (film), 423
*Burn, Baby Burn* (music video), 260
*Burn, Hollywood, Burn* (video), 270
Burnett, Carol, 98
Burnett, Charles, 280, 282
*Bless Their Little Hearts*, xiv–xv,
20–22, 26, 169, 269
*The Killer of Sheep* see *The Killer of
Sheep* (film)
*My Brother's Wedding*, 21, 26, 169
*To Sleep with Anger*, 169–171, 351,
373
Burns, Ken, 377
Burton, Richard, 330, 362
Burton, Tim, 126
Burum, Stephen H., 33
Bush, George, 261, 304
Bush administration
Akbar, 397
*Baker Boys* and, 145
Fab 5 Freddy and, 274
frustrations of, 376
*Home Alone* and, 184, 185
media and, 377
propriety of, 210

*Purple Rose* and, 379
young black professionals and, 230
Bushwick Bill (performer), 311, 354
Busia, Akosua, 45, 46, 406
"Bust a Move" (song), 260
Busy Bee (performer), 276
Butler, Paul, 170
Butler, Sam, Jr., 100, 101
Butts, Calvin, 355

C + C Music Factory (musical group),
190, 191, 192, 257
*Cabaret* (musical), 15
*Cabin in the Sky* (film), 14
*The Cactus Album*, 259
Caesar, Adolph, 9, 10–11, 47
Cagney, James, 159, 226
*Cagney and Lacey* (TV program), 23
Calhoun, William, 87
*Caligari* (film), 300
Calloway, Cab, 11, 195, 196
Cambridge, Godfrey, 14
Campbell, Joseph, 120
Campion, Jane, 392–394, 418
*Can't Truss It* (music video), 422
"Can't Truss It" (song), 423
*Cape Fear* (film), 226, 351, 376
Capone, Al, 178
*Car Wash* (film), 413
Cara, Irene, 13
*Les Carabiniers* (film), 380
*Caravaggio* (film), 294
Carlsberg, Hildur, 141
*Carmen Jones* (film), 29
Carpenter, John, 35
Carpenter, Karen, 135
Carrere, Tia, 382
*Carrie* (film), 34, 35, 176, 181, 183
Carroll, Diahann, 53, 199
Carter, Thomas, 409
Carver, Raymond, 388, 390, 391
*Casablanca* (film), 267
Cassandra Half-Pint (performer),
249, 250
Cassavetes, John, 22, 25
*Casualties of War* (film), 175, 177,
178, 179–180, 183
*Cats* (musical), 337
*The Caucasian Chalk Circle* (play), 195
"Caught, Can We Get a Witness?"
(song), 104–105
Cavalier, Alain, xv
"Cave Bitch" (song), 416
*CB4* (film), 343, 350
"Celebrate the Achievement" (event),
418
*The Celluloid Closet* (Russo), 296
Central Intelligence Agency, 321
*Chameleon Street* (film), xv, 187–189,
253–256, 280–282, 328
*Daughters of the Dust* and, 279, 281
*Menace II Society* and, 351
*Sanofka* and, 422
*Straight Out of Brooklyn* and, 208
"Chan Goes to Shanghai" (song), 56
Chaney, James, 109
"A Change Is Gone Come" (song),
423
Chaplin, Charles, 49
Chapman, Tracy, 218, 358
Charisma Records (firm), 211
Charisse, Cyd, 196
Charles, Ernestine, 289

Charles, Ray, 130
Cheap Trick (musical group), 88
"Check Yo Self" (song), 413
*Cheers* (TV program), 237
Cher (performer), 35
*Cherish* (music video), 197
Cherry, Neneh, 144
Chester, Craig, 295
Chic (musical group), 56, 87, 88
*Chico and the Man* (TV program),
172
*Children* (film), 338
"Children Play With Earth" (song), 273
"Children Will Listen" (song), 356,
357–358, 359
*A Chinese Ghost Story* (film), 119
*Chocolat* (film), 394
*Choose Me* (film), 143
Christgau, Robert, 351
Christianity, 19
*Christine* (film), 35
*The Chronic* (recording), 352, 353–355
Chuck D (performer)
*AmeriKKKa's Most Wanted*, 155
"Bring the Noise," 83
"Can't Truss It," 422
Ice Cube and, 157, 159, 412, 414
Ice-T and, 307
*It Takes a Nation*, 103, 104–105
J. Jackson and, 363
mainstream criticism of, 430, 432
Marky Mark and, 261
N.W.A. and, 156
radio and, 82
Sister Souljah and, 301
on white rock, 283
Willie D and, 311
CIA (Central Intelligence Agency),
321
"Cindy C" (song), 93
*The Circus* (recording), 333
Cisse, Souleymane, 140
*Citizen Kane* (film), 253, 255
*The City Sun* (newspaper), xvi, xvii,
256
*The Civil War* (TV film series), 377
"Clap Your Hands" (song), 167
Clarke, Shirley, 25
Clarke, Vince, 333–334, 335
Clash (musical group), 217
*The Clash of Races* (Madhabuti), 282
*Claudine* (film), 199
Clayburgh, Jill, 45
"Clean Up Man" (song), 309
*Cleopatra Jones* (film), 227
Clift, Montgomery, 297
Clinton, Bill
Elvisiana and, 316
Sister Souljah and, 285, 286, 301
Streisand and, 356, 358
Clinton, George
De La Soul and, 136
Dr. Dre and, 353
Funkadelic and, 137
Prince and, 90, 91
*Repo Man* and, 17, 18
Clinton administration, 435
Clivilles, Robert, 192, 193
*Close Encounters of the Third Kind*
(film), 176
*The Color Purple* and, 44
mothership in, 238